JESUS THE CENTRAL JEW

Society of Biblical Literature

Early Christianity and Its Literature

Gail R. O'Day, Editor

Warren Carter
Beverly Roberts Gaventa
David Horrell
Judith M. Lieu
Margaret Y. MacDonald

Number 15

JESUS THE CENTRAL JEW

HIS TIME AND HIS PEOPLE

by
André LaCocque

SBL Press
Atlanta

Copyright © 2015 by SBL Press

All rights reserved. No part of this work may be reproduced or transmitted in any form or by any means, electronic or mechanical, including photocopying and recording, or by means of any information storage or retrieval system, except as may be expressly permitted by the 1976 Copyright Act or in writing from the publisher. Requests for permission should be addressed in writing to the Rights and Permissions Office, SBL Press, 825 Houston Mill Road, Atlanta, GA 30329 USA.

Library of Congress Cataloging-in-Publication Data

LaCocque, André.
   Jesus the central Jew : his times and his people / André LaCocque.
      p. cm. — (Society of Biblical Literature early Christianity and its literature ; number 15)
   Includes bibliographical references and index.
   ISBN 978-1-62837-111-6 (paper binding : alk. paper) — ISBN 978-1-62837-113-0 (electronic format) — ISBN 978-1-62837-112-3 (hardcover binding : alk. paper)
   1. Jesus Christ—Jewishness. 2. Bible. Gospels—Criticism, interpretation, etc. I. Title.
BT590.J8L33 2015
232—dc23   2015005709

Printed on acid-free, recycled paper conforming to ANSI/NISO Z39.48-1992 (R1997) and ISO 9706:1994 standards for paper permanence.

Contents

Acknowledgments vii
Abbreviations ix

Introduction 1
1. The Gospel as Retrospective 11
2. Jesus the Messiah 15
3. Jesus Son of Man/Son of God 43
4. Jesus as Healer 53
5. Jesus and Torah 71
6. Jesus and Moses 131
7. Jesus and Israel 141
8. Jesus Taught in Parables 169
9. The Birth Narratives 183
10. Jesus's Baptism 193
11. Jesus's Self-Consciousness 197
12. Jesus Is Betrayed 211
13. The Trial of Jesus and His Passion 217
14. *Egō Eimi* in the Mouth of Jesus 239
15. The Great Cry of Jesus on the Cross 247
16. Jesus and the Resurrection 263
Conclusion 273
Bibliography 279

Index of Passages 295
Index of Subjects 333

Acknowledgments

The reader-friendly text of this book of mine owes much to the editing of my friend and former student David Strong. He has spared no time and effort in his task, and I am very much in his debt. As the talmudic aphorism states (y. Ber 2:8, 5c): "A person's student is as beloved to him as his son."

As to the contents of the present work, many a New Testament scholar has been a wonderful source of inspiration. I had the privilege to discuss things with a number of them. Further, I have tried to do justice to the works of those I was able to quote, and I apologize to specialists who will not find their names mentioned. This represents no negative judgment. There is an "ocean" of monographs about the historical Jesus on the shelves of the library. No one on earth is capable of referring to all of them. Unavoidably, I had to select some of them, and I hope not to have missed anything that would have changed my judgment or approach.

Reference should be made to a number of modern Jewish critics whose work on Jesus demonstrates a welcome and penetrating understanding of our topic. Their mentorship is, I believe, evident in my book. There is thus a sort of continuity from the ancient Hebrew, Aramaic, Mishnaic, and Palestinian Greek sources, on the one hand, to modern Jewish exegetical exploration into the labyrinth of the Gospels, on the other.

I also want to express gratitude to the staff of SBL Press. Their excellent work has brought this book's composition closer to flawlessness.

Abbreviations

Rabbinic Works

ʿAbod. Zar.	ʿAbodah Zarah
ARN	Abot de-Rabbi Natan
B. Bat.	Baba Batra
B. Qam.	Baba Qamma
Ber.	Berakot
Cant. Rab.	Canticles Rabbah
Deut. Rab.	Deuteronomy Rabbah
ʿEd.	ʿEduyyot
ʿErub.	ʿErubin
Exod. Rab.	Exodus Rabbah
Gen. Rab.	Genesis Rabbah
Giṭ.	Giṭṭim
Hag.	Hagigah
Ker.	Keritot
Ketub.	Ketubbot
Liv. Pro.	Lives of the Prophets
m.	Mishnah tractate
Mak.	Makkot
Meg.	Megillah
Mek.	Mekilta de Rabbi Ishmael
Menaḥ.	Menaḥot
Miqw.	Miqwaʾot
Moʿed Qaṭ.	Moʿed Qaṭan
Naz.	Nazir
Ned.	Nedarim
Nid.	Niddah
ʿOr.	ʿOrlah
Pirqe R. El.	Pirqe Rabbi Eliezer

Pesaḥ.	Pesaḥim
Pesiq. Rab.	Pesiqta Rabbati
Pesiq. Rab Kah.	Pesiqta de Rab Kahana
Qidd.	Qiddušin
Qoh. Rab.	Qohelet Rabbah
S. ʿOlam Rab.	Seder ʿOlam Rabbah
Šabb.	Šabbat
Sanh.	Sanhedrin
Šeqal.	Šeqalim
Sop.	Soperim
t.	Tosefta tractate
Taʿan.	Taʿanit
Teḥar.	Teḥarot
Tg. Isa.	Targum Isaiah
Tg. Mal.	Targum Malachi
Tg. Neof.	Targum Neofiti
Tg. Obad.	Targum Obadiah
Tg. Onq.	Targum Onqelos
Tg. Ps.	Targum Psalms
Tg. Ps.-Jon.	Targum Pseudo-Jonathan
Tg. Zech.	Targum Zechariah
y.	Jerusalem talmudic tractate
Yad.	Yadayim
Yal.	Yalquṭ
Yebam.	Yebamot
Zebaḥ.	Zebaḥim

Old Testament Pseudepigrepha

Liv. Pro.	Lives of the Prophets
T. Benj.	Testament of Benjamin
T. Iss.	Testament of Issachar
T. Jos.	Testament of Joshua
T. Levi	Testament of Levi
T. Mos.	Testament of Moses
T. Zeb.	Testament of Zebulun

Other Ancient Literature

Abr.	Philo of Alexandria, *De Abrahamo*
Ant.	Josephus, *Antiquities of the Jews*
Barn.	Barnabas
CD	Cairo Genizah copy of the Damascus Document
Cher.	Philo of Alexandria, *De cherubim*
Clem. Recogn.	*Clementis quae feruntur Recognitiones*
Did.	Didache
Gos. Eb.	Gospel of the Ebionites
Gos. Heb.	Gospel of the Hebrews
Gos. Mary	Gospel of Mary
Gos. Thom.	Gospel of Thomas
Hist.	Herodotus, *Historiae*
Hist. eccl.	Eusebius of Caesarea, *Historia ecclesiastica*
J.W.	Josephus, *Jewish War*
Jub.	Jubilees
LAB	Liber antiquitatum biblicarum (Pseudo-Philo)
Leg.	Philo of Alexandria, *Legum allegoriae*
Mos.	Philo of Alexandria, *De vita Mosis*
Post.	Philo of Alexandria, *De posteritate Caini*
Prob.	Philo of Alexandria, *Quod omnis probus liber sit*
Prot. Jas.	Protevangelium of James
Sib. Or.	Sibylline Oracles
Spec.	Philo of Alexandria, *De specialibus legibus*
Virt.	Philo of Alexandria, *De virtutibus*

Journals, Major Reference Works, and Series

AB	Anchor Bible
ABRL	Anchor Bible Reference Library
ABD	*Anchor Bible Dictionary*. Edited by David Noel Freedman. 6 vols. New York: Doubleday, 1992.
AGJU	Arbeiten zur Geschichte des antiken Judentums und des Urchristentums
BSac	*Bibliotheca Sacra*
DBSup	*Dictionnaire de la Bible: Supplément*. Edited by Louis Pirot and André Robert. Paris: Letouzey et Ané, 1928–.
ETR	*Etudes théologiques et religieuses*

ExpTim	*Expository Times*
IEJ	*Israel Exploration Journal*
HTR	*Harvard Theological Review*
HUCM	Monographs of the Hebrew Union College
IDB	*The Interpreter's Dictionary of the Bible*. Edited by George A. Buttrick. 4 vols. New York: Abingdon, 1962.
JBL	*Journal of Biblical Literature*
JJS	*Journal of Jewish Studies*
JQR	*Jewish Quarterly Review*
JTS	*Journal of Theological Studies*
LEC	Library of Early Christianity
NBS	*Nouvelle Bible Segond.* Villers-le-Bel: Societe Biblique Francaise, 2002.
NTS	*New Testament Studies*
NovT	*Novum Testamentum*
PL	Patrologia Latina [= *Patrologiae Cursus Completus*: Series Latina]. Edited by Jacques-Paul Migne. 217 vols. Paris: Migne, 1844–1864.
RGG	*Religion in Geschichte und Gegenwart.* Edited by Kurt Galling. 7 vols. 3rd ed. Tübingen: Mohr Siebeck, 1957–1965.
SBLDS	Society of Biblical Literature Dissertation Series
SBLMS	Society of Biblical Literature Monograph Series
SBT	Studies in Biblical Theology
SemeiaSup	Semeia Supplements
SPAW	Sitzungsberichte der preussischen Akademie der Wissenschaften
StPB	Studia Post-biblica
SJT	*Scottish Journal of Theology*
ST	*Studia Theologica*
TDNT	*Theological Dictionary of the New Testament.* Edited by Gerhard Kittel and Gerhard Friedrich. Translated by Geoffrey W. Bromiley. 10 vols. Grand Rapids: Eerdmans, 1964–1976.
USFSHJ	University of South Florida Studies in the History of Judaism
USQR	*Union Seminary Quarterly Review*
WUNT	Wissenschaftliche Untersuchungen zum Neuen Testament
VC	Vigiliae Christiane
ZTK	Zeitschrift für Theologie und Kirche

Introduction

"the most Jewish of all Jews ... I have found in Jesus my great brother. That Christianity has regarded and does regard him as God and Saviour has always appeared to me a fact of the highest importance which, for his sake and my own, I must endeavor to understand."
—Martin Buber, foreword to *Two Types of Faith*

"the Jew-of-Jews, the Jew proper"

—Harold Bloom[1]

A vast literature has been and is now dedicated to the rediscovery of the historical Jesus. It is beyond the scope of this present attempt to do justice to more than a fraction of that literature. I must, therefore, start with an apology to all those scholars whose work is not specifically mentioned in this book. That is not a sign of nonappreciation but of the limitations of the author.

The present book is not about Christianity as such. Nor is it a Christology. It purposely addresses restricted sources, namely, the Synoptic Gospels (Matthew, written between 80–90 CE; Mark, written ca. 70; and Luke, written between 80–90), for its aim is to contribute to the modern understanding of the historical—as opposed to the mythical or the "real"—Jesus. On this score, the Gospel of John is already somewhat off-limits, as are the

---

1. Harold Bloom, *Jesus and Yahweh: The Names Divine* (New York: Riverhead, 2005). Bloom also ironically writes, "Jesus has been an American nondenominational Protestant for the last two centuries" (22). Joseph Klausner: "In all this, Jesus is the most Jewish of Jews ... more Jewish than Hillel.... From the standpoint of general humanity, he is, indeed, 'a light to the Gentiles'" (*Jesus of Nazareth: His Life, Times, and Teaching* [New York: Macmillan, 1925], 363, 374, 413 (now New York: Bloch, 1997).

writings of the apostle Paul. However, none of these sources is taboo, and each of them will occasionally be consulted.[2]

If Daniel Boyarin is right in stating in his recent book that "Jesus and Christ were one from the very beginning of the Jesus movement,"[3] it remains that, from the beginning, the emphasis must fall on either the one or the other. Hence, this book is about the central Jew, not the central Christ, as it would be for students of John or Paul. Certainly no polemic is intended regarding John P. Meier's oeuvre, *A Marginal Jew*.[4] Sociologically, pedagogically, and historically, Jesus may be said to be marginal (that is, marginalized; see the perfunctory treatment of Jesus by Josephus). Furthermore, as Jesus's disciples' fear shows, the last pilgrimage to Jerusalem dangerously exposed the Master. What could be taught more or less with impunity in Galilee—or, as the Qumran community demonstrates, in the far-flung desert—was not so easily tolerated around the temple of Jerusalem. In that sense again, Jesus is seen as "marginal," as he represents a Judaism considered from Jerusalem as marginal. Spiritually and religiously, however, Jesus is the central Jew, and this study of mine into what can be retrieved of the historical Jesus can ignore neither the total Jewishness of the Nazarene nor his ultimate claim to be *verus Israel*. These paradoxical perceptions of Jesus's persona—marginality and centrality—make compelling Meier's distinction between "the real Jesus" forever irrecoverable and "the [recoverable] historical Jesus."[5] For instance, in the Synoptics

---

2. John comes with a series of intriguing parables, and Paul, although disregarding "details" in the life of Jesus, alludes to his sayings and considers them as normative. He insists on the Davidic ascendance and on the fact that Jesus's ministry originally addressed the Jews, not the gentiles (Rom 1:3; 15:8; cf. Matt 10:5–6). Let us note that the Synoptic textual parallels are "für die rabbinische Tradition charakteristisch," Gerhard Kittel says (*Die Probleme des palästinischen Spätjudentums und das Urchristentum* [Stuttgart: Kohlhammer, 1926], 63–65). Morton Smith has especially emphasized this fact in *Tannaitic Parallels to the Gospels*, SBLMS 6 (Philadelphia: Society of Biblical Literature, 1951).

3. Daniel Boyarin, *The Jewish Gospels: The Story of the Jewish Christ* (New York: New Press, 2012), 7.

4. John P. Meier, *The Roots of the Problem and the Person*, vol. 1 of *A Marginal Jew: Rethinking the Historical Jesus*, ABRL (New York: Doubleday, 1991).

5. But what an impossible task, when, with Joel Carmichael, we realize that the nineteenth-century critical method produced some 60,000 biographies of Jesus (*The Death of Jesus* [New York: Dorsert, 1995], ch. 1).

we hear about the last three to four years of Jesus's life and almost nothing before! I shall return to this issue below.

Furthermore, it would be self-defeating for the historian to ignore the fact that the gospels[6] were written some three to four decades after the facts. We are dealing with a *tradition*, more precisely with an oral tradition, eventually put into written form in the four canonical *evangelia*. The feverish expectation of the parousia (return in glory) among the early disciples (including the apostle Paul, who believed that Christ in glory would come before he, Paul, died; see 1 Thess 4:15) was one cause of this delay in writing. But as their Lord tarried, the second generation realized that they needed *teachers* (already in the time of Paul, see Gal 6:6; cf. Did. 13.2), that is, guardians of and witnesses for this oral tradition. We the readers meet the historical Jesus through the medium of how he was seen by his disciples and the evangelists. The latter are three degrees removed from the historical Jesus (the second degree being the disciples' vision), and we are at best four degrees removed from the real Jesus.

Jan Vansina calls the early Christian teachers "walking reference librar[ies]."[7] Jesus himself was a *didaskalos*, and his followers are *mathētai* (in Hebrew, *thalmidim*), "students." They must *remember* (1 Cor 11:2; 2 Thess 2:5; elsewhere in the Pauline literature; see also John 14:26; 15:27). Their remembrances eventually became the written gospels, in a form that James D. G. Dunn calls a biography of Jesus, but with the proviso that it is a "biography" as the ancients understood the genre. That is, the characters remain stable and unchanged, so that these portraits rely on what they did and said. Sean Freyne adds that their structure comprises a beginning (*archē*), a middle (*akmē*, on the subject's public life), and an end (*telos*, on the subject's demise or vindication).[8]

---

6. "Gospel," from "God-spel" = good news. In the OT the term *bsr* refers to bringing good news (of, e.g., a military victory). Here Second Isaiah is central: the prophet expects the good news. The *mebaser* proclaims it and thereby makes it a reality (as God speaks through the messenger; see Isa 51:16). The good news par excellence is the advent of the *makut shamayim* ("kingdom of God"). John the Baptist is its messenger (see Exod. Rab. 46 on Exod 34:1; also Pesiq. Rab. 35).

7. Jan Vansina, quoted by James D. G. Dunn, *Jesus Remembered*, vol. 1 of *Christianity in the Making* (Grand Rapids: Eerdmans, 2003), 177 (see Vansina, *Oral Tradition as History* [Madison: University of Wisconsin Press, 1985]).

8. Sean Freyne, *Jesus, A Jewish Galilean: A New Reading of the Jesus-Story* (London: T&T Clark, 2004), 5.

At this point, it is not too early to raise the vexing problem of texts' so-called authenticity. First, the gospels are no biographies in the modern meaning of the term. Second, it was unavoidable that the gospel writers be influenced by contemporary problems in their particular churches. They intimated that Jesus had responded to these issues already during his ministry, so that the modern reader must wonder apropos each text whether it authentically belongs to Jesus's ipsissima verba or whether it represents a later opinion current in the early Christian communities. As we shall see all along this study, a large amount of New Testament scholarship is dedicated to solving this problem, and the word *authentic* or *inauthentic* will appear time and again in our development. Nevertheless, I believe that scholars' anxiety not to appear naive has played a large role in pushing them to an exaggerated skepticism or even cynicism. More damaging is the tendency to isolate the Nazarene from his people and their traditions. Some scholars, as we shall see, even proposed as a "criterion of authenticity" the nonconformity of a given saying of Jesus with the teaching of the Judaism(s) of the time!

David Flusser's stance is more to my liking.[9] Contrasting the Synoptics with the Gospel of John, Flusser expresses confidence in the authenticity of Matthew, Mark, and Luke regarding the sayings and doings of the historical Jesus. Originally, he thinks, there was in existence a Hebrew or Aramaic tradition written by Mark. To this must be added Q (*Quelle*, a reconstructed compendium of Jesus's sayings). The present Gospel of Mark depends on the Greek translation of its original in Aramaic, but entirely rewritten. Matthew and Luke used both the old original Mark as well as the new one; Luke preceded the latter and was used by the "present" Mark. As Flusser insists, the Jewishness of the gospels' testimony vouches for their representing the historical Jesus: "The Jesus portrayed in these three Gospels is, therefore the historical Jesus." Changes in the texts, however, occurred "as a result of ecclesiastical tendentiousness" (col. 10). Flusser's examples include Jesus's birth narratives, which could not have been produced by anyone but Jews.[10] The same is true of the conversation with the high priests in Luke 22:67–72 or with Pharisees and scribes elsewhere.

---

9. David Flusser, "Jesus," in *Encyclopedia Judaica*, ed. Cecil Roth, 16 vols. (Jerusalem: Keter, 1972), 10:10–17.

10. See below, "The Birth Narratives," 183–91.

What I mean here by "historical Jesus" is the study of the insertion of the Galilean Jesus into the particular history of his environment, Jesus in the particular history of his time. The historical Jesus is thus to be distinguished from the "true" Jesus, which no one can ever retrieve. Were not the term loaded with dogmatic contents, we could speak of the "incarnate Jesus," the Jewish Jesus sharing flesh and blood with his people.

This definition explains why the Synoptic Gospels are of prime importance, by contrast with the Pauline Letters, which display little interest in Jesus's "biographical" events and sayings. They also contrast with the Gospel of John, which is a brilliant theological and mystical reflection on the transcendent meaning of Jesus Christ.

Not that the Jesus of the Synoptics should be literally deprived of religious meaning, however. On the contrary, the Synoptics are written *ad probandum* (to prove something); but they never lose sight of Jesus's actual deeds and sayings. Here, the biographical carries with it the transcendental. In reviewing the former, we must reckon with the latter. The term *historical* in "historical Jesus" is phenomenological, as in history of religion. The transcendent dimension cannot simply be evacuated from the historian's scrutiny; however, what we can suspect of being the outcome of later Christian consideration retroverted into the *kerygma* ("message") is to be put into parentheses.

In what follows, the reader will notice that I am rather conservative in dealing with the gospel texts. Where many of my predecessors in the field tend to use the scalpel, I sometimes do not find a compelling reason for concluding the inauthenticity of the text. I happen to have developed a great respect for the evangelists and their remarkable ability of discrimination regarding the "historical." All apocryphal gospels negatively testify to this fact.[11]

This, of course, does not mean that the Synoptics present a leveled-off text, all on the same height of historicity. There are, in fact, diverse rhetorical categories, which include legal (halakic), parabolic, sapiential,

---

11. Albert Einstein wrote in 1929, "No one can read the Gospels without feeling the actual presence of Jesus" ("What Life Means to Einstein: An Interview by George Sylvester Viereck," *Saturday Evening Post*, October 26, 1929,); and Joseph Klausner, "In [Jesus's] ethical code there is a sublimity, distinctiveness and originality in form unparalleled in any other Hebrew ethical code" (*Jesus of Nazareth: His Life, Times, and Teaching* [New York: Macmillan, 1925], 412; see 414).

devotional, hymnic, as well as the all-important midrashic genre.[12] The historian must perspicaciously identify the categories and draw appropriate critical conclusions within the framework each of them offers.

*

The gospel is *performed*, with audience interaction, so that, when we find series of Jesus's sayings or miracles, we can imagine early Christian assemblies asking for more from the witnesses/teachers: "Tell us more about Jesus's miracles!" or "Tell us more of Jesus's parables!" (e.g., Matt 13; Mark 4). This interaction explains why, in the Jesus tradition, the *impact* of Jesus's deeds and words outweighs what he actually did and said.[13] With Dunn I concur that

> whereas the concept of literary *layers* [à la Bultmann] implies increasing remoteness from an "original," "pure," or "authentic" layer, the concept of *performance* allows a directness, even an immediacy of interaction, with a living theme or core even when variously embroidered in various retellings.... [A tradition] that takes us with surprising immediacy to the heart of the first memories of Jesus.[14]

In what environment did the story develop? Anthropologically, the Mediterranean world offers "a strong urban orientation; a corresponding disdain for the peasant way of life and for manual labor ... an honor-and-shame syndrome which defines both sexuality and personal reputation.... Religion plays an important role in both north and south, as do priests, saints, and holy men."[15] Sociologically, in Galilee, landowners lived in cities and exploited the peasants; the latter often became debt-ridden, and eventually paid with their lands, thus becoming day laborers (see Matt

---

12. In this book, "midrash" is used in its modern elaborated meaning, that is, as a text displaying a subjective, creative exegesis of an ancient biblical tradition. As such, the "midrashic" is very much present in the gospel.

13. See James D. G. Dunn, "The Tradition," in *Jesus Remembered*, 241.

14. Ibid., 249, 254. See the section "Jesus and the Pharisees" in ch. 7 ("Jesus and Israel") below.

15. David D. Gilmore, "Anthropology of the Mediterranean Area," *Annual Reviews of Anthropology* 11 (1982): 175–205, cited by John Dominic Crossan in *The Historical Jesus: The Life of a Mediterranean Jewish Peasant* (San Francisco: HarperSanFrancisco, 1991), 7.

20:1–16; Mark 12:1–9). Poverty filled the ranks of highwaymen and prostitutes. Clearly this created a mutual hostility between city and countryside. The ruling classes were seen by the *chora* (rural region) as parasites. Those that the gospel calls "the poor" are mainly oppressed peasants, living from hand to mouth and often reduced to begging. They are what the anthropologist Gerhard Lenski calls "the expendables."[16]

Pride and shame were central to all. Pride is based on the fact that "an individual ... sees himself always through the eyes of others.... Respectability ... is the characteristic of a person who needs other people in order to grasp his own identity.... He who has lost his honor no longer exists."[17] In such an environment, we can imagine the perfect scandal of Jesus associating with marginalized people, with lepers,[18] crippled, prostitutes, toll collectors, "sinners," in short, the poorest people.[19] By attitude and by words, Jesus condemned social inequality. Text after text insists on this "program" of his: see Luke 6:20–21, 36–38, "blessed are you who are poor" and "the measure you give will be the measure you get back"; 12:16–21 on the rich man's foolish dreams; 12:33–34 (// Matt 6:19–21), "Where your treasure is, there your heart will be also"; 16:13 (// Matt 6:24), on God and mammon; and 16:19–31, on "poor Lazarus." Jesus claimed that "the reign of God was coming wherever good things happen to the poor," as José A. Pagola says.[20]

---

16. See Gerhard Lenski, *Power and Privilege: A Theory of Social Stratification* (Chapel Hill: University of North Carolina Press, 1984 [1966]). We must remember that, to the extent that Palestine was Hellenized—an incontrovertible fact—the Greek influence went toward despising the *chora*. Now, Jesus was a "Galilean peasant," as Crossan says. On the other hand, one has to reckon with a deep prophetic influence on the pious Jews, so that they almost equated "poor" with "righteous."

17. Pierre Bourdieu, "The Sentiment of Honour in Kabyle Society," in *Honour and Shame: The Values of Mediterranean Society*, ed. John G. Peristiany (Chicago: Chicago University Press, 1966), 211–12.

18. The lepers included people afflicted with psoriasis, eczema, and all skin diseases. Jesus neutralizes the principle sick = cursed, that is, sickness as a deserved fate; see Luke 13:4–5.

19. Jesus's companionship with such people (see Luke 14:21) is in clear opposition to the Essene rule that excludes from the sect "anyone impaired in one's flesh, with paralyzed feet or hands, limping or blind or deaf or mute or hit in one's flesh of an imperfection that the eye can see" (1QSa 2:5–7, a rule based on Lev 21:17–23 regarding the priests).

20. José A. Pagola, *Jesus: An Historical Approximation*, trans. Margaret Wilde (Miami: Convivium, 2009), 99.

Along the line of pride and shame, I would say anticipatively that crucifixion systematically involved a total loss of honor of the victim. After a merciless flogging, the victim was stripped and nailed naked to the cross. The death was slow, after which the corpse was left hanging for vultures and wild dogs to eat its flesh. The remains were buried in a common grave, so as to deprive the dead of all identity. Hence Trypho's horrified reaction to the Christian glorification of the crucified Jesus.[21] David Daube reports a saying by Rabbi Ishmael (ca. 130 CE) when facing martyrdom: "Do I weep because we are to be slain? No, but because we are to be slain like murderers and desecrators of the Sabbath."[22] It is in the context of shame that we read about the eagerness of the gospel to "protect" the integrity of Jesus's body on the cross (John 19:31–42; cf. Ps 34:21). Similarly, rather than allowing that Jesus's corpse be buried unanointed, like a criminal, Mark says that he was anointed in advance (14:3–29), and John says that he was so by Joseph and Nicodemus (19:39–40).

A Foreword

In what follows I intend to demonstrate that Jesus was totally and unquestionably a Jew. He lived as a Jew, thought as a Jew, debated as a Jew, acted as a Jew, and died as a Jew. He was not a Jew marginally, but centrally. He had no intention of creating a new religion; rather, he was a reformer of the Judaism of his day.[23] True, his critique went far beyond intellectual subversion. In fact, Jesus progressively thought of himself as the "Son of Man," inaugurating the advent of the kingdom of God on earth. So, although he was not the founder of a new religion, he proposed and incarnated a transfigured Judaism, such as into itself eternity changed it, to paraphrase Stéphane Mallarmé.

Step by step, I hope to go ever deeper into the soul of the historical Jesus. Among the formidable obstacles he had to face were Israel's various conceptions of messiahship. Was he himself the expected messiah (see ch. 2 below, "Jesus the Messiah," 15–42)? What do other "messianic" titles like "Son of God" and "Son of Man" imply and signify (see ch. 3, "Jesus Son of Man/Son of God," 43–52)? In what way did his recorded healings,

---

21. See Justin, *Dialogue with Trypho* 90.1.
22. David Daube, "Three Questions of Form in Matthew V," *JTS* 45 (1944): 21–31.
23. Paul's preference in terms of labeling those faithful to Jesus is to call them a Jewish sect known as "the Way" (Acts 9:2; 22:4; 24:14, 22).

INTRODUCTION 9

for instance, contribute to his extraordinary claim to centrality—and even his own emerging self-consciousness (see ch. 4, "Jesus as Healer")? His dealings with the sick, the crippled, the poor, and other victims of fate or society raised the problem of the forgiveness of sin (if only because of the then-prevalent notion of the close association of sickness and sinfulness; see).[24] An all-important issue is thus how Jesus read and understood Torah (see ch. 5, "Jesus and Torah," 71–130). In what way did he flesh out his own statement that he came to fulfill the law? Was he a new Moses, even more than the historical Moses (see ch. 6, "Jesus and Moses")? Jesus's way of thinking, teaching, and behaving stirred a perpetual controversy. True, he had disciples, but the number of his followers seems to have varied according to circumstances. His clashes with the so-called Pharisees were Homeric.[25] His relationship with the Jerusalem temple was ambiguous.[26] So it behooves us to explore his sense of belonging to his people (see ch. 7, "Jesus and Israel," 141–68).[27] Much of Jesus's impact is through his speaking in parables, most of which focus on the inconspicuous but powerful advent of the "kingdom of God," a central notion in Jesus's self-consciousness (see ch. 8, "Jesus and the Parables," 169–82; and ch. 11, "Jesus's Self-Consciousness" 197–209).

The final chapter in Jesus's life is highly dramatic. A disciple, pejoratively (?) called Judas, betrays him (see ch. 12, "Jesus Is Betrayed," 211–16); he is tried by religious and political authorities (see ch. 13, "The Trial of Jesus and His Passion," 217–38); and he is killed by the Romans on a cross (see ch. 15, "The Great Cry of Jesus on the Cross," 247–62). His death does not end the Jesus story, however, since his disciples subsequently proclaim his resurrection (see ch. 16, "Jesus and the Resurrection," 263–71). Beyond this point, Jesus becomes "Christ" for the early church, which is the ulti-

---

24. See Ps 41:4; Isa 33:24.
25. Clashes between rabbis were not unusual; see m. Hag. 2:2; m. Yebam. 16:7; t. 'Abod. Zar. 4:9. The apex of the diatribe against Pharisees comes when Jesus and the disciples go up for the last time to Jerusalem (see Mark 10:32, the disciples are afraid because they sense danger).
26. Jesus revered the temple ("my Father's house," John 2:16), but he was offended by some excesses in the cult, and by the laxity of some priests. See below the section "Jesus and the Temple" in the ch. 7, "Jesus and Israel."
27. James H. Charlesworth writes, "On the one hand, Jesus was a product of his time and spoke in the language of his country. On the other hand, as with all geniuses, Jesus transcended his time and was amazingly creative" (*The Historical Jesus: An Essential Guide*, Essential Guides [Nashville: Abingdon, 2008], 103).

mate limit for this research of ours. As a matter of fact, the thesis of the present book is to show Jesus assuming his vocation of "appointed human centre" of the kingdom of God.[28]

---

28. Martin Buber, *Two Types of Faith: A Study of the Interpenetration of Judaism and Christianity*, trans. Norman P. Goldhawk (New York: Harper & Row, 1961), 104. See Matt 11:5: "The blind receive their sight, the lame walk, the lepers are cleansed, the deaf hear, the dead are raised, and the poor have good news brought to them" (// Luke 7:22; cf. Isa 42:7; 61:2).

1
The Gospel as Retrospective

To speak of the man Jesus, I must start at the beginning. The gospel itself does so. It tells us, in Matthew and Luke, about Jesus's birth. Mark starts with his baptism by John the Baptist,[1] and John the Evangelist begins with the creation of the universe by invoking the *Logos* identified with the Christ, the Greek word for messiah.

But this ostensible chronology is defeated by an internal logic whereby the end is the beginning and the beginning is really the end. As a matter of fact, the evangelists wrote their pieces a posteriori, that is, after realizing that the man on the cross—"this man"—"was really righteous [innocent]" (Luke 23:47): "Then their eyes were opened, and they recognized him" (Luke 24:31). Thus it is the crucifixion—when it seemed that all had ended—that is the story's raison d'être. Before the disciples were able to fully grasp the meaning of Jesus's resurrection, they undoubtedly experienced a great bewilderment and sense of loss. They had nearly missed the whole affair. "We *had* hoped," they said, "that he was the one to redeem Israel.... It is true that some women ... had indeed seen a vision of angels who said that he was alive.... But besides all this, it is now the third day since these things took place" (Luke 24:21–23). Jesus's followers were gripped by the sense of a premature and disastrous end to their hopes and expectations. Their initial despair found them as "empty" as the tomb with "linen strips of cloth by themselves" (Luke 24:12), the pitiful remnants of the age of unbelief (Luke 24:11).[2]

---

1. In fact, all New Testament sources agree that Jesus's baptism constitutes the beginning of his ministry (see, e.g., Acts 10:37).

2. Elder Olson perceptively writes, "Because it fragments experience ... language must give successive expression even to attributes which are simultaneous in fact" (*The Theory of Comedy* [Bloomington: Indiana University Press, 1968], 43).

When they finally recognized Jesus, they had to reassess all that had preceded. "Remember how he told you while he was still in Galilee.... Then they remembered his words" (24:6–8). Until that reawakening, the words and the acts of the Jewish Jesus were shrouded in ambiguity. Even those who knew him best, those who had followed him from the beginning of his ministry, "did not understand these things at first" (John 12:16). It was only "when Jesus was glorified," John continues, that "they remembered." Yes, their eyes needed to be opened (Luke 24:31). Typically, after Easter, the disciples are urged to return to Galilee: "There you will see him" (Mark 16:7). It is a return to the beginning and a new assessment of Jesus's person and life.

Women had played a major role in Jesus's ministry and were again playing a central part in the last events of Jesus's life. Indeed, Jesus's attitude toward women during his ministry is vindicated by the role of women in the "discovery" of the empty tomb. He cured sick women (Mary Magdalena, for instance), and some of them probably saw this act as equivalent to a call to discipleship.[3] John P. Meier is puzzled by the reality of female discipleship without this title in the New Testament. One exception is the term *mathētria* in Acts 9:36, applied to Tabitha. But note the missing ingredient in female discipleship: being sent as missionaries to spread the gospel. (For one exception, however, see Junia in Rom 16:7).

It remains that women followed Jesus to the end. Luke 8:1–3 says, "and also some women"; Matt 27:55 speaks of "many women." They went without chaperone and thus exposed themselves to being shunned by a society that frowned on such behavior. This was "discontinuous with the Judaism of the time and with what Luke presents ... of the first generation Christian mission."[4] We find the faithful women again—and most noticeably—at the foot of the cross (Mark 15:47; 16:1–8; John 19:25).[5] Jesus remained celibate, like John the Baptist and, before them, the prophet Jeremiah.[6] He may even have been accused of being a eunuch (Matt 19:12). Jesus's

---

3. See John P. Meier, *Companions and Competitors*, vol. 3 of *A Marginal Jew: Rethinking the Historical Jesus*, ABRL (New York: Doubleday, 2001), 77.

4. Ibid., 76.

5. Common to all the lists is the name of Mary Magdalena.

6. Had Jesus been married, the least to be expected is that his wife be beneath the cross with the other women. Indirectly, Jesus's identification with Jeremiah by the crowd (Matt 16:14) may be an indication of his celibacy. Jeremiah stands off as sufferer but also as celibate.

passion was for the kingdom of God and the "good news of God" (Mark 1:14). Furthermore, his celibacy must be envisaged from the perspective of Jesus as manifestation of the kingdom of God, in which, he says, the just will be like angels and sexual distinction disappears (Mark 12:25). Furthermore, during his ministry, Jesus's commerce with women—a fact stressed by all the gospels—is of great importance. For the male genius tends "to bypass the woman and the species role of his own body.... The genius can try to procreate himself spiritually."[7]

*

The present study purposely limits itself to the Synoptic Gospels, except for occasional references to the writings of Paul and John. For their part, Paul and John could only draw their conclusions about the person of the Christ *after the fact*, that is, in the light of his resurrection.[8] In the Gospels of Matthew and Luke, such conclusions were retrofitted "horizontally" by recounting Jesus's miraculous birth. Paul and John introduced a "vertical" speculation about the Christ's preexistence and deification "in heaven" (his apotheosis). In both cases—the virgin birth and the divine Word made flesh—we move beyond the boundaries of the historical Jesus. From a historical point of view, we are either too early or too late. The phenomenological effect in both cases is an oversized "Jesus Christ" transcending all human limitations.[9]

---

7. Ernest Becker, *The Denial of Death* (New York: Free Press, 1973), 118.

8. According to Hans Conzelmann, three Synoptic passages are genuine: Mark 8:27–30 (Peter's confession); 12:35–37 (in relationship with David); 14:61 (before the Sanhedrin; for Conzelmann, this text, as such, is inauthentic) (Conzelmann, *Jesus: The Classic Article from RGG Expanded and Updated*, trans. J. Raymond Lord, ed. John Reumann (Philadelphia: Fortress, 1973, 42 [= "Jesus Christus," *RGG*, 3rd ed. vol. 3, cols. 619–53]).

9. Meier states, "For all practical purposes ... our early, independent sources for the historical Jesus boils down to the Four Gospels, a few scattered data elsewhere in the NT, and Josephus" (*The Roots of the Problem and the Person*, vol. 1 of *A Marginal Jew: Rethinking the Historical Jesus*, ABRL [New York: Doubleday, 1991], 140). Already in John 1:49–51, one can see that John establishes an equation between messiah, king of Israel, Son of God, and Son of Man (see John 1:24–42; cf. Gen 28:12–17). In John 3:13, the Son of Man has descended from heaven; in 5:18, he is "making himself equal to God"; in 5:27 the Son of Man is judge (in parallel with the Similitudes of Enoch, Q, Matthew, and Luke); in 9:35–39 and 6:62, his preexistence is again emphasized; in

The four gospels were redacted "late," while our earliest witness, Paul, wrote in the 50s, that is, some twenty years after the events. This fact may be interpreted ambiguously. For, in spite of this distance in time, we find a surprising persistence and vitality of the reality called Jesus. Twenty years after the crucifixion of the Nazarene, the ripples of his martyrdom had not diminished, a surprising fact as thousands of other people had been and were being tortured by the Romans. On the contrary, those ripples proved to have earthshaking consequences.

12:23, the Son of Man is glorified through his death (see vv. 24–25, 33); in 14:1–3, he draws his followers with him to heaven.

2
Jesus the Messiah

Jesus was born around 7 or 6 BCE, shortly before the death in 4 BCE of Herod the Great (who, incidentally, practiced state terrorism). He seems to have started his ministry at the age of thirty-three or thirty-four, after his baptism by John the Baptist, probably in 27 or 28 CE. The gospels cover about two and a half years of Jesus's life. On April 6 or 7 of the year 30 CE, at the age of thirty-six, he was arrested and crucified.

We know few details about Jesus's life before he became a public figure in Galilee and, later, in Judea.[1] He was a disciple of John in the desert. "More than anyone else, [John the Baptist] influenced the trajectory of Jesus."[2] He was preaching conversion at the very place where Joshua, successor of Moses, had led the people just before crossing the Jordan River, opposite Jericho. His baptism was symbolic of a new beginning by crossing again to the other shore and occupying anew the land of the promise. Ezekiel 36:25–38 ("I will sprinkle clean water upon you") would thus be fulfilled.

As a disciple, Jesus repeatedly heard that someone "who was to come" was on his way. At some point, Jesus realized that he himself might be this someone (Mark 1:7). His baptism by John shows that he agreed with the necessity of Israel's radical conversion before the kingdom could come. However, the yawning gap in the approach of the two men grew with time.

---

1. We do not know anything of Jesus before the beginning of his ministry. In parallel to this, note that, according to Jewish tradition, the great Rabbi Aqiba remained an unschooled shepherd until he was forty (b. Pesaḥ. 49b). Schalom Ben-Chorin stresses the "new birth" of Jesus when baptized by John the Baptist (*Brother Jesus. The Nazarene Through Jewish Eyes*, trans. Jared S. Klein and Max Reinhart (Athens: University of Georgia Press, 2001), see, e.g., 26).

2. José A. Pagola, *Jesus: An Historical Approximation*, trans. Margaret Wilde (Miami: Convivium, 2009), 78.

Gerd Theissen, John Dominic Crossan, and others rightly insist on the shift that occurred from the people going to John in the desert to Jesus going to the people as an itinerant prophet. We should keep in mind the important distinction between the people in pilgrimage and Jesus as himself a pilgrim, thus emphasizing the centrality of Israel.

These pieces of information are welcome, but they hardly fill the decades of Jesus's life before his ministry. We do not know, for example, what language he spoke—although it was likely Aramaic—or to what extent, or even whether he was educated. Jesus's being born in Nazareth (not in Bethlehem)[3] and living in what was an obscure village, which is not mentioned in most Jewish sources either before or after the first century CE,[4] one wonders what kind of education, if any, he could have received and through what channels. The Mishnah, it is true, describes quite a widespread educational system throughout the country, but the Mishnah was written some two hundred years after Jesus's time, and Emil Schürer says that this is a "later legend."[5] I shall return to this point below.

We do know that Palestine was a quadrilingual nation in Jesus's time. On the one hand, Latin was the language of power. On the other hand, Greek had become the lingua franca around the Mediterranean as a result of the Hellenization process that had begun at least in the third century BCE.[6] To a large extent, Judea also was Hellenized. Among the Hellenized Jews of Jerusalem (like Stephen in the book of Acts), normal discourse must have been in Greek. (Did Andrew or Philip serve as interpreters?) The subsequent Maccabean revolt reimposed Hebrew and Aramaic in the land, but with limited success. Josephus himself was once invited by Titus to speak with him by in Aramaic, since it was the language that the people

---

3. According to John 7:42, Jesus was not born in Bethlehem, nor of the Davidic line. Let us add that he cannot have been born under King Herod who died in 4 BCE.

4. Archaeology uncovered an extensive settlement from the second century BCE. Nazareth is isolated but lies not far off the north-south highway from Jerusalem to Damascus. Lower Galilee was one of the most densely populated areas of the Roman Empire. Furthermore, the city of Sepphoris was only four miles from Nazareth, about an hour's walk.

5. Emil Schürer, *A History of the Jewish People in the Time of Jesus Christ: 175 B.C.–A.D. 135*, rev. and ed. Geza Vermes, Fergus Millar, and Martin Goodman, 5 vols. (Edinburgh: T&T Clark, 1986), 78.

6. That explains why the gospels were written in Greek.

2. JESUS THE MESSIAH

knew best.[7] Hebrew was by far the language most used at Qumran, which led to mishnaic Hebrew. The targumim, however, are written in Aramaic.[8]

Jesus preached in synagogues, including the one in Nazareth. It is true that we probably have to understand "synagogue" as the assembly itself, rather than a building. He read from the scrolls, which shows that he knew at least some Hebrew, although he assuredly spoke in Aramaic. Jesus's sayings contain Aramaisms[9]—including phrases such as "thalitha qum" (Mark 5:41), "abba" (14:36), "ephatha" (7:34), "eli, eli, lema sevakhthani." We should also note the relative absence of Hebraisms in his sayings.

In John 8:6, a highly loaded text about the denunciation to Jesus of an adulterous woman, Jesus is described as writing on the ground. Or was he simply doodling? Raymond Brown says that Jesus was just indicating his lack of interest or impatience with the accusers.[10] As is well known, Jesus shames the vociferous crowd and remains alone with the woman. Since all of the accusers had left, he tells her, "Neither do I accuse you. Go home and sin no more."

Does John 8:6 shed light on Jesus's education? Probably not. However, in my opinion based on the portrait of the Nazarene provided by the gospel, Jesus was a man who was intimate with the Scriptures and who was entirely dedicated to scriptural exposition and interpretation. That he was also a carpenter (*textōn*, Mark 6:3; Matt 13:55) like his father becomes at most an aside in his life.[11]

---

7. Flavius Josephus (ca. 37–106 CE) was a Jewish historian and an apologist for Judaism. His works are very biased and are thus to be used with caution. Among his classics, see *Antiquities of the Jews* and *The Wars of the Jews*, both of which shed light on the postbiblical period.

8. At Qumran, 11QtgJob is a translation, not a commentary. Let us also mention in Aramaic 1QapGen and 4QprNab. There are also extent copies of Tobit and 4QtgLev.

9. Aramaic only can explain the use of "debts" in the "Our Father" prayer; only in Aramaic does the noun "debt" serve as a metaphor for sin (*hovah*).

10. Raymond E. Brown, *The Gospel According to John 1–12*, AB 29 (Garden City, NY: Doubleday, 1966), 333–34. John 7:15 says that Jesus "had not studied." But Jesus could comment on the Hebrew Scriptures! In Luke 4:16–30, he reads Isa 61:1–2 in the synagogue—but the authenticity of the pericope is questioned. (On this pericope, see further ch. 15, "The Great Cry of Jesus on the Cross.")

11. According to Geza Vermes, "carpenter" and "carpenter's son" were metaphors to mean "scholar" (*Jesus the Jew: A Historian's Reading of the Gospels* [New York: Macmillan, 1973], 21–22). This identification is doubtful. At any rate, the city of Sepphoris, after the Romans razed it to the ground when Jesus was five, was quickly rebuilt by

Luke 24:44 summarizes Jesus's use of the Scriptures, that is, the three subdivisions of the MT: "These are my words that I spoke to you while I was still with you—that everything written about me in the Law of Moses, the Prophets, and the Psalms must be fulfilled." We find the same acknowledgment of "Scripture" in Ben Sira (ca. 130 BCE), prologue 1, 3, 7, "the Law, the Prophets, and the Writings of the fathers." The Qumranic text 4QMMT 7:10 has "the book of Moses, the Prophets, and David." Hence, it is inconceivable that Jesus would fail to exploit all the sources of information available to him. Where he found them must be guesswork on our part, but in all certainty the Nazareth synagogue—not necessarily a building, as noted above—played a major role. It was also a school, to which Jesus once returned to teach (Mark 6:1–6 and parr.). Furthermore, education occurred in the family, with the father in charge of the children's "studies." Nor do we know how long it took for Jesus to build his solid "scholarship," but since Jesus's preaching started late in his life (see Luke 3:23), he had plenty of time to prepare himself.[12] This means that any statistical discussion of the literacy or illiteracy of the Galileans in general is of little value.[13] As far as Jesus is concerned, the problem is not general but specific. As a matter of fact, gospel tradition does not present Jesus as an ignoramus, but rather to the contrary. As a token of his literacy, I cite his recurrent question to Jewish authorities, "Haven't you ever read …?" In Luke 10:25–37 Jesus asks the lawyer, "How do you read?" In the Gospel of John, of course, God is Jesus's teacher (8:28).

At times, Jesus was called rabbi or teacher (e.g., Mark 9:5; 11:21; see Mark, M, L, and John). In addition, James the famous brother of Jesus demonstrated the mettle of a leader after Jesus's death in Jerusalem. In conclusion, John P. Meier's statement is incontrovertible: "One … has to allow for a high degree of natural talent—perhaps even genius—that more than compensated for the [alleged] low level of Jesus' formal education."[14]

Antipas and thus provided work for craftsmen (including father and son?). The reconstruction took twenty years.

12. During the so-called hidden years.

13. We must remember that Rabbi Yohanan ben Zakkai taught for seventeen years in 'Arab in Galilee, halfway between Nazareth and Capernaum, probably between 25 and 45 CE. 'Arab, to be sure, was no scholarly desert.

14. John P. Meier, *The Roots of the Problem and the Person*, vol. 1 of *A Marginal Jew: Rethinking the Historical Jesus*, ABRL (New York: Doubleday, 1991), 278. In support of Meier's judgment, see Matt 11:25–27.

2. JESUS THE MESSIAH

Martin Hengel speaks of him as a charismatic and refers to John 7:15 ("How does this man have such learning?") and Mark 6:2–3 ("What is this wisdom that has been given to him?").[15] Marcus Borg, in his turn, prefers "mystic."[16]

Speaking of instructors, the functions of a priest in Israel bear notice. He was more than an offerer of sacrifices. As priest, he was an official interpreter of the Torah. This implied a judicial function as well.[17] Presiding over sacrifices, instruction, and judgment, the priest was the most powerful religious functionary in Israel. Independently of Jesus's opposition to the establishment, to centers of power and to institutions in general, the innovation of the synagogue—where the Torah was read and interpreted by lay teachers—constituted competition with the temple. Besides, the rivalry between Pharisees and the priesthood was born already around 170 BCE, when Ptolemaic authorities made of the high priest the supreme leader in Israel. This stirred a laity reaction in the name of its right to call to account royal and priestly polity, like the ancient prophets did.[18] The supporters of the priests were the Sadducees.

At the time of Jesus, John the Baptist had made an inexpensive rite of purification generally available, in preparation for the imminent advent of the kingdom of God, in contrast to the expensive services in the temple.[19] Then, when the Romans destroyed the temple in 70 CE, the synagogue appeared as the providential tool of the people to survive the ruin of their religious center. Jesus had prophetically announced the coming of this terrible event. Paradoxically, this does not signal the end of the world, but is a catastrophe that can be remedied ("Within three days, I shall rebuild it").

---

15. Martin Hengel, *The Charismatic Leader and His Followers* (Edinburgh: T&T Clark, 1981), *passim*.

16. Marcus J. Borg, *Jesus: Uncovering the Life, Teachings, and Relevance of a Religious Revolutionary* (San Francisco: HarperSanFrancisco, 2006), 110 and 131ff. As such, Jesus leaves the boundaries of self-consciousness and opens himself up to experience connection.

17. See, e.g., Deut 17:9–13; Ezek 44:23; Mic 3:11; Hag 2:11–13; Mal 2:6–7. See Sir 45:1–5 (on Moses), "[God] gave him the commandments face to face, the law of life and knowledge, so that he might teach Jacob the covenant and Israel his decrees" (v. 5).

18. It is not the first time that the prophet collides with the priest. Hosea speaks of "gangs of priests" (6:9) lying in wait and willfully assassinating "defenseless people for spoil."

19. See Morton Smith, *The Secret Gospel: The Discovery of Interpretation of the Secret Gospel According to Mark* (Middletown CA: Dawn Horse Press, 1973), 208.

We saw that, at times, Jesus himself is called "rabbi," which for all practical purposes identifies him as belonging to the synagogal, not the priestly, form of Judaism.[20]

This point is important. As a teacher, Jesus competed with the priests who held the privilege of instructing the people and can be considered as having challenged the priestly leadership. As a matter of fact, many priests, in contrast with the rabbis (see below), had lost all rights to instruct the people because they were "defilers" (Matt 12:5), they envied the authority of Jesus (Mark 15:10), showing, by the way, how indifferent they were to human suffering (Luke 10:31).[21] We shall encounter this same competition with the priesthood when Jesus assumes the authority to forgive sins. As a matter of fact, the priests would normally determine whether atonement had actually been made through the offering of appropriate sacrifices.

Besides, several contemporary sources, in addition to the gospel, denounce the Jerusalem priesthood as having mixed motives, to say the least. The covenanters of Qumran come to mind. It seems incontrovertible, for instance, that some priests, especially among the leaders, were opportunistic in their interaction with the Roman authorities. This is in the background of the Enochial literature's secularization of the title "Son of Man," which initially was a priestly title.[22] We should also keep in mind that a Pharisee named Eleazar invited the Hasmonean Hyrcanus II (63–40 BCE) to relinquish the high priesthood in favor of civil power only. Official prerogatives, as a result, shifted to the Sadducees by royal fiat!

We find a different kind of criticism regarding another group of contemporary teachers, namely, the Pharisee rabbis (teachers).[23] Although at points Jesus's competition with them was "professional," he acknowl-

---

20. In a tour de force, the author of Hebrews hails Jesus Christ as the high priest!

21. A tactless high priest once greeted the converts Rabbis Shemaya and Abtalion, the masters of R. Hillel: "Shalom to the sons of gentiles," to which they replied, "Shalom to the sons of gentiles who perform Aaron's work, but not to the sons of Aaron who do not do the work of Aaron" (Yoma 71b).

22. See my *The Book of Daniel*, trans. David Pellauer (London: SPCK; Atlanta: John Knox, 1979), on Dan 7, 122–34, 145–48.

23. Not all Pharisees are rabbis, and not all rabbis are Pharisees. But Jacob Neusner writes, "The rabbis after 70 assuredly regarded themselves as the continuators of Pharisaism" (*The Idea of Purity in Ancient Judaism*, The Haskell Lectures, 1972-1973 [Leiden: Brill, 1973], 65). See also Hyam Maccoby, *Early Rabbinic Writings* (Cambridge: Cambridge University Press, 1988) (who seems to have missed the Neusner quote that precedes).

edged that they occupied the seat of Moses (Matt 23:2–3).[24] Nevertheless, as distinguished from them, Jesus did not base his teachings on the exposition of the Torah but rather on the radical authority of the charismatic *exousia* ("power") that he had (Mark 1:22, 27 // Matt 7:29; cf. Luke 4:32, 36). His parables, for instance, "never, in the rabbinic fashion, serve the purpose of expounding the Torah, but are for the explanation of his eschatological message."[25]

It remains that Jesus, disputing with Pharisees, honored their questions. Decisively, however, the responses coming from the one and from the others are very different, but they are, generally speaking, a matter of interpretation. Meier calls the Nazarene "a rabbinic teacher of the Law."[26] Amy-Jill Levine, although adamantly opposed to counting Jesus among the Pharisees, recalls for instance Jesus's lesson on divorce (Matt 19), on the great commandment (Luke 10), on the fig tree (a biblical image, as is also the vineyard in Mark 13:28; Matt 20:1–16), on the "Son of Man," and so on. Further, Jesus repeatedly uses a rabbinic argument based on *qal wahomer* (a fortiori, e.g., Luke 13:15; 14:5), and so on.[27]

In addition—and the material that follows should be considered with caution due to its relatively late composition—some charismatic figures around the time of the Nazarene serve as striking partial parallels. Following Geza Vermes, I refer to Honi (the circle-maker) and Hanina ben Dosa.[28] These figures, around whom legends later coalesced, are important to us—whether they are historical or legendary—for multiple reasons. They were charismatic miracle-workers (see Josephus, *Ant.* 14.22

---

24. Matt 5:20 adds, "Unless your righteousness exceeds that of the scribes and Pharisees...," which is an indirect compliment.

25. On this, see Hengel, *The Charismatic Leader*, 48–49, 67–68.

26. John P. Meier, *Mentor, Message and Miracles*, vol. 2 of *A Marginal Jew: Rethinking the Historical Jesus*, ABRL (New York: Doubleday, 1994), 434.

27. Personal communication.

28. See Vermes, *Jesus the Jew*, 69ff. Of the same, Vermes, "Hanina ben Dosa: A Controversial Galilean Saint from the First Century of the Christian Era," *JJS* 23 (1972): 28–50, and 24 (1973): 51–64. Vermes rightly says that historiography is "a literary genre completely alien to talmudic and midrashic writings" ("Hanina ben Dosa," 1972, 28). Hence it is a methodological mistake to attempt to reconstruct a historical profile of Honi (the circle-maker or circle-drawer) and Hanina ben Dosa. Clearly Honi draws a circle like Elijah did on the Mount Carmel (1 Kgs 18:30–38, 41–45), and Hanina prays with his head between his knees (Ber. 34b) like Elijah did in 1 Kgs 18:42. The control of rainfall recalls that of Elijah's in 1 Kgs 18 (see Ta'an. 24b = Yoma 53b).

about a certain "Onias" [Honi?], who died in 65 BCE). In m. Ta'an. 3:8, Honi is said to have used God's "great Name!" Flabbergasted, Simeon ben Shetach (first-century-BCE president of the Sanhedrin) considered excommunicating him (for blasphemy, presumably). He was, nevertheless, an eminently nonclassical model of piety and part of the orthodox tradition. In Ta'an. 23, he is called "rabbi."[29] His rabbinic colleagues saw him as a (spoiled) son of God and treated as such by the divinity. In short, he looms large in the Jewish tradition, although not as an expounder of the Torah. Strikingly, Honi called God *abba* ("father"), thus stressing his intimacy with God. Note that the mentioning by Honi of God thrice as *abba* is unique in Jewish tradition outside of the gospel, with the exception of his grandson, Rabbi Hani'a ha-Nehba (end of first century BCE) in Ta'an. 23b.[30]

Meier minimizes the importance of all this, but the point, as I see it, lies neither in ostensible nor actual chronology, but elsewhere. Jewish tradition could embrace these charismatic figures even though they used unorthodox means, such as uttering the Tetragrammaton and thus, at a minimum, were subject to suspicion of blasphemy.

In other words, had the tradition surrounding Honi (the circle-maker) and Hanina ben Dosa[31] been written before the time of Jesus, it would

---

29. But John Dominic Crossan may be right in his judgment: "Terms such as *hasid* or rabbi and emphases on prayer or legal observance are all parts of the rabbinization process necessary to have these popular and famous magicians included in the rabbinical corpus" (*The Historical Jesus: The Life of a Mediterranean Jewish Peasant* [San Francisco: HarperSanFrancisco, 1991], 157).

30. Joachim Jeremias adds, "but not as an address to God" (in contrast with Jesus using *abba* in prayers). See Jeremias, "Abba as an Address to God," in *New Testament Theology: The Proclamation of Jesus* (New York: Scribner's Sons, 1971), 62–68. The term *abba* appears especially in targumim; see Tg. Ps. 89:27, where *'abi* is translated *'abba*, and Tg. Mal. 2:20, where *'ab* is translated similarly; but even here it is not a direct address to God. In a tenth-century CE document called Seder Eliahu Rabba, the address to God is in the words, *'abi shebashamayim* ("my Father, who are in heaven"), an exceptional case but also a very late one. God is also addressed as Father in pseudepigraphic literature: Sir 23:1, 4 LXX; 3 Macc 6:3, 8; Apocryphon of Ezekiel, frag. 3; Wis 14:3; see Jeremias, "Abba as an Address to God."

31. On Hanina ben Dosa, there are three mishnaic traditions: m. 'Abot 3:10–11, where he is called "Rabbi" and teaches ethical lessons to the effect that compassion toward others is determinative. M. Soṭah 9:15 tells us that Hanina was a "man of deed," presumably of kindly deeds. In m. Ber. 5:5, Hanina ben Dosa's feeling of easiness or uneasiness when praying forecasts for him whether the person he is interceding for

have served as a precedent. Chronologically, the reverse order took place, leading us to wonder whether the traditions around these charismatic mystics were influenced by the Nazarene figure, my presupposition being that there may have been some permeability between formative Judaism and formative Christianity, as adversarial as they may seem.[32] At any rate, these dramaturgical "holy" men perturb the status quo of a rigid system of sacred times and places, that is, the prescribed ways of relating to God.

One thing is certain: the Pharisees' problems were also Jesus's problems, and like most of them, Jesus was a nonordained teacher. So, as regards Jesus's education, we note the incredible courage of a layman (probably without academic training, although assuredly not an ʿam haʾarets) confronting the highest authorities of his people. A parallel with the prophet Amos, for instance, comes to mind.

Even Paul's antithesis of Judaism and Christianity rests on the basis of a preestablished kinship between the two (see Rom 9–11): they have a common trunk but represent different branches. Both acknowledge a common traditional authority: the Scriptures.

*

The term *messiah* means "the anointed one." This notion goes back in time to ancient Near Eastern royal ideology and practice. In the Hebrew Scriptures, "messiah" designates the reigning king, who receives unction and sits on his throne as part of the enthronement festival. The word "messiah" was attached to the Davidic dynasty in Judah in this sense. It is also used on occasion to describe other high functionaries in Israel, for example, the high priest during the Second Temple era. However, the technical—that is, eschatological—meaning of "messiah" does not appear until the first century BCE. This shift in meaning is due to a general disappointment

---

will live or die. He is credited with healing from a distance (Ber. 34b) for he was a miracle-worker in Taʿan. 24b–25a.

32. See Ulrich Luz, *Matthew 1–7*, trans. J. E. Crouch, Hermeneia (Minneapolis: Fortress, 2007), 55: "The similarity between the Gospel of Matthew and many of the traditions about [Yohanan ben Zakkai] is amazing." Andrew Simmonds: "'Woe to You … Hypocrites': Rereading Matthew 23:13–36" *BSac* 166 (July–September 2009): 336n2: "Shabbat 116b seems to know Matthew 5:17–18. There was clearly a unilateral influence of Qumran (cf. the Ebionites) and a bilateral influence of the Baptist's group on early Christianity."

regarding the rulers of Judea and Galilee and, eventually, to the absence of a king to lead the nation. In fact, messianism remained largely dormant during the Hellenistic period until the revolt of the Maccabees.[33] Hasmonean ambitions, however, were rebuked within orthodox milieus, and messianic expectations were reinterpreted eschatologically and apocalyptically. Since the Hasmoneans were not descendants of David, the parties of the opposition insisted on a Davidide Messiah.

There are three texts that bear witness to this crucial metamorphosis of messiahship:

1. Psalms of Solomon 17–19; Parables of Enoch 37–71 (see 48:10; 52:4); and the Eighteen Benedictions synagogal prayer.
2. The Qumran literature: 1QSa and other texts.
3. The Jerusalem Talmud (see y. Ta'an. 4:8, 68d) and Philo (see *On Rewards and Punishments* 95). The witness of 1 Enoch 48:4, for instance, claims that the messiah will be a *shebet*, a ruler's staff, as found in Gen 49:10; Num 24:17; Testament of Judah 24 and Qumran texts claim a Davidic messiah (as distinguished from the priestly messiah). He will also be the "light of the nations," as in Isa 42:6 and 49:6 (cf. 2:2 and 9:1) and "the hope of the afflicted" (see Isa 49:10; 61:1; 66:2). He or an angelic figure is preexistent as far as his name is concerned in 1 Enoch.[34] I note that he is not associated here with the line of David.

Among the covenanters of the Judean desert (mainly from the first half of the first century BCE), we find a revival of messianic expectations. So, in Pesher Isaiah on 11:1-5, the messiah's coming is "at the end of days." The expression "Branch of David" is used on the model of Isa 11:1; Jer 23:5; 33:15; and Zech 3:8; 6:12. In 4Q252 (Pesher Genesis), it is a matter of the "messiah of righteousness." In 4Q285, the Branch of David is the "prince of the congregation," as he is in 1QSb 5:20 (= 29) or CD 7:17.[35]

---

33. Note the absence of a messiah in Daniel and Enoch books, where the "Son of Man" figure is rather angelic.

34. He is, in 48:10 and 52:4, the Messiah; in chapter 71 [perhaps not authentic] Enoch himself is "Son of Man."

35. Note the parallel with Pss. Sol. 17. Here the Messiah is a mighty warrior who will drive out the gentiles, that is, the Roman occupiers.

2. JESUS THE MESSIAH

As is well known, Qumran texts refer to a double messiah. Scroll 1QS 9:11 speaks of *meshihey 'aharon weisrael* while CD uses the singular in the expression *meshiah 'aharon weisrael*.[36] The "Son of God" text, 4Q246, says that someone will be called a "Son of God" and "Son of the Most High" and that his kingdom will be everlasting (cf. Luke 1:32). As for 4Q521, it evokes a messiah whom heaven and earth will obey. He is described as healing the sick, reviving the dead, and preaching good news to the poor. The parallel with Matt 11:2-6—where the rising of the dead is mentioned although not included in the model text of Isa 35:3-6—is unmistakable. Let us add to this powerful image the text of 4Q541, where the messiah is a redeemer, compared with the servant of the Lord of Isa 53, and hailed as a priest as in Testament of Levi 18.[37] On the poor inheriting the earth (see Matt 5:35; cf. Isa 61:1-3; 66:2), David Flusser rather refers to 1QH 18:14-15.[38] In all of this, there is "a strong overtone of social protest and it [Isa 40:29 LXX] became an expression of eschatological hope."[39]

---

36. Cf. the "two sons of oil" in Zech 4:14; furthermore, the Hasmoneans had combined for themselves both the kingship and the supreme priesthood.

37. In the New Testament, the use of Isa 53 is surprisingly scarce (Matt 12:18; Acts 3:13, 26; 4:27, 30; 1 Pet 2:22-25). In Assumption of Moses 3:11, the reference is rather to the redeeming suffering of Moses: he suffered much in Egypt, at the Red Sea, and in the desert for forty years. In 11:17 Moses declares, "[Dominus] me constituit pro eis et pro peccatis eorum." Cf. Deut 9:18, where his death expiates the sin of the golden calf (see Num 25:3, 5, 18; 31:16) and the sin of Peor (see Deut 34:6 and its Targum; also Soṭah 14a). On the other hand, while 4 Ezra and 2 Baruch speak of the death of the messiah, it has no atoning dimension. The Targum on Isa 52-53 bypasses the servant's suffering altogether.

38. David Flusser, *Judaism and the Origins of Christianity* (Jerusalem: Magnes, 1988), 102ff. But Florentino García Martínez's translation is different! (*The Dead Sea Scrolls Translated: The Qumran Texts in English*, 2nd ed. [Leiden: Brill; Grand Rapids: Eerdmans, 1994], 359). The poor shall inherit the earth (cf. Ps 37:11) is given a symbolic meaning, as in m. Sanh. 10:1 and m. Qidd. 1:10. In 1QM 10:9, 13, the poor seem to be the community. See 1QS 10:26–11:1 on the oppressed, those with a stray spirit and the meek. In summary, Flusser writes, "The clear literary parallel to Matt. 5:3-5 in the *Thanksgiving Scroll [1QH]* (xviii: 14-15) is a part of a whole ideological complex in the literature and thought of the Dead Sea Sect; the passages quoted from sectarian literature contain identical and similar designations of those whom God loves and who will be saved as the Beatitudes: paupers" (*Judaism and the Origins of Christianity*, 146).

39. Flusser, *Judaism and the Origins of Christianity*, 119. Further, let us note that the strong social motif we find in the Magnificat, for example, has precedents in 4 Ezra 11:42 and in 1 Enoch, esp. chs. 94-104; see also 5:7. In 1QM, as in the Magnificat, the social is linked with the nationalistic. In the view of Flusser (ibid., 143-44), John the

Did the covenanters identify the Davidic messiah with their teacher of righteousness? The latter, it is true, understood himself as the servant of YHWH, but there is no evidence that he himself was regarded as the messiah.

*

Listing the functions of the messiah indicates the variety of achievements expected of him. And this is only the tip of the iceberg. According to Jewish traditions, the messiah must meet a number of contradictory demands.[40] For instance, in the view of Hayim Vital (1543–1620)[41] and Martin Buber, he may not indulge in self-proclamation. (The Markan concept of messianic secrecy comes to mind; cf. John 8:14–15). The messiah must be kingly but humble, even, according again to mystical kabbalah, considering himself as 'ayin ("nothing") (Jesus, recall, enters Jerusalem riding a donkey; see Zech 9:9). He is the son of David (as in Matt 1–2; Rom 1:3), but viewed by others he is a foreigner (like Cyrus in Isa 45:1). He is to be a prophet (see Deut 18; Isa 61:1), a priest,[42] a sage, a magician, a mystic, a theurgist, and, at the same time, both a law-abiding "patriot" and a reformer. But he is also Adamic, Enochic, preexistent, and divinized (but only a posteriori, says Nathan of Gaza, the "prophet" follower of Sabbatai Zwi in the seventeenth century). Some go so far as proclaiming the messiah as creator and redeemer, but he is also to suffer and even to die to atone for our sins.[43] He

---

Baptist's disciples composed this song. John offered his baptism of repentance to all Israel and not to the members of the sect of Qumran only.

40. See John J. Collins, *The Scepter and the Star: The Messiahs of the Dead Sea Scrolls and Other Ancient Literature* (New York: Doubleday, 1995), 195. Moshe Idel speaks of the "diverging types of Kabbalah" and of eschatological visions in Jewish mysticism (see his *Messianic Mystics* [New Haven: Yale University Press, 1998], 204, 248).

41. A disciple of the famous kabbalist Isaac Luria.

42. As in (First) Zechariah where the anointment is granted to Zerubbabel as king and to Joshua as high priest. See Hebrews; possibly Rom 8:34; see also Pss. Sol. 17:30 (restoration of the Davidic dynasty and the priestly functions by a sinless leader whose mere word shall establish purity of Israel); Testament of Levi 14–18 // Mark 1:9–11.

43. In the late first century CE, see 4 Ezra, 2 Baruch and Wisdom of Solomon. Fourth Ezra 7:28–29 reads, "My son the Messiah shall die and all who draw human breath" (// 2 Bar 30:1; a Christian redactional addition is conspicuous in both texts). Fourth Ezra 13 is central: "something like the figure of a man" comes out of the sea and flies with the clouds. He is preexistent but born from the line of David.

2. JESUS THE MESSIAH

is a representative of his people but is also universal, a savior of his people first, then of the world. He is to be just and innocent, extroverted and meditative, dynamic and visionary. He is to practice *mitsvoth* ("good deeds"), *tiqun* (the repair of the fragmented divine "vases" at creation), and *devekut* (the mystical attachment to God). Apocalyptic and transcendent, he belongs to heaven.[44] He is the restorer of the temple—unless he replaces it corporeally.[45] This list of the protean qualities of the messianic figure is not exhaustive, to the point that its flexibility leads some to even conclude, with William Scott Green, "In early Jewish literature, 'messiah' is all signifier with no signified; the term is notable primarily for its indeterminacy."[46] More to the point, Matthew Novenson writes, "Every [Jewish] messiah text drew its own creative conclusions."[47]

In the Pharisaic tradition, the messiah is the eschatological king. However, he plays practically no role in the Mishnah,[48] where we find only two references, m. Ber. 1.5 and m. Soṭah 9:15 (about "the footprints of the messiah," *'iqewoth meshiha'*). However, in the synagogal prayer called Eighteen Benedictions, in parallel with the targumic literature (see Tg. Ps.-Jon. on Genesis 49), one prays for the coming of the Branch of David. It is only

---

44. See 1 Enoch 48:8–49:3; the "Son of Man" in the gospel and 1 Enoch 37–71 (the parables of Enoch): here is a transcendent heavenly figure, an exalted Son of Man, on the model of Dan 7:13; he is also an exalted servant of the Lord on the model of Isa 49; 53:4–12; anointed by YHWH in 1 Enoch 48:10; 52:4; Acts 7:56; Heb 2:5–9).

45. See the Targums: the Messiah is the eschatological Davidide, coming at the end of days; an apocalyptic figure (warrior); he will restore the temple. In the gospel, the verb "restore" appears in Matt 17:11 // Mark 9:12 (cf. Mal 4:5 [3:24] and Acts 1:6).

46. William S. Green, "Introduction: Messiah in Judaism: Rethinking the Question," in *Judaisms and Their Messiahs at the Turn of the Christian Era*, ed. Jacob Neusner, William S. Green, and Ernest Frerichs (Cambridge: Cambridge University Press, 1987), 4.

47. Matthew V. Novenson, *Christ among the Messiahs: Christ Language in Paul and Messiah Language in Ancient Judaism* (Oxford: Oxford University Press, 2012), 178.

48. When comparing Christian and formative Jewish writings, caution demands the realization that for the former the messiah has come and therefore occupies center stage, while for the latter the messiah remains a complex figure and cannot in consequence be elaborated. Israel is central in both views, at least within the gospel if not in the later patristic literature. From a sociological perspective, the omnipresence of Christ in Christian literature constitutes a strong bulwark against an elitist governance of "the church" during the pristine era of Christianity, that is, before its complete institutionalization. By contrast, compare the rabbinic reorganization of Judaism, which has the relationship of master-disciple at center.

after 400 CE and the Christianization of the Roman Empire that we find messianic speculations in the two Talmuds and in Genesis Rabbah. At that point, the messiah became the centerpiece of salvation history.[49] For the sages in general, the messiah's coming is dependent on the full obedience of Israel to God's rule.[50] He will evince the full extent of the torah and make it fully work in the world. This and other issues, as we saw earlier, created tension with charismatic figures of the first century CE, including Jesus, Honi, and Hanina ben Dosa.[51] As a matter of fact, messianism can represent a religion of opposition, even of subversion. Henri Desroche, in his introduction to *Dieux d'hommes*,[52] says of it that it is "le sacré à l'état sauvage" within a space between the one *who* waits and *what* he waits for. Messianism subverts institutions and, therefore, remains somewhat vague both in its formulation and in its expected outcome. As such, messianism must be distinguished from utopianism, which specifies what will come. When the institution triumphs, messianism fades away. It becomes, in

---

49. The text is more explicit in Sanh. 96b–99a: the messiah is son of David; he comes at a time that cannot be calculated; his coming depends on Israel's repentance, but God may decide to bypass that requirement (97b); and before he comes, there will be a time of sufferings during which the Torah is forgotten and the people indulge in reprehensible behavior (this belongs to the motif of the *havelei ha-mashiah* [the pangs of the messiah]).

50. Some texts evoke the total observation of two Sabbaths (see Šabb. 118b), or even of one Sabbath by the whole people as a precondition for the advent of the messiah. There is no such conditionality in Jesus's teaching. He appeals merely to faith. Noteworthy is the reversal of terms of dependence. Now the acknowledged centrality of the messiah makes Israel dependent on its relationship with him. There is some kinship with the Jewish siddur (prayer book), which can be dated at shortly before or after 70 CE.

51. Each of them was called "God's son." Honi says to God, "I am as a son in the house before Thee" (m. Ta'an. 3:8). R. Simeon ben Shetah said to Honi, "Though you importune God, he does what you wish in the same way that a father does whatever his importuning son asks him" (m. Ta'an. 3:8). Cf. Luke 18:1–8. The importance of these parallels between the charismatic Jesus and Honi/Hanina is tempered, however, by what Alan J. Avery-Peck cautions, that they "reflect more about the attitudes and theologies of the third through sixth centuries, when the documents in which they were contained were edited, than about these individuals and their historical periods" ("The Galilean Charismatic and Rabbinic Piety: The Holy Man in the Talmudic Literature," in *The Historical Jesus in Context*, ed. Amy-Jill Levine, Dale C. Allison Jr., and John Dominic Crossan [Princeton: Princeton University Press, 2006], 152).

52. Henri Desroche, "Contribution à une sociologie de l'attente," *Dictionnaire des Messianismes et des Millénarismes* (Paris: Mouton, 1969).

Émile Durkheim's words, the administration of the sacred, which ceases for all practical purposes to be "sauvage." As Alfred Loisy said, instead of the kingdom of God, the church came.

The messianic expectation is that a redeemer will bring the present order, considered as disorder, to an end. Its main dimension is *time*, within which the unpredictability of the events makes the whole structure problematic. This point is important because it emphasizes the uncertainty within which the messianic "candidate" finds himself wavering. He either claims to be the messiah, or he is so proclaimed by others. In fact, more often than not he makes the claim after being so hailed by others. This is true, I contend, also for Jesus (see Luke 12:50 and John 12:27). Whether or not this point is conceded, it remains that there are messianisms without a messiah, as, for instance, in Second Isaiah's "songs" of the servant of the Lord,[53] and in Dan 7 on the "Son of Man." The mention of the term is no conditio sine qua non for the text to be messianic (see, e.g., Jer 23:5–6).[54] For some time before his end, Jesus moves in a "messianic" atmosphere to which a sociology of waiting applies.

The collapse of time is a common trait of messianisms. The expected end is very similar to the beginning, affecting a return of the past. The literary recourse to ancient witnesses is, therefore, routine. "Le messianisme en appelle du *présent* à un *passé* lointain pour fonder son projet d'*avenir*," says Georges Crespy.[55] Yes, it is a project, a purpose that all too often remains no more than that. All messianism is more or less a failure—Sabbatianism and Frankism come to mind. This is not merely a historical observation but a condition that is inherent to the phenomenon: if messianism were to realize its goal, it would become triumphalism and commit suicide. It would be a total failure, demonstrating that it cannot last. The sole remedy is *remembrance*, that is, the reactivation of the original energy (see "Do this in remembrance of me"). The immense risk, of course, is the deaxiologization and the rise of technocracy. Issuing from the failure of

---

53. "[A] modification of the image of the Messiah" (Martin Buber, *Two Types of Faith: A Study of the Interpenetration of Judaism and Christianity*, trans. Norman P. Goldhawk [New York: Harper & Row, 1961], 105).

54. Is the text "authentic"? It seems to contradict Jer 22:30, but it plays with the name of King Zedekiah (597–587). That the messiah be from the line of David jibes with Ezek 34:23–24; 37:24–25 ("my servant David").

55. Georges Crespy, "Sociologie et Théologie des Messianismes" *ETR* 54, no. 2 (1976): 196.

messianism, the church strives, through accommodations, to render the absolute energy viable in "this world" (*ha'olam hazeh*) and Christ is recast in an image fashioned by society. There is a "European American Christ," an "African American Christ," an "Asian Christ," a "liberation theology Christ," "my Christ" (who is not yours), and so on. Remarkably, there is no central Jew Christ!

Perhaps I should not be so negative. After all, as regards bimillenarian Christendom, we must acknowledge both failure and success. Georges Crespy's metaphor is wonderful. He says, "The caravels of the Renaissance failed in their quest to find Paradise, but they were finding new continents!"[56] Furthermore, the institution of the church is not entirely responsible for its betrayal because, with Christ's individual resurrection, there is an intrinsic tension between *waiting* and *presence*. Each day is potentially the last, an aphorism that calls to mind the talmudic saying that one must repent one day before one's last![57]

In the Synoptics (Jesus as the Son of God)

Strikingly, Mark starts his gospel with the following words, "The beginning of the good news of Jesus Christ, the Son of God. As it is written in the prophet Isaiah," after which comes the baptism of Jesus by John the Baptist, when Jesus "saw the heavens torn apart and the Spirit descending like a dove on him. And a voice came from heaven, 'You are my Son, the Beloved; with you I am well pleased'" (Mark 1:9-11; see Ezek 1:1; Isa 61:1; 64:1). This initial Markan pericope forms a montage with Ps 2 and Isa 42. The "Son of God" is clearly not a warrior but a prophet (cf. also Matt 21:11).[58] In Mark 3:7-12, he is a cautious miracle worker and an exorcist (see ch. 4, "Jesus as Healer," 53-70). He presents himself as God's agent in all he does, surrounded by an aura that makes him "divine" (that is, numinous). Using other prophetic texts (2 Kgs 9:13; Zech 9:9; 14:4), Mark and its Synoptic parallels describe Jesus's majestic entry into Jerusalem mounted on a colt. The "very large crowd" (Matt 21:8; "the whole multitude of the disciples," says Luke 19:37) salutes him as "the coming one,"

---

56. Ibid., 201.
57. See y. Ta'an. 1:1, 64a V (R. Aqiba).
58. See also Gos. Heb. 2: "My son, in all the prophets was I waiting for you that you should come and I may rest in you"; Gos. Eb. 4: "thus it is fitting that everything should be fulfilled."

the son of David (Matt 21:9; cf. Luke 19:38; John 12:13, 15), a divinely/ numinously "clouded" man.[59] He is bringing about the kingdom of God (Matt 21:9, which is a spontaneous popular acclamation).

Let us take those designations one by one. First, however, an absence: the title "messiah" has not been used as yet. Jesus is the "son of David"[60] and the "beloved son of God." (In the scene of Jesus's transfiguration, he is again declared by a *bath qol*, "My Son, the Beloved.") But here, as in several other contexts, an unexpected motif is introduced: the "Son of Man." Jesus generally used this term, instead of the first person singular, to designate himself: "This son of man [= I] is to go through many sufferings and be treated with contempt" (Mark 9:12).[61] But this device is highly ambiguous since the notion of the Son of Man encompasses a broad area, from the common meaning of "someone" or "myself," to the transcendent figure in Dan 7, "the Son of Man coming in clouds with great power and glory" (Mark 13:26). This ambiguity is due to the daring juxtaposition of the earthly and the heavenly.[62] As the earthly "son of man," Jesus can be

---

59. Note that the reigning king is called *'elohim* in Ps 45:6, although subordinate to the Most High (v. 7). See Ps 21:4. In Isa 9, a human character is called "Mighty God"!

60. Cf. Matt 1:1. In the angel's announcement to Mary in Luke 1:32, Jesus is to be called "Son of the Most High," and he will occupy "the throne of his ancestor David," and his reign is "forever, no end." In fact, "he will be called Son of God" (1:35). Matthew uses the title "son of David" ten times, by contrast with Mark and Luke, and still more so with John, who never uses it. It is never found in Jesus's or his disciples' mouths. See the contrast in Rom 1:3-4 between "son of David according to the flesh" and "Son of God."

61. On the suffering Son of Man in the Gospel of Mark, see also Mark 8:31; 9:31; 10:33-34, 45). One can invoke the "criterion of dissimilarity," although the gospels use texts from the Tanak like Isa 53:11-12, of course, and also 43:3-5. It is difficult here to follow John Dominic Crossan, who says that there is no evidence that "son of man" in Hebrew or Aramaic designated "I" or "me." Even in the mouth of Jesus, he says, the sense is always generic (= everyone) or indefinite (= anyone), unless the context shows that the allusion is to Dan 7:13, like in Mark 13:24-27 // Matt 24:29-31 // Luke 21:25-28. Matthew 24:30 has "the sign of the Son of Man in heaven" (// Didache 16.6-8, but with "the Lord"), and in Mark 9:12, however, "son of man" is neither generic nor indefinite! True, the generic sense is most important in those texts that say, "The son of man has nowhere to lay his head" (Luke 9:57-58 // Matt 8:19-20; cf. Gos. Thom. 86).

62. This, in the image, we could say of Jesus's God, who describes himself as dwelling in the high and holy place but also as being with those who are contrite and humble in spirit (Isa 57:15). On the notion of Son of Man, see ch. 3, "Jesus Son of Man/ Son of God," 43-52.

humiliated and crucified, but on the heavenly side of the title ("Son of Man"), he rises from the dead and returns in power and glory. The dropping here of the simile in Dan 7, "*like* a son of man" (to designate a being that is angelic) is noteworthy.[63] How is it possible for someone to blend, within him, the lowest as well as the highest? No other title given to Jesus approaches the scope and the stature of "Son of Man."[64]

A similar and unlikely juxtaposition occurs when Peter, the spokesman for the disciples, calls Jesus messiah (Mark 8:27–30 // Matt 16:16 // Luke 9:20). Peter undoubtedly is thinking of the messiahship of the Davidic line, but Jesus responds by again shifting the emphasis to the self-designation "son of man" and insisting that he must suffer and die (Mark 8:31)!

This matter of suffering and death, of course, does not jibe with the traditional understanding of messiahship[65] Thus the title "messiah" is handled with great caution in the Synoptics. Perhaps surprisingly, the "son of man" label that Jesus adopts is more suggestive of suffering and death. During the last chapter in the Nazarene's life, at the time of his interrogation in the courts of the Sanhedrin and of the Roman governor, the identification between "Son of Man" and "messiah" seems to be an accomplished fact (Mark 14:53–65). But continuing the ambiguity, Jesus's response to Pilate, "you say so," is evasive (Mark 15:2), and the centurion's exclamation that "this man was God's son" may need explication. Does it necessarily mean that he is the messiah (15:39)? Jesus's subsequent acceptance of suffering belongs to the period of the "hiddenness" of the Son of Man, as well as that of the figure of the servant of the Lord in Isa 49:2—like "an arrow hidden in the quiver of the Lord";[66] his messiahship cannot start until after his resurrection and exaltation.

---

63. The same simile occurs in 1 Enoch 46:1, "like the appearance of a man."

64. Phil 2:6 makes the same point: Christ is *en morphē theou*, that is, human par excellence as all humans are the *morphē theou* (although the LXX term in Gen 1:26–27 is *eikōn*. Also in 2 Cor 4:4 and Col 1:15, Christ is the *eikōn tou theou*). In Phil 2, the term *morphē* is appropriate, however, as Christ is said to adopt another "form," namely, of a slave. The word *eikōn* is here out of the question, obviously.

65. See Raphael Patai, *The Messiah Texts* (New York: Avon, 1979), 83. Although this notion may have been vague in the first century or for centuries after (see Sanh. 98a), a fragmentary midrash gives a vivid image of the messiah as he was expected to be.

66. This is what Martin Buber calls the "state of concealment" (*Two Types*, 104).

Jesus's passion, to the extent that he was messiah or Son of Man, was shocking and scandalous, but it was not outside the Jewish concept of messiahship. Note that the messianic pangs (*havelei ha-mashiah*) are well illustrated in the midrashic and talmudic traditions (see, e.g., Sanh. 96b–99a). Here the pangs are due to the unrighteousness of the people. Thus the days of the messiah's advent are preceded by apocalyptic tribulations and by a dire corruption within the people (see, e.g., m. Soṭah 9:15; Soṭah 49b; Cant. Rab. 2.13.4). Some sages even expressed the hope never to see the messiah coming (see Sanh. 98b)! He is another Job suffering for centuries or millennia.[67] A midrash says, "Pains have adopted him." He is heir to the suffering servant, and the collective sufferings are projected onto him. He sits "with the poor who suffer of diseases."[68] When asked when he will be coming, he answers, "Today!" referring to Ps 95:7: "Today, if you but hearken to his voice" (Sanh. 98a). He accepts his unspeakable suffering with joy because it saves the children of Israel. He is compared with the "first redeemer," that is, with Moses; he will reveal himself and then be hidden (Ruth Rab. 5.6).[69] Furthermore, his suffering is like God's suffering at the hands of the wicked nations (Pesiq. Rab. 36–37). Thus the torments and death of the Lord's servant in Isaiah 53 were messianically interpreted, at least in Jewish literature after 70 CE.[70]

To recall, the term *'ebed* ("servant") was applied to prophets (such as Moses) and to kings (such as David), for the ideal king is a *servant-prophet* (see Isa 50:4). In Second Isaiah's time, the king was granted prophetic abilities, for, like Moses, he was supposed to take his people from Babylon back to the promised land. This may imply a royal passion (on the model of the servant of the Lord) especially during the exilic period (so Ringgren)[71] (cf. Pss 18; 22; 49; 88; 116). This may be in the background of the title

---

67. On the suffering messiah, see Pesiq. Rab. 36–37.

68. Jesus adopted the status of utter poverty (Matt 6:25–33; 8:20; Mark 10:21; Luke 9:58). The principle of biblical poverty is enunciated by m. 'Abot 5:10, "What is mine is yours, and what is yours is your own."

69. See Patai, *Messiah Texts*, 99.

70. See description in m. Soṭah 9:15 again and esp. Sanh. 97–98. See also Patai, *Messiah Texts*, 112–13. In fact, 1 Cor 15:3 is the first historical example of this. The reading of Isa 53 as applied to the messiah supposes identity between Jesus and Israel because the servant refers to the people collectively and, perhaps, to his personification in the prophet.

71. Helmer Ringgren, *The Messiah in the Old Testament*, SBT 18 (London: SCM, 1961).

"son of David" in the narratives on Jesus's miracles (e.g., Mark 10:46-52; Luke 18:35-43; Matt 20:29-34; 9:27-31; 15:21-28; 12:22-23). But Jesus expressly rejects this kind of expectation. The only text showing Jesus's thoughts about "son of David" is Mark 12:35-37 and its parallels. Though Matthew insists on that title, it is only as a secondary motif.

There are three types of references to the title "Son of God" in the Hebrew Scriptures. It can designate heavenly or angelic beings (Gen 6:2, 4; Deut 32:8; Ps 29:1; Dan 3:25), or Israel as a people (e.g., Exod 4:22; Jer 31:20) or again kings of Israel (2 Sam 7:14; Ps 2:7 [the king is called "god" in 2:2]; 89:26-27). The latter served as the basis for the postbiblical expectation of the king messiah of the end time. The use of "Son of God" was addressed to the just and saintly men (inclusive of women?): see the Greek version of Sir 4:10, Wis 2:17-18 and Jub. 1:24-25.

In the course of this study, I stress the point that the king in Israel is "Son of God" by adoption only. Now, it is true, Adela Yarbro Collins and John J. Collins state, that "he is begotten, not adopted."[72] But they add, "This language is mythical and metaphorical.... It does not employ ontological categories."[73] Events, however, shook this belief in the kingly sonhood of God, so that there is left only one mention of it among the prophets (Isa 9). In the Deuteronomic Holiness Code, we find, "I will be a father to him and he will be a son to me" (see 2 Cor 6:11; based on 2 Sam 7:14; cf. Jer 31:9). While the royal ideology of Judah had died out, the language remained and was applied to the end time in the person of messiah to come.[74]

Let us note with Gerd Theissen that the context of social revolution introduced by the Nazarene affects the meaning of the Son of God title. It was initially applied to kings in Israel, then to the people (Hos 1:10; 11:1),

---

72. In Adela Yarbro Collins and John J. Collins, *King and Messiah as Son of God: Divine, Human, and Angelic Figures in Biblical and Related Literature* (Grand Rapids: Eerdmans, 2008), 204.

73. Günther Bornkamm's rejection of the distinction between functional and ontic (ontological) is unfortunate. See *Jesus of Nazareth* (New York: Harper & Brothers, 1960). The fact that "the preexistent Christ participates in God's unique activity of creation" (28-29, 35-40) proves nothing. Wisdom participates in creation although being a creature, see LXX Prov 8:22 (in MT, idem; see Gen 4:1); 8:24-31; Sir 24:9. To recall, there is textual insistence on the subordination of the Son to the Father, see Mark 13:32 // Matt 24:36; cf. 1 Cor 15:27-28; Matt 16:16.

74. See esp. the Similitudes of Enoch: he is heavenly, preexistent judge, and also messiah (48:10, on the basis of Dan 7:13).

but Jesus applied it now to the "little people" (Matt 5:9, 44–45). Besides, the assigned task of spreading peace and generosity toward enemies is a princely one. Jesus expects the "little people" to behave like kings (see Luke 6:35).[75]

Various voices called Jesus "Son of God" in the Synoptics. In the mouth of demons, it means messiah—"You are the Messiah, the Son of God" (Matt 16:16 // Mark 14:16; Matt 26:63; cf. John 11:27; 20:31)—and it stresses the ability to perform miracles (e.g., Mark 3:11 // Luke 4:41; Mark 5:7; cf. Luke 8:28). This same messianic sense is true in the declaration of the angel Gabriel to Mary in Luke 1:31–35. As such, it is also echoed by human beings (see Matt 14:33, "Truly, you are the Son of God"), by Jesus himself ("He said, I am the Son of God," Matt 27:42–43), and again, during his baptism, by a heavenly voice (*bat qol*, Matt 3:17 // Mark 1:11).[76]

And in Paul (A Few Reflections)

Paul, however, speaks in Gal 5:11 and 1 Cor 1:23 of "the scandal of the cross," and, in Gal 3:10–14, he calls forth the text of Deut 21:23, "Anyone hung on a tree is under God's curse." Paula Fredriksen rightly argues against Paul on this, as the Deuteronomic text speaks of the curse of being guilty of a crime liable of capital punishment, not of being exposed on a tree after death. Whether this detracts from Paul's main point that Jesus's crucifixion was seen as scandalous by his opponents is another matter. Paul's circumvention in Gal 3 may well be "snarled," but the fact remains: many saw in the cross a sign of curse *as far as messianic claimants were concerned*. Not being scholars like Fredriksen, they may even have invoked Deut 21 as a proof text. This was wrong, say scholars, but so also was the accusation that Jesus threatened to destroy the temple. The consequences were no less tragic for being ill-grounded.

Besides, the gospel is *skandalon* (Matt 11:5–6; Mark 8:35). It demands a *metanoia* ("conversion"). It is also a stumbling block, since it contains the suffering and death of the Messiah. Nevertheless it is "good news" that will

---

75. Gerd Theissen, "Le mouvement de Jésus, révolution charismatique des valeurs," *NTS* 35 (1989): 343–60.

76. For Luke's version, see 3:22 and the parallels in Tg. Isa. 41:8–9; cf. 43:20; 44:1: God is well pleased with Jacob/Israel/the messiah (43:10), while the MT speaks only of God's choice of these figures.

eventually spread and cover the whole world (Mark 13:10 // Matt 24:14; Mark 16:15).

The word *christos* ("anointed one") appears some 270 times in Paul's letters, as if it had become some sort of a surname of Jesus. After World War II, several scholars stated that, as used by Paul, the word *christos* lost its conventional range of meaning. It was no longer a title but simply a name.[77] For Hengel, *christos* is a cognomen and *kyrios* ("Lord") is the title favored by Paul.[78] Matthew V. Novenson, in his magisterial study of the topic, follows the lead of John J. Collins[79] and says that we must make a clear distinction between the linguistic phenomenon (of messiah language)—always kept alive even when the social phenomenon ebbed low—on the one hand, and the psychological (messianic hope) and social (messianism) phenomena on the other. Novenson concludes, "People could know what the words meant whether or not they shared the sentiment expressed."[80]

The term "anointed" (as *mashiah*) appears some thirty-eight times in the Hebrew Bible. Even the temple's furniture was anointed, that is, consecrated to God. The practice of anointing, however, fell into desuetude, except for linguistic use. Later references to messiah mostly interpret scriptural texts, with the idea that there was a messianic expectation already in the Hebrew Bible (see the Qumran literature, the targumim, etc.). Characteristically, Paul refers only to a few Hebrew Scriptures' messianic texts, but in the texts that he quotes, the word "messiah" is absent (so Gen 49:10; Num 24:17; 2 Sam 7:12-13; Isa 11:1-2; Amos 9:11 and Dan 7:13)! Paul believed that Jesus was the Jewish messiah (see Rom 9:5). For him, he was even a Davidide (Rom 1:3).[81] However, as said above, he preferred to use the term *kyrios*, "Lord," which appears about 180 times, and his focus is on the death and the resurrection of the Christ. *Christos* is an

---

77. So Lloyd Gaston, *Paul and the Torah* (Vancouver: University of British Columbia Press, 1987).

78. Hengel, *The Charismatic Leader*.

79. John J. Collins, "Messiahs in Context: Method in the Study of Messianism in the Dead Sea Scrolls," in *Method of Investigation in the Dead Sea Scrolls and the Khirbet Qumran Site: Present Realities and Future Prospects*, ed. Michael O. Wise et al., Annals of the New York Academy of Sciences 722 (New York: New York Academy of Sciences, 1994), 213-29.

80. Novenson, *Christ among the Messiahs*, 47.

81. See especially passages on David ruling over gentile nations (e.g., Isa 11:10; 2 Sam 22 = Ps 18).

honorific; it is axiomatic for Paul, but not an appellation (a name of a class, as in Acts 17:3) as it fits only one person. "Lord" tends to replace "messiah" for all practical purposes. It is Jesus's obedience to death that makes him the Lord of all as God has elevated him (see Phil 2:5–11).

The Greek title *kyrios* has been thoroughly investigated by Geza Vermes, from its earliest use to its New Testament avatars.[82] *Kyrios* corresponds to the Aramaic *mar* as in *marana tha* ("come, Lord!" in 1 Cor 16:22; cf. Rev 22:20). *Mar* means "sir" and is used as a courteous address to Jesus. It is a degree higher than "rabbi," as it can even be used specifically for miracle workers.[83] The term is originally used by gentiles in the gospel, as in the Syro-Phoenician woman in Mark 7:28 and the centurion from Capernaum in Matt 8:8. In such contexts, the word conveys no christological significance. In Hebrew, it is equivalent with *'adoni*, "my lord," as in 1 Kgs 18:13 and 2 Kgs 8:12.

Vermes reviews the use of this title in the Synoptics.[84] In Mark, aside from 7:28 (the Syro-Phoenician woman), *kyrios* is in absolute form in 11:3. In Matthew, the term is not exclusively used by gentiles but also by disciples, and only in the vocative. Compare with Matt 8:25 and Luke 8:24, where *kyrios* is replaced by *epistatēs* ("chief, master"). In Luke, we find the title used only three times, in miracle-working contexts. In thirteen other texts, it means "teacher."

Furthermore, Mark 11:3 is the only text in Mark (and Matthew) to apply the title "Lord" to Jesus. (This clearly reflects the influence of usage in the early church after the resurrection.) In these gospels, we find the same restraint as regards the title "Savior," which appears once in John (4:42) and in Luke, and twice in Acts (5:31 and 13:23). In Luke 2:11, *christos kyrios* is unique and, in truth, suspect. In the LXX, it is always in the form of *christos kyriou* (with the exception of Lam 4:20 and Pss. Sol. 17:36 [ca. 63–48 BCE]); see Acts 2:36 and John 20:28. In Luke 1–2 (by another author?), *kyrios* (some twenty-five times!) always designates God.

In the background is the historic passage from YHWH to *'adonay* ("my Lord"), with emphasis on of the divine name's meaning. This evolution to the absolute form is critical. John offers God's kingship and lordship. By using the Septuagint's term *kyrios* for Jesus, the gospels hail Jesus as the manifestation of the full spectrum of uses, from "Sir" to Thomas's

---

82. Vermes, *Jesus the Jew*, 103ff.
83. Ibid., 121.
84. Ibid., 122ff.

exclamation, "My Lord and my God!" (John 20:28).[85] Under the pen of Paul, the word takes a much more aloof meaning, and it displays the same ambivalence that we met with "Son of Man" (see Mark 12:35–37, interpreting Ps 110:1 LXX).[86]

Paul's preference of *kyrios* over *christos* is due to his Christology, which depends *essentially* on the apostle's conviction that Christ opened the door to allow gentiles to become part of the people of God,[87] even though his mission was originally for Israel's sake (Rom 15:8). The Israelite notion of "messiah" was too restrictive. *Kyrios* emphasized the Christ's universal dimension and suggested a subversive contrast with Caesar's pretensions. Note in passing that this Pauline insistence put gentile Christians in the awkward position of resisting the official religious-political system on the one hand, but depriving them of the state protection granted to Jews on the other hand. The latter were indeed exempt from participating in the official Roman religion.

Paul's extension of Jewish "privileges" to all gentiles must be envisaged within the context of the first century CE. First, one must stress the understandable religious and political hatred of the Roman occupiers, who never understood the Jewish way of thinking and living. They continually wavered between noninterference—for instance, the legions abandoning their banners and eagles before entering Jerusalem—and fiercely crushing any suspected attempt at revolt. They were generally seen as "goyim" (in the sense of barbarians) par excellence, and one should not be surprised to find repeated expressions of exclusivity in the contemporary Jewish literature. For instance, Sipre Deuteronomy (7:12), states that the torah was given exclusively to the Jews; to extend it outside of Judaism would

---

85. Vermes (ibid., 111) says that the title "Lord" postdates the historical Jesus and, as an acknowledgment of divinity, arose from Hellenistic milieus. As correspondent to the Aramaic *mar*, it is applied in the NT to "persons of authority in the family … or in society at large" (ibid., 120).

86. After the crucifixion, Jesus was identified as the Son of Man that he had proclaimed and also with the figure seated with God as in Ps 110:1 (see Collins and Collins, *King and Messiah*, 173).

87. Much of the modern Jewish resentment toward Paul is due to the lack of attention to this crucial point. Even Buber's study in *Two Types of Faith* is flawed in this regard. Paul is moved by his conviction of being an apocalyptic apostle: the conversion of the gentiles is a prerequisite to the eschatological coming of the kingdom of God (see, e.g., Rom 15:16; 11:13–16).

amount to adultery.⁸⁸ More surprising are contrasting traditional declarations as, for example, in Mekilta de Rabbi Ishmael 6.1 (on Exod 19:2): the torah was given in a no-man's-land so that it was not stamped with a national accent.⁸⁹ The torah was offered to all nations; its occasional observance by gentiles was welcomed.⁹⁰ In Sipra Ahare Mot 13:3 to Lev 18:1–2, a non-Jew practicing the torah is greater than the high priest! Philo also insists that the Jews "have a mission to the whole world as the priest has to the whole Jewish people" (*Spec.* 2.61–62). And in *De praemis et poenis* 16.152, Philo utters the great statement that no race but "virtue" matters to God, "who takes no account of the roots [the gentile or Jewish origins] but accepts the full-grown stems."⁹¹ In a way, such a Philonian universalism was vindicated by the fact that, in the first centuries CE, many gentiles becoming Christians were intimately acquainted with Jewish traditions. Mark 3:1–8 and 4:35–40 speak of a "multitude."⁹²

Understandably, because of the temple's destruction by the Romans, rabbinic attitude vis-à-vis gentiles varied but was in general negative. As Jacob Neusner insists, "gentiles" meant idolaters—so that Neusner goes so far as to translate the Hebrew term by idolaters. As regards the access to the temple, Zebaḥ. 22b unequivocally tells us that "non-Jews would be disqualified [from entering the temple] even if they had circumcised hearts and circumcised flesh."⁹³

Paul is not antinomian. This is a sad misunderstanding, since Paul thinks that the gentiles should not observe the torah-as-law *the way that Jews do*.⁹⁴ Consequently, a gentile conversion to Judaism in order that the

---

88. Magnus Zetterholm adds also m. 'Abot 3:14, but I think he has misunderstood the text (see Zetterholm, *The Messiah in Early Judaism and Christianity* [Minneapolis: Fortress, 2007], 48).

89. R. Ishmael was a Tanna of the first and second centuries CE.

90. I refer to Marc G. Hirshman, "Rabbinic Universalism in the Second and Third Centuries" *HTR* 93 (2000): 101–15.

91. Quoted by Paula Fredriksen, *From Jesus to Christ: The Origins of the New Testament Images of Jesus* (New Haven: Yale University Press, 1988), 150n35.

92. Among the Second Temple literature, some documents were not antigentile (Sirach and Wisdom of Solomon), while others were quite inclusive of the gentiles (Testaments of the Twelve Patriarchs; Josephus, *J.W.*; Jewish strata of Odes of Solomon).

93. Contrast with Gal 3:26–4:6.

94. See Rom 3:20: "whatever the law says, it speaks to those who are under the law"; 3:21: "but now, apart from the law, the righteousness of God has been disclosed, as is attested by the Law [Torah] and the Prophets"; 3:28: "a person is justified by faith

law may cleanse and justify is an aberration. The fulfillment of the *mitsvoth* does not justify anybody since they are in response to the grace of God (see Rom 3:23-24) and therefore do not entail any reward. If anything, "through the law comes the knowledge of sin" (3:20). That is, the torah's revelation sets an exceedingly high standard of purity and morality. No one in the world is capable of fulfilling it entirely, for if there were such a "boasting," "it is excluded" in advance (3:27), as it would be itself a disobedience to the law. Paul's argument does not remove him from a Jewish context. He does not repudiate the torah, but he identifies it with God's acts in Jesus Christ. Since the present Jewish "blindness" opens the door of God's compassion to the gentiles, so the justification of all, Jews and gentiles, in Christ sets the law in its right place, that is, not as a means of justification (that would compete with the divine grace in Christ) but as a thanksgiving on the part of those who fulfill the *mitzvoth*.[95] Within the people of God—without anything like a supersession of one "race" over the other—Jews should remain Jews and gentiles, non-Jews.[96] In the sight of God, however, there is no Jew or gentile, in the same sense that there is no male or female, servant or master, and so on (Gal 3:26-28).[97]

When Paul, in the same Epistle to the Romans, speaks of the "curse of the law" (3:13), he means that the law displays a *side* that amounts to being a curse as it plumbs the depth of human sinfulness. That side we today call "legalism." Paul evokes Deut 27:26, "Cursed is everyone who

---

apart from works prescribed by the law"; and Gal 2:16: "justified by faith and not by doing the works of the law, because no one will be justified by the works of the law." Jack Miles, in his foreword to Daniel Boyarin's *The Jewish Gospels: The Story of the Jewish Christ* (New York: New Press, 2012), xviii, says that Paul was far more rabbinically Jewish than Jesus.

95. Like Paul himself; see decisive texts like Acts 21:20-30; 18:18; 22:3; 23:6; 24:11-17; 26:5; Phil 3:4-11.

96. See Gal 2:14; 5:1-6 (see the historical context in Acts 15:1, 5); 1 Cor 7:17-18.

97. Cf. Rom 10:12; 1 Cor 12:13; Col 3:11. There might be a parallel in Tanna de-be Eliahu 48. Amy-Jill Levine refers to Seder Eliahu Rabba and Seder Eliahu Zutra (*The Misunderstood Jew: The Church and the Scandal of the Jewish Jesus* [San Francisco: HarperSanFrancisco, 2006], 159). On both, see Šabb. 53 and Qidd.. 41. Along this line of thought, reference should be made to Jacob Neusner's conclusion after reviewing the haggadah regarding the gentiles (steadily identified as idolaters): "Those who accept the Torah are called Israel, the others, who reject the Torah in favor of idolatry, are called gentiles" (*Performing Israel's Faith: Narrative and Law in Rabbinic Theology* [Waco, TX: Baylor University Press, 2005], 39).

does not observe and obey all the things written in the book of the law." If it is permissible to draw an analogy, we could say that there is also a curse attached to the Jerusalem temple. True, there is no biblical tradition to that effect, but Jesus actually deals with the issue in different places. Particularly illuminating is Jesus's dialogue in John 4 with the Samaritan woman. The latter, as expected in a conversation with a Judean, raises the vexing problem of where to worship God, in the Jerusalem temple or on Mount Gerizim.[98] The question involves judgment on "the other." Who is right, you or we? Who is the alien here? You in Samaria or I in the company of a Judean? Is there ever a solution to this problem in the future? Jesus's answer is striking: the true worship of God is not an institutional matter. It is "neither in this mountain [of Gerizim] nor in Jerusalem.... The true worshipers shall worship the Father in spirit and in truth" (John 4:24).

The "curse" of the temple is that it camouflages the true problem of worshiping. It can be so ritualistic—and how could this be avoided when literally thousands of animals were sacrificed in the temple during the festivals?—as to create a false sense of self-rectitude. Rather than facing the real question of what is spiritual worship, people choose an escape and they dispute the appropriate location of prayer, what kind of animals must be offered, how many of them and how they are to be slaughtered. This leads to divisiveness and internecine hatred—and God in the process is not worshiped! It is therefore probable that Jesus spoke ill of the temple as he is accused of having done during his trial. Jesus was not questioning the temple as such, but the use of it by the establishment: "My house shall be called a house of prayer for all the nations, but you have made it a den of robbers" (Mark 11:17; an echo of Jer 7:11, "Has this house, which is called by my name, become a den of robbers in your sight? You know, I too am watching, says the Lord.")

Jesus's insistence on the temple as house of prayer for all nations is another way to "neutralize" the temple establishment. The formula was revolutionary at the time, in spite of the temple's special precinct meant for the non-Jews.[99] Jesus seems here to envisage the whole temple welcoming Jews and non-Jews, that is, a complete reform of the temple theology, for, in the time of Jesus, "all nations" would primarily include the Romans, an

---

98. The Samaritan temple was probably built under Alexander the Great. It made final the schism between Jews and Samaritans.

99. But a Greek inscription in the Herodian temple forbade non-Jews to cross over the limits of the gentile Court under penalty of death (see Acts 21:28; Ezek 44:7).

outrageous statement for the temple personnel. In Jesus's mind, the alternative is the destruction of the shrine.

It is noteworthy that Jesus's criticism unexpectedly finds an echo in a famous declaration by Rabbi Yohanan ben Zakkai, the "father" of rabbinic Judaism after the destruction of the temple in 70 CE. ARN (A) 4:11a tells us that he said to Rabbi Joshua, "Grieve not, we have an atonement equal to the Temple, the doing of loving deeds, as it is said, 'I desire love, and not sacrifice.'"[100]

Strange as it may seem, the sublime fares like the trivial or even worse.[101] Jesus saw as part of his mission the denunciation of the religious abuses. His friendship with "sinners" and those of the lowest classes is already an implicit criticism of the bien-pensant. The latter, called scribes, Pharisees, and chief priests, did not miss the point. They endlessly scolded Jesus over his acquaintances. If the gospel can be trusted on this, Jesus once exploded and called them vipers and serpents (see Matt 23:29–33). Apparently there is a curse also attached to being religionists. Sin spares no one. Now, Paul says clearly in his Epistle to the Romans that the outcome of sin is death. The law shows death as ineluctable. In the Sermon on the Mount, Jesus shows unequivocally that no one escapes sinfulness; even anger is already murder!

It is from this perspective that Paul looks to the cross. "Christ died for us" (Rom 5:8); that is, he is the ultimate and unique victim of death and, in a radical way, of universal sin. Jesus's death is thus the decisive breakthrough, as it deprives death of its sting, of its seemingly unbeatable triumph (see 1 Cor 15:55; cf. Rom 8:39; 2 Cor 5:18).[102]

(On Jesus's conception of messiahship, see also below chapter 11, "Jesus's Self-Consciousness.")

---

100. See Judah Goldin, trans. *The Fathers according to Rabbi Nathan* (New Haven: Yale University Press, 1955), 34–35. Deut. Rab. 5.3 reads, "The Holy One blessed be He says, Rightness and justice that you do are to Me dearer than the Temple." See 1QS, which stresses the same point.

101. Those who forsake Jesus at the end had been witnesses of his transfiguration (Matt 17:2)!

102. Paul's Jesus was abused and crucified (see, e.g., Rom 15:3; 1 Cor 15:3; Gal 2:20; 3:13). He was raised from the dead (1 Cor 15:4) and seen by witnesses, including later by Paul himself (1 Cor 15:5–8).

3
Jesus Son of Man/Son of God

In spite of Daniel Boyarin's thesis in *The Jewish Gospels*, the title "Son of God" or, as we shall see below, "Son of Man" does not qualify Jesus as a second person of an alleged Trinity or Binity. We may not disregard other biblical entities also called "son(s) of God" and "son of Man" in Scripture. Israel as a people is called "sons of God" in Deut 14:1; Ps 82:6; 103:13; Hos 11:1; so is their king in Ps 2:7, and he is even "divinized" in Ps 110:1, where we see him sitting on a throne at the right hand of God (or is it at His left? see v. 5), an image that reappears in Daniel 7 as the one "who is like a son of man." The Bible, as a matter of fact, does not hesitate sometimes to use hyperbolic language to speak of the transcendent.

True, the gospels present an amalgam of features making Jesus a kind of half-human, half-divine persona, something like an Achilles! The birth narratives in Matthew and Luke bear much of the responsibility for this. I shall dedicate a chapter below to this all-important aspect of these two Synoptics (ch. 9, "The Birth Narratives," 183–92). At any rate, Jesus is made *the* Son of God, representing all the sons of God. There is a perfect identity between God's thinking and Jesus's ministry, thus creating between the two an actual and historic identity (John 1:51; 5:20; 10:30; 12:45; 14:9).

The title Son of Man appears only in the gospels, Acts 7:56, and Rev 1:13 and 14:14.[1] It is generally used to avoid appearing arrogant or self-centered. As I have said, I do not concur with Boyarin that "Son of Man"

---

1. In the Synoptics, sixty-nine times and thirteen times in John. Ignoring the parallels, there are thirty-eight independent instances of the phrase "Son of Man." It is not a normal Greek expression, but rather a translation from the Aramaic *bar-nash(a)*. It was not generally used in the early church and is thus undoubtedly an authentic usage by Jesus.

does not designate "a human being at all."[2] The human component of the expression must be safeguarded. So, for instance, when Jesus says, in Mark 2:28, that "a son of man is master even of the Sabbath," he means any human being, since the Sabbath "was created for the human," and the disciples, qua humans, are entitled to pick up grains during the Sabbath according to Jesus's halakic decision.[3] The same is true of Mark 3:28 (see Matt 12:31-32 // Luke 12:10; Gos. Thom. 44): sinning "against a 'son of man' [including Jesus himself] shall be forgiven." Not so when the sin is "against the Holy Spirit." Accusing Jesus of exorcizing by Beelzebub amounts to such a sin. The "highly charged nature of the situation"[4] made Jesus use indirect expressions wherewith "everyone" means you, "son of man," me, and "Holy Spirit," God. Jesus could expect a "widespread agreement at its general level."[5] In Mark 14:21, "a son of man goes as it is written of him" means that everyone is mortal. "But woe to that one by whom the Son of Man is betrayed" shows that a "son" like Judas—alluded to in general terms—included all traitors, so that everyone around can agree.

Maurice Casey does not consider Mark 14:61-62 as authentic. Not so Peter Stuhlmacher in his article "The Messianic Son of Man: Jesus' Claim to Deity."[6] The problem is partially a linguistic one. The questioning high priest uses a composite expression, "Are you the Messiah, the Son of God?" Scholars such as Eduard Lohse, Hans Conzelmann, and Albert Lindemann say that this is a "non-Jewish linguistic impossibility." But Stuhlmacher

---

2. Daniel Boyarin, *The Jewish Gospels: The Story of the Jewish Christ* (New York: New Press, 2012), 26.

3. On this and the following texts, see Maurice P. Casey, *From Jewish Prophet to Gentile God: The Origins and Development of New Testament Theology* (Louisville: Westminster John Knox, 1991), 46–56. On the general human privilege superseding the rest of Sabbath, I refer to Qoh 3:11, with a possible rendering in English as: "[God] placed in the human mind a notion of eternity." In the sixteenth century, Sir Philip Sidney wrote, "[Let us] give right honor to the heavenly Maker of that maker [the poet], who ... set [man] beyond and over all the works of that second nature [the poet's creation]" (*Elizabethan Critical Essays*, ed. G. G. Smith [Oxford: Oxford University Press, 1953], 1:156–57; cited by M. H. Abrams, *The Mirror and the Lamp: Romantic Theory and the Critical Tradition* [Oxford: Oxford University Press, 1953], 273).

4. Casey, *From Jewish Prophet*, 50.

5. Ibid.

6. Peter Stuhlmacher, "The Messianic Son of Man: Jesus' Claim to Deity," in *The Historical Jesus in Recent Research*, ed. James D. G. Dunn and Scot McKnight (Winona Lake IN: Eisenbrauns, 2005), 325–44.

cites early Jewish texts such as 11QMelch 13; 1 Enoch 45–50, 61–64, and 4 Ezra 13, where messianic titles are used *cumulatively*. See now 4Q246 (4QapocrDan ar). He concludes that "*Mark 14:61-62* [was] *completely possible linguistically and conceptually in Jewish tradition before Easter.*"[7] In 1 Enoch 37–71 (first century BCE or CE), the Son of Man is preexistent and the end-time judge-redeemer (62:14). In 48:10, for example, he is identified with the messiah. In Dan 7, the "one like a son of man" points to the angel Michael who appears as a human being in the vision. Michael is heavenly and "divine" (like the king of Israel in Ps 2), but he is not God. The same can be said of Enoch in 1 En. 71:17 or of "Metatron" in 3 Enoch (fourth–fifth centuries CE).

As for "Jesus' claim to Deity," quoting Stuhlmacher's essay title, let me stress that we should keep the distinction between *theos* and *theios*—or between *elohim* and *elohi* in the medieval Jewish philosophical idiom. Regarding Jesus, the most that can be said is that he became a *theios anēr*, a far cry from a mythological figure à la Zeus or Hermes.[8] Metaphorical or hyperbolic language should never be understood literally. The Danielic figure is *like a* "son of man," that is, like a human being; he is angelical and has chosen humanity over the animality of the monstrous nations of the vision (cf. Matt 8:20 and parr.).[9]

It is not without surprise that we read from the pen of T. Francis Glasson the statement, "When a Messiah is mentioned he is of the warrior type. There is no transcendent figure descending in glory to conduct the last judgment."[10] E. P. Sanders approves. He does not mention Dan 7 even once in *Jesus and Judaism*![11] Both critics wrongly dismiss as late another document, the Similitudes of Enoch in 1 Enoch. The scholarly consensus

---

7. Ibid., 335 (emphasis original).

8. I may firmly believe that my late wife was an angel of God, but not that she was a goddess! It is true that, in the Greco-Roman world, the *theios anēr* was worshiped as a living theophany.

9. Rabbi Rami M. Shapiro writes, "Jesus makes it plain that it is not Jesus who is God, but God who is Jesus" ("Listening to Jesus with an Ear for God," in *Jesus through Jewish Eyes: Rabbis and Scholars Engage an Ancient Brother in a new Conversation*, ed. Beatrice Bruteau [Maryknoll, NY: Orbis, 2001], 177).

10. T. Francis Glasson, "Schweitzer's Influence—Blessing or Bane?" *JTS* 28 (1977): 289–302, 299.

11. E. P. Sanders, *Jesus and Judaism* (Philadelphia: Fortress, 1985). In spite of direct references to Dan 7 in Mark 13:26 // Matt 24:30 // Luke 21:27; and Mark 14:62 // Matt 26:64 // Luke 22:69. There is an indirect reference to the same in Mark 8:38

is to date the Similitudes early, and to stress their (non-Christian) Jewishness. Two historical events are referred to in the document: the invasion of Palestine by the Parthians in 40 BCE (56:5-7), and the Herodian attempt at healing himself in the waters of Callirhoe (67:7-9). "Scenes of judgment dominate the entire work.... Cosmic transformation of heaven and earth is explicitly promised in 45:4-5.... The righteous enjoy a heavenly afterlife ... (39:5)."[12]

The Similitudes speak of the preexistence of the Son of Man and of his eschatological manifestation (48:3-5; in the whole document [= 1 Enoch 37-71], the Son of Man appears sixteen times, distinguishing the Danielic Son of Man from any other human being by using the demonstrative "*that* Son of Man" (unless the context does not support it); see 62:7; 69:27. The central theme is the last judgment and the role then played by the Elect One/Son of Man: it emphasizes the correspondence between the human righteous and their heavenly counterparts. As an example, Enoch himself is identified with the Son of Man (71:14; more generally, see 62:14 and 71:17).

As for Dan 7:13, it reads, "Behold, with the clouds of heaven came one like a son of man, he reached up to He-Who-Endures, and was brought before him. He was offered dominion, glory, and kingship, and the humans of every people, nation, and language served him. His dominion is eternal and will not be taken away, and his kingdom is indestructible" (my trans.). The coming down of the Son of Man on a cloud (so also, e.g., 1 Thess 4:16; Sanh. 98a; Tanḥ. B, 706; Num. Rab. 13.14) recalls the descent of God on a cloud in 2 Sam 22:10. It is a scene of coronation, the recipient being collectively *verus Israel*, and individually the angel Michael. God sits as a judge (see Ps 122:5), flanked by the Son of Man.[13] The parallel with the god El of Ugarit is striking. He is enthroned as king and judge.

Fire, another ingredient of a theophany, like cloud,[14] is here dependent

---

// Matt 16:27 // Luke 9:26. Sanders does not consider Mark 14:62 and parr. and Matt 16:27-28 as authentically from Jesus.

12. See John J. Collins, "The Early Christian Apocalypses," *Semeia* 14, *Apocalypse: The Morphology of a Genre*, ed. John J. Collins (1979): 39.

13. See Rashi: one throne for judgment and one for justice. Note that all people serve the Son of Man. The term "serve" always refers to divine service (see Dan 3:12, 14, 17, 18, 28; 6:17, 21; Ezek 7:24). Gentiles serve collective Israel and thus indirectly God himself.

14. About 70 percent of a total of about one hundred references to clouds in Scripture refer to Sinai or the temple (e.g., 1 Kgs 8:10-11; 2 Chr 5:13-14) or to eschatological theophanies (Isa 4:5; Ps 97:2; Nah 1:3).

on Ezek 1 and 10. It is a sign of divine judgment, as several texts testify.[15] The kingdom in Dan 7 is de facto messianic (pace Glasson; see my note 10 above).[16]

It is evident that the Apocalyptist's chosen vocabulary in chapter 7 constitutes a designed shift in the conception of messianism. The redeemer-judge is no longer the "son of David." The historical circumstances in the second century BCE are now beyond Jewish control. The redeemer is now a sort of prelapsary Adam, Adam redivivus, himself "son of God" (Luke 3:18). The accent is on the humanity of the salvational figure. He is Man par excellence. The power he displays is less kingly by divine right than judicial by spiritual and ethical authority, as opposed to the "animality" of the nations (Dan 7:3–27).

The beast metaphor demanded that its opposite be described in terms of humanity. Adhering to the classic "Messiah ben David" would only be valid in the event that his foes had been described as kings. In other words, as often happens in the history of ideas, the nature of the evil agent determines the nature of the St. George-like champion, fervently hoped for and expected.

Then a further aspect of messianism is transformed. The Davidic political messiah was to deal with the nations on a horizontal plane (spatial and historical). The Son of Man, by contrast, is effective on the vertical plane. He is cosmic and transcendent. He embraces the totality of space and time. In short, he has become atemporal and nonspatial. Hence, the circumstances that were beyond control have become obsolete and fade into inconsequence.

This is a totally different messianism. It is the messianism adopted by Jesus according to the gospel. The Romans hold power, and the Jewish people ardently expect their defeat and departure from the Holy Land. Jesus's response to this is different from the political one: the Roman presence is transient and thus inconsequential. "Give back to Caesar" implies disengagement from the radical hatred of Rome; Rome is—not yet but already—nonexistent. Jesus reverses the terms of the equation: The Roman Empire is a phantom; the spiritual kingdom of God is the concrete reality.

---

15. See Ps 50:3; 56:9; Mal 3:16; Ezek 13:9; Rev 3:5; 20:12; Pss. Sol. 15:6–7; Apocalypse of Abraham 31. Sanh. 38b speaks of the "tribunal on high"; see also 1 Enoch 1:9; 71:8, 13; 91:15.

16. On this reflection on Dan 7, see my *The Book of Daniel*, trans. David Pellauer (London: SPCK; Atlanta: John Knox, 1979), esp. 134–48.

Toward his last breath, Jesus dealt with the tormenting Roman governor as if he was unreal and contemptible ("God would send a legion of angels ...").

With the Dan 7 vision of the Son of Man, the sacral, preapocalyptic, myth-and-ritual view of the king is neutralized. Typically, crucial notions such as the temple, the land, and the torah remain unmentioned. A conception of this kind is worlds apart from the literalism of some trends in Judaism—but it is still Jewish. It is driven by the idea that "there is here something greater than Solomon" (Matt 12:42; cf. John 8:53–58).

There is an unmistakable tension between Jesus's self-designation as the "Son of Man" (or is it a "son of man"?) and his own expectation of the ultimate manifestation of *the* Son of Man in the eschaton (see Mark 14:61–62). Carsten Colpe writes, "Whether Jesus thinks of himself directly as the apocalyptic Son of Man is hard to say for certain.... Direct identification, however, destroys the dynamic element in the relation and robs the preaching of its prophetic character.... It is difficult to equate him directly with the Son of Man."[17] The expression is ambivalent. It appears ninety-seven times in the book of Ezekiel, where it clearly means "man," as well as another fourteen times "as a term for man."[18] More impressive for our query is Ps 80:18, where either Israel is meant or its king as *ben adam*. It means "I, me" (and subtly something more) in texts like Mark 14:21; Luke 22:48; and Mark 10:45. In Matt 5:11 we find "for my sake" (Jesus's), while the parallel Luke 6:22 has "for the Son of Man's sake."

In Dan 7:13, the comparative "like" shows that "there is no exact equation with earthly humanity."[19] Nor, I would add, is there an exact equation with God, since the Son of Man figure is brought to the face of the Ancient of Days. In the Danielic interpretation part, the figure represents *verus Israel*, and we should note its collective feature (see Dan 7:22). Furthermore, throughout Daniel B (Dan 7–12), angels are called "men," as in 8:15–16: "one [angel] who looked like a man [with] a human voice." See also 9:21 and 12:1: "Michael, the great prince, the one who stands beside the sons of your people." True, angels are called *benei (ha) elohim* in Job 1:6; 2:1; 38:7 after Gen 6:1–4, but Ps 89:7 cannot be clearer: "Who in the

---

17. Carsten Colpe, "υἱός," in *The Theological Dictionary of the New Testament: Abridged in One Volume*, ed. and trans. Geoffrey W. Bromiley (Grand Rapids: Eerdmans, 1985), 1219. See further idem, "ὁ υἱὸς τοῦ ἀνθρώπου," *TDNT* 8:400–477.

18. Colpe, "υἱός," 1215.

19. Ibid., 1217.

skies can equal the LORD, can compare with the LORD among the divine beings [*benei 'elim*]?" (see also 1 Kgs 22:19–23).

In 1 Enoch Similitudes (37–71), "Son of Man" is not really a title (there are three different forms of the expression), but he is preexistent, and in the third Similitude he is identified with Enoch himself. This, says Colpe, implies "the institution of Enoch into *the office and function* of the eschatological Son of Man."[20]

In 4 Ezra the Son of Man is "the national leader of Israel,"[21] that is, the guardian angel of Israel, as is clear in Dan 10:13, 20–21.

At any rate, it is striking how careful Jesus is to speak of himself indirectly. He thus provisionally avoids identifying himself with the specific *egō eimi* that will play a great role later on in the Jerusalem chapter of his life (see below, ch. 11, "Jesus's Self-Consciousness"). For example, in the parable of the "strong man" (see Mark 3:24–25; Matt 12:25–26 // Luke 11:17–18), Jesus is the "stronger man" who plunders the possessions of the (less) "strong man" (i.e., Satan).[22] When he speaks of the kingdom of God, a central theme indeed, Jesus again uses "Son of Man" as a screen to cover his identity. So also in Matt 11:2–5, responding to John the Baptist's inquiry, Jesus does not directly refer to himself, so that the performer of miracles is not mentioned. Furthermore, in Luke 10:22–24 (blessings) the call is to be witness to the kingdom, not to its mediator.[23] The miracle stories show that Jesus's power was in fact his ability to call on the power of God rather than to act himself as a supernatural being.[24]

Why did Jesus display such reluctance? Humility should be considered, although it does not exhaust the meaning of this indirectness. An inchoate messianic consciousness is surely another element. A third possibility is his eagerness to thwart popular misunderstanding as to who he

---

20. Ibid., 1218 (emphasis added).
21. Ibid.
22. On the parable of the "strong man," see John P. Meier, *Mentor, Message, and Miracles*, vol. 2 of *A Marginal Jew: Rethinking the Historical Jesus*, ABRL (New York: Doubleday, 1994), 419–20.
23. On this, see ibid., 438.
24. The disciples saw him as a holy man, intimate with God. Only the resurrection persuaded them that the miracles had been signs of the coming kingdom of God. Note that the disciples are to tell people, "The kingdom has come near to you" after they heal the sick (Luke 10:9, 11). Before Jesus, we find no combination of charismatic miracles with apocalyptic ideas (see Gerd Theissen, *The Miracle Stories of the Early Christian Tradition*, trans. F. McDonagh [Edinburgh: T&T Clark, 1983], 279).

actually was. (I shall return to this point below when dealing with the principle of secrecy in the Gospel of Mark.) But, more importantly, by using indirectness as a rhetorical device, Jesus acknowledges the transcendence of notions like the kingdom of God and of titles like Son of Man and Son of God, notions and titles that he is in the *process* of fulfilling with his person. These notions are as much goals to be reached as they are immanent in his sayings and his deeds. This is the key to Jesus's eschatology, both in its remote/prophetic *and* in its proximate/realized aspects. In the words of Joachim Jeremias, Jesus's eschatology is *proleptic*.[25] *It is so because his whole messianism is proleptic*. Even in the great christological declaration of Martha, sister of Lazarus, who says in John 11:27, "You are the Messiah, the Son of God, *who is to come* into the world" (*ho eis ton kosmon erchomenos*). Jesus stands at the point of midnight, when it is both today and tomorrow. Today is pregnant with tomorrow, and tomorrow will fulfill the promise of today's pregnancy.[26]

My reading sheds light, I think, on a text like Luke 17:20–21: the kingdom of God does not descend from heaven like a UFO. It is, instead, a dynamic reality, already in our midst. It grows within us, like yeast in the dough, like a mustard seed in the soil. It does not belong to a sacral geography (it is not "here or there"), but it is, rather, a force. Nor, as such, does it belong to a sacral calendar; it instead spans time from beginning to end.[27] True, the kingdom is coming and has come, but the phrasing is metaphorical. "Your kingdom come! [in full force, at the parousia]."[28] John P. Meier judiciously refers to Luke 10:23–24, in which Jesus's beatitudes are in the present tense, fulfilling in the present the hopes entertained by kings and

---

25. See Joachim Jeremias, *The Parables of Jesus*, rev. ed. (New York: Charles Scribner's Sons, 1982). The point is particularly emphasized by Heb 8:5, "image and shadow of celestial realities"; and 10:1, "shadow of things to come." John 2:11 shows the connection between Christ's glory (*doxa*) and its manifestation (*phanerōsis*) on earth. See also John 3:13–14 on the Son of Man's descent and ascension (cf. 1 Enoch 70:2; 71:1; T. Levi 2:5–12).

26. E.g., the Bethany woman's anointment of Jesus' feet in John 19, the prolepsis of his body's anointment after his death.

27. See Mark 1:15, "the time is fulfilled"; cf. Matt 10:7; Luke 10:9. Marvin Meyer quotes Gos. Mary 8.11–22: "The child of humankind is within you" (*The Gospel of Thomas: The Hidden Sayings of Jesus* [San Francisco: HarperSanFrancisco, 1992], 108).

28. See Meier's discussion of *engiken* in the past tense, with the meaning of "has drawn near," as an action that is "now over and done with" (*Mentor, Message, and Miracles*, 433).

prophets of the past. The eschatology is "realized," in contradistinction with the Sermon on the Mount, where we have a future eschatology.

Matthew 11:4–5 and the miracles in general are signs that the kingdom is already present and also future. But these signs are sporadic and temporary instead of being continuous and permanent. Hence, the kingdom is echoing the garden of Eden of origins. In other words, Jesus's miracles are proleptic. They can be "seen" and "heard" now, for the kingdom "has come near," but they are also harbingers of things to come.[29]

This is what Rudolf Bultmann called the "presence of eternity."[30] This notion is so central in Jesus's ministry that even his "festive" meals prefigure the eschatological banquet (see Matt 8:11–12 [cf. 1 Enoch 62:14, "in the company of the Son of Man"]; Luke 13:28–29). The ultimate transition to the heavenly banquet is the "Last Supper" (Mark 14:22–25 and parr.). It is a Passover meal (the festival of liberation) according to Mark 14:24 and Matt 26:28. John 6:63–58 and 1 Cor 10:1–5 refer to the manna in the desert, while Luke 22:20 and 1 Cor 11:25 evoke the "new covenant" with the wine of the *cena* representing the "blood of the covenant" in Exod 24:8. True, the exodus of Israel from Egypt is not mentioned in the reports on the last meal of Jesus with his disciples. It follows, however, the Seder ritual. Jesus distributes the matzo and shares the final cup of wine, declaring them his body and blood (Matt 26:28). Now, the fourth cup of wine in the Seder is called the cup of wrath, based on the words of Ps 79:6, "Pour out your anger on the nations that do not know you." Hans Kosmala argues that here Jesus replaced the divine anger invoked with the fourth cup with the covenantal words, "for many in his blood," "in which God's love and mercy are revealed."[31]

On this, Schalom Ben-Chorin is right to remind us that the gospel did not find such mention essential when addressing knowledgeable Jews or, alternatively, a Hellenistic non-Jewish public. The gospel wants to make the point of Jesus instituting the "new covenant." The central motif is

---

29. A comparison is provided by the Sabbath that is considered by Jewish tradition as the foretaste of the *'olam haba'* ("the world to come"). The same notion is the basis of the eucharistic "Lord's Table."

30. Rudolf Bultmann, *Presence of Eternity: History and Eschatology* (Edinburgh: Edinburgh University Press, 1975).

31. Hans Kosmala, *Essener, Christen: Studien zur Vorgeschichte der früh-christlichen Verkündigung* (Leiden: Brill, 1959), 186.

remembrance, which, from remembering the exodus is now directed to remembering "me," as Jesus says (Luke 22:19).

4
Jesus as Healer

Jesus went throughout Galilee, teaching in their synagogues and proclaiming the good news of the kingdom and curing every disease and every sickness among the people. (Matt 4:23)

One of the main expectations of first-century charismatics was that they be healers. Even a cursory look at the four gospels reveals that Jesus was seen as a healer. Healing, evidently, played a major role in Jesus's ministry.[1] There are some fifteen stories of healing by Jesus. For the sake of argument, even if the historian comes to the conclusion that such-and-such miracle stories are not authentic—say, for instance, the changing of water into wine at Cana—the story as creation of the early church says some significant things about the historical Jesus: his participation in a banquet; his tense relationship with his mother; the absence of his father; his reluctance to perform a miracle in order to satisfy others' expectations; his mysterious relation with wine; and so on. All this is true to character and can be compared with miracle stories that probably reflect historical events, like the paralytic lifted down through the roof (Mark 2:1–12), the paralytic by the pool of Bethesda (John 5:1–9), the healing of the Roman centurion's son (or servant, John 4:46–54 and Matt 8:5–13 // Luke 7:1–10), the restoration of sight to blind people (Mark 10:46–52; 8:22–26 and John 9:1; cf., e.g., Matt 11:5). A counterproof is a text like Mark 6:5–6 with the note that Jesus was incapable of accomplishing miracles in Nazareth. As Schalom Ben-Chorin says, "A relationship of trust between the physician and his patient is a precondition for these healings."[2] Mark 6:5–6 puts the matter squarely on a psychological plane. It is not that psychology would

---

1. A collection of Jesus's miracles is found in Matt 8–9.
2. Schalom Ben-Chorin, *Brother Jesus: The Nazarene through Jewish Eyes*, trans. Jared S. Klein and Max Reinhart (Athens: University of Georgia Press, 2001), 44.

be enough to explain the phenomenon of miraculous healings, but it certainly plays a role, and the gospel acknowledges it.

The first question to ask is whether this jibes with Jewish traditional literature. In a famous letter written by the Besht (the Baal Shem Tov, founder of the Hasidic mystical sect in eighteenth-century eastern Europe) to his brother-in-law Rabbi Gershom of Kutov, "messianism" is put at the level of *personal* healing of the body and the perfection of the soul (by imitation of the Besht's ascent on high).³ What is interesting in this instance is the notion of *tiqun* already encountered and to which I shall return. Moshe Idel stresses this anomian aspect "reminiscent of Abulafia's mystical techniques, which are also anomian." The center of gravity, so to speak, has shifted from the rigorous practice of the *mitsvoth* to a mystical presence of power, which the individual attains by an ascent to heaven. "The Besht can function messianically," and so arguably and at a minimum did Jesus of Nazareth.⁴ My point is that the mystical techniques touted by Abulafia (thirteenth century) and the Besht (eighteenth century), on the one hand, converge on the other hand with the acts of power—the healings performed by Jesus as preserved in the gospel tradition. In both cases, the human soul experiences a vivid consciousness of the intervening divine providence or, in the words of the gospel, of the Holy Spirit. The Holy Spirit favors individuals, since *every individual Jew is invited to repair the personal messianic vocation that belongs to their soul.*⁵ Seen from this perspective, the messianic dimension of the Nazarene does not isolate him as another *theios anēr* of Greek mythology,⁶ but involves calling his people, Israel, to complete with him (as a "corporate personality") "Adam's initial stature," as Hasidic masters would say.⁷ They are all sons of God like their

---

3. See Moshe Idel, *Messianic Mystics* (New Haven: Yale University Press, 1998), 217–18.

4. See ibid., 219.

5. Already in 1520, Martin Luther stated that Christ shares his powers as king and priest with all Christians, see *On Christian Freedom*, in *First Principles of the Reformation, or The Ninety-Five Theses and the Three Primary Works of Luther Translated into English*, trans. H. Wace and C. A. Buckheim (1883; repr., Digireads.com, 2011).

6. For the Greeks, accustomed to the mysteries, the conception of the Christ as a *theios anēr* was what made him credible. Within this perspective, the individual resurrection of Jesus could be accepted, on the model of the dying and rising gods. In fact, *theios anēr* rather refers to Moses: see Josephus, *Ant.* 2.201–204, 233, 331; 4.326; Assumption of Moses 11:16.

7. Jesus's favorite self-designation as "Son of Man" is striking.

Master Jesus, provided that they become what they are,[8] a notion that Paul particularly well understood (see, e.g., Gal 3:26; fundamental texts in the background include Deut 14:1 and Jub. 1:23-28).

True, having recourse to the Hasidism of the eighteenth century CE may be questionable. However, since Jewish tradition is constantly building on the basis of historic "normative Judaism," it is graced with a striking consistency. The main criterion of a new tradition's receptivity is whether it inscribes itself in the line of former expressions of the Jewish tradition.[9] If we raise the issue of what prompted Jesus to be a healer in the first place, we must return to the roots of the problem of healing. Mark identifies Jesus's feeling of compassion (see 1:41; cf. John 11:1-45) as being the motive. We may also think of healing as a means of authentication. But in Matt 16:1-4 and 12:38-39 and their parallels, Jesus distances himself from this view by refusing to give a sign as requested by his opponents.

Isaianic texts such as Isa 35:5-6 and 61:1-3b provide a key. The former reads, "Then the eyes of the blind shall be opened, and the ears of the deaf unstopped; then the lame shall leap like a deer, and the tongue of the speechless sing for joy." And the latter text says, "The spirit of the Lord is upon me,[10] because the Lord has anointed me; he has sent me to bring good news to the oppressed, to bind up the brokenhearted, to proclaim liberty to the captives, and release to the prisoners … to comfort all who mourn in Zion."[11] In view of these prophecies, we shall follow the conclusion of A. E. Harvey that the healings performed by Jesus "were eschatological miracles" and that they pointed to the new age.[12] E. P. Sanders's reminder of the Elisha cycle moves in the same direction. The prophet is credited with curing a leper (2 Kgs 5:1-14; cf. Mark 1:40-45 and parr.) and with raising a dead child (2 Kgs 4:32-37; cf. Mark 5:21-43).

---

8. See Martin Buber, *Two Types of Faith: A Study of the Interpenetration of Judaism and Christianity*, trans. Norman P. Goldhawk (New York: Harper & Row, 1961), 75.

9. See again m. 'Abot 1:1; ARN (A) 1:1.

10. In 1 Enoch 46:3, "The Lord of Spirit has chosen him."

11. We find about the same formulation, based on Isa 58:6; 61:1; and Ps 146:7-8 in 4Q521 (Messianic Apocalypse) col. 2, lines 8, 12-13.

12. Anthony E. Harvey, *Jesus and the Constraints of History* (Philadelphia, Westminster, 1982), 113. E. P. Sanders approves but, unfortunately, adds that the kinship with the Isaianic texts is "more coincidental than determinative" (*Jesus and Judaism* [Philadelphia: Fortress, 1985], 161, 164).

So the argument in favor of the uniqueness of Jesus's healings does not hold as such. The point, it seems to me, is that healings and exorcisms[13] *restore* the immunity that humans enjoyed in Eden. This is as true of Elisha's interventions as of Jesus's. We may speak of Jesus's uniqueness, not in statistical, but rather in existential terms, "Urzeit wird Endzeit," as Herman Gunkel said. In this connection, Jesus's healing by command alone is striking (as in the case of the blind beggar from Jericho, the centurion's servant, and the man with a "dry" hand).[14] The parallel with creation by fiat is unmistakable. Besides, the gratitude expressed by those who have been healed and by witnesses is consistently directed toward God, not toward the miracle worker.[15]

Before Jesus decisively commands the demons to leave the sick, the gospel describes his exorcisms as violent confrontations with the possessing spirits. These toe-to-toe battles affect the healer as well. For example, Jesus feels a loss of energy when the woman with a flux of blood touches his tzitzit, garment fringes (Mark 5:24-34). Perhaps the impact of these confrontations led Jesus's family to think that he was "out of his mind" (see Mark 3:22; John 7:20). This way, Jesus's exorcisms were presented by opponents as fights between demons, hence the retort of the Nazarene in Matt 12:26.

Scholars generally isolate Isa 61:1 from the rest of the prophet's oracle. In what precedes, I have quoted 61:1-3 as a condensed unit. As such, it includes "all who mourn in Zion," which is Isaiah's reference to Israel. It thus creates an inclusive and beneficial context, where magic would demand an exclusive and ambivalent one. Now, as is well known, Morton Smith tried to make the case that Jesus was a magician, *like those Greek magicians described in the Greek Magical Papyri* (from the second century BCE to the fifth century CE).[16] Josephus tells us that the Essenes were adept

---

13. There are four stories of exorcism in Mark (1:21-28; 5:1-20; 7:24-30; 9:14-29); Mark 1:34, 39, provide summaries (cf. Luke 6:18). See here below.

14. Mark 3:1-5; Matt 12:9-13; Luke 6:6-10. Rabbi Hanina ben Dosa (before 70 CE) also "healed from a distance" (b. Ber. 34b; y. Ber. 5:4-5, 9d; cf. Matt 8:5-13 and parr.).

15. Although, as Hans Conzelmann rightly says: with the miracle, "das Da-Sein Jesu" (the present Jesus) "is drawn into the proclamation about God" (*Jesus*, trans. J. Raymond Lord, ed. John Reumann [Philadelphia: Fortress, 1973], 55 [= "Jesus Christus," *RGG*, 3rd ed., vol. 3, cols. 619-53]).

16. Morton Smith, *Jesus the Magician* (New York: Gollancz, 1978). Jesus seems to have performed acts of magic (Mark 7:31-37 and 8:22-26 [texts not picked up by Mat-

at practicing magic, and there was no shortage of charismatic personalities during the time of Jesus. I prefer to look for parallels in traditional Jewish literature—even those written later than the gospels—rather than in Greek sources. I for one think that Smith's alleged parallels are far-fetched. It is true that we find in the gospels odd echoes of popular opinions about Jesus according to which some saw him as either possessed by an impure spirit or plagued by a psychological imbalance.[17] Rather than using foreign terms—that is, coming from a totally different worldview—like "magician," we should instead see the Nazarene as a prophet.[18] An important point in this respect is Josephus's testimony that Theudas and "the Egyptian," in imitation of Moses, rejected the accusations of being sorcerers. They claimed that their signs were eschatological because they recalled the exodus.

There was at the time an attitude of suspicion toward the claims of some prophets, (see Matt 7:15 and parr.; 24:11, 24). Following the promotion of the priestly function, that is, subsequent to the return from exile in Babylon, some crucial functions within Israel faded away, sometimes to reappear for a while, like those of kingship and prophecy. Withy regard to these two ministries, Jews expected the imminent coming of *the* king, son of David, and of *the* prophet, Elijah redivivus. When Jesus asks his

---

thew and Luke!]). But Jesus's miracles neither harmed nor cursed anyone. The papyri show that the name of Jesus was used as a magical formula by magicians and called "the god of the Hebrews." A true parallel is rather with the prophetic acts of Elijah and Elisha (with the exception of Elisha's cursing to death children who were mocking him). Note that, for Smith, the term "magician" is used by the foes of the gifted man. "Skeptical but reverent admirers" use rather the title *theios anēr*. "Believers" would call him "son of God." This diversity stresses the constant misunderstandings, even on the part of the disciples (cf. Matt 16:9).

17. See Mark 3:19–21, 30–31. Dementia may be a by-product as well as a means of resistance against conditions bringing despair, providing an escape strategy and a protest against the abuses of the socioeconomic system (so David S. Hollenbach, *The Common Good and Christian Ethics* [Cambridge: Cambridge University Press, 2002]; Richard A. Horsley, *Jesus and the Spiral of Violence: Popular Jewish Resistance in Roman Palestine* [San Francisco: Harper & Row, 1987], Sanders, Crossan, and others. See José A. Pagola, *Jesus: An Historical Approximation*, trans. Margaret Wilde [Miami: Convivium, 2009], 170).

18. But with the caveat sounded by Geza Vermes (*Jesus the Jew: A Historian's Reading of the Gospels* [New York: Macmillan, 1973], 97): As "promises [by first-century prophets] remained unfulfilled and … miracles failed to materialize … the term 'prophet' … between the years AD 50 and 70 not surprisingly acquired distinctly pejorative overtones in the bourgeois and aristocratic idiom of Pharisees and Sadducees."

disciples what the populace thinks of him,[19] one answer is that he is *the* prophet (John 6:14; cf. 1:14–18; Acts 3:22–23; 7:37). The claim of prophecy was thus associated with messiahship. Deuteronomy 18:18 also played a great role: "I will raise up for them a prophet like you [Moses] from among their own people; I will put my words in the mouth of the prophet, who shall speak to them everything that I command." To the extent that Jesus was indeed *the* prophet, he revitalized prophecy among his followers. On this basis, the church came to claim to be in toto prophetic—and thus nonconformist and open to the unconventional. This implied that the church's radical involvement in history and its pronouncements about politics, economics, ecology, and so on assume the authority of prophecy.

Along these lines of thought, the popular opinion expressed by Peter that Jesus is Elijah redivivus is important. We must remember that Elijah is credited with having power over rain, food, and death, that is, over all of life. This provides a striking parallel with the role of the temple according to King Solomon's prayer at its dedication, in 1 Kgs 8:35–36; 2 Chr 7:26–27.

*

"There are some fifteen distinct stories of healing, plus the general Q list in Matthew 11:2–6 // Luke 7:18–23," says John P. Meier.[20] Let us take as an example Mark 2:1–12, with the *paralytikos* being let down through the roof of a house in Capernaum. Jesus declares that the crippled man's sins are forgiven, and his opponents react immediately, accusing Jesus of "blasphemy." Another example is the man with a withered hand in Mark 3:1–6. The scene is set in a synagogue on the Sabbath. The healing again angers some. Jesus had declared, in 2:28, that the Son of Man (or son of man) is the lord even of the Sabbath. This provides a striking contrast between Jesus's restoration of life and the plot to kill him (verse 6). In both stories of healing, the supreme authority of the Nazarene is stressed. The healings per se do not raise a problem to the people around, but rather the forgiveness of sin and, more pointedly, the halakah on the Sabbath,

---

19. Cf. Luke 9:18–21 // Matt 16:13. A sign of anxiety, of not being sure about his own identity? A need for reassurance regarding himself and his impact on "the crowds"?

20. John P. Meier, *Mentor, Message, and Miracles*, vol. 2 of *A Marginal Jew: Rethinking the Historical Jesus*, ABRL (New York: Doubleday, 1994), 678. To recall, "Q" is material common to Matthew and Luke but not present in Mark.

the day of rest.[21] Meier says that critical analysis shows that the Synoptic stories of healing on the Sabbath are not authentic, while the Johannine stories on healing are authentic but not their setting during the Sabbath! But perhaps the point is elsewhere. The intervention of "the ruler of the synagogue" in Luke 13:10–17 shows, I believe, that the distraction from prayer and liturgical continuum (13:14, whether authentic or not) were the cause of the commotion. This "distraction" affected the worshipers' motivation for gathering in the house of prayer because some came to be healed or to witness healings.

But not just this. The rest of the story in Mark 2:11 shows Jesus shockingly ordering the former paralytic to pick up his mat and walk—on a Sabbath day! Retrospectively, the healing itself was already a "transgression" of the Sabbath rules as set by the Pharisees. So it was not "easier" to declare the remission of the sick man's sins, or to command him to violate the Sabbath rest by carrying his bed to go home.[22] In both cases, Jesus takes it upon himself to twist the letter of the rules, and at this point the bearing of the episode moves way beyond the boundaries of this particular incident. Jesus is acting with messianic authority and affirms it publicly. A text like Yebamot 90 comes to mind: (speaking of the messiah to come, rabbis said) "Even if he tells you to transgress any of the commandments of the torah, obey him in every respect."

The issue of the Sabbath plays a great role in the conflict between Jesus and some "Pharisees." In fact, however, they differ on halakic interpretation, as was true, for instance, between the house of Shammai and the house of Hillel in m. Šabb. 1:5. The Qumran community is the strictest of all (see CD 10:14–11:18, but esp. 11:16): here, even if a human being falls into a pit on the Sabbath, he cannot be rescued! By contrast, in rabbinic thinking, medical treatment is permitted on Sabbath to save a life (see m. Yoma 8:6). Clearly, the whole question centers on a definition of "work" and "rest." Against Qumran rigidity, Tanhuma Massei 1 (fourth century) closely resembles Jesus's conception. The text focuses on Lev 12:3, which orders circumcision even during a Sabbath. Tanhuma provides the

---

21. John P. Meier, *Law and Love*, vol. 4 of *A Marginal Jew: Rethinking the Historical Jesus*, ABRL (New Haven: Yale University Press, 2009), 259. Ben-Chorin notes that the opposition to Jesus on these occasions is less directed against the physician than against the teacher: the problem is not the healing per se, but the halakic interpretation of the torah (Mark 2:28; Luke 6:5). See Ben-Chorin, *Brother Jesus*, 45.

22. See the perfect parallel in John 5:8.

rationale that, since circumcision "sets right just one of the 248 limbs of a person, then the whole body of a person should certainly be able to be set right."[23]

Remarkably, Jesus does not work but merely utters a word in the healing stories, so that it should not stir controversy, except perhaps with Qumran sectarians (The adversaries remain unnamed in the narrative of Mark 3:1–6.) To them, curing may have been forbidden on a Sabbath. Furthermore, for both Mark 2 and 3, it is not a matter of saving life, and Jesus could have waited until sundown to heal them. Hence, Jesus is not arguing that he is rescuing a man from the grasp of death, but he is "doing good" as opposed to "doing harm" by ignoring the condition of the crippled man.

Thus Jesus's point of view is radically different. A legalistic approach to the Sabbath requires strictly maintaining the status quo. The Sabbath then results in time being frozen, with moves of all kinds being reduced to a strict vital minimum. (At Qumran, the monks abstained from defecating on the Sabbath!) The Nazarene changes the criteria for respecting the Sabbath, and he presents a novel viewpoint: is respect for the Sabbath expressed by *doing* good or by *doing* harm? This is a tremendous hermeneutic shift that entirely changes the perspective. Jesus's opponents are dumbfounded, so foreign to them is this new approach (3:4). The parallel with the parable of the good Samaritan—in which Jesus also reverses the terms of the problem (of whom am I the neighbor?)—is remarkable.

In conclusion, I see no grounds for dismissing these narratives by arguing that they cannot go back to a historical event.[24]

This brings us to another healing story, mentioned above, in Mark 5:24–34, where a woman with a hemorrhage—that is, with a constant source of ritual impurity (see Lev 15:25) and its accompanying religious and social marginalization—comes to Jesus to be healed.[25] She touches the

---

23. See John 7:21–23; cf. Matt 12:10–12; Luke 13:14–16; Mark 2:23–28.

24. *Pace* E. P. Sanders, Meier, and many others.

25. There is a clear tendency among Jewish New Testament scholars to present the first-century CE Judaism in an idealized manner. Words like "ostracized," "outcast," disenfranchised," or "marginalized" raise a red flag, since they would not necessarily correspond with what we know of Jesus's social environment. Now, although this Jewish caveat is welcome as far as the "ideal" literature of the time is concerned, it should not be overstressed. Jesus says that he came "to set at liberty those who are oppressed" (Luke 4:18–21, quoting Isa 61:1–2). As in the time of Third Isaiah, there were actually oppressed people in Jesus's time—even if Luke 4:18–21 is the outcome of Luke's compositional work.

fringes of Jesus's garment[26] and thus communicates to him her uncleanness (see Lev 15:27). Of course, she is frightened and does it by stealth (Mark 5:28).[27] This external contact (with vestment fringes) goes much deeper than being "skin deep," which is demonstrated by Jesus's feeling that power has gone out of him. The tzitzit prove to be a conduit, a channel between Jesus and the woman. Not surprisingly, Jesus declares to her that her faith has "saved her."

The story smacks of magic: Jesus feels a power flowing from him—like the blood of the woman. One might stress this overtone of the story, but more impressive, I think, is the indication that Jesus's healings exact a price from him. The rebbes of the Hasidic movement in the eighteenth century are also described as healers, and they became exhausted in the process. Jesus's healings are not without cost: besides the criticism of foes (absent in the present narrative), he experiences a depletion of his personal power.

Mark 1:40–45 presents the healing of a leper. The curious point I'd like to focus on is perhaps a secondary element in the story as told, but may illumine an aspect of the person of Jesus. In verse 41, some authoritative versions, in lieu of "pity," have "anger" ("moved by anger, Jesus stretched out his hand"). It is obviously the *lectio difficilior*. It could be dismissed as making no sense in the present context of the narrative, but it echoes a similar quote encountered in Mark 3:5. About what would Jesus be angry in Mark 1:41? The answer seems to be: about an unspecified attitude of bystanders. Then Mark may allude to a gapping element of his story on the healing of the leper. It is easy to imagine the scandal in the eyes of some who see a banished leper being singled out by Jesus and healed in front of them with the words (v. 41), "I do choose. Be made clean." Where? When? We do not know.

Another possibility to entertain, of course, is that Jesus's anger is directed against the evil in the world, which is responsible for the terrible infirmities and illnesses that deface the good creation of God. This interpretation is buttressed by the ostensible absence of opponents in this particular case. We must remember that the leper was ostracized according to Lev 13–14. Hence it was necessary to obtain an official priestly certifica-

---

26. On "fringes" (tzitzit), see Num 15:37–40; cf. Mark 6:56.
27. The issue of impurity is not mentioned in the gospel text, however. The same is true of the resurrection of Lazarus and the dead girl in Matt 9:18–26 // Mark 5:21–43 // Luke 8:40–56. More remarkably, there is a similar absence of mention when Jesus touches a leper in Matt 8:1–4 to heal him.

tion that the sick man was made "clean" (*katharizō*, Mark 1:40, 41, 42, 44) and could be reintegrated as a bona fide member of the community.

Returning to one of Jesus's functions mentioned above—namely, the relationship of the healing by Jesus and the temple's claim to be the locus of healing—is fundamental. N. T. Wright has argued that Jesus and his followers are themselves the temple as it was intended to be[28]—an idea close to my stress on the teleological fulfillment of "Israel," "the torah," and now the temple (see ch. 5, "Jesus and Torah," 71–130; and ch. 7, "Jesus and Israel," 141–68, below). That is why Jesus establishes an intimate correspondence between healing and the forgiveness of sin (cf. Matt 9:5–6), which is a prerogative tied to the sacrificial offerings in the temple. Now, the temple is microcosm, and world equilibrium depends on the practice therein. As Joel 1–2 shows, the cessation of the Tamid sacrifice and the disregard for Sukkoth would entail the cessation of the proper order of the heavenly bodies and of rainfall. Claiming to be the veritable temple would thus mean that Jesus and his disciples claimed to be the transfigured heaven and earth. The physical destruction of the temple will, therefore, no longer cause creation to return to the primordial chaos (see Mark 14:58). "While the old Jerusalem Temple cosmology would *literally* disappear, he believed the physical world would then be sustained by himself, his words (Mark 13:31b), and his people, who would embody the new Temple as well as the new heaven and the new earth."[29]

Along this line of thought, some sources connect sickness and sinfulness.[30] Two of these sources, Ps 103 and 4QprNab, are particularly clear. In Ps 103, the terms "forgive" and "heal" as well as "sins" and "sickness" are set in parallel. In 4QprNab, the king is afflicted by malady (1) and a Jewish "exorcist forgave [his] sin" (4). Similarly, in Mark 2:1–12 and parallels, Jesus's healing of the paralytic is through forgiving his sin (see Matt

---

28. N. T. Wright, *Jesus and the Victory of God* (Minneapolis: Fortress Press, 1992).

29. Crispin H. T. Fletcher-Louis, "Jesus, the Temple and the Dissolution of Heaven and Earth," in *Apocalyptic in History and Tradition*, ed. Christopher Rowland and John Barton (Sheffield: Sheffield Academic, 2002), 141. On the new temple, see Ezek 43:1–9. It is probably correct to note, with Pagola (*Jesus*, 64), that, while Jews prayed turning to Jerusalem, Jesus is reported to have prayed "looking toward heaven" (Mark 6:45; 7:34; Luke 9:16), thus relativizing the importance of the temple.

30. In the Hebrew Bible, see Lev 26:14–17; Ps 103:3; 2 Chr 21:12–15. In Qumran, see 1QS 3:20–24; 4QprNab. In the Talmud, see t. Ber. 6:3. *The Jewish Annotated New Testament*, ed. Amy-Jill Levine and Marc Zvi Brettler (Oxford: Oxford University Press, 2011), 17–18, provides these texts, with others less convincing.

9:2). It is a "strange thing" (Luke 5:26), never seen before (Mark 2:12), and praiseworthy because God "has given such authority to human beings [*anthrōpois*]" (Matt 9:8).

The principle of distributive justice too often made individual sin the cause of suffering as a punishment (in spite of the book of Job). The gospel tells us that once Jesus's disciples asked him what to think about the victims of a fallen tower (of Siloam). Jesus responded with a clear dissociation between the alleged cause and that effect. Strikingly, he said, "Do you think that [those who were killed by the tower's fall] were worse offenders than all the others living in Jerusalem? No, I tell you; but unless you repent, you will all perish just as they did" (Luke 13:4–5; Matt 4:17). In the same spot, if we believe John's report about the healing of a man blind from birth (9:1–41), Jesus said to his disciples, "neither this man nor his parents sinned" (v. 3). The point seems to be that "this world" (*ha'olam hazeh*) is itself sick because it is sinful. The general sickness of an unbalanced universe also affects individuals, whether righteous like the author of Ps 103 or wicked like Nabonidus. But whether (relatively) righteous or all but wicked, individuals participate in this general sinfulness/sickness. A text such as m. 'Abot 2:8 leaves no doubt about this: "More flesh, more worms" said Rabbi Hillel.

The Jewish world was unanimous in acknowledging a tight connection between sin and sickness.[31] By contrast, sickness and death were absent in Eden. Thus Jesus's irony in Matt 9:5 ("Which is easier to say, 'Your sins are forgiven,'[32] or to say, 'Stand up and walk'?") squarely equates healing and the forgiveness of sin. One is not "easier" than the other.[33]

---

31. Vermes (*Jesus the Jew*, 69) writes, "Rabbis of the second- and third-century AD were still voicing the opinion that no one could recover from illness until his sins were remitted" (see Ned. 41a).

32. It is easier to say, "your sins are forgiven" than to say, "Your individual participation in universal sin is forgiven." On the text of Matt 9:5 or Mark 2:1–12 and parr., see Sanders, *Jesus and Judaism*, 273–74; and Vermes, *Jesus the Jew*, 66–67. Rabbi Hanina ben Dosa (a contemporary of Jesus) is reported to have been bitten by a snake … that died on the spot! Hanina said, "It is not the snake that kills, but sin" (Ber. 33a). Cf. Mark 16:18.

33. On Jesus's display of irony, see Dale C. Allison, *The Intertextual Jesus: Scripture in Question* (Harrisburg, PA: Trinity Press International, 2000). He quotes texts such as Luke 6:27–45 (subverting Lev 19); 9:58 (an ironic reapplication of Ps 8:5); 12:22–31 ("do not worry" in contrast to wisdom exhortations; see Prov 6:6–11); and 14:26, "hate father and mother."

Many around Jesus seemed to be ready to tolerate an exorcist/magician in their midst, but they were outraged by the claim of a man to be able to forgive sins. God is the only one with that authority (Exod 34:7; Num 14:37; 2 Sam 12:13; Isa 6:7; 43:25; 44:22; Dan 9:9).[34] The astonishing thing is that God has given that authority to human beings. It is a delegation of power; therefore, the crowd praised *God*. What is awe-inspiring is less the power itself than its transmission from the heavenly realm. Along the same line, Peter, as representative of the disciples, receives "the keys of the kingdom of heaven" (Matt 16:17-19; cf. 2 Bar. 10:18; 4 Bar. 4:4; ARN [A] 4), just as they were first given to the priests in Isa 22:22.[35] Peter is granted the authority to forgive or not to forgive. The correspondence with Jesus's authority in Matt 9:8 is striking and emphasizes once more the collective aspect of messiahship.[36]

Luke 13:10-17 sheds additional light on the topic. It is the story of a woman who has been crippled for eighteen years. Jesus heals her on the Sabbath in a synagogue with words that echo the language of liberation from slavery and exile. In other words, healing amounts to a new exodus, this time from demonic powers, and Jesus is a new Moses; under his leadership, Israel enters the kingdom of God ("it has come unto you," Luke 11:20 and parr.; cf. Luke 17:21). Note that Jesus's response to the inquiry of John the Baptist in Matt 11:5 and parallels refers to Isaiah, for whom such miracles symbolize God's redemption of Israel from the Babylonian exile. The good news to the poor, for instance, refers to Isa 61:1. John the Baptist was awaiting the end time; Jesus tells him that it is now come. Matthew 11:11 implies an already-present kingdom of God.

Jesus's drawing a parallel between healing and the liberation from Egypt is decisive. Instead of reading Exod 20:10 and Deut 5:14 as restraining orders, Jesus reads these texts as liberation manifestos. They express good news, not divine favor on condition of performance. The introductory words of Exod 20:2 and Deut 5:6 are crucial: "I am the lord your God who brought you out of the land of Egypt, out of the house of slavery."

---

34. Texts cited in Levine and Brettler, *The Jewish Annotated New Testament*, ad loc.

35. In rabbinic literature, what is bound and what is loosed means what is forbidden and what is permissible.

36. See John 1:12; Gos. Thom. 3; 108. Andrew N. Wilson writes about the Fourth Gospel that "we ourselves who read it ... are meant to be characters within the story" (*Jesus: A Life* [New York: Fawcett Columbine, 1992], 61).

The Decalogue is the constitution of a free people. It does not so much prohibit working as free from the slavery of work. In a striking text that has all chances of being authentic, Luke 6:4 Codex D reports that Jesus, seeing a man plowing on a Sabbath day, tells him, "Man, if you know what you are doing, blessed are you; but if you know not, accursed are you and a transgressor of the law."

As usual, Jesus's deed according to Luke 13 provokes anger among some witnesses. The leader of the synagogue is "indignant because Jesus had cured on the Sabbath" (v. 14). So it is clear that some people considered healing a work. Further, while they interpret ailment as the outcome of sin, Jesus interprets it as bondage/exile, that is, the universal human condition but particularly the life experience of the Jewish people. Therefore, healing becomes a metaphor for liberation from the human condition.[37]

In a cogent reflection on what constitutes rest during the Sabbath, the halakah in Šebiʿit, Šabbat, and ʿErubin bases its prescription on the generative model of the divine activity as Creator and his rest on the first Sabbath day (Gen 2:2–3). As Israel's cultic work (see ʿAbodah) replicates God's act of creation, so must Israel desist from working during the Sabbath.[38]

This powerful talmudic halakah, probably in force among the Pharisees before 70 CE, may be the source of the judgment we find in Luke 13:10–17, about healing on the Sabbath. A prima facie assessment would be that healing is creating new conditions that are to last, a forbidden "work" according to the halakah. Jesus transforms this judgment into the view that healing provides rest to the weary—a liberation from "exile." We shall discover a similar approach in the parable of the good Samaritan. For Jesus, the problem is not so much how to observe rest on the Sabbath, but how to provide rest to others. A similar principle is wrought in the above-mentioned parable: the problem is not, Who is my neighbor? but, To whom shall I be the helping neighbor?

This is the very meaning of the Sabbath for the Nazarene, a meaning paradoxically missed by theologians of the time (but not by "the entire crowd" in the synagogue, see v. 17). They preached the sanctity of the day,

---

37. Only those who believe that they are without sickness—that is, sinless in their own eyes—do not need the help of the physician (see Mark 2:17).

38. See Jacob Neusner, *Performing Israel's Faith: Narrative and Law in Rabbinic Theology* (Waco, TX: Baylor University Press, 2005), 184ff.

but in fact they were the blind leading the blind, the dead burying their dead (Luke 9:60-62; Matt 8:22).[39]

This principle also applies to the parable of the sower (Matt 13:1-23 // Mark 4:1-20 // Luke 8:4-15 // Gos. Thom. 9). N. T. Wright sees in this parable an apocalyptic "subversive retelling of the story of Israel, which ... belongs exactly with [Jesus'] action in the Temple."[40] He cites numerous textual warrants wherein "seed" is a metaphor for "remnant" or *verus Israel* that will be "sowed" again in the land.[41] Now God continues to sow, but much of the seed goes to waste. Jesus's audience is challenged to have ears to hear: the Jesus-event is the momentous turning point and "encapsulation" of Israel's story. Since this is a story of rejected prophets, Jesus cannot expect anything better because he recapitulates that prophetic heritage; hence the quotation of Isa 6:9-10 ("so that they may not ... comprehend with their minds and turn and be healed").

Jesus's healings are at times presented as exorcisms. In fact, all healings are in one way or another exorcisms.[42] In the narrative of Luke 13, there is no direct reference to Jesus expelling demons, but verse 16 clearly says, "Satan bound [her] for eighteen long years." In every case, Jesus's intervention is a demonstration of power, be it expressed as *dynameis* ("mighty deeds"), *semeia, terata*, or *paradoxa* ("astounding deeds"), or again as *thaumasia* ("wondrous deeds").[43] I shall take as an example Mark 9:14-29, the boy possessed by an unclean spirit (v. 25). It is a clear episode of some kind of epilepsy. Modern science would dismiss this as an alleged possession. "Our modern mental horizon [is] light-years away from the worldview of Jesus and the evangelists."[44] Nevertheless, had Jesus and the gospel writers been medically knowledgeable, I suspect that they would stick to their own

---

39. The Mishnah lists thirty-nine categories of work forbidden on the Sabbath (Šabb. 49b). But elsewhere, the Mishnah concludes, "The laws of the Sabbath are like mountains hanging on a hair" (m. Ḥag. 1:8).

40. N. T. Wright, *Jesus and the Victory of God* (Minneapolis: Fortress, 1996), 232.

41. See ibid., 233 and n26.

42. Sigmund Freud, speaking of a thirty-five-year-old woman with occasional stomach trouble, said, "Why not keep it, I told her, because if we are able to take away those attacks that come once in a fortnight or so, we do not know what problem we shall discover beneath it" (quoted by Jessie Taft, *Otto Rank* [New York: Julian, 1958], 139). Or, as Ernest Becker puts it, "Men are doomed to live in an overwhelming tragic and demonic world" (*The Denial of Death* [New York: Free Press, 1973], 281).

43. So Meier, *Mentor, Message, and Miracles*, 646.

44. Ibid., 647.

diagnosis of demonic possession. This opinion is not the result of scientific ignorance. Anything that endangers human integrity (*shalom*) is deemed demonic. Disease is no mere accident; it is not a hiccup. Within Jesus's "mental horizon," everything has a theological meaning. Regardless of the outrageous conclusion by some hypocrites that the boy deserved his fate, illness as phenomenon is not natural in God's creation. It is an evil power corrupting the goodness of "Eden" here and now. Hence, Jesus's healings are either "by the finger of God" or by Satan (Luke 11:20), *tertium non datur*.[45] Nor can any scientific third term neutralize this understanding or judgment. Thus, as I have said, all of Jesus's healings are exorcisms—something that a medical cure is not, although, *by implication*, even a medical cure becomes a testament to God's compassion.

In conclusion, the modern scientific point of view does not supersede that of the allegedly unsophisticated evangelists. The spiritual abnormality of illness (versus its physiological inevitability/accidentalness) is what is at stake. This does not detract from the eminent nobility of the physician. On the contrary, her intervention is set under the umbrella of "healing" beside Jesus's exorcisms.

The multiplication of loaves and fish in order to feed the crowd (Mark 6:32–44) is, of course, not a healing story strictly speaking, but its importance in Jesus's miracle working is strongly stressed by the gospels. In fact, it is the only miracle reported in all four gospels, and it is also the only one to be recounted twice, that is, in two variant forms, in both Mark and Matthew. The second account is in Mark 8:1–10 // Matt 15:32–39. Furthermore, the version of it in John 6:1–15 is independent of those in the Synoptics. But there are some parallels between the second version in Mark 8 and John 6. Strangely enough, in the second occurrence of the miracle, the disciples show no awareness of the precedent, a proof that the second narrative is independent of the first.

The evident parallel in the Hebrew Scriptures is Elisha feeding a hundred people with twenty loaves (2 Kgs 4:43–44; in 1 Kgs 17:8–16, Elijah

---

45. The expression "the finger of God" appears only one time in the Hebrew Bible, in Exod 8:15 (the third plague in Egypt). So here Jesus associates himself with Moses and Aaron. Meier, after Manson and Perrin, refers to Exod. Rab. 10.7, where the Egyptian magicians say, "This is the work of God and not the work of demons." The use of "the finger of God" in Luke 11:20 and parr. is unique also in the New Testament; see John P. Meier, *Companions and Competitors*, vol. 3 of *A Marginal Jew: Rethinking the Historical Jesus*, ABRL (New York: Doubleday, 2001), 231.

increases the amount of oil of the widow of Zarephath). There are also rabbinic parallels.[46] For example, the Midrash Qoh on 1:9 (9b) draws a parallel between the "first liberator" (Moses) and the last one (the messiah): "As the first liberator let rain bread (Exod 16:4) ... so with the last liberator, he will rain bread."

In the multiplication stories, Jesus acts as a paterfamilias. He "gives thanks" over the bread, then "blesses" the fish, setting a parallel with the Eucharist (where the wine has replaced the fish). John, by setting this latter scene around Passover, emphasizes the parallel. The people are many; the food, abundant; and Jesus and his people eat the flesh and drink the blood of the Son of Man, thus infinitely extending the collective dimension of messiahship.[47]

Raising the Dead

Several statements in the gospel claim that Jesus restored people to life. Peter is also credited (Acts 9:36–43) with the same miracle in the person of Tabitha. Resurrecting the dead was initially recorded in the legends around Elijah and Elisha (1 Kgs 17:17–24; 2 Kgs 4:18–37, cf. 2 Kgs 13:20–21). The raising of the dead is less frequent in rabbinic literature, but it is recorded (more or less in a comic mode) in Meg. 7b and 'Abod. Zar. 10b.

Jesus performs three such raisings in the gospel: the daughter of Jairus (Mark 5:21–43), the son of the widow of Nain (Luke 7:11–17), and Lazarus (John 11:1–46). Meier calls them "extreme examples of healing."[48] We shall concentrate on the raising of Lazarus, which serves as the culmination of Jesus's miraculous signs in John.[49] John proclaims Jesus as life giver (10:10); he also sees in the reviving of Lazarus the cause of Jesus's arrest and execution (see 11:47–53).

---

46. See Jean-Marie van Cangh, "La multiplication des pains dans l'Evangile de Marc. Essai d'exégèse globale," in *L'Evangile selon Marc: Tradition et rédaction*, ed. M. Sabbe, BETL 34 (Gembloux: Duculot, 1974), 309–46.

47. On the collective messianism in the gospel, see the very important text of Isa 52:7 ("How beautiful on the mountains are the feet of the messenger..."). The MT or the LXX has "messenger" in the singular. So is it also in Acts 10:36 and Eph 2:17. But the plural is used in Rom 10:15 (*evangitzomenōn*) and Acts 5:42.

48. Meier, *Mentor, Message, and Miracles*, 776.

49. John 1–12 builds a Book of Signs.

4. JESUS AS HEALER

The Johannine text is well written in general and introduces a keen sense of suspense. Jesus appears to delay his intervention as much as he can. The result is that Lazarus dies and is entombed four days before Jesus arrives. Even mentioning that Bethany is close to Jerusalem (11:18) is ambiguous, since the text does not say that Jesus and disciples were in Jerusalem (in Judea, says v. 7), in which case it is stressed that Jesus could easily have walked some two miles to be with his friend Lazarus and heal him. At any rate, there is no need to attribute this geographical information to unknowing Christians living outside of Palestine.

Verses 33–38 are awkward, with multiple references to Jesus's emotion (vv. 33, 35, 38). Clearly, their purpose is to show the deep love Jesus felt for his friend and, incidentally, that his delay before coming to Bethany was not due to indifference. These verses also show that Jesus was no magician. The raising of Lazarus will be a drama, not the intervention of a deus ex machina. This also implies that Jesus will have to struggle with death, changing lifelessness into life-fullness, like the Creator God at the "beginning." True, these verses may be a later addition to the narrative,[50] but they certainly are not superfluous to this story.

A similar judgment may apply to the possible adjoining of verses 21–27 (the Martha encounter). They interrupt the flow of the narrative and appear as secondary in light of verse 45, where Mary is the centerpiece, not Martha.[51] On the other hand, the excision of these verses would deprive the reader of some of Jesus's key statements regarding resurrection and life (eternal), and also of Martha's regarding Jesus's messiahship. If, therefore, verses 21–27 are later, they were a felicitous addition.

Furthermore, John is prone to using the device of *inclusio* in his narratives. In our text he started with "Mary and her sister Martha" (v. 1) plus a note on Mary (who anointed Jesus's feet with perfume; John 12:1–8; to recall, Luke 7:36–50 narrates the anointment of Jesus's feet by an anonymous woman). Therefore, it is not unexpected that she would appear again at the end of the story (v. 45). The character of Martha is *included* and literarily parenthetical—but what a magnificent parenthesis! Within it, we note the presence of "the Jews who were with Martha in the house, consoling her" (John 11:31). It is not often that John offers a positive note on "the Jews"![52]

---

50. So Meier, *Mentor, Message, and Miracles*, 816.
51. That Mary and Martha were really two sisters is confirmed by Luke 10:38–42.
52. The phrase "the Jews" in the Gospel of John needs to be reinterpreted. This

expression designates both the Judeans, seen from the standpoint of a Galilean (hence "the Judeans") and the Pharisees (to the extent that the word means "the separated ones"). After 70 CE, however, there are no grounds for this distinction. They become simply "the Jews" (until the emergence of other dissidences). More on this below in "Excursus: John's Use of the Term 'the Jews'" (166–67).

5
Jesus and Torah

For Jesus, the absolute of the spirit of the law[1] takes precedence over the absolute of the letter of the law. As an example, let us focus on Jesus healing the man with a lame hand on the Sabbath (Luke 6:6). At stake is the principle that the double Torah (written and oral) strives toward its own transcendence when, from being the rule of Israel *kata sarka* ("Israel after the flesh"/the contingent Israel), it becomes, at last, the rule of the kingdom of God.[2] The former carries the seed of its own transformation. Thus, here and now, the law of the Sabbath is violated in favor of even a one-day-old infant, but not for someone dead, even if he were King David. "As long as someone lives and observes the commandments the Sabbath is violated for them" (t. Šabb. 17:19); Šabb. 151b adds, "The Torah says 'profane a Sabbath for human beings, that they may observe many Sabbaths.'"[3]

By transcendence, I mean the promise that strives toward a coming fulfillment of its hopes, like we find in the entire prophetic corpus. This means that the present is pregnant with things to come—that is, the king-

---

1. Although the word *torah* also means "law," its basic sense is instruction, direction(s), from the Hebrew root *yrh*, "to shoot an arrow" (see 1 Sam 20:35–38). *Nomos* in the Synoptics refers to the written Pentateuch (as reinterpreted by Jesus), while in Jewish tradition in general it may mean the whole corpus of Scripture and, later, include the two Torahs, written and oral.

2. Can "Sinai" be transcended? Yes. Pesiq. Rab Kah., pisqa 21, says that the restoration of Zion in the time of the messiah will surpass the glory of the revelation at Sinai. So also does the exodus; it aims to its own fulfillment (see Mek. 2.3 [on Exod. 14:15]). Note that this idea was not without danger. In the second century BCE Posidonius Apamea advanced the suggestion that the original Mosaic law had been simple and "natural." Priests later falsified it!

3. M. Soṭah 9 comes with a litany of rule cancellations, all due to a change of circumstances (the main one, of course, being the temple destruction, as m. Roš Haš. 4:1–4 demonstrates).

dom of God—a notion that permeated Jesus's kerygma. The time of the divine promise has now come to an end. A new era has started, the era of its accomplishment.[4]

Let us take as an example Jer 31: the covenant will be new, that is, renewed in such a way that "Israel will finally be Israel, in its own place in time," as Kornelis Miskotte writes.[5] The torah must be written on hearts, rather than on stone. Then there will be full "knowledge of YHWH" (cf. Jeremiah and, before him, Hosea). The same is true regarding kingship. While Jeremiah sees the royal dynasty as a grave problem (see 22:13-18, 24-30), he also "promises that one will arise from that dynasty who will do what kings are supposed to do, namely, practice justice and righteousness (Ps 72:1-4; cf. Jer 22:15-17)," as Walter Brueggemann says.[6]

Martin Buber, writing about Matt 5:48 ("Ye therefore shall be perfect, as your heavenly Father is perfect"),[7] astutely contrasts the "as" in Jesus's saying with the "for" in the corresponding Leviticus texts that exhort Israel to be holy "*for* I am holy." The "as" is possible only when one is speaking eschatologically, for "there is no perfection in the course of history."[8] In talmudic literature, there is a parallel in b. Šabb. 133b, y. Pe'ah 1:1, 15b: "Be thou compassionate and merciful as He is compassionate and merciful."

Quite a number of New Testament scholars think that Jesus opposed the law.[9] But, even more than for other gospel issues, nuance is of utmost

---

4. A tensive era, nevertheless, during which Christians continue praying, "Thy kingdom come!" and *marana tha* ("Lord, come!").

5. Kornelis Miskotte, *When the Gods Are Silent* (New York: Harper & Row, 1967), 413.

6. Walter Brueggemann, *A Commentary on Jeremiah: Exile and Homecoming* (Grand Rapids: Eerdmans, 1998), 318.

7. God is Father in the four gospels, sometimes in the Aramaic form *abba*, which stresses intimacy (see Isa 63:16-17; 64:8; 1Q36 [Hymns] 9:34-35). It is especially used in this way by Jewish charismatics. We note the special use of "Son of God" to designate the royal messiah in 2 Sam 8:14; Ps 5:7; Rom 1:1-4.

8. Martin Buber, *Two Types of Faith: A Study of the Interpenetration of Judaism and Christianity*, trans. Norman P. Goldhawk (New York: Harper & Row, 1961), 60. See also 4 Ezra 3:20-22: in the day of revelation "you did not take away from them the evil heart.... The good disappeared and the evil remained." On this, see Jon D. Levenson, *Creation and the Persistence of Evil: The Jewish Drama of Divine Omnipotence* (San Francisco: Harper & Row, 1988).

9. So for Werner Georg Kümmel, e.g., Jesus rejected all the torah; for Rudolf Bultmann, followed by E. P. Sanders, Jesus opposed only a selection of laws. See Sanders, *Jesus and Judaism* (Philadelphia: Fortress, 1985), 246.

5. JESUS AND TORAH

importance. Even the rabbis opposed the "letter" of some laws. For instance, they took exception with Exod 20:5 (God visiting the iniquity of the fathers upon the children to the third and the fourth generation).[10] But, as Sanders remarks, this was not construed as a denial of the torah. The soon-to-come "Oral Torah" (*hatorah shebe'al peh*) modifies, alters, deletes but at the same time paradoxically *confirms*. Jesus's attitude toward the temple—whose rites are based on the torah—shows he understood that the current dispensation was *not* final.[11]

With regard to a text such as Matt 8:21–22 // Luke 9:59–60 ("let the dead bury their dead")—clearly an authentic logion—there is no parallel in Jewish literature. It directly contravenes basic ordinance as found in Gen 23:3–4; Exod 20:12; Tob 6:13-15; Ber. 3:1. In short, "Jesus consciously requires disobedience of a commandment ... given by God."[12] This astonishing declaration by Jesus did not become a new statute. As Martin Hengel says, Jesus at times formulates ad hoc maxims.[13] The present one starkly contrasts Jesus as life-bearer[14] and the *derek 'erets* (the habitual living manners), which is a foil to life. To follow him—which is what the young man wanted—demands the leaving behind of all worldly care. That's probably what the logion means, but it certainly implies that, with Jesus's presence, something immensely important is happening that supersedes even a sacred duty and the natural desire to take care of one's dead father.[15] It is true that in Ezek 24:15, God forbids the prophet to lament his wife's death, and Jeremiah cannot take part in the lament for the dead (16:5–7). In both cases, these are signs of God's judgment. The parallels with prophetic texts are striking in more than one way, for, in Matt 8:21–22, Jesus demands obedience just as God did with individual prophets, for specific purposes.[16] At other times, we see Jesus disrupting family cohesion, comparable to demands by Essenes on neophytes (see

---

10. Mek. R. Shim. b. Yohai (to Exod 20:5).
11. See Sanders, *Jesus and Judaism*, 252.
12. Ibid., 254.
13. Martin Hengel, *The Charismatic Leader and His Followers*, trans. James Greg (Edinburgh: T&T Clark, 1981), 7.
14. Cf. Acts 3:15, against the background of Hebrew *meqor* [*mayim*] *hayim* in Ps 36:10; Prov 10:11; 13:14; 14:27; 16:22; 18:4; Jer 2:13; 17:13.
15. Hengel reminds us that the care of dead has "primacy among all good works" (see Ber. 3:1a; m. 'Ed. 8.4; 'Abod. Zar. 37b).
16. See Hengel, *The Charismatic Leader*, 12.

4QTest 16–20).[17] While offensive to Jewish sensitivities, Jesus's saying to the young man illustrates his "unique authority as the proclaimer of the *imminent Kingdom of God*."[18] This message is far from being benign; we remember Jesus's saying that he came to cast fire on the earth (Luke 12:49; Gos. Thom. 10; cf. Mic 7:6; also 1 Enoch 100:21 and Sanh. 97a ["when the Son of David comes"]).[19]

A scriptural parallel to this can be found in the calling of Elisha by Elijah in 1 Kgs 19. In 19:19–21, Elijah seems to forbid Elisha to say farewell to his parents. The MT is ambiguous; Josephus understood that Elisha actually said adieu to his parents (*Ant.* 8.354), in which case Jesus in Matt 8 imposes a more radical demand. Another possible parallel is found in 1 Macc 2:27–28, 39–48, where those called to follow Mattathias are to leave "all their possessions behind in the town."

This is an antiestablishment atmosphere. The disciple makes himself dependent on the personality of a charismatic, like John the Baptist, for instance, or for that matter Jesus himself.[20]

We find a comparable situation in his own conviction that accepting him is enough, emphasizes the centrality of Jesus's person.[21] Neither formal repentance (actualized by the offer of sacrifice in the temple) nor restitution (of ill-gotten gains, in the case of tax collectors, e.g.)—as required by the law—are necessary to inherit the kingdom of God. Rather, Jesus asked those who would follow him to minister to the sick and downtrodden.[22] This certainly stirred indignation in some.

---

17. See, e.g., Matt 10:34 // Luke 12:51; Matt 10:37 // Luke 14:26.

18. Hengel, *Charismatic Leader*, 15.

19. This apocalyptic language evokes a time of tribulations when chaos reigns and children rise against their parents.

20. Sean Freyne speaks of the "inevitable clash of perspectives between the guardians of the institution and the charismatic 'outsider'" (*Jesus, A Jewish Galilean: A New Reading of the Jesus-story* [London: T&T Clark, 2004], 113). The fate of Jeremiah is an example (see 18:18–23; 26:1–24).

21. David Rhoads, Donald Michie, and Joanna Dewey say that Jesus "interprets the desire for healing as an indication of repentance" (*Mark as Story: An Introduction to the Narrative of a Gospel* [Philadelphia: Fortress, 1982], 110).

22. "The humble of the earth" (Ps 76:10). Jesus pronounces a clear beatitude of the poor (see Matt 5:3–6). At Qumran, the covenanters call themselves *'ebyonim* ("poor"). This is in glaring contrast to a certain trend in wisdom literature that blames the poor for bringing their own wretchedness upon themselves (see, e.g., Prov 6:6–11; 10:4–5; cf. Sir 18:32–33; 25:2–3; 40:28–30).

As to Mark 7:15 (on purity/impurity), I do not think E. P. Sanders is correct in suggesting that the meaning of Jesus's saying is: "not *only* what goes in defiles, but even more, what goes out."[23] Jesus, once more, radicalized the law.[24] The disciples themselves should, indeed, be more righteous than (even) the Pharisees are (see Matt 5:20). The Pharisees were Jesus's "most *worthy* opponents."[25]

Another test of Jesus's attitude toward the law is exemplified by his saying about divorce (in Matt 5:31–32; 19:3–9 // Mark 10:2–12; Luke 16:18, and confirmed by Paul in 1 Cor 7:10–16). This is explicitly in reference to *Urzeit*, in Gen 1:27 and 2:24. It is also in contrast with Deut 24:1–4 (on the modalities of divorce, given through Moses's leniency "because of your hardness of heart," says Jesus in Mark 10:5).[26] Jesus does not invite violation of the law but, as Sanders says, introduces a statute where there was none by "excluding the situation in which [the other statutes] were relevant."[27] In 1 Cor 7, cited above, Paul repeats this prohibition in the name of "the Lord"—which, incidentally, confirms the authenticity of Jesus's logion—but then discusses its repercussion in the present economy, where some allowance is necessary. Paul, "a Jew of the torah," thus finds in himself two contradictory laws, the torah and "another law in my members ... that takes me captive" (Rom 7, see especially vv. 18–19). Unable, as it were, to rescue humanity without destroying the created freedom in the process, God allows his Son to atone for all.

In fact, Jesus's attitude toward divorce reveals, once more, his conception that the new order dawns with his ministry. As I underscored, it is a return to *Urzeit*, to Gen 1 and 2. Concomitantly, the torah is thus acceding

---

23. At any rate, John P. Meier, *Law and Love*, vol. 4 of *A Marginal Jew: Rethinking the Historical Jesus*, ABRL (New Haven: Yale University Press, 2009), 17, concludes that the saying is a product of the early church. Parenthetically, I'd like to quote the following, taken from Yann Martel's *Life of Pi* (New York: Harcourt, 2001): "Evil in the open is but evil from within that has been let out" (71).

24. See below the section "Purity/Impurity," 102–7.

25. Andrew Simmonds, " 'Woe to You ... Hypocrites': Rereading Matthew 23:13–36," *BSac* 166 (2009): 348.

26. To Moses's leniency in the law, one could add the building of a temple "made with hands" (Mark 14:58); see Mek. 1.16 (on Exod 13:2), referring to Isa 66:1 ("what is the house that you would build me?"). See Acts 7:7; 17:24.

27. Sanders, *Jesus and Judaism*, 257.

to its transcendental form, into which "at last eternity transforms" it (see Matt 5:17).[28]

Note that the contrast established by Sanders between this strict abiding Jesus and the Jesus "friend of collectors" and "sinners" is uncalled for. Jesus abides to a transcendental torah, which extends its compassionate wings to harbor the downtrodden, the collectors, and the alleged "sinners."[29] I do not see a gap between these two aspects of Jesus's torah. The same is true of Sanders's contrast with Paul's argument in favor of his mission to the gentiles. The clash between the present economy and the "new age" economy suffices to explain the early church's (and the modern scholars') embarrassment. I for one do not see why "no one will attribute to Jesus" Matt 5:17 (rather Matt 5:18), as Sanders says.[30] Jesus's claim is to reveal the ultimate form of the torah, not the alteration of even one iota of it.[31] This is a claim echoed by Paul in Rom 3:31. The point is that we must distinguish between the economy inaugurated and *actualized* by Jesus's presence among "us," on the one hand, and the interim economy in which "we" now live in Jesus's temporary absence. While the "bridegroom" is living, the disciples should not fast (Matt 9:15); when "he is taken away from them, then they will fast" (Matt 6:16–18), and they will tithe mint, dill, and cumin according to the law (Matt 23:23). Meanwhile, Matt 11:16–19 (and parr.) says, "The Son of Man came eating and drinking," presumably because it was time for a wedding, a wedding between him and his people.[32]

Within this perspective, Paul's pragmatism is in full sway. He is, like all the followers of "Christ," caught between the two economies, whereby the eschatological impinges on the present reality. This certainly marks the respect for the Mosaic law in that day as transient, provisional, and "approximate," and of its interpretation as proclaimed by Jesus's teaching, especially in the Sermon on the Mount, permanent and final.[33] This inter-

---

28. Quoting Stéphane Mallarmé, "The Tomb of Edgar Allan Poe."

29. See Mark 2:15: "And many toll collectors and sinners were reclining at table with Jesus."

30. Sanders, *Jesus and Judaism*, 262.

31. Note with Geza Vermes (*Jesus the Jew: A Historian's Reading of the Gospels* [New York: Macmillan, 1973], 137) that "messianic speculation turning on the verb, 'to be revealed,' was in great vogue from the latter part of the first-century AD onward."

32. Meier refers to *megillat ta'anit*: in the calendar, there are days of joy during which it is not permitted to fast.

33. See ch. 6 below, "Jesus and Moses," 131–40.

pretation was inspired by love that proceeds by amplification (versus justice that proceeds by reduction according to the principle of reciprocity) as I shall expound below. Here, the principle is the presence of eternity within time.

If we take as an example the so-called rejection of the food laws—on the basis of Mark 7:20 (cf. Matt 15:10–20)—it must be explicated in the sense that all human food, by amplification, has become kosher, not that the *kashrut* has been abolished (see, e.g., Acts 10:14). This is a critical difference: now every meal is eucharistic. In consequence, the righteousness of Jesus's disciples surpasses that of the Pharisees themselves.

When Jesus says that he has come to fulfill the torah (Matt 5:17),[34] one must remember that, in the view of the Pharisees, the coming messiah would reveal the authentic torah, that is, in its eschatological dimension.[35] Jesus's teaching in the Sermon on the Mount claims to fulfill this requirement. (Recall what he has to say about murder, adultery, oaths, divorce, the *lex talionis*, and love of the neighbor.)[36] In Buber's words, "Fulfillment of the Torah … means here disclosure of the Torah."[37] With the coming of the messiah, the sages say, God teaches a new torah, and gives thirty new commandments. In Leviticus Rabbah (fifth century), all sacrifices and prayers will be abolished, as there will be no sin to atone for.[38] It is thus no

---

34. In the words of Harold Bloom, "No Jew known at all to history can be regarded as more loyal to the Covenant than was Jesus of Nazareth" (*Jesus and Yahweh: The Names Divine* [New York: Riverhead, 2005], 12).

35. See, e. g., m. 'Ed. 8:7.

36. About these rules, it can be said in more general terms what Daniel Harrington says about the talion: "[Jesus's] teaching on non-retaliation pushes the biblical law of retaliation (see Exod 21:23–24, Lev 24:19–20, Deut 19:21) to the point of abrogation" ("The Jewishness of Jesus," in *Jesus' Jewishness: Exploring the Place of Jesus in Early Judaism*, ed. James Charlesworth [New York: Crossroad, 1991], 11).

37. Buber, *Two Types of Faith*, 67. Note that, within the Sabbateanist movement, Nathan of Gaza offers also an eschatological interpretation of Scriptures. The emphasis is on the messianic vicissitudes. In terms of the law, both Christianity and Sabbateanism claimed that their respective messiahs had introduced "the beginning of a new era … and the foundation of a new reality. Hence they had to adopt a radically different attitude toward the values … dominant until then, namely, the Law of Moses and the halakhic tradition of Rabbinic Judaism respectively" (Gershom Scholem, *Sabbatai Sevi: The Mystical Messiah*, trans. R. J. Zwi Werblowsky [Princeton: Princeton University Press, 1973], 797–98).

38. The Zohar says that the letters of the Torah of Moses will be rearranged into different words with new prescriptions. See also, e.g., Gen. Rab. 98.9; Lev. Rab. 9.7.

surprise that Matthew sees Moses redivivus in Jesus delivering "his" law from the mountaintop.

It behooves us to reflect some more about the central notion of fulfillment. That the torah needs fulfillment means that it is a promise and an expectation ("till all [of the law] be fulfilled" [Matt 5:18; see 5:17; Rom 13:8, 10; cf. Gal 5:14; 6:2; Jas 2:8]). The era of the law is a period of expectation that lasted till the days of John the Baptist (Matt 11:13). When Jesus begins to fulfill the torah, a new era starts, in which expectation is over—there is no duplication of the fulfillment. The life of the pious is now spent within the embrace of the torah fulfilled. It has reached its telos, in both senses of the word. This is not an abrogation of the law, but a triumph. The human incapacity to fulfill the commandment is transcended by the Son of Man's supreme sacrifice—a love as strong as death—according to the demands of the torah, when correctly understood (see Isa 53). Such love includes the enemy. The lover's diet includes all foods—it is the all-inclusiveness of *kashrut*. Love includes all people, as all people can be dealt with in a neighborly fashion. It is antipodal to murder, for it gives life. It excludes divorce, on the grounds that wife and husband become one unit, as intended by the Creator.

So the torah's very terms themselves are transcended. Quibbling will never fulfill the law—admirable though the enormous effort may be. The ultimate fulfillment can never be reached until the Pious dies for love (see John 15:13). Anything short of this remains within the parameters of the provisional. It is only good until it is not.

Excursus: Amy-Jill Levine's Development on the Prohibition of Divorce in Mark 10:2[39]

Professor Levine remarks that, since Deut 24:1–4, which is in the background of the discussion between Jesus and the Pharisees, clearly allows divorce, the Pharisees' question on whether it is lawful to divorce one's wife is somewhat odd. I would imagine, however, that this was not the first time Jesus had spoken about divorce, but it remained unclear to his audience whether he actually wanted to question the text of Deut 24. The testing questions of the "Pharisees" allow Jesus, as usual, to become more

---

39. Amy-Jill Levine, *The Misunderstood Jew: The Church and the Scandal of the Jewish Jesus* (San Francisco: HarperSanFrancisco, 2006), 139–43.

specific in his stance. First, Jesus acknowledges the torah's commandment (Mark 10:3–4). Then Jesus takes exception with it on the grounds of Gen 1:27 and 2:24 (Mark 10:5–9). (Note that Jesus's interpretation is echoed by Paul in 1 Cor 7:10–11 and, with some practical margin of interpretation, in Matt 5:31 and 19:9.)

Levine rejects critics' conclusion that Jesus is protecting women from arbitrary divorces. The oft-referenced m. Giṭ. 9:10, allowing a husband to divorce his wife for having spoiled his food or because he found another woman more beautiful (so, R. Aqiba), is counterbalanced by other rabbis' opinions (Shammai, for instance). In the Gemara, R. Eleazar, says, "If a man divorces his wife, even the altar sheds tears" (Giṭ. 90b). Incidentally, Levine adds that Josephus, in *Ant*. 15.529, wrongly says that only men are permitted to divorce their wives. (On this, perhaps Josephus's statement is a pique against Herod's household's practices, with women divorcing their husbands.)

I think that Professor Levine's discussion is well put and useful. I remain, however, somewhat unsatisfied. Granted, there is nothing anti-Judaic in Jesus's statement. Mishnah Giṭṭin only gives voice to a particular understanding of Deut 24, especially the extreme license given to men by R. Aqiba to divorce their wives. His opinion is typically contradicted (in part) by other rabbinic voices, R. Eleazar's, for instance. All the same, Giṭṭin is *mishnaic*, and the other opinions are not! What is mishnaic is vested with a special authority.

Furthermore, and on a different level of understanding Mark 10, this is much more than a conflict of opinions between Jesus and "some Pharisees." After all, Jesus pits one text of the Torah against another, namely, Gen 1 and 2 against Deut 24! He says that Deut 24—used to spell out a lax rule that favors men only—has become obsolete. Jesus's grounds for such a daring stance, although not specified here, refer evidently to the new era inaugurated by the Nazarene. In other words, not all toratic laws are created equal! The irruption of the kingdom of God, through the person, sayings, and deeds of Jesus, has changed the equation. Deuteronomy 24—and presumably many other commandments and prohibitions in the Torah—was valid for an era of transition, but it came to an end with John the Baptist (see Matt 11:13–14). Now, however, "Urzeit wird Endzeit" (what used to be "in the beginning" is newly realized at the end). This implies that provisional allowances are no longer valid. The end has come near, which entails the end of an era. But it does not cancel out the torah (see Matt 5:17–20); it fulfills the torah, if only by solving the contradiction between Gen 1:27 and Deut 24. By doing so, Jesus relativizes a polity that was valid for historical Israel but only until the advent of the messianic kingdom.[40]

Taking this stand, Jesus demonstrates that what is at stake in the present discussion with the "Pharisees" is much more than a wisdom teaching. Jesus's radicalism is revolutionary. From his hermeneutic perspective, Deut 24:1–4 was, *ab origine*, set under the umbrella of Gen 1:27. It was, from its incipience, no more than an expedient, a provisional amendment to Gen 1 and 2. Therefore, it could not last forever, and its validity came to an end when the messianic telos arrived. By analogy, we could say that commandments in the torah, when given "because of hardness of heart" (Mark 10:5), are set on the level of prophetic oracles, for example. As oracles are time-bound, so are they. For instance, Amos 5:21–27; Isa 1:10–20; and Ps 51:16–17 come with a prophetic amendment to the pentateuchal requirements of sacrifices.[41]

"Hardness of heart" begs reflection. Rabbinic teaching says that there must be a *siyag latorah* (a fence around the torah) (see m. 'Abot 1:1); that is, sages should make explicit how to avoid transgressions, and so on. But the torah itself is already a *siyag*. Yebamot 21a and B. Qam. 5a expound, "Make a *siyag* around My *siyag*."[42] Many commandments and prohibitions in the torah are preventive. They are given because of the "hardness of human hearts." For Jesus, this fact stamps them as provisional. In the messianic kingdom, there can be no "hardness of heart"!

Thus Deut 24:1–4 does not constitute a unique case of relativity. Jesus applies the same "sliding scale" criterion to a variety of notions, like "neighbor," purity/impurity, *kashrut*, Sabbath keeping, fasting, temple ritual, sacrifices, family ties, honor due to parents, divorce, oaths, vows, and so on. He asked which of the torah commandments is the greatest—hence there are many that are less great! True, there are rabbinic parallels to this inquiry (Rabbi Hillel's pronouncement comes to mind [see Šabb. 31a] or, even earlier, Tob 4:15), but these are not perfect parallels. Hillel, for one, provides a

---

40. On the perennial validity of Deut 24, see below.

41. The relevance of those texts in the Torah and the prophetic literature remains unquestioned.

42. The Maharal of Prague (sixteenth century), in his *Derekh Hayim* (a commentary on 'Abot), reflects on the wording of the Mishnah that Moses received the Torah "from Sinai." It should have been "from the mouth of God," he says. But "Sinai" had become the "indispensable intermediary."

summary of the whole torah, not with a principle according to which some parts of the law are relative while others are absolute. Jesus used a different touchstone. It introduced a hierarchy, within which the ethical is recognized as the supreme criterion, thus expressing an implicit criticism against a "formalism" that confuses the essential with the accessory.[43] Jesus's viewpoint depends entirely on the nature of the kingdom of God that he both announces and realizes. We shall thus turn to this notion, which is central in Jesus's weltanschauung.[44] But first, additional reflections on Jesus's prohibition of divorce in Mark 10:9 and Luke 16:18 are in order.[45]

The marriage of two human beings makes manifest God's joining them together, as written in Gen 1–2. This makes the marriage unbreakable. Cutting it asunder is anathema. From such a viewpoint, the rules on divorce in Deut 24:1–4 must be considered as laxist and provisional, filling the period between the beginning (Genesis) and the end (apocalyptic).

I submit that Jesus's reasoning is entirely based on the assumption that *God* has joined the two spouses. This, however, leaves a gapping margin of interpretation, when wedded people discover that God did *not* join them. A mutual attraction without real basis was mistakenly interpreted as "sacred." In other words, Jesus's negative judgment on Deut 24 denounces a lack of distinction between a divinely focused union and one that is all-too-human. When such confusion prevails, this casuistry allows the dissolution of the former as if it belonged to the latter—an abomination.[46]

---

43. Of course, in the subversive literature of the Israelite prophets, moral imperatives take precedence over the offering of sacrifices (Isa 1:10–17; Hos 6:6; Amos 5:21–25; Mic 6:6–8).

44. Jesus's stance depended to a large extent on his conviction that the end was indeed near. It was generally believed that when the messianic age comes, some commandments—like sacrifices, prayers, festivals (with the exception of Purim), and *kashrut*—would be canceled. Since the parousia was delayed sine die, however, the church found itself standing between two worlds: that of the present and that to come, hence, having so to speak one foot in *ha'olam ha-zeh* and the other foot in *ha'olam ha-ba'*, an uncomfortable dialectical situation where Jesus's torah would make life impossible in the present economy (see Matt 5:38–42), while ignoring it would marginalize the Jesus-event.

45. Perhaps extending to ordinary people laws applied only to the high priest (so William Loader, *Jesus' Attitude towards the Law. A Study of the Gospels* [Grand Rapids: Eerdmans, 2002 [1997], 521).

46. See the novelistic example signed by Eliatte Abécassis, *La Répudiée* (Paris: Albin Michel, 2000).

Jesus and the Kingdom of God

The "kingdom of God" was not a central concept or symbol before Jesus's time—although the kingship of God is abundantly illustrated in the whole of Jewish literature, especially in Hellenistic times (see Tobit; 2 Maccabees; 3 Maccabees; Sibylline Oracles [esp. the third and fourth oracles, which speak of an earthly kingdom around refashioned Jerusalem]; Wisdom of Solomon [where the kingdom of God is identified with wisdom, righteousness, and immortality] // Philo). The expression "kingdom of God" thus does not appear as such in the apocalyptic literature.[47] In rabbinic tradition, we occasionally find "kingdom of heavens" (see also Matthew). Bruce Chilton, however, presents us with a heuristic exploration of eight targumic texts where the kingdom of God or of YHWH is to be "revealed" as already being a reality (so in Tg. Zech. 14:9 // Tg. Obad. 21, both from the first century CE). In all cases, Chilton says, "'the Kingdom of God' refers to God himself, as it were, personally," and he quotes Tg. Isa. 31:4 (cf. 24:23), where the prophet's "the Lord of Hosts" is rendered by "the kingdom of the Lord." A similar shift is found in Matt 18:23-35; 22:1-14; Mark 4:26-29. The kingdom of God is the activity of God (cf. Tg. Isa. 40:9; 52:7); the kingdom *is* God ("Deus est").[48] The Tg. Isa. 24:23 associates the kingdom of YHWH with God's self-revelation on Mount Zion, which occasions a feast for all nations (see 25:6-8; cf. Matt 8:4; Luke 13:28-29). Targum Isaiah 31:4 speaks of YHWH descending on Mount Zion as an unafraid lion, which finds an ideological parallel in Jesus's kingdom of God being violent. The language of Tg. Job 36:7 ("upon the throne of his kingdom with established kings") is akin to that of Luke 22:28-30 and Matt 19:28.[49]

---

47. John Dominic Crossan (*The Historical Jesus: The Life of a Mediterranean Jewish Peasant* [San Francisco: HarperSanFrancisco, 1991], 290) contrasts the view of the kingdom as apocalyptic and the view that "[based on the Wisdom of Solomon, the] kingdom of God is the kingdom of Wisdom eternally present, available ... to anyone who heeds her call and ... punitively transcendent to all the evil rulers of the world."

48. See also Tg. Exod. 15:18 and Tg. Ezek. 7:7. Bruce Chilton, "Regnum Dei Deus Est," *SJT* 31, no. 3 (1978): 261-70. See also Chilton, "Targum, Jesus, and the Gospels" in *The Historical Jesus in Context*, ed. Amy-Jill Levine, Dale C. Allison Jr., and John Dominic Crossan (Princeton: Princeton University Press, 2006), 238-55.

49. Against the relatively late date of the targumic literature—Tg. Onq., ca. end of third century; Tg. Neof. I, ca. end of third century; Tg. Ps.-Jon., after the seventh century—"at issue is not merely Rabbis' exegesis but common interpretation.... In

Malkhuta' di 'elaha' in Aramaic, *hē basileia tou theou* in Greek, is, for Norman Perrin, a tensive symbol, that is, something that tells a story and is a masterpiece of art.[50] This means that the kingdom of God should not be thought of either as present or future, because it is not a conception but rather a kind of personal experience. E. P. Sanders rightly counters that kingdom in Paul's letters is clearly in the future (1 Cor 6:9–10; 15:50; Gal 5:21). It will be handed over to God by Christ (1 Cor 15:29: it is otherworldly). It is also present (1 Cor 4:20), that is, "wherever and whenever God's power is active."[51] Christians are already justified and transformed (Rom 5:1; 2 Cor 5:17; 3:18; 4:16), but salvation is to come (e.g., Rom 5:9–10; 10:13), as Rom 8 (esp. v. 23) clarifies with the notion of the firstfruits, until all opposing power is eliminated.

The Kingdom of God in Mark

The kingdom of God is revealed to insiders (4:10–12 [Isa 6:9–10], 26–32) in contrast to outsiders, including religious authorities, but also the rich (10:25) since entering the kingdom requires virtues that are opposed to the social norms (10:31).

---

any case, no one would seriously argue that rabbinic sources were simply made up by authors on the spot at the time of written composition. By means of both oral and written transmission, their heritage reaches back behind the period of the New Testament" (Chilton, "Targum, Jesus, and the Gospels," 252). The following quote on the evidence of the Qumran scrolls comes from Laurence Schiffman: "The Talmudic materials are far more accurate than previously thought … the terminology, and even some of the very laws as recorded in rabbinic sources (some in the name of the Pharisees, and others attributed to anonymous first-century sages), were actually used and espoused by the Pharisees. In other words—and this is extremely important—rabbinic Judaism as embodied in the Talmud is not a post-destruction invention, as some scholars had maintained; on the contrary, the roots of rabbinic Judaism reach back at least to the Hasmonean period" ("The Significance of the Dead Sea Scrolls," *Bible Review* 6, no. 5 [October 1990]: 25).

50. See Norman Perrin, *The Kingdom of God in the Teaching of Jesus* (Philadelphia: Westminster, 1963), 16–23; and Perrin, *Jesus and the Language of the Kingdom: Symbol and Metaphor in New Testament Interpretation* (Philadelphia: Fortress, 1976), 29–32.

51. Sanders, *Jesus and Judaism*, 126. His reminder of the sense of "covenant" to explain the kingdom is helpful. He refers in Jewish literature to, e.g., m. Ber. 2:2; Sipra, Ahare Mot, 13:3 (to Lev 18:1–2).

The Kingdom of God in Matthew

We find here fifty-four mentions of the kingdom and thirty-eight of the "kingdom of God/heaven," but note especially the saying about the alternative kingdom, the one belonging to the Son of Man (13:41; 16:28; cf. 20:21). In 13:41–43, the kingdom of the Son includes both the righteous and the unrighteous (in the Matthean community?), but the kingdom of the Father includes only the righteous (through the last judgment, 25:31–46; see the parable of the weeds, 13:24–30; of the net, 13:47–50; of the ten maidens, 25:1–13).

The Kingdom of God in Luke

The statistics show that "kingdom" is mentioned forty-six times and eight times in Acts (see 11:20; cf. 9:2, 11). The person of Jesus is at the notion's center, spreading the good news to the poor and marginalized, healing for gentiles (4:16–30), and performing miracles (4:31–41). To witness the kingdom of God is to continue its proclamation (e.g., 9:60; 10:9; Acts 1:8).

Luke's second diptych, the so-called book of Acts, completes the picture of the advent of the kingdom. In the relentless social field of the struggle for survival, early Christianity strove to give power to the powerless, property to the dispossessed, wisdom to the cultureless, and hope to those who despair. Social status or the lack thereof becomes insignificant (see 1 Pet 2:9).

The Kingdom of God in John

There are here only two explicit sayings on the kingdom of God (3:3, 5, and "my kingdom" in 18:36). See the dialogue with Nicodemus in John 3.

In Summary: The Transformation of Values

The kingdom of God appears to be subversive (see the beatitudes about the poor, Luke 6:20), because it includes the hungry, the sorrow stricken, and the persecuted. See what Jesus says about the commandment to bury one's parents (Luke 9:60–62; cf. m. Ber. 3:1); about "sons of the kingdom" being excluded and gentiles being included (Matt 8:11–12; Luke 13:28–29); about the kingdom of God being hidden like a mustard seed (Luke 13:18); and about being likened to leaven in the dough (Luke 13:20). It is paradoxically already present (Mark 1:14–15) in spite of all the evidence to the contrary, and this is the "good news." See Jdt 9:11: "But you are the God of the lowly, helper of the oppressed, upholder of the weak, protector of the forsaken, savior of those without hope." Paul says, "My grace is sufficient for you, for power is made perfect in weakness" (2 Cor 12:9), an echo of Jesus's remark that the sick are those who need the physician (Mark 2:17). In other words, there is a curse attached to being strong, rich, powerful, that is, to being self-sufficient.[52]

While everyone was expecting the grandiose advent of the messiah, Jesus spoke of the kingdom as a mustard seed, that is, the smallest grain he knew of, but still capable of growing to the size of a three-to-four-meter-high bush, where birds can nest. John Dominic Crossan calls attention to the corrected parallel with Ezek 17:27–28 (a vision of a powerful cedar harboring birds, etc.).[53] Jesus's unexpected interpretation of Scriptures demonstrates a great freedom, reversing at times the negative nature of the parable's model into the positive. For example, he speaks of "yeast" in the same way as the mustard seed (Luke 13:21). Now, yeast is uniformly used negatively in biblical tradition (including some texts of the gospel); see Exod 12:15; Lev 2:4; Deut 16:3; Mark 8:15 // Luke 12:1; 22:1.

This process of reversal is of crucial import. What is true as regards the kingdom is also true of the poverty Jesus finds everywhere around him: while Ps 23:1 and 34:10, for instance, bless the wealth of the rich, Jesus locates God's blessing with the poor. Consolidating the notions of the kingdom and poverty, the parable of the "poor Lazarus" bestows paradise on Lazarus rather than on the rich man (Luke 16:19–31).

This same reversal applies to the laws of purity. God's holiness does not segregate the impure as undesirable (Matt 5:48; Luke 6:36), for God's mercy is unconditional. It does not even demand repentance as a precondition. God's compassion (the love of the enemy, for example) is a reversal of God's wrath (see Matt 5:43–45; Luke 6:28; see the discussion of the Last Supper above in ch. 3, "Jesus Son of Man/Son of God," 43–52). Jesus's focus on the spirit of Scriptures, by the way, facilitates these reversals. He shows

---

52. Power is the greatest temptation of some Christian branches; see Luke 16:13. José Ortega y Gasset writes, "He who does not really feel himself lost, is without remission, that is to say, he never finds himself, never comes up against his own reality" (*The Revolt of the Masses* [New York: Norton, 1957], 157).

53. John Dominic Crossan, *In Parables: The Challenge of the Historical Jesus* (New York: Harper & Row, 1973), 45–49 (45 and 47).

an amazing liberty of interpretation, always in the name of love superseding justice. Indeed, love is the ultimate superabundance of justice, as we have seen. *Lex talionis*, for instance, was decreed as a way to control and limit retaliation: only an eye can be taken for the damage to an eye. This restriction in the name of compassion eventually leads to the ultimate limitation called forgiveness (Matt 6:14; 26:28; 1 Cor 13:7). Matthew 7:1 (Luke 6:37) shows, from the same perspective, that God will use in his judgment the very "measure" we use to judge others. We find the very same idea in m. Soṭah 1:7. Hans Conzelmann concludes, "In this the unitary meaning is uncovered, viz., the command to love, which tolerates no limitation—thus it even includes the love of enemies."[54]

A hotly discussed text is Matt 12:28 // Luke 11:20 ("If it is by the Spirit of God that I cast out demons, then the kingdom of God has come to you."). C. H. Dodd—also referring to Mark 1:15—writes, "The Eschatological Kingdom of God is proclaimed as a present fact."[55] When Jesus says, according to verse 27, "by whom do your sons cast [demons] out," he thus implies that these sons also make "the kingdom of God come to you," and thus addresses the "fathers'" convictions, without any further implication. The issue is not whether "the kingdom has come to you" through exorcisms; Jesus demonstrates that he is acting by the Spirit of God and, *therefore*, brings the kingdom to his people (*pace* Werner G. Kümmel[56]). At a minimum, Jesus says that his casting out demons "was no sure proof of an alliance with Satan than was the same activity in the case of others."[57]

---

54. Hans Conzelmann, *Jesus*, trans. J. Raymond Lord, ed. John Reumann (Philadelphia: Fortress, 1973), 62 (= "Jesus Christus," *RGG*, 3rd ed., vol. 3, cols. 619–53). So, e.g., the rules around oath giving are transcended by the command of truthfulness. Swearing becomes superfluous.

55. Charles H. Dodd, *The Parables of the Kingdom* (London: Collins, 1961 [1935]), 28–29. On the presence of the kingdom in the words and deeds of Jesus, see also Matt 11:5-6; Mark 1:14–15 and parr. Dodd used the expression "realized eschatology," a formula he later regretted. A better word, says Charlesworth, is "a realizing eschatology." Besides the gospel, a mixture of realizing and futuristic eschatology can be found in Sib. Or. 3.46–48 and T. Mos. 10.1 (*The Historical Jesus: An Essential Guide*, Essential Guides [Nashville: Abingdon, 2008], 98, 99).

56. Werner G. Kümmel, *Promise and Fulfillment: The Eschatological Message of Jesus*, SBT 23 (London: SCM, 1957), 105–6.

57. Sanders, *Jesus and Judaism*, 135. In a pericope that sounds like a summary or a catch-all, Matt 9:32-34, "the Pharisees" say that Jesus expels demons by the power of "the prince of demons."

Akin to this Matthean text, Luke 17:21 says that the kingdom is "in your midst" but that it cannot be observed. A striking parallel is drawn by Gos. Thom. 113: "The Father's kingdom is spread over the earth, and people do not see it" (cf. Luke 11:9; Matt 7:7). Marcus Borg comes with the useful expression "participatory/collaborative eschatology" and refers to Matt 6:33 and Luke 12:31.[58]

There is a heated scholarly debate about the data. Indeed, they seem inconsistent, with some stressing the presence of the kingdom within the works of Jesus, but others insisting on the eschatological *coming* of the kingdom. A possible reconciliation between these two alternatives, I suggest, is by distinguishing between the *eventuality* of the kingdom and its *nature*. As to the *when* of the kingdom of God (its eventuality), only God knows (Mark 13:32; see Matt 24:36), but as to its *what* (its nature), Jesus's ministry is its demonstration. The *what*, however, impinges on the *when* as, in parallel with the messianic advent, "il n'en finit pas de venir." The kingdom is also "ever-coming" since Jesus made it manifest within history and our world. To that extent, the future of the kingdom is decisive as regards its "presentness," for, as Conzelmann says, "the kingdom is not the continuation and perfection of conditions of this world, but their end."[59] He also says, "The future is effective now."[60]

Although the signs of the kingdom are present and demand to be acknowledged (see Mark 13:28–29; cf. Luke 12:54–56), the kingdom will come suddenly, without signs warning of its coming (Luke 17:20). Such a dialectical tension is understandable. It is also true of the parousia, as it was also true for the disciples regarding Jesus's crucifixion. All previous announcements to that effect proved to be of little avail when the event occurred.

Jesus's proclamation of the advent of the kingdom of God is clearly crucial to his ministry.[61] It is the fifth and everlasting kingdom that crowns

---

58. Marcus Borg, *Jesus: Uncovering the Life, Teachings, and Relevance of a Religious Revolutionary* (San Francisco: HarperSanFrancisco, 2006), 259 (emphasis added).

59. Conzelmann, *Jesus*, 69.

60. Ibid., 79.

61. In a useful list of motifs about Jesus in the gospel, Harvey K. McArthur ("The Burden of Proof in Historical Jesus Research," *ExpTim* 82 [1970–1971]: 116–19) says that the following items are witnessed by the four strands of the Synoptic tradition (i.e., Mark, Q, M, and L): the proclamation of the kingdom of God, the disciples around Jesus, healing miracles, relationship with John the Baptist, the use of parables, the concern for the outcasts, a radical ethic, the stress on love and on forgiveness, clashes

the four-kingdom schema of Dan 2, for example. Note that Jesus hails the coming of the kingdom at a time when Rome considered itself the ultimate power that would not be followed by any other. Hesiod shares that pretension in *Works and Days*, and so does Virgil, who declares Rome as "boundless," and as an *imperium sine fine* (see *Aeneid* 1.278–279).[62] At an earlier time, Babylon had also believed itself to be a "realized eschatology" of sorts.

We must approach the kingdom of God in the gospel by asking discrete questions: *when?* (its eventuality), *what?* (its nature), *where?* (its universality). The kingdom is clearly an eschatological reality. A number of texts leave no doubt about it: Mark 13:32 and Matt 24:36,[63] as well as Mark 14:25 and Luke 22:16.[64] On the other hand, the coming of this eschatological reality is felt to be imminent, according to Matt 10:23; Mark 9:1; 13:30; and Matt 24:34. The kingdom will come suddenly, says Rev 3:3 // 16:15 // 2 Pet 3:10, "like a thief," like a homeowner returning home at night suddenly (see Mark 13:33–37 and parr.; Did. 16.1; cf. 1 Thess 5:2; Gos. Thom. 21; 103). Matthew 10:23 says that the kingdom of God (or rather the Son of Man) will come before the disciples "have gone through all the towns of Israel," which admittedly is rather vague. Mark 9:1 is more precise: "Some standing here will not taste death until they see that the kingdom of God has come with power," an allusion to Jesus's parousia (see 8:38). Mark 13:30 and Matt 24:34 broaden the preceding saying to include

---

about the Sabbath observance, sayings about the Son of Man, and the use of the word "Amen" to introduce some sayings (118).

62. At the time, Rome had some one million inhabitants. (Compare with Alexandria, half a million.)

63. Both Mark 13:32 and Matt 24:36 read, "But about that day or hour no one knows, neither the angels in heaven nor the Son but only the Father." Charlesworth calls attention to 4 Ezra 4:42: the archangel Uriel does not know the time either (*Historical Jesus*, 101).

64. In Mark 14:25, Jesus says, "Truly I tell you, I will never again drink of the fruit of the vine until that day when I drink it new in the kingdom of God." Note that wine drinking—an unusual beverage among the poor—suggests some disreputable company. The principle is that purity is communicated, rather the other way around. Jesus eats the last festive meal of his life (Mark 14:25)—a Passover meal for Luke 22:15–20—as a sign of the final banquet. Cf., e.g., Mark 2:19; Luke 13:28–29 and parr.; 14:15–24 and parr. In Luke 22:16, Jesus says, "For I tell you, I will not eat [this Passover] until it is fulfilled in the kingdom of God." Why did Luke create this Passover environment? Perhaps to allude to the sacrificial, atoning death of Jesus. This stressed the concomitance of the catastrophe and the reign of God.

"this generation." True, Mark 9:1, for instance, is probably not authentic, nor is Mark 13:30. They rather reflect the feverish expectation of the parousia by the first Christians,[65] and those Markan texts in chapter 13 belong to a medley of traditions not always mutually consistent.[66] It may be that Mark tried to patch things up by having the scene of the transfiguration follow 9:1 immediately in 9:2: "Six days later, Jesus took with him Peter and James and John ..." so that, indeed, "some standing here" saw the coming of the kingdom of God in the transfiguration of Jesus. But, as John P. Meier stresses, the transfiguration occurs six days after the prophecy that many will not die before the coming of the kingdom. As for Mark 13:30 ("This generation will not pass away until all these things have taken place"), which refers to the apocalyptic signs that precede the advent of the kingdom, it is canceled out by the addition of verses 32–33: no one but the Father knows the *when*. Verse 32 reflects the bewilderment felt by Mark's generation.

The conclusion seems incontrovertible: early Christians were convinced that their Lord would soon come back in glory, and they put assurances to that effect in Jesus's mouth. The only hurdle on this path is that those gospel texts were written long "after the fact" at a time when the evangelists must have realized that the coming of the parousia was unexpectedly delayed. "This generation" (that is, Jesus's) had passed, and so had "some standing here"!

It seems clear that the evangelists brought their understanding of these sayings to another level, namely, to a level where the *what* interferes with the *when*. For the *what* of the kingdom also has a temporal dimension, to the same extent that the *when* has an ontological dimension. Let us refer to a central text, Luke 7:22 (Matt 11:5): "Go and tell John ... the blind receive their sight, the lame walk, the lepers are cleansed, the deaf hear, the dead are raised, the poor have good news brought to them" (cf. Luke 4:16–21, citing Isa 6:1–2). In other words, the healings are signs of the kingdom

---

65. See 1 Thess 4:15; 1 Cor 15:51. Cf. Matt 24:30–31 and parr.; Matt 16:27–28 and parr.

66. The study by John P. Meier, *Mentor, Message, and Miracles*, vol. 2 of *A Marginal Jew: Rethinking the Historical Jesus*, ABRL (New York: Doubleday, 1994), 317, is well summarized thusly: "In sum, according to Matt 8:11–12 par., the historical Jesus did expect a future coming of God's kingdom, and in some way a transcendent one, surmounting this world's barriers of time, space, hostility between Jews and Gentiles, and finally death itself."

that has come near in and with the person of Jesus. It is an "already/not yet" reality.[67] When one witnesses the transformation of the human condition through Jesus's bringing peace and healing, consolation and life, one realizes that the kingdom of God has been fundamentally substantiated. Each miracle is an epiphany, says Gerd Theissen. It is an activation of the kingdom among humanity.[68] One knows *what* the kingdom is all about: it is primarily Jesus himself and all that this implies in terms of peace, healing, and good news.

What Jesus says here concerning divorce must be counterbalanced with his making allowance for human weakness, as the torah itself did before him. In another context, Jesus says that he should not pay tax for the temple, for he is the son of God and, hence, should be exempt. But he recommends that Peter not "scandalize [the other Jews]" (Matt 17:27). When we bring together the concessions of the torah and of Jesus, we realize once again the improbability of the balance of the terms *coincidentia oppositorum* in the already/not yet dialectic.

Besides, we must realize that Jesus's miracles remain particular and not universal. Not all the blind recover their sight, nor are all the captives released. Jesus's healings are therefore a foretaste of things to come. They are prophetic deeds, a stamp of authenticity applied to the promise. They restore Eden apocalyptically: "The kingdom has come unto you"; "the kingdom is in your midst." But these miracles are not yet *in* the kingdom. "Thy kingdom come!"

The kingdom of God, therefore, is a dialectical reality; it both is and is to be, like the parousia itself. Controversial statements, such as those we have cited in Mark and Matthew, are thus open to more than a literal understanding. "This generation" or "those who are now standing" correspond to the scriptural "today," which stresses the urgency to make a move. "Today, if you hear his voice …" (Heb 3:7; on the basis of Ps 95:7). It is always a matter of here and now, of "this generation." "And if it is not now, then when?" asks Rabbi Hillel.

---

67. Note the present indicative in John 3:16 ("has the eternal life") // 5:25, while in 4:14 the tense is future ("will become"). The same ambivalence is present in the notion of parousia (either on the last day, as in 21:22, or now as in 14:20). The model prayer "Our Father" starts and ends with the petition that the kingdom come (Matt 6:9–13). Contrast with Luke 17:21, "the kingdom of God is among you."

68. Gerd Theissen, *Urchristliche Wundergeschichten*, Gütersloh: Gütersloher Verlagshaus, 1974), 102.

This dialectical dimension of the kingdom of God is stressed in Luke 17:21: "Nor will they say, 'look, here it is!' or 'There it is!' For, in fact, the kingdom of God is among you." Here, the Greek preposition *entos* ("among") designates Jesus's presence among the faithful (see v. 24). Its realization is dependent on faith here and now. A purely eschatological kingdom would have rendered Jesus's work and person obsolete. The kingdom is to come *and* is already present "among you." "The kingdom of heaven has come near" (Matt 10:7).[69]

"Should we expect someone else?" asks the Baptist. The answer of the gospel is, not someone else, but Jesus glorified. In the meantime, the kingdom grows, like a grain of mustard, and some will not die before the kingdom is as fully present to them as it is for the Nazarene (Mark 9:1; Luke 21:31-35; cf. John 11:25-26). The same dialectical tension exists regarding Jesus's resurrection, which is "the firstfruits of those who have fallen asleep" (1 Cor 15:20).

Note the contrast with the declaration of Matt 11:12-13 and Luke 16:16 ("the violent take it [the kingdom] by force").[70] Who are the violent ones? The text is obscure, and no decisive exegesis of it has emerged so far. According to one view, the "violent" designate, negatively, messianic pretenders. So an era has come to its end with the demise of the prophets, including John the Baptist, the last of them. They have been murdered (see Matt 5:12; Luke 6:23). Only the violent, the murderers, remain. They may pretend to bring about the kingdom with their call to rebellion against the Roman occupation, as it happened so often in Jesus's time. This certainly includes false prophets, but also—more allusively—the aristocrats of the temple personnel, who assault heaven with thousands of animal sacrifices and other rituals meant to force God's hand. Meier says that they oppose the kingdom of God by making the transcendent immanent and palpable; it is that aspect of the kingdom that "suffers violence."[71] All messianic royal

---

69. The Gospel of Thomas has rather understood the saying as speaking of the kingdom "inside of you, and it is outside of you" (saying 3). In 51, the kingdom "has already come, but you do not recognize it." In 113, "The kingdom of the Father is spread out upon the earth, and people do not see it."

70. Note that the three verbs in the Matthew text are in the negative, and that the order of the words "all the Prophets and the Torah" is unique, as is also the verb *epropheteusan* ("have prophesied") applied to the Torah. The vocabulary of violence (*biazomai* and *biastes*) is striking. All of this militates for authenticity.

71. Meier, *Mentor, Message, and Miracles*, 161. The theme is again evident in the Lord's prayer (Matt 6:10 // Luke 11:2), "Your kingdom come," which expresses the

pretenders were militant. Their favorite Hebrew traditions were the scepter of Balaam's oracle, Isaiah's "shoot of the stump of Jesse," and such texts implying violence. In Qumran, of course, the "sons of light" are fighting the "sons of darkness." As far as Jesus is concerned, the sole episode along that line would be his entry into Jerusalem on "Palm Sunday" (Matt 21:1-11; Mark 11:1-10; Luke 19:29-38; John 12:12-16). Matthew and John quote Zech 9:9, but this text is never used as messianic in the Qumran scrolls or in the Pseudepigrapha.[72] "Here Jesus appears to change roles, from that of prophetic herald of the kingdom to that of king to usher it in," says John J. Collins.[73]

Other exegetes offer a totally different interpretation. For Gerd Theissen, for example, the violent ones are the Jesus movement that violates all social conventions. By conjuring up the name of John the Baptist, we have a terminus a quo of the movement. Note that the self-designation with the evident negative aspect of it serves as a self-stigmatization; it borrows the language and opinion of opponents.[74]

As to the *where*, that is evidently what prompted Jesus, at the end of his career, to come to Jerusalem in the first place. Jerusalem is, and continues to be, the navel of the world, of history, of space and of time. The most important point here is the daring amalgamation of the kingdom of God, the person of Jesus, and the very center of Israel's history. A text like Luke 19:11 is illuminating: "He was near Jerusalem, and they supposed that the kingdom of God was to appear immediately." If everything had been "normal," the temple would have played a decisive role in the advent of the kingdom, but it had disqualified itself, and anyway, it was soon to be destroyed. The kingdom transcends institutions, and this means that what

---

apocalyptic hope that God will come to save his people by coming to rule as King (see ibid., 299). It parallels the synagogal Qaddish and Shemoneh Esreh 11. Rabbi Pinhas ben Yair (end of second century) said that when the temple was destroyed, "men of violence ['anshey zeroa'] and loud tongue prevailed" (m. Soṭah 9.15; BM 118a; Sanh. 58b (cf. Job 22:8). There must be no forcing of the end, which is known exclusively by God (see 1QpHab; 1QSa 1; Ber. 64a).

72. Its earliest messianic use is in Sanh. 98a.

73. John J. Collins, *The Scepter and the Star: The Messiahs of the Dead Sea Scrolls and Other Ancient Literature* (New York: Doubleday, 1995), 206.

74. Gerd Theissen, "Le mouvement de Jésus, révolution charismatique des valeurs," *NTS* 35 (1989): 343-60.

was expected from the temple is now fulfilled in an overflowing way by what as in itself "at last eternity transforms" it.[75]

The transformation of the world—on which Judaism generally insists as the stamp of authenticity on messiahship—can, of course, be interpreted in various ways. First, the question arises, what is the source of this conviction? The expected Davidic restoration envisages a glorious reign of Israel's king, the "king of the Jews." Nations will recognize Jerusalem and its sovereign as a beacon of peace (shalom). Nowhere, however, is it described how deeply this acknowledgment will change the universe. The change, at any rate, is significant from a spiritual point of view. For the New Testament, it is palpable in the fact that "the word of God has come out of Jerusalem, and the torah from Zion" to the extremities of the world (see Isa 2:3 and Mic 4:1–4). The best of the Jewish scholars, such as Franz Rosenzweig, Martin Buber, Abraham Heschel, and Leo Beck, think that this phenomenon is decisive. True, we could have expected that there would be no more war, and the world is actually submerged under a flood of hatred. But what does this mean? The wishful divine withdrawing of control from the humans so that, even if they want to vent their rage, they are unable to do so? Or does it mean that people may now realize that the world has been touched by the boundless power of peace and love? Corruption and impurity are contagious, but purity is also contagious.[76] But unless this virtue is incarnate,[77] it remains utopian. From the point of view of the gospel, utopia ceases when innocence reaches its apex by consenting to the supreme sacrifice. From then on, the rhetorical realm makes room for the historical and the theoretical for the concrete.

The sin of Adam is paradigmatic, so human beings inherit this onus, but only to the extent that they repeat and duplicate their ancestor's transgression. Similarly, the transformation brought by innocence is operational to the extent that the heirs of this new paradigm concretize it in

---

75. Mallarmé, "The Tomb of Edgar Allan Poe." See the striking text of Heb 9:23–25.

76. When Jesus touches the leper, the latter is purified, but Jesus is not made impure (Mark 1:40–42). The Beatitudes affirm that purity is contagious. There is a *middah keneged middah* ("measure for measure") in "Blessed are the merciful, for they will receive mercy," and "blessed are the pure in heart, for they will see God" (Matt 5:7–8). On the third beatitude ("blessed are the meek") see Ps 37:9, 11. For a parallel (from the third century CE), see Rav in Sukkah 29b.

77. "The crowd was amazed when they saw the mute speaking, the maimed whole, the lame walking, and the blind seeing. And they praised the God of Israel" (Matt 10:31).

their lives. No one's freedom is obliterated in the process. On the contrary, for the first time ever, individual and collective are free to choose good and life, rather than evil and death. The Jewish sages had experienced the disastrous reality of impurity as contagious, but Jesus taught that the reverse is also true: purity, like love, is contagious.[78] Mark 1:15 is of prime importance. It reads, "The time is fulfilled, and the kingdom of God has come near; repent, and believe in the good news" (see also Mark 3:2).

Excursus: On the Parousia

Contrary to the expectation of the first generation of Christians, the parousia tarried. Had it dawned when, as it was once said, "some standing here will not taste death until they see that the kingdom of God has come with power" (Mark 9:1; see 8:38),[79] the vindication of the gospel—oral, as it would have been unnecessary to write it down—would have been complete, so we can understand the fervor of Christians' hope. With its delay, however, the question of Jesus's messiahship became critical. Indeed, it is true to this day. How can Jesus be the Messiah while the world, objectively speaking, remains unchanged? What use is there of a messiahship without the restoration of Eden? This constitutes a major stumbling block for many Jews and others, from the first century CE on.

The chasm between the de jure and the de facto, that is, between promise and fulfillment, between the already and the not-yet, is far from being a new phenomenon in the faith of Israel. Let us consider, for instance, the so-called 'Orlah commandments in Lev 19: God, owner of the land, sets the terms for its utilization, so that the people treat the land of Israel as Eden restored. The Levitical text clearly established a parallel between Israel's cultic agricultural actions and the divine creation of the world. Here we also find the already/not yet dialectic tension, and the same applies, of course, to the Sabbath, Sabbatical year, and Jubilee observances.

The Christian expectation of the parousia belongs to the well-illustrated "forking" category of "Eden now" and Eden in the world to come. It underlines once more, I believe, the fact that Christianity is a branch

---

78. If killing one individual amounts to killing humanity as a whole, as the rabbis and the Qur'an teach, loving one individual—healing a paralytic on a Sabbath day—is world changing. Much of Jesus's kerygma is so summarized.

79. Mark 13:30 and Matt 24:34 broaden the preceding saying to include "this generation."

5. JESUS AND TORAH

of Judaism. The issue that divides them is not the (relative) absence of world renovation with the advent of the Nazarene, but the interpretation of the ever-coming kingdom of God.[80] The enormous actual event of the spreading of the "good news" to reach the ends of the world and the end of history—a messianic feature, if not, in the eyes of some, *the* messianic seal of reality—is to be considered.

*

Jesus claimed to be (or to become) the ultimate manifestation on earth of the kingdom he heralded: he inaugurated the realm of the eschatological torah, which is characterized by unconditional love, a love independent of time and space and subject neither to opportunity nor to any legal limitation. Such love extends—for the first time and in a unique way in Jewish literature[81]—to embrace even one's enemy.[82] Aside from Jesus, no one has gone further than this regarding the unconditionality of love, and the truth of the matter is, no one else can, because he paid the ultimate price for it.[83] Jesus's logion about the love of the enemy is found in Matt 5:44 (// Luke 6:27–28, 32–36). At its basis is Lev 19:18, on the love of the neighbor. As God's love is unconditional, so must be human love. To the authenticity of this logion militate not only the criterion of discontinuity, as we just saw, but also the abruptness of the command. This discontinuity is clear when we compare the saying with the Hebrew Bible, the Dead Sea Scrolls, the Pseudepigrapha, Philo, Josephus, and the rest of the New Testament testimony (with the exception of Rom 12:9–21 [see esp. v. 14]; cf. Matt

---

80. Il n'en finit pas de venir, as I said above. As Patai writes, "I will give them one whom they will never see but whose presence they will feel all the time; who will never come but will always be a-coming … who will be found only in their heart of hearts" (Raphael Patai, *The Messiah Texts* [New York: Avon, 1979], prologue, XIX).

81. In T. Zeb. 6:8, we find an exhortation to love the strangers; in T. Jos. 18:2, to pray for the evildoer; in t. B. Qam. 9:29–30, to forgive even the offender who does not relent. Jesus's commandment starkly contrasts with the later composition of the Mishnah (ca. 200 CE). Here, any new or unique event is readily absorbed into unchanging categories. The uniqueness is illusory, for the event has already occurred before, but in a different form.

82. See also Paul and Peter on this: Rom 12:14, 17–20; 1 Thess 5:15; 1 Cor 4:12; 1 Pet 3:9.

83. Buber concludes, "Nowhere else is love to man precisely made the presupposition of the realized sonship to God as here" (*Two Types of Faith*, 76).

5:44; Luke 6:28 [but without echo of the love of enemy]). To be added to this is the criterion of coherence.[84]

The license to hate one's enemy—Matt 5:43 and parallels, contradicting Exod 23:4-5—was not without qualifications. Deuteronomy 25:17-19 declares the Amalekites enemies forever to be hated. The Qumran scroll 1QM says that one must hate the sons of Belial, sons of darkness. The foe to be rejected is the enemy of God, "the haters of God" in Ps 139:21-22. Jesus's commandment is to love *my* enemy, not God's enemy. Jewish tradition recalls that God has created all people in his image (see Gen. Rab. 24; Pesiq. Zutra on Num 8; ARN 16:32 says, "Love all—and hate the heretics, the apostates and the informers.")[85]

It is within this perspective that, ab initio, Jesus can call God his Father. The torah—such as into itself eternity changes it—must now reflect the fatherhood of God, rather than his judgment. The transcended torah is a torah of freedom and joy, as the Mosaic law always promised to be (Gal 5:1). All limitations to the love of God and of the other ("neighbor") are eliminated. Within this perspective, the so-called Golden Rule (Matt 7:12 // Luke 6:31) raises a problem for the critic. Meier is very reluctant to consider the text as authentic. It displays, he says, an "ethic of reciprocity" that we find, for sure, under the pen of a number of pagan authors,[86] but that contradicts Jesus's rejection of such ethics (see, e.g., Luke 6:32-36). The parallel with religious declarations found elsewhere is often invoked. Tobit 4:15 sounds similar: "What you hate, do to no one." In Šabb. 31a, Rabbi Hillel says that the love of others "is the whole torah in its entirety." Starting with this aphorism, Hillel then invites the gentile to learn "the rest" as he will discover that it does not contradict the Golden Rule.

To return to the issue of absolute love, according to Jesus, let us note that, while the Mosaic stage of the torah established a historic distinction between the pure and the impure, as well as between Israel and the nations, the "new" (that is, the renewed—its ultimate and glorious

---

84. See, e.g., "Let the dead bury their dead"; "Whoever loses his life will save it."

85. For more on Jesus regarding the core of the law, see the section "Jesus and the Pharisees" in ch. 7 below (143-58).

86. See, e.g., from the fifth century BCE, Herodotus, *Histories* 3.142 (in a negative form); Isocrates (436-338). See John P. Meier, *Law and Love*, vol. 4 of *A Marginal Jew: Rethinking the Historical Jesus*, ABRL (New Haven: Yale University Press, 2009), 553. Let us add Confucius, *Analects* 12.22; 17.6.

stage—cf. Mark 1:27) torah removes all barriers.[87] The temple's "curtain is torn in two" (Luke 23:45). Jesus declares to the gentile Syro-Phoenician woman, "For saying that, you may go—the demon has left your daughter" (Mark 7:24–30). And about the centurion, "Not even in Israel have I found such faith" (Luke 7:9).[88]

This declaration to the Syro-Phoenician woman or to the Roman centurion marks a turn in Jesus's self-consciousness. It behooves us to elaborate. The gospel shows an evolution in Jesus's understanding of the role of the nations in God's plan. At the outset of his ministry, Jesus makes clear that he conceives his mission as strictly limited to the Jewish people and to "the lost sheep of the house of Israel."[89] His first reaction to the Syro-Phoenician woman's plea for her daughter is incredibly arrogant and cruel: "It is not fair to take the children's food and throw it to the dogs" (Mark 7:27). We find a similar reluctance of Jesus in the case of the centurion's servant (Matt 8:5–13 // Luke 7:1–10) and the royal official's son (or servant) in John 4:46–54.

The "pagan" woman's reply displays a grandeur of soul that would be difficult not to reckon as teaching a lesson to the master: under the table, the dogs eat the crumbs left of the children's bread (7:28)![90] The remainder of the Markan text shows that Jesus has learned the lesson.[91]

Furthermore, the context of Mark 7:24–30 is one of purity or impurity of food (vv. 1–23). On this, Jesus is said to have extended the category of

---

87. In T. Levi 16:3–5 (perhaps a Christian gloss), we read: "A man who by the power of the Most High renews the Law you name 'Deceiver,' and finally you shall plot to kill him ... [thus] you take innocent blood on your heads." (In punishment, the temple will be razed, no place will be clean, and they shall be dispersed among the nations until God has compassion). According to Luke 16:16, the "old" torah lasted until the days of John the Baptist.

88. Regarding texts that condemn Israel and praise gentiles, we are, of course, entitled to suspect that they are examples of the church's apologetics (see, e.g., Matt 11:21–24; 12:41–42), but it is clear that Paul's mission was based entirely on his conviction that Jesus ordained such mission.

89. See also Matt 15:24 (only to Israel); 19:28 (the apostles will judge the twelve tribes of Israel). Note also the collective dimension of the receivers of the message (Matt 10:5–6; 12:39, "generation" as in Mark 8:11–13).

90. Something of the same idea is found in Matt 8:11–12 // Luke 13:28–29; non-Jews will eat in the kingdom with Abraham, Isaac, and Jacob, although the Israelites are "the heirs of the kingdom" (see also Matt 13:38).

91. After all, the dominant Hellenistic culture taught that to be a "Hellene" was less a matter of birth than of disposition (*paideia*).

the *kashrut* to include anything that enters the mouth (7:18–19). In Matt 6:25, he is reported as asking the rhetorical question, "Is not life more than food and the body more than clothing?" which parallels another of his sayings, about the Sabbath being made for humans, not humans for the Sabbath.[92] He thus straddles the barrier between Jews and gentiles, with the proviso that he came "first to the Jews and then to the gentiles" (Rom 1:16).

I believe that this episode makes it clear that Jesus had no dogmatic opinion regarding non-Jews. He learned what to think and what to do empirically.[93] His discourse changed accordingly. His dialogue with a Samaritan woman demonstrates this much again (John 4:7–26). In fact, Jesus's attitude toward the Samaritans provides a touchstone. At first, it corresponded to the general Jewish contempt for this "mixed race" (see, e.g., John 4:4, 9; Matt 10:5).[94] But soon Jesus goes through a remarkable transformation, crowning it with the sublime statement, "Salvation is from the Jews. But the hour is coming, and is now here, when the true worshipers will worship the Father in spirit and truth, for the Father seeks such as these to worship him. God is spirit, and those who worship him must worship in spirit and truth" (John 4:22–24).[95]

In Matt 8:11–12 // Luke 13:28–29, non-Jews will eat in the kingdom with Abraham, Isaac, and Jacob. The text recalls several MT declarations regarding the nations, especially in the end time. Here, they join Israel "from east and west" at the final banquet. Those who are "thrown into the

---

92. Mekilta 9.1 says, "The Sabbath is given to you, but you are not given to the Sabbath" (R. Shimeon b. Menashia, end of second century CE).

93. The Galilean origin of Jesus made him ill-prepared to deal with non-Jews, for Isa 9:1, for example, describes Galilee as the "district of the gentiles," thus provoking a sense of inferiority among its people. Jewish tradition is generally critical of the Galileans. The Mishnah, although Galilean in origin, denounces the Galilean ignorance of ritual purity, etc. (see ARN [A] 27). They are *'am ha'arets* ("like unclean animals, and their wives like reptiles," (b. Pesaḥ. 49b; cf. the remarkable text of John 7:41, 45–52). Herod Antipas (4 BCE–39 CE) proceeded with an intensive Romanization of the Galilee country; he founded Tiberias on the lake and compelled people to live there.

94. See m. Nid. 4:2: Samaritan women are considered to be as unclean as menstruants "from their cradle." (But so are the daughters of Sadducees who abide by Sadduceeism.) This point of view is not shared by R. Joshua ha-Nasi in Nid. 31b.

95. See the striking Lukan texts of 9:51–56 (Jesus's restraint vis-à-vis the Samaritans); 17:11–19 (with the Samaritan leper); and 10:30–37 (the parable of the "good Samaritan," to which I refer below).

5. JESUS AND TORAH 99

outer darkness," although being entitled by birth to the kingdom, are the opponents of Jesus. For Meier, the logion is authentic on the basis of the late coming of the gentiles into the picture drawn by Jesus, for Israel is "the heirs of the kingdom" (cf. Matt 13:38). Note with the critic the absence of Jesus (he plays no role here) and the transcendence of death, with the three patriarchs alive and eating, and the exiles regathering from all places and all times.[96]

In short, one can only concur with Sanders that the evangelists, interested as they were in having the gospel preached to the gentiles, found little material during Jesus's ministry to back it up.[97] Jesus seems to have broached the issue of the non-Jews on an ad hoc basis—as he did, by the way, in his interpretation of legal matters while responding to insistent and specific questions of "Pharisees." He did this "with authority," says Matt 7:28–29, which means without hiding himself behind tradition or the Oral Law, but rather speaking as a charismatic eschatological prophet ("Amen, I say unto you"). With this, Jesus was probably consciously fulfilling the role of the eschatological Elijah as foretold by Mal 3:22–24. First Maccabees shows that people expected the coming of an eschatological prophet who would make decisions regarding unresolved legal dilemmas (see 1 Macc 4:46; 14:41). Sages in the Mishnah concurred.[98] Meier does not mention obvious New Testament texts like Mark 8:28 ("Elijah," "one of the prophets"); Matt 16:14 ("Elijah," "Jeremiah," "one of the prophets"); Luke 9:19 ("Elijah," "one of the ancient prophets has arisen"). Luke's text especially seems to allude to the popular expectation of *the* prophet, attested in 1 Maccabees, on the basis of Deut 18:15–19. About the latter, let us note that, in the eyes of his followers, Jesus himself became *the* living tradition. So thought Paul, eminently (see 1 Cor 7:10–12, on divorce).[99]

Again, regarding Matt 13:38, we may ask: was there a scriptural justification in including gentiles among "the heirs of the kingdom"? Against Joachim Jeremias's discriminatory selection of positive texts from the Hebrew prophets and negative texts of "late Judaism" (that is, rabbinic

---

96. Meier, *Mentor, Message, and Miracles*, 317.
97. E. P. Sanders, *The Historical Figure of Jesus* (London: Penguin, 1993), 192.
98. Meier (*Law and Love*, 656) lists m. ʿEd. 8:7 (cf. t. ʿEd. 3:4); m. B. Meṣ. 1:8; 3:4–5; m. Šeqal. 2:5; m. Soṭah 9:15.
99. From then on there was a bifurcation in the Jewish historical trajectory, between the rabbinic chain of transmission and the Christian reference to Jesus's authoritative pronouncements.

literature) regarding the gentiles, Sanders has no difficulty in choosing six passages from prophetic literature that display a more varied conception, from moderate to utter negativity.[100] By contrast, rabbinic tradition is predominantly favorable to gentiles (in spite of the dire situation in Palestine under Roman occupation and brutality), see t. Sanh. 13:2; Sanh. 26ab. Qumran is atypical and sectarian.

Speaking of nuances, even Paul, the apostle to the gentiles, happens to be a harsh critic of gentile "sinners" (see Gal 2:15; cf. Rom 1:18–32; 1 Thess 4:5). As to Pss. Sol. 17, it forecasts the total defeat of gentiles and their submission to Israel. They will come to Jerusalem's temple. In short, Jeremias has been wrong on this score. There is a most unfortunate tendency in modern New Testament scholarship to set a cheap contrast between normative Judaism (mostly bad) and the gospel (all good). The "uniqueness" of Jesus is thus badly misplaced, and groundless. Jesus is indeed unique in history, but for other reasons.[101]

With regard to Jesus's relationship with the Jewish sects of the time, the gospel reports an endless clash with "the Pharisees." Now it is clear that, when the gospels were redacted, the Pharisees were the great surviving party after the Roman destruction of the temple in 70 CE. They were consequently *the* Jewish rivals of the early Christians. In reality, chances are that, during his ministry, Jesus felt little empathy with the Sadducees or with the Zealots.[102]

Excursus: The Zealots

The designation *zēlotēs* alluded to God's jealousy (see, e.g., Exod 20:5; 34:14) and thus provided the sectarians who adopted it with the slogan, "No other Lord!" We note that, among Jesus's disciples, there was a Simon the Zealot (Luke 6:15; Acts 1:13) or Simon the Canaanite (Matt 10:4; Mark 3:18; Greek *zēlotēs* is, in Aramaic, *qenaʾana*), as well as his foil, Matthew the tax collector.[103] In his description of the scene of the "cleansing of

---

100. Sanders (*Historical Figure*) cites Isa 45:14; 49:23; 49:6; 54:3; Mic 5:10–15; Joel 3:17; and for each of these six texts several cognates.

101. See below on Martin Hengel and also ch. 13, "The Trial of Jesus and His Passion," 217–38 below.

102. In spite of S. G. F. Brandon, *Jesus and the Zealots* (New York: Scribner, 1967).

103. That the gospel labels Simon as a Zealot indicates that he constituted an exception.

the temple," John says that Jesus acted like a zealot (John 2:17, citing Ps 69:10 LXX, *zēlos*). Paul, reminiscing on his earlier zeal against the Christian church, says in Gal 1:13–14, "so strict a Zealot I was," and in Phil 3:6, "as to *zēlos*, a persecutor." Ironically, now that Paul had left their ranks, the Zealots wanted to kill him since he relaxed the Mosaic laws among the Diaspora Jews (Acts 21:20–21). Paul's response was that he is *"zēlotēs* as you all are today" (22:3). Some of them—probably far-right extremists called *sicarii*, that is, assassins—took an oath not to eat or drink until they had slaughtered Paul.

Who were the Zealots? Speaking of the Zealots of 66–70 CE, Richard Horsley says that they were "peasants-turned-brigands-turned-Zealots."[104] They made alliance with lower-class priests, especially Eleazar ben Simon, and started a reign of terror. The Zealots regarded allegiance to the Romans as idolatry (the emperor called himself *kyrios*). They assassinated the high priest Jonathan and other high officials (Josephus, *J.W.* 2.254–257; *Ant.* 20.165, 186, 204, 208–210). As a matter of fact, families of the high-priest caste bribed the Roman procurators in their efforts to gain power. When lower-class priests rebelled against the Jewish aristocracy, the royalist troops, and the Roman contingent in 66 CE, they gained an initial victory (*J.W.* 2.409–421) and thus rallied a large social spectrum of supporters to their cause. They started by cleansing the temple of all gentile influence (2.418–256). They then elected new high priests by lot instead of heredity—for instance a certain Phanni, whom Josephus called a clown (*J.W.* 4.153–157). They also conducted purges against the nobility for, as they were planning a *social* revolution, the upper classes were their foes. They are called Zealots by Josephus (*J.W.* 4.161), who blames them for the eventual destruction of the temple by Rome in 70 CE.

This may be the place to reflect on the Roman occupation of the land. The Romans' lack of understanding of the Jewish religion and way of life took them to incredible brutality and blood thirst. There were several rebellions against the Romans during the first century CE: in 4 BCE already after Herod's death; in 41 CE when the emperor threatened to desecrate the temple; in 52 again; and in 66–70.[105] Then the Romans conducted the

---

104. Richard A. Horsley, "The Zealots: Their Origin, Relationships and Importance in the Jewish Revolt," *NovT* 27 (1986): 174.

105. It is indirectly due to the heavy Roman taxation of the peasants that "the war [a few years after Jesus's death] was not only a national revolt against Rome, it was also a class war among the Jews" (Rhoads, Michie, and Dewey, *Mark as Story*, 178.

second Holocaust (the first was organized by Antiochus IV in the second century BCE). Thousands and thousands of people were massacred. Josephus (*J.W.* 6.283–285) reports, without showing empathy, one such episode: the temple was on fire in 70 CE, and "the poor [Jewish] women and children … numbering 6,000" were burned alive in "one remaining portico of the outer court."[106]

*

Jesus shared with the Pharisees, the Qumran covenanters, and the Sadducees the sense that life was a cultic act. This point leads to the incontrovertible conclusion that the disputations reported in the gospel occurred within Judaism, among kin: in brief they were a family affair. True—and this is crucial—life as a cultic act was interpreted and practiced differently according to the tenets of each Jewish sect. Neusner's words about the Pharisaic transposition of the temple ritual to the quotidian family life of the pious come to mind: "By making the laws of ritual purity incumbent upon the ordinary Jew, the Pharisees already had effectively limited the importance of the Temple and its cult."[107] This Neusner citation brings us to the all-important notion of purity/impurity in ancient Judaism.

Purity/Impurity

Purity/impurity was indeed a major issue during the Second Temple era.[108] Differences regarding its nature wrought divisions among the people according to their affiliations (as noted by Josephus, Philo, and the Mishnah). The archaeological remains of *miqvaoth* (ritual baths) everywhere in the Judean and Galilean areas of the time attest to the popular concern for

---

106. The parallel with the Nazi burning of Oradour Church, crammed with people, is stunning.

107. Jacob Neusner, *The Idea of Purity in Ancient Judaism: The Haskell Lectures, 1972–73* (Leiden: Brill, 1973), 69. See R. Yohanan b. Zakkai's opinion on the substitution of good deeds for the sacrifices in the temple (m. 'Abot 6).

108. As Richard A. Horsley rightly remarks (*Jesus and the Spiral of Violence: Popular Jewish Resistance in Roman Palestine* [San Francisco: Harper & Row, 1987], 128), colonized people stick all the more to their ancestral and religious customs "as symbols of their former freedom and self-determination."

purity.¹⁰⁹ The priests (mainly Sadducees) were expected to perform their ritual in absolute purity.

The divine commandment to be holy (see Lev 11:44; 20:7) made Israel into a people of priests (Exod 19:6; cf. Isa 61:6), intimately attached to the temple and its system of rites. Although the temple was acknowledged as the center of the purity system, the Pharisees seem to have made holiness a matter of the daily practice as well. The home table became a private altar; and the paterfamilias, the officeholder. Thus they recognized the presence of the absolute in the contingent. For the Pharisees, as for all other "parties,"¹¹⁰ purity was a central concern that permeated "bread and board." This meant avoiding nonkosher food and contact with people and things impure (such as menstruating women or a corpse).¹¹¹ The result was the creation of a sect.

Not unexpectedly in a community that considered itself as God's temple "personalized," the Qumran community considered purity crucial (see CD 12:1–2).¹¹² The covenanters went through repeated ablutions to purify themselves. The rite, however, was recognized as insufficient in itself. In 1QS 3:8, ablution without a spirit of repentance is spurned: "By the spirit of uprightness and of humility [only] his sin is atoned."¹¹³ The Jerusalem temple service is defiled; hence the community of covenanters forms a new temple (CD 5:6–7, 11–12). There is, therefore, a sacred ritual at Qumran as it was in the temple of Jerusalem (CD 10:12–13; 11:19–22;

---

109. In Mark 5, on the bleeding woman, the accent is on the power of faith, but we note with Thomas Klazen (*Jesus and Purity Halakhah: Was Jesus Indifferent to Impurity?* [Winona Lake, IN: Eisenbrauns, 2010]), that the description of the woman's problem is very close to the LXX text of Lev 15:19, 25, as in both texts we find a recurrence of the motif of "touching," a redundancy present also in the raising of Jairus's daughter.

110. The term "parties" is used by Josephus to designate the different major sects of the time. Y. Ḥag. calls them *kitot* (classes, sects; 2:2, 77d).

111. According to the Temple Scroll (11QTemple 50:10–19), a pregnant woman with a dead fetus renders the whole house she enters impure.

112. In the Mishnah and the Tosefta, the community is the counterpart and the mirror image of the temple (says Jacob Neusner, *Messiah in Context: Israel's History and Destiny in Formative Judaism*, The Foundations of Judaism: Method, Theology, Doctrine 2 [Philadelphia: Fortress, 1984], 72 and 76). The rabbis and the just are individual messiahs (ibid., 71). Sanders writes, "Judaism elevated all of life to the same level as worship of God" (*Historical Figure*, 38).

113. We shall see the same strong caveat in rabbinic literature (below).

12:1–2), but all who transgress God's word are unclean (1QS 5:13–14), and impurity was identified with sin. So, for instance, a person speaking with arrogance "was regarded as impure and could not touch the pure food or water of the community."[114]

We hear a similar tune when we turn to the prophetic corpus of the Tanak. Here also, the prophets stress moral purity (called *tahor* like the ritual one), as in Isa 1:16, 25; Jer 33:8; Zeph 3:9; and Ezek 36:33. Isaiah 56:3–8 and 66:21 display a reinterpretation of the Deuteronomic laws (on the presence of strangers and eunuchs in the community). See also the book of Jonah and Zech 14, which broadens the narrow frame of the Levitical laws of purity. Amos 5:21–24 is particularly devastating: "I hate, I despise your festivals, and I take no delight in your solemn assemblies.... But let justice roll down like waters, and righteousness like an overflowing stream." Jesus will draw his inspiration from this line of thinking (see Matt 11:13).[115]

Mark 7 on Purity/Impurity

The text of Mark 7:1–23, on purity/impurity, has its parallel in Matt 15:1–20 (cf. Luke 11:37–41). Leviticus 11–15 and Num 19 are in the background. Already Leviticus distinguishes between ritual and moral purity/impurity. The latter is identified with sexual improprieties (Lev 18:24–30), idolatry (Lev 19:31; 20:1–3), and bloodshed (Num 35:33–34). While ritual impurity is not sinful, moral impurity is. However, since sin does not result in ritual defilement, sinners are not excluded from the temple.

There are various layers of tradition put together in Mark 7:1–23, Meier says.[116] He distinguishes three parts: (1) 7:1–13, debate about the ritual washing of hands; (2) 7:14–15—the pivot of the pericope—an aphorism about defilement; and (3) 7:16–23, teaching about impurity from without and from within. In fact, Rabbi John Fischer's foursome division is to be preferred.[117] Jesus, in Mark 7, is said to have used a pattern that we find repeated in rabbinic parallels. It starts with an opponent's question

---

114. Neusner, *The Idea of Purity*, 67.

115. This contrasts with the later Mishnah, which no longer had an interest in history or in the prophetic. While Jesus's teaching is inseparable from his life, the sages in the Mishnah are mainly remembered for what they said.

116. See Meier, *Law and Love*, 353ff.

117. John Fischer, "Jesus through Jewish Eyes: A Rabbi Examines the Life and

(Mark 7:5); the Master retorts with a general declaration (5:15); in private, the Master's followers ask for further explanation (7:17); a private elaboration follows (7:18–23).[118]

The protagonists in the dialogue are "the Pharisees and some of the scribes." They ask a question regarding the nonwashing of hands by Jesus's disciples. Jesus answers with a quotation of Isa 29:13 and Exod 20:12, accusing the questioners of being hypocrites. He brings the example of the traditional notion of *qorban* (that is, an offering to God). After that, Jesus summons the crowd and he enters a house, where he utters an aphorism on what really pollutes, (vv. 14–15). The disciples had requested an explanation in the same wording in verse 17 as the Pharisees and scribes had in verse 5. Verse 19 comes with a final interpretive aside by the narrator: "(Thus he declares all foods clean.)"

Ideologically, the pericope starts in its first half with a polemical note: "the tradition of the elders" does not come from God. It can even be opposed to God's commandment in the torah. In the second half of the narrative, the scope becomes universal: consuming food can defile no human being. The quote of Isa 29:13 in verse 6 is according to the LXX text, which is somewhat different from the MT. It is surprising that Jesus would use it here. It brings Meier to conclude that the passage is not authentic.[119]

Verses 9–13: The "tradition of the elders" is but "tradition of [mere] men." Jesus now accuses his opponents of intentionally altering God's commandment. The example invoked is the *qorban*. This, however, may be a non sequitur, but Meier allows for a historical tradition going back to an actual halakah of Jesus's.[120] It may well be based on an actual legal subterfuge, as is attested by CD 16:14–20. As in the case of the divorce prohibited by Jesus on the basis of Gen 1–3 (see Mark 10:2–12), the *qorban* case refers

---

Teachings of Jesus," Menorah Ministries, 2004, http://www.menorahministries.com/Scriptorium/JesusThruJewishEyes.htm.

118. See texts in David Daube, *The New Testament and Rabbinic Judaism* (London: Athlone, 1956; repr., Peabody MA: Hendrickson, 1990), 141ff.

119. Meier, *Law and Love*, 373. Note that Paul uses the same LXX text of Isa 29:13 in Col 2:21–22. And this sheds doubt, I think, on Meier's radical conclusion regarding Mark 7. For both the Markan and the Pauline texts may have had recourse to an oral or written tradition (in the first century CE there is still no MT extent). All the more so if, as Meier writes, "Colossians is not literarily dependent on Mark for its use of LXX Isaiah 29:13" (ibid., 374).

120. Ibid., 378.

back to Exod 20:12 (on the respect due to one's parents).[121] Hence, per se, the unit looks authentic.

Mark 7:15: Is the aphorism on the purity of all foods historical? Is it conceivable that Jesus would annul the food laws of Leviticus and Deuteronomy? Doubt is shed on this by the fact that the issue remained a burning one in Paul's epistles and in Acts. All the same, invoking discontinuity with the Judaism of the day, Ernst Käsemann and Norman Perrin declare the aphorism authentic.[122] More gingerly, Meier calls attention to the prophetic expression "not *x* but *y*" that actually means "more *y* than *x*" (see Hos 6:6). In Mark 9:37, Jesus says, "not me but the One who sent me," which amounts to a "dialectical negation" emphasizing priorities (see Matt 15:11). Gospel of Thomas 14 harps on this latter text of Matthew, which introduces the word "mouth" (*stoma*) within the two halves of the sentence: "what goes into the mouth/what comes out of the mouth." Hence, the Matthean text looks like a reworking of Mark's; and Gos. Thom. 14, a reworking of Matthew's. But is this tradition authentic? Meier calls attention to the fact that Jesus and his disciples did not eat forbidden foods. Further, Mark 7:15 stirred no reaction from the crowd. Paul and Luke remained silent about this teaching, which, besides, is not backed up by multiple attestations.

Can we at this point draw a conclusion from this analysis of Mark 7? In summary, there is here a sharp contrast between what goes in and what goes out of human mouth. The pericope is true to Jesus's character. It fits the recurring opposition to external ritualistic manifestations that we find everywhere in the gospel. Mark 7:15, however, is Mark's personal conclusion that he drew from within the context of dietary controversies of early Christianity, especially for gentile converts. The same may be said of verse 19 and of verses 21-23 (the defilement coming from the human heart). But if these verses are not authentic, their spirit remains authentic (cf. Matt 23:27-36; Mark 12:38-40). It is out of the question to concur with Meier's assumption that Mark 7:1-23 "drops out of consideration."[123] We must maintain a profound difference between an idea and its traditional transmission. It is inconceivable that Jesus would have ignored the issue

---

121. M. Ned. 9:1 remains somewhat indecisive. In m. Ned. 5:6, *qorban* is annulled through a complicated legal fiction.

122. See John P. Meier, *The Roots of the Problem and the Person*, vol. 1 of *A Marginal Jew: Rethinking the Historical Jesus*, ABRL (New York: Doubleday, 1991), 17.

123. Ibid., 405.

of purity/impurity. What we learn of his dealing with it corresponds with what we know of his stance regarding the ritual(s) of corpse impurity, for instance: Jesus touches Jairus's daughter (Mark 5:41), goes into Lazarus's grave (John 11:38), and touches the bier of the widow's son (Luke 7:14). The touching of lepers or of the woman with a flow of blood, the commerce with ostracized individuals, and so on go in the same direction. Another striking example of Jesus's rejection of ritual—when not prompted by an inner devotion—is found in Matt 23:25–26 ("first clean the inside of the cup that the outside of it may become clean").[124] In Luke 11:44, Jesus deals with a halakah on the impurity of walking on an unseen grave (see Temurah 4:11). Here as elsewhere, Jesus's personalization is remarkable: "Woe to you [specialists of torah's interpretation] ..." for they themselves are unseen graves. The effect is a moralization of the meaning of the law.

The otherwise fine analysis of Mark 7 by Meier surprisingly missed an important element: In Mark 7:17, we find the unexpected characterization of Jesus's aphorism as being a *parable*! This constitutes a significant downgrade from the level of dogma or authorized statement. A parable opens up a "large margin of interpretation" (Paul Ricoeur). Jesus's saying is seen as figurative. The parable is not the appropriate means to convey a halakic statement able to annul, in one stroke, the entirety of dietary law in the torah. The parable is meant as a way for the reader to meditate. It *laisse à penser*.

*

In fact, Jesus upholds the torah in its entirety. Pharisees abuse the taw with hypocrisy (so in Q; see also Matt 5:17). True, many of the Pharisaic applications are valid, but Jesus warns against hairsplitting. The torah itself remains central as long as compassion is primordial. There is on the part of Matthew an effort to remove from Mark all disparaging statements on the law, the abuses of which will bring about the destruction of the temple. Luke, in his turn, gives much attention to the ritual and cultic laws. The

---

124. For the parallel text of Luke 11:39–41, the "inside cleaning" means giving alms. Later, Maimonides made the same comment: "For to confine oneself to cleaning the outward appearance through washing and cleaning the garment, while having at the same time a lust for various pleasures and unbridled license ... merits the utmost blame" (*The Guide of the Perplexed*, trans. Shlomo Pines (Chicago: University of Chicago Press, 1974), vol. 2 bk. 3, 533).

torah is universal. All animals are pure for consumption. Obedience means keeping the law, but there are degrees of validity in the commandments, for first comes compassion (see the parable of the good Samaritan in Luke 10). John's assessment follows a Platonic model: the torah is patterned on a higher reality (see 2:17). In summary, we may follow William Loader's conclusion to his book on Jesus's attitude toward the law. He notes: "A reconstruction of Jesus' attitude toward the Law needs to take into account diverse strands of tradition: the radically humane Jesus; the culturally conservative Jesus; the theologically strict Jesus in issues of morality."[125]

For Jesus, moral impurity *does defile a person*. Matthew 15:19 lists such defiling things: "fornication, theft, murder, adultery, avarice, wickedness, deceit, licentiousness, envy, blasphemy, pride and folly. All these things come from within, and they defile."[126] This contrasts with rabbinic halakah, which is more interested in ritual impurity than in moral impurity.[127] The rabbis keep those two categories separate, in spite, should we say, of Ps 24:3-4; 51; 2 Chr 30:8-20, and others, which make no such distinction.

So while Jonathan Klawans is certainly right when he says that Jesus's declarations "themselves do not constitute a rejection of anything," he is short of the mark when he concludes that "Jesus explicitly prioritized the maintenance of moral purity over the maintenance of ritual purity."[128] Jesus did more than that. He took a stance that happens to fall in parallel with that of the Qumran covenanters, who did not distinguish between the two notions.[129] In Jesus's case, "prioritizing" is insufficient. *For Jesus, ritual purity/impurity belongs to the ethical realm*. For him, there is a moral rationale behind cleaning the exterior of the cup; otherwise, it is the banging of "empty cymbals" (see Matt 23:25-26; Gos. Thom. 14). And, indeed, one does not offer a sacrifice in the temple for the ritual's

---

125. Loader, *Jesus' Attitude*, 523-24.

126. We find a comparable list of moral impurities in the book of Jubilees, several copies of which have been found at Qumran: fornication, uncleanness, iniquity: these were the cause of the flood (7:20-21).

127. Amy-Jill Levine and Marc Zvi Brettler, eds., *The Jewish Annotated New Testament* (Oxford: Oxford University Press, 2008), at Matt 15:19, send the reader to rabbinic documents, m. Yad. 1:1-2:4; Ber. 53b; Giṭ. 15b; Pesaḥ. 115ab and Sukkah 26b; 27a.

128. Jonathan Klawans, "Moral and Ritual Purity," in Levine, Allison, and Crossan, *The Historical Jesus in Context*, 281-82.

129. Klawans refers to CD 2:25-3:6; 4:9-11; 5:13-14, 18-19; 6:24-26; 8:16-18; 4Q512, frags. 29-32, lines 8-10.

5. JESUS AND TORAH

sake. Nor does one practice circumcision simply in blind obedience to a commandment—that would be fundamentalistic. Therefore, rabbinic literature justifies with care the moral validity of commandments through exegesis of texts that are deemed appropriate.

As an example, for the Pharisees around Jesus, not washing hands has nothing to do with sin, but only with ritual. As one may not approach the altar in the temple until one's hands are clean, so the Pharisees saw eating at home as a cultic act and therefore transferred to the home many of the laws pertaining to the temple. Furthermore, Pharisees avoided contact with non-Jews. In a multinational country, as Palestine had become, this was nearly impossible and required at least a symbolic washing of hands before meals. By contrast, for Jesus, the washing of hands has everything to do with the ethical. As such, the ritual itself is not rejected, but when Jesus and his disciples do not wash hands, they proclaim an ethical principle.

We saw that in the Hebrew Scriptures, impurity may be used as metaphor for moral evil. Even the land may become unclean (Isa 35:8; Ezek 14:11). We are thus witnessing a process of what Neusner calls "neutralization of the force of impurity.... The actual process of contamination or purification is made entirely relative," a prophetic move that clashes with the priestly laws.[130] It is clearly this prophetic trend that informs the Pauline understanding of the notion of pure and impure. Romans 14:14-23 says (in a context of food consumption), "nothing is unclean in itself; everything is indeed clean" (cf. 1 Cor 6:12-13; Gal 2:11). Romans 6:19 equates impurity and iniquity—in 1 Thess 4:7, for instance, sex can be subject to impurity. Besides, the church is the new temple (1 Cor 3:16-17), which implies that Christian behavior is to be constantly immersed in holiness.

Shifting from Paul to the Synoptics presents no problem. Impurity affects different existential areas. One of these lies in bodily afflictions. The gospel insists therefore on Jesus's healings and Jesus's consorting with sick people, in particular with lepers, that is, the impure par excellence.[131] Each time Jesus is in contact with one of them, the notion of purity is mentioned (Mark 1:40 // Luke 5:12 [Jesus *touches* the man]; Luke 7:22 and 17:12-19, where the lepers are "purified"). Mark 14:3 // Matt 26:16 is puzzling. Jesus is in the home of Simon the leper on the eve of Passover

---

130. Neusner, *The Idea of Purity*, 17.
131. One remembers that Job was a "leper" (2:7-8; cf. 18:13). So also was the suffering servant, according to Bernhard Duhm, *Das Buch Jesaia übersetzt und erklärt*, HKAT (Göttingen: Vandenhoeck & Ruprecht, 1902) (on Isa 53:3).

in Jerusalem! The situation is so odd that Luke 7:36–50 does not mention that Simon is a leper. Neusner suggests that Simon was formerly a leper but is not anymore when Jesus visits with him.[132] Perhaps. But Jesus's striking association with lepers makes his visit with Simon the leper less surprising, even at the eve of a festival that would play a decisive role in Jesus's destiny.

It behooves us to consider leprosy further within the context of rabbinic Judaism and the gospel. The book of Leviticus is in the background for both approaches. Impurity is akin to disorder, so permanent, physical defects are listed as impurities in Lev 21:17–24 (regarding priesthood without blemish) and in Deut 17:1 (animals' defects). They are submitted to the priests for their decision as to whether they are pure or impure (Ezek 22:26; 44:23). Sickness—especially leprosy—is a source of impurity (Lev 13–14; 2 Kgs 5:10–14). Incidentally, this is why Jesus's exorcisms are directed toward "impure spirits" (see Mark 5:1–13). As for the rabbis, the issue of purity/impurity raised a vexing issue. It was one of their major problems.

Early rabbinism, says Neusner, viewed "impurity (leprosy) not as a metaphor for sin in general, but as a sign that a *specific* sin had been committed."[133] The rabbis saw a parallel between Israel's historical troubles and the individual's impairments. "The leper was excluded from the community as well as from the temple; he suffered all sorts of disabilities."[134] With this, we come to the core of the question, namely, the problem of theodicy. The rabbis reasserted the principle of divine distributive justice: *middah keneged middah* ("measure for measure"). The sufferings of a person are set on the same level as the sufferings of the people: they are deserved. A woman dies in childbirth because she transgressed menstrual rules. Leprosy is due to gossiping. And so on.[135] Impurity is contagious, while purity is not (Hag 2:12–19). Therefore, it must be contained or eradicated (Isa 6:5–7; cf. Ps 51:4, 9). It is contained when the "culprit" is sick (leprosy, croup, etc.). It is eradicated when he or she dies, or through repentance. Purity is not treated in this way. It is not contagious, as we just said. Hence, separateness must accompany purity. It needs to be walled in,

---

132. Neusner, *The Idea of Purity*, 60.
133. Ibid., 88.
134. Ibid., 118. In Num 5:1–4, the leper is expelled from the Israelite camp in the desert.
135. See m. Šabb. 2:6; Šabb. 31b; Sipra Metsora' 5:9 (cf. Num 12:1–16).

5. JESUS AND TORAH

untouched by sources of uncleanness.[136] Thus Mary Douglas says, "The laws of nature are dragged in to sanction the moral code: this kind of disease is caused by adultery; that by incest; this meteorological disaster is the effect of political disloyalty; that the effect of impiety."[137]

The disastrous consequences of this theodicy-bound concept are evident, leading to some kind of Manichaeism before its time. In his critique of Mary Douglas's *Purity and Danger: An Analysis of Concepts of Pollution and Taboo*, Neusner writes (about Judaic ideas of purity), "Whatever pollutions people have incurred they may remove by a single act of purification,"[138] but then he forgets the leper or the woman with a constant blood issue.[139] As a general rule, we may agree with Neusner that rabbis do not suggest that "a rite of purification takes away the guilt or moral effects of sin,"[140] in spite of Douglas' statement that "pollutions are easier to cancel than moral defects." Neusner writes, "There must be an advantage for society at large in attempting to reduce moral offences to pollution offences which can be instantly scrubbed out by ritual."[141] It seems evident, however, that the rabbis took exception with a popular misconception about the efficacy of the ritual.[142]

Earlier, in chapter 4, "Jesus as Healer" (53–70), I broached the principle of distributive justice in the New Testament. I cited texts on the victims of the fallen tower of Siloam. Jesus's response, to recall, was, "Do you think that [those who were killed by the tower's fall] were worse offenders than all the others living in Jerusalem? No, I tell you; but unless you repent, you will all perish just as they did" (Luke 13:4–5; Matt 4:17). Then, if we believe John's report about the healing of a man blind from birth (9:1–41),

---

136. Especially as regards priests, see Num 8:14; 16:19; Deut 10:8; 1 Chr 23:13.
137. Mary Douglas, *Purity and Danger: An Analysis of Concepts of Pollution and Taboo* (London: Routledge, 1966), 2–3.
138. Neusner, *The Idea of Purity*, 121.
139. Not to be confused with a menstruating woman; hence, it is not a matter of purity, Meier says (*Law and Love*, 409). He may be wrong, however.
140. Neusner, *The Idea of Purity*, 126–27.
141. Douglas, *Purity and Danger*, 129–37, cited by Neusner, *The Idea of Purity*, 126.
142. I know for a fact that, until today, some 1800 years after the rabbis' protest, the *ex opere operato* of the ritual is still very much cultivated, especially in religious confessional systems. The simplistic and hypocritical illusion persists that "a rite of purification [a repetition of a certain formulaic prayer, for instance] takes away the guilt or moral effects of sin."

Jesus said to his disciples, "Neither this man nor his parents sinned" (v. 3). It is perfectly understandable within the Judaisms of his day that Jesus would address the priority of distributive justice or theodicy. He repudiates it in his teaching, as we just saw, but perhaps more powerfully yet by associating with the "impure," that is, the sick, lepers, the possessed, morally questionable characters such as prostitutes and tax collectors, the poor (who, in the eyes of some, may deserve their wretchedness), even the dead (Jairus's daughter, Lazarus), and so on. This sinfulness is not individual, but rather collective. The individual sufferings may be systemic, inflicted by others, as Jas 5:1–6 strongly insists. They may be endowed with a redeeming effect, as 1 Cor 15:3 and John 1:29 intimate, in reference to Isa 52:13–53:12. The New Testament declaration that Jesus did not sin[143] is the seal that confirms this notion (2 Cor 5:21; cf. John 8:46; 14:30; Heb 4:14). As to the Christian herself, she is said to benefit from a new life that is no longer stamped by sin (Rom 8:3; 1 John 3:6, 9).

I do not think we can overemphasize the enormous import of Jesus's repudiation of the purity/impurity system. The latter had been a very central concern as long as the temple was standing. Even before its destruction by the Romans, Jesus brought a major shift in the religious landscape. True, in the early church, the criterion for doing so was spelled out in christological terms, but it also implied a fundamental criticism of the theodicy as understood by the Pharisees-rabbis in particular, and already so powerfully denounced by the book of Job, a major work hardly ever cited in rabbinic Judaism.

It is not surprising that food, as another source of potential uncleanness, would also be among Jesus's concerns. On this point as well, we have seen that, for the gospel, *kashrut* had been extended to include all foods (e.g., Matt 15:10–20; Rom 14:14–23). Within this context, the parenthetical addition in the text of Mark 7:19 ("Thus he declared all foods clean") becomes much more than an aside. By refusing to distinguish between ritual purity/impurity and moral purity/impurity, Jesus indeed broached the principle of *kashrut*. At the very least, he raised the question of the ethical rationale behind kosher eating: What does it *mean*? In what way are "all foods" to be segregated between the pure and the impure? When will all foods be integrated into the kosher category?

---

143. Like Enoch, who was morally perfect and hence did not die.

5. JESUS AND TORAH

Jesus certainly deemphasized the priestly categories of *tahor* ("pure") or *tame'* ("impure") as spelled out in Lev 10:10; 11:47; and elsewhere. A whole world of thought, a whole weltanschauung, is thus questioned. We must remember that the priests were in charge of sorting out the pure and the impure from among both people and things (Ezek 27:26). They deal with whole classes of impure items, including nonkosher animals, living beings with physical defects, men and women with or after genital issues, and so on (see Lev 21:17-23; cf. 1QM 7:4-8). The important principle is that *impurity is contagious* (see Lev 10:10; 11:32-47; Hag 2:12-14).

In sharp contrast to this principle, Jesus advanced the revolutionary idea that *purity is contagious*. Jesus's acts purify! (Mark 1:23-26, 40-44). In his doctrine, purity is synonymous with holiness and commitment (Matt 5:8; John 15:2; Rom 6:19).[144]

Mark, like Matthew, spoke of the healing of the leper (1:40-45), of the bleeding woman, and of the resurrection of Jairus's daughter (in 5:21-34), thus exemplifying how Jesus dealt with the three main sources of impurity: skin disease, genital discharge, and corpses (see Lev 12-15; 21; Num 19:1-22). In the first instance, the tradition unanimously testifies that Jesus came in contact with lepers. He expressed dismay with the way they were marginalized by society (see the Synoptics and Papyrus Egerton 2). He could not accept the judgmental attitude of some who complacently set themselves apart. They were actually more sick than those they spurned and whose ailments were aggravated by the arrogance of others who fared well. In all cases, Jesus shifts the issue from the cultic to the ethical and hence from the plane of the bodily impurity of the sufferers to the moral inadequacy of "healthy ones" who violate the rules of social justice and compassion.[145]

---

144. In the foundation of normative Judaism, the Mishnah, "Messiahs ... were merely a species of priest" without historical role, according to Neusner (*The Idea of Purity*, 18). Also in contrast with the gospel, the Mishnah seldom appeals to the Scriptures. In Leviticus, however, purity is associated at times with holiness (11:44-45; 16:19; cf. 2 Chr 29:15-19) and, in the prophetic books, purity has a moral sense (Isa 1:16; 6:5; Jer 33:8; Ezek 36:33; Hab 1:13). In Psalms, the idea is common (18:21, 25; 24:3-4; 51:12; 73:1, 13). In the NT, beside Gal 2:12, see especially Acts 10:15 and Titus 1:15.

145. Mark 12:34 (on the greatest commandment) leads to the realization that the ethical supersedes the ritual and makes one closer to the kingdom of God. In Jewish tradition, what gives precedence to the house of Hillel over the house of Shammai is the former's sense of compassion. What give the advantage to the house of Hillel is its

Far from canceling the law, Jesus's teaching makes it absolute.[146] He eliminates all limits on its application in the name of ethics. The Sabbath, for example, is not violated but sees its original intent fulfilled when the man with a lame hand is healed on that very day. For the veritable aim of the Sabbath laws has always been to attain *shalom*, but no one can be *shalem*, and hence in God's *shalom*, as long as he or she is handicapped. The healing of his lame hand opens for the crippled man the gate to the true Sabbath.[147] This implies that everyone on earth and throughout history is similarly handicapped. All humans strive to be restored in soul and body so that the Sabbath can at last start for them as well. As for the people who are prey to the illusion that they are in a position to observe the Sabbath without having to be healed—because they are not in need of the "physician" (see Mark 2:17)—they deprive themselves of the Way, the Truth, and the Life (John 14:6). They may be called hypocrites, a judgment that does not spare anyone on earth, for it so happens that all people are indeed sick *and* deny it; that is, they deny their ethical duty vis-à-vis others and themselves, and eventually their mortality. Paradoxically, they do not really enjoy the Sabbath and its *shalom*, but they "hypocritically" claim to be among the chosen ones who observe the Sabbath!

The parallel with the rule of *kashrut* is evident. All foods are now absorbed into the category of *kashrut*, and all ritual restrictions are now transcended. It is not what goes in but what goes out that soils, a crucial saying, as we saw, that Matt 15:18 put in these words: "Whatever goes into the mouth … goes out into the sewers. But what comes out of the mouth proceeds from the heart, and that is what defiles."[148] "Thus," Mark adds, "[Jesus] declared all foods clean" (7:19; cf. Rom 14:20).

---

humility and its kindness. Yet, in 'Erub. 13b, a *bath qol* declares that both the Shammaite and the Hillelite interpretations are "words of the living God."

146. This notion is close to the later one of *devekut* (a person's entire dedication) in the Zohar and the eighteenth-century Hasidism. In the early Zohar, however, there is a clear trend of antinomianism. In 1668, Abraham Miguel Cardozo, a Sabbatian kabbalist, wrote *Magen Abraham*, in which he says that, in the messianic era, the law becomes unnecessary.

147. Note, as it is made clear in the parable of the good Samaritan, that the main point is always to allow *others* to be treated as a neighbor (rather than gaining for oneself "eternal life") and to enjoy the wholeness of Sabbath (rather than personally fulfilling its rules of performance).

148. In *The Jewish Annotated New Testament*, Levine and Brettler refer to Pesiq. Rab Kah. 4.7 and Pesiq. Rab. 14.14.

Jesus sets up a sliding scale in the torah's commandments, giving priority (but not exclusivity) to the "moral," that is, the soul of the "ritual," not its substitute (see Matt 23:23).[149] He severely criticizes the priestly establishment (Mark 11:15–18, in parallel with Jer 7), invoking his own divine sonship (12:1–12). This tolls the end of the political instrument that the temple of the time had become. It is declared impure and obsolete (13:1–2; cf. 14:58) in the name of the advent of the kingdom of God.

The Sermon on the Mount depends on this principle of absolute ethics. Anger is murder, lust is adultery, and so on. The critical consensus is that those commandments are impractical and are contingent on Jesus's mistaken belief that the kingdom was at hand. Hence, the fulfillment of the maxims put forward by the Nazarene would be of short duration, thus softening somewhat their "impossibility." This, however, is a partial explanation that amounts to evading the question. In fact, as I shall expound below, Jesus gave absolute priority to loving amplification—so poetically developed by Paul in 1 Cor 13—over the legally restricting principle of reciprocity.[150] But this is not a time-limited maxim.

In all of this, Jesus's relationship with the Pharisees is more complex than appears from their numerous disputations with Jesus. These disputes always involve differing interpretations of the law, not questioning the Pharisees' authority (see Matt 23:2–3). Had Jesus taught a systematic opposition to Pharisaism as such, he would not have shared meals (and possibly accommodations) with some of them (see Mark 14:3–9; Luke 7:36; 11:37; 14:1). As noted above, Jesus made friends with members of the Sanhedrin, such as Nicodemus and Joseph of Arimathea. Furthermore, Jesus's rejection of the Sadducees and their opposition to the Pharisees' "traditions of the fathers" is proof enough.

However, the gospel insists, Jesus taught with authority, not like the scribes (Luke 5:20; Matt 9:2; Mark 2:5). What distinguishes Jesus's teaching from that of the scribes is the respective sources of their authority. For one thing, the recourse to Scriptures in the gospel is abundantly illustrated as the touchstone of Jesus's authenticity. The rabbinic practical ignorance

---

149. This prioritizing of the ethical is less revolutionary than it may appear when one remembers that torah means much more than "law." Buber is right when he states that the reductionist translation of torah by *nomos* made possible "the Pauline dualism of law and faith, life from works and life from grace" (*Two Types of Faith*, 57).

150. Cf. Gos. Thom. 95.

of "all forms and styles of Hebrew Scriptures" is striking.[151] Further, the "scribes" speak in the name of former rabbis ("so and so says in the name of so and so"), that is, in the name of tradition, while Jesus vests authority in himself ("you have heard that it was taught to the elders ... but I say unto you").[152] A rabbinic teaching may be anonymously transmitted (through oblivion of its author or for any other reason), but the teaching of Jesus is inseparable from his person. The exhortation to love even one's enemy, for instance, would make no sense coming from anyone else, as we have seen. A traditional authority is likely to be questioned or to become obsolete under new circumstances, but this is not so in the case of teaching that is incarnate in the teacher; its "obsolescence" would imply the obsolescence of the Master.[153]

In Matt 21:23–27 and parallels, they ask Jesus by what authority he speaks and acts. The question is, "Who gave you this authority?" that is—within the perspective of traditional rabbis' concatenated traditions—who was your Master (your 'ab)? Jesus then asks whether the baptism of John the Baptist came from earth or heaven. Since they will not answer, Jesus also refuses to say. Like John, Jesus was more than a rabbi, or a prophet, but rather someone who got his *reshut* ("legitimacy") from God, not from a teacher. Jesus was a disciple of John, but he got his *reshut*, like John, from God. So there is no response that Jesus could give that would fit the questioners' worldview.[154]

---

151. See Jacob Neusner, *The Pharisees: Rabbinic Perspectives* (New York: Ktav, 1973), 155.

152. Behind the term "authority" (of Jesus), there is the rabbinic *geburah*, that is, divine power (so Marcus Borg, *Jesus: A New Vision* [New York: HarperCollins, 2009], 46). What people have heard is typically the rabbinic tradition and its "Rabbi So-and-So says."

153. Indeed, the tradition's backup is not always probative. Hama bar Hanina (third century) says in Exod. Rab. 4.18 that Moses was removed from his father's house when he was twelve. Thus, when he revealed the Name of God, he could not be suspect of forwarding a tradition passed down from his father Amram. Then, "the people believed" (Exod 4:31), but Hama's argument is atemporal.

154. Note the difference of conception here from m. 'Abot 1, where it is said that the Torah was transmitted from Moses to Joshua, from Joshua to the elders, from the elders to the prophets, etc. Thus the prophets also got their authorization from tradition. Paul uses the same pattern in 1 Cor 11:23–25 (one of the first creedal statements of the church) and 15:3–5.

5. JESUS AND TORAH

One of the major issues of that time was, who are the true teachers? Or even, who is the true teacher? This problem was paramount in Qumran, in formative Judaism, and in the Matthew's Gospel. Matthew, for example, stresses equality and mutuality (Matt 18:1-4, and the use of the term *adelphos* ["brother"] in the Sermon on the Mount). Matthew 23:7-12 shows Jesus's concern about hierarchy; he calls instead for a mutuality without prerogatives.[155] Authority comes directly from God, and tradition cannot become a substitute.

Notwithstanding this, the formula "You have heard ... but I say unto you" belongs to rabbinic parlance![156] The frequent talmudic expression *shomea' 'ani* means "I might understand" (although it is not so). An example is Mek. 6.8 (on Exod. 20:12): God descended on Mount Sinai and left heaven empty! And the *shomea'* is the one who sticks to the literal meaning of the text. He then explicates the text with additional "conclusions" that are not in the MT and belong to a narrow, literal interpretation. To this, the rabbinic authority reacts by saying, *'amartha*, "you must [rather] say."

The rabbinic setting, as can be seen, is academic. In the case of Jesus's Sermon on the Mount, however, the public is not composed of the teaching rabbi's peers, but of "blind" people, to whom Jesus now says, "but I say unto you," in a prophetic tone and without any reasoning (that is, "with authority, not like the scribes"). For Jesus is not just a law interpreter, in the dialectic understanding of the term, but he is lawgiver, like Moses, while surpassing Moses with a torah that goes beyond all quibbling.

To be sure, whatever Jesus taught about this issue, he forbade the creation of a caste-forming elitism by his adherents: "You are not to be called rabbi.... And call no one your father on earth.... Nor are you to be called instructors.... The greatest among you will be your servant" (Matt 23:8-12). Scandalously in the eyes of many, Jesus had commerce with "shudras"—publicans, lepers, prostitutes, and the downtrodden of all kinds (Mark 2:15-17). Consequently, the early church welcomed into its community, without qualification, sinners, tax collectors, eunuchs, and gentiles. Besides, the church had no formal name: Christians were called, often derogatorily, *christianoi* (see Acts 11:26; 26:28; as a self-designation, 1 Pet 4:16), *hagioi* (see Rom 15:25; 2 Cor 1:2), *hē ekklēsia* (esp. in Matthew), *hē hodos* (see Acts 18:25-26; 22:4; 24:14), *ho oikos* (see Eph 2:19;

---

155. Pointedly, Matthew speaks of their (*autōn*) synagogues (e.g., 4:23; 9:35; 10:17). Also in Mark, see 1:23, 39; and in Luke, 4:15.

156. On this, see Daube, *New Testament and Rabbinic Judaism*, 55ff.

1 Thess 3:15). The rationale, as we saw, lies in the teaching of a doctrine of purity based on the principle that impurity does *not* come from outside, but from inside the human heart.[157] Jesus may well react, here, against the Pharisaic oral rule about the washing of hands to prevent impurity through contact (so Daniel Boyarin),[158] but, as I said, it seems evident that the controversy goes beyond the ritual level, and is not "about *whether* to observe it [the law]," as says Boyarin.[159] Let me add the following quote of David Roads, "Jesus' ideology was to spread holiness through mercy so that holiness in the land might be attained not by suppression or exclusion but by the transformation of what was unclean through healing, forgiveness, and a renewal of the temple and Torah."[160]

Within this context, let us note that, at the time, "rabbi" as an honorific was already evolving toward becoming a title among the Pharisees. The promotion to prominence of the "rabbi" even led at times to regarding him as messianic. Matthew therefore calls not just to humility but also to faithfulness to *the* rabbi's teaching: "You have only one teacher, one father, one master."[161] The interpretation of the torah is not up to the "fathers/elders" (Matt 5:21–48). Matthew denounces the plurality of teachers and of teachings. The Matthean Jesus is primarily *the* teacher (cf. Matt 5; 18), and so the disciples are taught with one teaching (Matt 28:19–20). The disciple is a "scribe trained for the kingdom of heaven … who brings out of his treasure what is new and what is old" (13:52; cf. Ezra 7:6).[162] The Matthean disciples understand (see 16:16–17), but the Markan disciples do not (see Mark 9:32). Both evangelists are right, of course.

I used the word "transcendence" to characterize the ultimate nature of the torah and all the rules therein. Perhaps, no prophetic text is more decisive on that score than Zech 14:20, "In that day [*bayom hahu'*], … the

---

157. See Gos. Thom. 45.

158. Daniel Boyarin, *The Jewish Gospels: The Story of the Jewish Christ* (New York: New Press, 2012), ch. 3 (102ff.).

159. Ibid., 103.

160. David Rhoads, "Zealots," *ABD* 6:1052b.

161. The contrast between the disciples of the sages and those of the Nazarene is relativized when we turn to a rabbinic text such as y. Ber. 2:8, 5c: "A person's student is as beloved to him as his son."

162. As such, there is a kind of competition between Jesus's disciples and the "scribes." When the early Hasidim questioned the Hasmonean religious leadership, the scribe (i.e., the scholar, a layman) eventually took over. After 70 CE, the scribe becomes the rabbi of rabbinic Judaism.

cooking pots of the house of the Lord shall be as holy as the bowls in front of the altar, and every cooking pot in Jerusalem and Judah shall be sacred to the Lord of hosts ... and there shall no longer be traders in the house of the Lord of hosts on that day." Just as the prophet Zechariah did not cancel the opposition between holy and common, or between pure and impure, but hailed the eschatological extension of the holy to include the common, the pure and the impure (see Lev 10:10), so Jesus takes ownership of the same vision and declares its fulfillment in his days (that is, *bayom hahu'*): "Purity codes are not set aside, but people are cleansed of their impurity."[163]

The Parable of the Good Samaritan: A Hermeneutics of the Law[164]

Although I will reflect on Jesus's parables in a coming chapter, I review here one of the most striking. It is found only in Luke (chapter 10) and is customarily called the parable of the good Samaritan (verses 25-37). Its clear exposition of Jesus's understanding of the law justifies its study here.

Our reading of this Lukan parable must start with the verse 25. "Just then a lawyer stood up to test Jesus. 'Teacher,' he said, 'what must I do to inherit eternal life?'" The following verse sets up Jesus's terms of the problem: "What is your reading [of the law]?" The lawyer happens to have a sharp intelligence, but his hidden agenda is to justify himself (v. 29).[165] To do so, he is *using* Scripture. When he and Jesus have agreed that the core of the torah is love of God and love of the neighbor (Deut 6:5 and Lev 19:18),[166] the issue becomes one of the neighbor's identity: "And who is my neighbor?" the lawyer asks (v. 29).

The discussion seems academic, but in fact all the characters involved in Luke 10:25-37, including Jesus and the lawyer, are "doers." Priests and Levites are functionaries; in the parable, they represent their clerical func-

---

163. Levine and Brettler, *Jewish Annotated New Testament*, 63.

164. A more detailed study of the parable can be found in my article "Jesus's Hermeneutics of the Law, Rereading the Parable of the Good Samaritan," in *Creation, Life, and Hope: Essays in Honor of Jacques B. Doukhan*, ed. Jiri Moskala (Berrien Springs, MI: Andrews University, 2000), 251-76.

165. See the series of "woes" against the lawyers (scribes) in Luke 11:45-52 (from Q [?]).

166. Compare with Rabbi Aqiba's opinion that Lev 19:18 is the greatest commandment (Sipra Qedoshim 4). See the same combination of Deut 6 and Lev 19 in T. Iss. 5:2 and T. Dan 5:3; Philo, *Spec.* 2.63-64.

tions. In the case of the Samaritan, his representation is self-evident to all Jews. At the end of the pericope, the lawyer will be invited *to do* (v. 37).

Yet the one who is mugged in the parable is simply called "the man" and remains anonymous. More than that, he has been stripped of his clothes, that is, of all his distinctive dress that might have shown where he stands in society, and he cannot speak. It is impossible to know his origins—Jew or non-Jew, rich or poor, native or stranger, *alive or dead*. Is this what paralyzes the priest and the Levite? They do not know—or affect not to know—whether "the man" is a "neighbor," and they choose to ignore whether he is now dead or beyond life-saving intervention. We do not know for sure, but, as good literary critics, we might be inclined to provide them with some kind of motivation. One of the best gap-fillers is by Martin Luther King Jr., who suggested that the priest and the Levite were afraid. He imagines them asking, "If I stop to help this man, what will happen to me—for there are bandits on the road?" The Samaritan asks the right question: "If I do not stop to help this man, what will happen to him?"[167] So the clergymen try to ignore the man and pass by him. Only a hated stranger, a Samaritan, is "moved by pity" and "shows mercy" (vv. 33, 37).[168] Clearly, it takes a stranger—who is not encumbered by the legal definition of "neighbor"—to be really helpful. To be sure, the point of the parable is not the issue of purity versus impurity. The point, instead, is made through the starkest possible contrast between people who should be expected to help and people who would be expected to show hostility. The former, men of the system, pitifully fail, while the one who allows himself to be "moved by compassion and show mercy" becomes a spiritual giant.[169]

As Amy-Jill Levine stresses, after the mention of "priest and Levite," one would have expected the traditional third category, Israelite. These are the three major divisions among the Jews. For Jesus to substitute a Samaritan for the Israelite is shocking.[170]

---

167. I owe this information to Amy-Jill Levine, with thanks.

168. See the pejorative view of the Samaritans in Josephus's *Ant.* 18.29-35; 11.114-119; 20.118-124.

169. No one will, however, ignore at this point Lev 21:1-3 forbidding the priest to touch a corpse except in the case of close kin. Ezek 44:25 confirms it. Num 19:11-22 associates impurity by contact with a corpse with committing a sin. (If the impure person does not remove his sin, he is expelled from Israel! Ezek 44:27 makes the same association.) In Qumran, the priest cannot approach the slain (1QM 7:4-5).

170. Levine, *The Misunderstood Jew*, 147. On priest, Levite, and Israelite, see, e.g., Sipra 194 on Lev 19:2, 15, where the triad appears no less than five times!

The contrast between the lawyer's—probably exemplifying his colleagues among contemporary "theologians"—and Jesus's understandings of the law is stark. Levine demonstrates in *The Jewish Annotated New Testament* that both the biblical texts on "neighbor" and their rabbinic interpretations go clearly in the inclusive sense adopted here by Jesus.[171] If so, the lawyer's question is futile, as it is without object. I therefore suggest a chronological sequence:

- First, the Hebrew Bible is clear about a broad understanding of "neighbor."
- Second, the political and economic circumstances during the first century CE exacerbated the populace's uneasiness regarding strangers in their midst, like Romans, Samaritans, and other hostile people. These were considered more as "enemies" than "neighbors," it seems. It is within this environment that the lawyer's question takes place.
- Third, as usual it is in response to the people's needs that the Pharisaic rabbis issued their halakic commentaries. They confirm the Scripture's broadmindedness on "neighbor."
- Fourth, Jesus's drift would go roughly in the same direction, but consistent with his striking and characteristic radicalism, he shows that the lawyer's question, as posed, was intended for self-justification. The problem is not one of definition, but one of creation: how shall *I* become the other's (any other's) neighbor?[172]

Jesus's agenda is to demonstrate that even one's enemy can become one's neighbor—or, shall we say, one's opportunity and invitation to be "neighboring."[173] The guardians of the Oral Law tend to proceed by legal

---

171. For Simmonds as well ("Woe to You," 339n18): "The Good Samaritan story is very much in the Pharisaic tradition. See Ta'anit 21a2–3 and n. 20 [Simmonds refers to the ArtScroll Series of the *Babylonian Talmud*, 73 vols. (New York: Mesorah, 1995)]; Sanhedrin 108b5–109a1; Sotah 45b5 and n. 40, etc."

172. Jesus's teaching in this case is again an irritant, no doubt, to other contemporary thinkers.

173. José Pagola paraphrases Jesus's command to love one's enemy thus: "Don't be enemies to anyone, not even to your enemies" (*Jesus: An Historical Approximation*, trans. Margaret Wilde [Miami: Convivium, 2009], 253).

restriction, while Jesus proceeds by loving amplification (to use Paul Ricoeur's categories[174]). The *lex talionis*, as noted above, defines justice as reciprocity: *only* an eye for an eye. Love transcends justice and reveals its ultimate purpose, which is the redemption of all, neighbor and enemy.[175] Is the Samaritan an enemy? No doubt about it. A daily Jewish prayer petitions God to prevent the Samaritans from *inheriting eternal life*! How, then, can they be considered "neighbors"? It is shocking that Jesus selects a Samaritan here as a role model.

And he certainly becomes a role model. For the truth of the matter is that the Samaritan was stepping on dangerous ground. He might well be suspected of having had a hand in the mugging of "the man."[176] In the background is a text from the torah that some suspicious people might have applied here, namely, Exod 21:18-19: "When individuals quarrel and one strikes the other with a stone or fist so that the injured party, though not dead, is confined to bed, but recovers and walks around outside with the help of a staff, then the assailant shall be free of liability, *except to pay for the loss of time, and to arrange for full recovery*" (NRSV, emphasis added). Also striking is y. B. Qam. 8:2, 6c = m. B. Qam. 8:1 (83b), "[If] he hit him, he is liable to provide for his medical care."

From this perspective, the Samaritan is thus dangerously exposing himself, first by interrupting his trip on a perilous road down to Jericho, but also—and especially—by taking care of a Jew (in all probability) and by bringing him to an inn (playing here the role of a clinic) where he also spends the night. He increases his endangerment by identifying himself openly and, last but not least, by announcing that he would come back. Not only is he under suspicion in Judea as a Samaritan and lacks proof that he did not participate in the attack on the poor man and, perhaps, was belatedly stricken by remorse, but also, according to the pentateuchal text of Exod 21:19 (a text common to Jews and Samaritans), he acts as if

---

174. Paul Ricoeur, "Love and Justice," in *Radical Pluralism and Truth: David Tracy and the Hermeneutics of Religion*, ed. Werner G. Jeanrond and J. L. Rike (New York: Crossroad, 1991), 187-202.

175. The same applies to the parable of the grape harvesters who are paid equally whether they worked the whole day in the vineyard or only one hour (Matt 20:1-15). This clearly goes beyond justice. In talmudic language, it is *huts mishurath ha-din*. At any rate, it makes obsolete the principle of performance (*mitsvoth*).

176. See Kenneth Bailey, *Through Peasant Eyes: More Lucan Parables, Their Culture and Style* (Grand Rapids: Eerdmans, 1980), 52-53.

5. JESUS AND TORAH

he indeed were liable for the maiming. His behavior thus follows, point by point, the prescribed compensation to be paid by the guilty party: "to pay for the loss of time, and to arrange for full recovery." Conversely, in retrospect, one can better understand the reasons why priest and Levite gingerly pass by the wounded man.

In short, prudence dictated that the Samaritan would have had more reason to "pass by" than either the Jewish priest or the Levite. What he chooses to do, by contrast, is at the apex of audacity. On that score, the parable of the good Samaritan is on a par with many of Jesus's parables on the kingdom of God. Throughout his ministry, Jesus extols an extraordinary understanding of God's expectations of his people and dedication to his service. Love means loving even one's enemy. To follow Christ is to carry one's own cross. The response to being hit in the face is to present the other cheek. To commit oneself to God means to leave everything behind and to let the dead bury their dead. Only a Jesus-like Samaritan can love so much and have such a broad understanding of the law. The parable is cryptically christological.[177]

Another—and the most important—lesson taught by the parable bears emphasis at this point. As will be stressed below, the lawyer's question regarding the identity of "my neighbor" is perfectly legitimate. Jesus's response, to the effect that one is a neighbor who is made so through the neighborliness of a "good Samaritan," transcends the national and ethnic boundaries initially envisaged by Lev 19:18.[178] The Samaritan's intervention in this parable is thus astounding, as is the anonymity of the wounded man, who may or may not be a Jew.[179]

The pure altruism of the Samaritan of the parable stands in stark contrast to the position adopted by the questioning lawyer, who puts himself at the center of his worldview. In his eyes, the neighbor is an *associate* and even instrumental to the lawyer's effort to inheriting eternal life. In his

---

177. More on this below. Cf. John 8:48. While Jesus's understanding of God's will is sheer folly, terms like "exaggeration" and "fantasy" ("the parable is a fantasy"), however, used by Robert W. Funk, are most unfortunate as they emasculate a strong message (see *Honest to Jesus* [San Francisco: HarperSanFrancisco, 1997], 177).

178. But see Lev 19:34! Furthermore, in view of the parallel established by Jesus between Deut 6:5 and Lev 19:18, the declaration by God, "I am compassionate," *eleēmōn gar eimi* in Exod 22:27b (cf. *eleos*, in the parable) is striking.

179. In spite of Robert W. Funk, who with great assurance says, "undoubtedly a Judean" (*Honest to Jesus*, 171).

exposition of the issue, the neighbor comes as an adjunct or a stimulant to the lawyer's performance.

Jesus redirects and reorients the question. The true problem is not the one raised, which betrays the inquirer's blindness to human suffering. Eternal life is not the share of pious "professionals," who spare no effort to stay beyond reproach. Rather, eternal life is for those whose concern for heavenly reward is minimal at best but who act out of compassion for a half-dead fellow man and did not fail to respond to his need.[180]

As a Pharisee, and hence a believer in the "world to come," the lawyer is thinking of an eternal life after death. But on this matter also, Jesus redirects his perspective to the hic et nunc of existence. The existential problem must not to be projected beyond death but is to be faced this side of death. The rest belongs to God.[181]

The man in dialogue with Jesus is a jurist. It is thus expected that he would stand on the ground of the law. His existential problem is the administration of justice. Now, *justice* is entirely based on the principle of equivalence (so that the priest and the Levite can in good conscience pass by and ignore someone who perhaps is not a Jew, or if he is a Jew is perhaps unworthy of compassion, or again is already dead and would make them "impure" by contact).[182] But *love* is founded on the logic of superabundance. Justice sets limits around the normal and the permissible; love transcends all limits and inaugurates an economy of *gift*, which makes all juridical allocation of rights secondary to compassion. Whether the stricken man of the parable is a Jew or a gentile, whether he is worthy or unworthy, alive or dead, pure

---

180. Helmut Gollwitzer speaks of the "non-miraculous, even irreligious, sober, and profane" nature of the parable of the good Samaritan (*Das Gleichnis vom barmherzigen Samariter* [Neukirchen-Vluyn: Neukirchener Verlag, 1967], 55).

181. Gollwitzer (ibid., 46) writes, "Zwischen diesem Tun und dem ewigen Leben steht nichts mehr, keine Distanz, kein Tod, keine Unsicherheit."

182. As I have said, the point of the parable is not a matter of purity versus impurity. But the fear of impurity may be the reason the two religious functionaries ignored the plight of the poor man. See Lev 21:1–3 on priestly defilement by contact with corpses. It is forbidden except for close relatives. Later, in m. Naz. 7:1, the priestly duty was extended to "a neglected corpse." Whether this is done as required, it remains that, according to Sipre Num. 127, "In the open, whoever touches a person who was slain by the sword or who dies naturally, or a human bone, or a grave, shall be unclean seven days" (Num 19:16). True, the priest and the Levite of the parable are not going to the temple, but from the temple toward Jericho, but can they afford to stay "unclean seven days"?

or impure, kin or alien—whether he is even an enemy—becomes irrelevant. He is someone in need of a "neighbor." Juridical reciprocity as a principle does not apply. There shall not be any kind of equivalence: the Samaritan expects nothing in return for his compassion, not even gratitude.

With this kind of conviction, Jesus does not fall into the trap set by the lawyer—who, we should not forget, "stood up to test Jesus." Even though the audience of the parable can easily empathize with the questioning lawyer and his openness, it remains that he does not come to Jesus with pure intentions. He may have been a temple scribe, and we must realize that the gospel references to chief priests and Levites are uniformly negative, on the model of Mark 12:38–40 (ending with the words, "They devour widows' houses and for the sake of appearance say long prayers. They will receive the greater condemnation").

Jesus does not supply a definition of the term "neighbor," as the rabbis of old do.[183] Instead, in Jesus's mouth, "neighbor" ceases to remain a static category, as it was, implicitly, in the lawyer's understanding, and becomes performative.

Bernard B. Scott has been sensitive to another striking shift from the initial question of the lawyer to the eventual rephrasing of it by Jesus. In his words, "So ... to have mercy is to give life and thus live eternally."[184] To recall, the lawyer's basic question had been, "What shall I do to inherit eternal life?" (v. 25).[185] The pattern of reversal is evident. To access eternal life is to give life to the neighbor. On that score again, the lawyer's self-centeredness is broken down. The lawyer raised his questions to justify himself. Surely, he thought, no one can be expected to love the unlovable as oneself! And indeed, in the Leviticus text read narrowly, "Thou shalt love thy neighbor as thyself" seems to set the "neighbor" as object. In

---

183. Midr. Ruth 4 says, "The Gentiles, amongst whom and us there is no war, and so those that are keepers of sheep amongst the Israelites, and the like, we are not to contrive their death; but if they be in any danger of death, we are not bound to deliver them ... such a one is not thy neighbor" (quoted after John Lightfoot by Bailey, *Through Peasant Eyes*, 40, see above note 176). Lightfoot also adds a reference to Maimonides in *Rozeh* chap. 2,4: the killing of an alien is not liable of the capital punishment, for the alien is not a neighbor.

184. Bernard B. Scott, *Hear Then the Parable: A Commentary on the Parables of Jesus* (Minneapolis: Fortress, 1989), 191.

185. The question resonates in several texts of the New Testament, and particularly in the Lukan corpus; see Luke 18:18; Acts 2:37; 16:30. The interrogation is typical of the Pharisaic understanding of torah.

Jesus's rephrasing of it, the neighbor becomes the subject of the action. The action becomes one of behaving in a neighborly fashion.[186] As the whole dialogue, including the "example story"[187] or parable, centers on the right interpretation of the law, it is clear that Jesus furnishes us with a hermeneutic key to the Leviticus text and, more generally, to the torah in general.

When the lawyer asks Jesus, "Who is my neighbor?" Jesus does not protest the raising of such a question. His answer, however, rejects any definition of "neighbor" that would be *restrictive* in defiance of the extravagance of the divine law. In another saying, very much akin with the present parable, Jesus extends love to include the enemy (Luke 6:27; Matt 5:47). In this parable, the lawyer's enemy is the Samaritan!

Luke 10:27 sets the Leviticus text in parallel with Deut 6:5 on the love of God. God must be loved "with all your heart, and with all your soul, and with all your strength, and with all your mind," which in the Leviticus text corresponds to the element "as yourself."[188] Clearly, in both cases the love commanded by the torah is a total commitment without any kind of restriction, for any limitation in one case would also apply in the other. That is, as soon as one starts to look for definitional parameters around the terms "love" or "neighbor," the absoluteness of the commitment is denied,

---

186. Franz Leenhardt ("La Parabole du Samaritain: Schéma d'une exégèse existentialiste," in *Aux Sources de la tradition chrétienne. Mélanges offerts à Maurice Goguel* [Neuchatel: Delachaux & Niestle, 1950], 136): "Such a relationship is no stasis, it only exists when being created."

187. Robert Funk takes exception with this designation. The parable "is metaphorical and therefore not an example story" (*Jesus as Precursor*, SemeiaSup 2 [Philadelphia: Fortress, 1975], 74). I do not agree with Funk on this. The parable of the good Samaritan is not a metaphor. Dan O. Via (*The Parables: Their Literary and Existential Dimension* [Philadelphia: Fortress, 1967], 12), by contrast, says that the "good Samaritan" is not a real parable but an example story because "the symbolic, figurative, or indirect elements are missing," and the point of the story is "present in the story. The story is an example of it." In the words of E. P. Sanders and Margaret Davies, the exemplary stories (among which the good Samaritan is paramount) "in one respect are not parables at all," but they are assimilated with parables because "they are narrative stories about one-time, non-recurrent behaviour, told as if the events actually took place; … they are used in the same way as are parables [and] they are commonly called 'parables'" (*Studying the Synoptic Gospels* [London: SCM; Philadelphia: Trinity Press International, 1989], 181).

188. Leenhardt ("La Parabole du Samaritain," 136) says of the expression "like yourself" that it must be understood quantitatively (as much as yourself) and qualitatively (inasmuch as she or he is yourself).

and the extravagance of the divine order is reduced to an innocuous aphorism that also opens the door to a similar restrictive understanding of Deut 6:4 on the love of God.

The purpose of Jesus's reversing of the terms in the lawyer's question about the neighbor resides exactly here: there is no categorical limit to the term "neighbor," as there is, axiomatically, no limit to the term "love." To love God and to love the neighbor are the two sides of an integral paradigm. God is "my God" when he is loved, but not, for example, when I posit his existence philosophically. The neighbor is "my neighbor" when he or she is loved as such but not, for example, when I apply a diacritical judgment on who does—or does not—fulfill a preconceived definition. Accordingly, only Jesus's reversing of the question's content into, "Who proved to be a neighbor?" is able to convey the fundamental intent of the Leviticus text. My neighbor is anyone and everyone who needs to be cared for, comforted, confirmed, and shown mercy. Jesus's understanding "explodes" the parameters of the interpretation of Lev 19:18. Who, for that matter, does not need the care of others? Thus, in Jesus's conception of the law, compassionate "neighboring" is wrought in favor of someone who is always "wounded." It falls to the one who would be a neighbor to acknowledge and respond to another human in distress. At this point, what Emmanuel Levinas says of the human face must be remembered: it bears the supplication, "do not kill me!"

Apart from the victim, only one character in the parable is not a killer: the Samaritan. All others, and they might include by analogy the lawyer, whose concern is to justify himself, contribute to the mugging of the victim. For not to be a killer means infinitely more than just "passing by on the other side." The bystanders, including the behind-the-kitchen-curtains peepers, are also among the killers. "Thou shalt not kill [commit murder]" is no exhortation to passivity. It takes a whole life not to kill, much less to even get "angry with a brother or sister" (Matt 5:22).

In this parable, the priest and the Levite personae serve as foils. They "kill" the wounded man, if only by neglect, by their refusal to help him. This is the veritable motive for the story's specification that the highway hoodlums left their victim "half-dead" (*hēmithanē*). What is intended is not just the possible confusion with a corpse, but rather that the priest and the Levite virtually give a fatal blow to the half-dead man.[189] For them, not

---

189. In this staggering story told by Jesus, it is made clear that "the law kills"—lit-

to "come near" (*proselthōn*) and to "pass by" (*antiparēlthen*) abets and aids the thugs. As far as the man left bleeding in the ditch is concerned, any distinction between the muggers and the nonhelpers is irrelevant; both groups stand to rob him of his life.

There is also an eschatological dimension to the parable of the good Samaritan, as indirect as it may appear. The radicalization of the divine law, on the one hand, and the hermeneutic opposition to the establishment personified by the priest and the Levite, on the other hand, make, as I said above, the parable implicitly christological. Again, Jesus's interpretation of Scripture is no academic stance, on a par with other possible interpretations. The reader knows—if the lawyer does not—that Jesus's teaching will cost him his life.[190] There is in Jesus's life no hiatus between "theory" (or storytelling) and "practice" (or the existential actualization of the conviction). He is from start to finish the neighbor par excellence. At times, his disciples must take him aboard a boat to spare him the pressure of the crowd (see Luke 5:1–3). At other times, he feels exhausted by the demands placed on him (see Luke 8:45–46). His life will not be taken from him, but eventually, he will offer it, thus becoming the ultimate and perfect "neighbor" of Jews and gentiles alike.

In summary, Jesus's hermeneutics does not allow the law to remain merely a law! It does, so to speak, take exception with the mere translation of *torah* by *nomos*. Torah, for Jesus, is never merely a legal apparatus. The rabbinic explication of torah as a corpus of 613 commandments and prohibitions is, in spite of appearances, reductionist. The torah qua law demands its own transcendence. The love of the neighbor is no less absolute than the love of God. As the latter is all-inclusive, so the former embraces all humans, even those called enemies. Not exclusive in its object, the torah is not exclusive either in its subject. Anyone, even a Samaritan, is able to accomplish the will of God. This tolls the end for all elitism.[191]

---

erally! (2 Cor 3:6). Leenhardt ("La Parabole du Samaritain," 133) writes: "Those two 'absent' men, who have killed their presence as well as God's, are also murderers as regards the stricken man, whom in turn they render absent."

190. In the parable itself, as Gollwitzer stresses, the last question addressed by Jesus to the lawyer ("Which of these three?") squarely puts the victim at center stage (*Das Gleichnis vom barmherzigen Samariter*, 59).

191. At Qumran, for instance, the covenanters are invited to love the sons of light and to hate the sons of darkness: 1QS 1:9–10; cf. 2:24; 5:25; 1QM 1:1.

5. JESUS AND TORAH 129

Put negatively, this means that no one is "my neighbor" whom I do not turn into a neighbor by my neighboring care. The Samaritan of the parable has made of "the wounded man" his neighbor by being neighborly to him.

Note that Luke 10:25–28 parallels Mark 12:28–34 and Matt 22:34–40.[192] Remarkably, the scribe/lawyer in both pericopes appears to have a penetrating mind. In Mark, for instance, he is praised by Jesus, who tells him that he is "not far from the kingdom of God." Strikingly common to both pericopes is the summary of the law that is given. In Mark, it is Jesus who utters it; in Luke, the lawyer. More important still is that for both, the issue is the understanding of the law, and in both narratives there is a similar insistence on the centrality of love. A significant corollary is that the love of God and the love of neighbor are two sides of the same coin. Jesus uses a trope called *gezera shawa*, that is, he brings together two different texts for mutual interpretation, based on the presence in both of key words, such as "and you shall love." The scribe must understand that the commandment of love supersedes the commandments governing the sacrifice ritual. Logically, once both parties agree on the summary of the law, Luke 10 addresses the theme: "Who is my neighbor?"[193]

---

192. See Matt 7:12, a parallel also drawn by Adolf Jülicher (*Die Gleichnisreden Jesu*, 2nd ed. [Tübingen: Mohr Siebeck, 1910 (1888)], 2:196). Jülicher seems to have been the first to sunder dialogue and parable here, because he feels unable to reconcile logically the lawyer's question (v. 29) and Jesus's answer (v. 37); so do Erich Klostermann, *Das Lukasevangelium*, 4th ed. (Tübingen: Mohr Siebeck, 1975); Rudolf Bultmann, who sees a discrepancy between the two parts of the Lukan text (*The History of the Synoptic Tradition*, trans. John Marsh [Oxford: Blackwell, 1968], 192); Wilhelm Michaelis, *Die Gleichnisse Jesu*, 3rd ed. (Zurich: Zwingli-Verlag, 1963); Gollwitzer, *Das Gleichnis vom barmherzigen Samariter*; Gerhard Schneider, *Das Evangelium nach Lukas*, 2 vols. (Gütersloh: Mohn, 1977); Joseph Schmid, *Das Evangelium nach Lukas* (Regensburg: Pustet, 1955)—against T. W. Manson, *The Sayings of Jesus* (London: SCM, 1949). See also Geoffrey Eichholz, *Jesus Christus und der Nächste*, BibS(N) 9 (Neukirchen-Vluyn: Neukirchener Verlag, 1953), 9, quoted by Gollwitzer, *Das Gleichnis vom barmherzigen Samariter*, 37. The reworking of Mark 12:28–31 in Luke 10 is rejected by Joseph A. Fitzmyer (*The Gospel According to Luke (x–xxv)*, AB 28A [Garden City, NY: Doubleday, 1985], 877); but is defended by Robert Funk and Roy Hoover, eds., *The Five Gospels: The Search for the Authentic Words of Jesus* (San Francisco: HarperSanFrancisco, 1997), 323.

193. First-century CE Judaism was interested in pinpointing the core of the torah. The summaries given by Paul (Rom 13:10; Gal 5:14), and the "Golden Rule" given by Rabbi Hillel testify to it, "What you hate, do not do to any one" (Šabb. 31a; cf. Tobit

If the lawyer accepts the lesson ("go and do like [the Samaritan]"),[194] he has no choice but to cease being preoccupied with his own purity and with his anxiety to determine who qualifies as his neighbor, and instead turn toward the suffering of others, all those human beings, Jews and gentiles, whose faces beg, "do not kill me!"

4:15; Philo, *Hypothetica* 2.63–64; 7.6: "What someone hates to experience, he should not do"). See, from late BCE, T. Iss. 5:2; 7:6; T. Dan 5:3 (cf. T. Benj. 3:3–4).

194. Schalom Ben-Chorin writes (*Brother Jesus: The Nazarene through Jewish Eyes*, trans. Jared S. Klein and Max Reinhart [Athens: University of Georgia Press, 2001], 85), "The unprecedented provocation that this exhortation represents becomes clear only when one grasps that an expert in scriptural law is being challenged to take a Samaritan as his model and to behave accordingly—in other words, to learn from *him* the proper meaning of Torah."

6
Jesus and Moses

This book seeks to understand what can be retrieved of the historical Jesus; this does not always jibe with what the gospel writers thought of him. At no point, for instance, does Jesus claim to be Moses redivivus. However, the gospel brings Moses and Jesus together, and clearly the conjunction of the two imposed itself on the disciples. Sometimes texts are rather subtle and the name of Moses does not necessarily appear in them, although he serves as a model. With Paul Achtemeier, mention must be made of Jesus's feeding of the five thousand, in parallel with the manna in the desert (Mark 6:30–44). More indirectly, Moses's profile is visible in Jesus's feeding the crowd in imitation of the Red Sea crossing leading to the feeding miracle, possibly mediated through the first wonder reported of Elisha as a water miracle (2 Kgs 2:12–14; cf. 2:8–10 [Elijah]).[1] Let us note at this point that, according to Jewish tradition, the manna belongs to the world to come, so in John 6:32 and in other documents: 2 Bar. 29.8; Qoh. Rab. 1.28; Mek. 6.1 (on Exod 19.2); Hag. 12b. (In John 6:35 the manna is Jesus himself.)

In fact, Jesus as miracle worker was expected to be "like Moses." Harald Sählin says that, according to 1 Cor 10:1–2 and Rom 6:3–4, Christ's death and resurrection have the "same meaning for the Church as the crossing of the Red Sea has for Israel."[2]

Of Jesus casting Moses's shadow during his ministry, the New Testament provides two striking examples: Jesus delivering the Sermon on the Mount, and the scene of the transfiguration. In what follows, I shall

---

1. Paul Achtemeier, "The Origin and Function of the Pre-Marcan Miracle Catenae," *JBL* 91 (1972): 202–5.
2. Harald Sählin, "The New Exodus of Salvation according to St Paul," in *The Root of the Vine: Essays in Biblical Theology*, ed. Anton Fridrichsen (New York: Philosophical Library, 1953), 82–83.

expound on these two features and argue for a more hidden presence of Moses in Jesus's portrait in the gospel.

The Sermon on the Mount[3]

We saw the decisive role the confrontations with the "Pharisees" played during Jesus's ministry. A major problem was a hermeneutic one. Jesus's halakic interpretation differed from other teachers', but he never denigrated "the subjects themselves."[4] For him, Moses is the great lawgiver, the veritable founder of Israel's religion. He is the "author" of the torah that is called *torat moshe*, or in the Greek of the New Testament *nomos Mōuseōs*. His torah is normative; hence Jesus quotes Deut 6:4–5 and Lev 19:18 in Mark 10:28–34 and parallels as constituting a powerful summary of the law.[5] The debate about the proper respect for the Sabbath day, on the plucking of grain on the Sabbath in spite of Exod 20:10 and Deut 5:14 (or again m. Šabb. 7:2), and on the role of the altar in the temple are matters of interpretation.[6] Jesus reacts against a rigid understanding of the torah's letter. He thus places himself in the wake of the prophets, particularly Jer 7:21–26; Hos 6:6; Amos 5:21–24; Mic 6:6–8.[7]

We shall note in passing Jesus's use of the rabbinic exegetical rule called *qal wahomer* (from a "light" case to a "weighted, loaded" one). In Luke 13:15 and 14:5, Jesus's argument is based on a *qal*: the Sabbath for the scribes is inviolable, but they make provisions in case of animals in danger or of a major loss if an animal would perish through negligence of the owner (m. Šabb. 18:1; Šabb. 128b). The *homer* is passing from an animal to

---

3. I refer the reader, of course, to ch. 5, "Jesus and Torah," above, 71–130.

4. Craig A. Evans, "The Misplaced Jesus: Interpreting Jesus in a Judaic Context," in *The Missing Jesus: Rabbinic Judaism and the New Testament*, ed. Bruce Chilton, Craig A. Evans, and Jacob Neusner (Leiden: Brill, 2002), 18.

5. Other summaries can be found in T. Iss. 5:2; 7:6; T. Dan 5:3; Philo, *Virt.* 51.95; *Spec.* 2.63; *Abr.* 208. Note that even the sitting position of Jesus on the side of the mountain (Matt 5:1–2) corresponds to "Moses sat" in Exod 23:2.

6. On the respect for the Sabbath, see Mark 3:1–6; Luke 14:1–6; John 5:9–17; 7:22–24; 9:14–16. On plucking grain: Mark 2:23–28. On the altar: Matt 5:23–24. The law of restitution in Matt 5:23–26 is affirmed in t. B. Qam. 10:18; B. Qam. 110a; cf. Sipra 68 (texts provided by Jacob Neusner, "Contexts of Comparison: Reciprocally Reading Gospels' and Rabbis' Parables," in Chilton, Evans, and Neusner, *The Missing Jesus*, 45–68).

7. See also Sir 7:8–9; 34:18–19; m. Pesaḥ. 3:7; Philo, *Mos.* 2.107–108.

a human being. The same a fortiori rule is illustrated in Matt 12:1–8; Mark 2:23–28; and Luke 6:1–5, about the plucking of the grain sheaves. The *qal* is what King David did in Nob; the *homer* is based on the principle that "the Son of Man is lord of the Sabbath"—hence implicitly, someone greater than David or Moses.[8] The *qal* may also be found in the Sabbath activity of temple personnel whose sacred duty supersedes scribal laws on the Sabbath; but the Son of Man is even greater than the temple (the Sabbath is *qal*, the temple is *homer*). There is, besides, no violation of the Sabbath by healing someone, according to Šabb.128a and t. Šabb. 9.[9]

Since we are evoking the rabbinics, let us proceed to the talmudic Hag. 12a, in which the primordial light shone before—but not after—Adam's sin. It shone again, however, with the gift of the torah to Moses and will shine again in the days of the messiah (see Gen. Rab. 2.3). In John 1:9, 17, nevertheless, the definitive light is in Jesus, not in Moses. Moses has been the mediator of the covenant, says T. Mos. 1:14; 3:12. He was "sent" (*shalah*), and thus became a *shaliah* (*apostolos*, a prophet).[10] Jesus also is "sent" (*apostellein*, e.g., John 3:17, 34; 5:36, 38). As the people murmured against Moses, so people murmur against Jesus (John 6:31–32, 35, 41, 43, 48, 51–56, 61).

---

8. It is self-evident that the setting of the alleged Pharisaic opposition, in the midst of a grain field on a Sabbath day, does not make sense. So the pericope of Mark 2:23–28 might well be a Markan invention. At any rate, it doubtlessly reflects the subject of conflict between two conceptions of the Sabbath. From this point of view, the physical setting becomes irrelevant. On the "event" of Jesus being superior to Moses, see John 6:32. Strikingly, Abraham Abulafia (thirteenth century CE) thought of himself as superior to Moses. In his *Sefer hahaftarah*, he writes, "Innovate a new Torah," a more spiritual one, conducive to mystical experiences. The point is to "know the supreme name" (See Moshe Idel, *Messianic Mystics* [New Haven: Yale University Press, 1998], 307).

9. One may be surprised by Jesus's argument regarding David at Nob (in Matt 12:1–8 // Mark 2:23–28 // Luke 6:1–5). But according to Menaḥ. 95b (which, incidentally, justifies David in this episode), though a biblical text may not be supplied as a *re'ayah* ("proof"), yet it may supply a *zeker* ("allusion"), as when it is said that Abraham, after ten years without heir coming from Sarah, took Hagar, a sign that a husband in such conditions should take a second wife, say the rabbis.

10. See Exod 3:10, 13, 14, 15; 4:28; 7:16; Deut 34:11; John 12:49 // Num 16:28; Sipre Deut. 5 (on Deut 1:6).

The Transfiguration (Matt 17:1–8 // Mark 9:2–8 // Luke 9:28–36)

Even before Jesus, Elijah's life pattern, as recorded in the Hebrew Bible, follows that of Moses. The prime example is the famous climbing of Mount Horeb (Sinai; see Exod 3:1–6) in 1 Kgs 19, where Elijah benefits from a theophany comparable with that of Moses. In both instances YHWH is "passing by" (1 Kgs 19:11–13 and Exod 33:19–23).[11]

On the mountain of the transfiguration, the disciples Peter, John, and James witness a conversation among Moses, Elijah, and Jesus. Such a threesome appears in Jewish literature only once, according to Neusner (Mid. Teh. on Ps 43),[12] citing Isa 42:1 as does also the gospel (see esp. Luke 9:35).[13] The motif of tents (Luke 9:33) recalls Ps 43:3 or the huts of Sukkoth (prospective day of deliverance).

This, by the way, takes us to the convenient list of parallel characteristics of the scene of the transfiguration and Mosaic texts drawn up by Craig Evans (he takes the text of Mark 9 as the basis):[14]

- "Six days" in Mark 9:2 // Exod 24:16.
- "A cloud overshadowed them" (Mark 9:7) // Exod 24:16.
- The voice of God coming from the cloud (Mark 9:2) // Exod 24:16.
- The threesome in Mark 9:2 // Exod 24:1–9.
- The twosome, Moses and Elijah; cf. Deut. Rab. 3.17 on Deut 10:1. Moses went to heaven (cf. Exod 19:3) in parallel with Elijah (cf. 2 Kgs 2:1).[15]
- Transformed appearance in Mark 9:3 // Exod 34:30.
- "They were terrified" in Mark 9:6 // Exod 34:30.
- In Exod 24:13, Joshua (// Jeshua/Jesus) goes up on the mountain with Moses.

---

11. Moses is called "the teacher of Elijah," see Pesiq. Rab., ch. 4.
12. From Yalkut Shim'oni to Ps 43.
13. The text refers specifically to Tg. Isa. 42:1. In the gospel, "that one" of the Isaianic text means Jesus.
14. Evans, "Misplaced Jesus," 104–5.
15. Adela Yarbro Collins says that in the first century CE, Moses, in parallel with Elijah, "was believed to have been taken up to heaven in bodily form" ("The Messiah as Son of God in the Synoptic Gospels," in *The Messiah in Early Judaism and Christianity*, ed. Magnus Zetterholm [Minneapolis: Fortress, 2007], 26).

- Peter offers to build *sukkoth*.

The figure of Moses soon became mythical.[16] In the Synoptics, Moses and Elijah speak with Jesus about his *exodos* ("departure") to Jerusalem (Luke 9:31). There is agreement among the gospels about the fate of Jesus, and this implicitly justifies the constant use of Scripture texts in the gospel. Everything is happening according to prophetic predictions in the Hebrew Bible.[17] This theme is further developed in John: the law is fulfilled (1:17). Even the brass serpent brandished by Moses to cure the serpents' bites in the desert, in fact, refers to the future Son of Man being elevated; the manna is superseded by "the true bread from heaven," that is, Jesus himself (6:32). Since Moses wrote of Jesus in the torah (John 1:45; 5:46), the rejection of Jesus leads Moses to be the accuser of "the Jews" before the Father (5:45).

Paul introduces the intriguing idea of a baptism "in Moses" (*eis Mōusēn*) in 1 Cor 10:2, a probable allusion to the crossing of the Sea of Reeds. The point is that gentiles, like Jews, can claim to be "in Moses," now that they are "in Christ" (cf. 12:13). In 2 Cor 3:7–8, Paul also uses a *qal wahomer* argument. This *qal* regards the veil on Moses's face after his encounter with God on Mount Sinai. The veil, says Paul, hid the passing splendor that Moses mirrored, but the dispensation of the Spirit is permanent (3:11). Jews have a veil over their minds, while Christians are unveiled, and they behold the glory of the Lord while being "changed into his likeness" (3:18). Such is the *homer*.

In Acts—as in John 5:45 (see above)—Stephen uses Moses as an indictment against those who reject Jesus. In doing so, they in fact reject Moses (Acts 7:2–53). In Hebrews, Jesus is superior to Moses, who was in God's house as a servant (3:5; cf. Num 12:7; Deut 34:5; Josh 12:7; 14:7) while Jesus is the son (3:6). In Heb 11:23, Moses must be emulated. In Revelation, angels sing "the song of Moses [Exod 14–15] and the song of the Lamb" (15:2–4). Moses similarly occupies a place of honor outside of the New Testament. In Qumran, for instance, the era of Moses is a model for the messianic age. Moses ascended three times to heaven, from the burning bush, from Mount Sinai and from Mount Nebo, where he visited with the messiah. In Philo, Moses is a "divine man," as we saw. As an inspired

---

16. As is clear in Jude 1:9 and 2 Tim 3:8. On what follows here, see Florence M. Gillman, "Moses," *ABD* 4:909–20.

17. Cf. Wilhelm Vischer, *Das Christuszeugnis des Alten Testaments* (Munich: Kaiser, 1934).

prophet, he declares what reason cannot understand (see *Mos.* II.2.3, 137). For Josephus also, Moses is a "divine man" who surpassed all men. He was a "soulful" man. In all his utterances, "one seemed to hear the speech of God himself" (*Ant.* 4.329). We find two striking ideas in the next document: T. Mos. 11. Moses was a "divine prophet for the whole world" (v. 16). "The whole world is his sepulcher" (v. 8). In Gen. Rab. 85, Moses is the first savior of his people, the forerunner of the messiah. He was raised among Israel's enemies, and so the messiah is raised in Rome.

We shall encounter additional mentions of Moses permeating the birth narratives of Jesus in Matthew and Luke. I thus refer the reader to the chapter on this theme, "The Birth Narratives" below (ch. 9, 183–92). Meanwhile, I shall turn to the (quasi-)identification of John the Baptist with Elijah redivivus, but perhaps more subtly with Aaron. John is priest (Luke 1), and he preaches in the desert (Mark 1; Luke 3; Matt 3). He is a prophet (Mark 6:15, in reference to Deut 18:15, 18; see Luke 1:76; 9:8; John 6:14; Acts 3:22–23).

The Gospel of Matthew

For this purpose let us turn to a characterization of Matthew's Gospel. As noted earlier, the Gospel of Matthew is prominently inspired by texts of the Scriptures. It uses the verb "fulfill" sixteen times, especially to introduce prophecies of the Hebrew Scripture that Jesus "accomplishes" (*pleroō*). This is typical of the so-called Matthean fulfillment theology.

Written approximately in 80–90 CE in Antioch or in Galilee, the gospel's opening genealogy goes back to David and Abraham and ties it with the Hebrew Scripture. Matthew divides his *euangelion* into five discourses of Jesus, which correspond to the Pentateuch and the book of Psalms (Matt 5–7; 10; 13; 18; 24–25). He refers to the LXX—especially with the motif of Jesus fulfilling the Bible—some fifty times. He credits his audience with knowledge of Palestinian topography; he never situates the locations he speaks about, nor explains national mores. The parallels he draws between John the Baptist and Elijah (also Aaron) and between Jesus and Moses are striking. Let us note that the binding together of Moses, Aaron, and Elijah is especially characteristic as regards the midrash.[18] Jesus's baptism

---

18. I refer to Josephus, *Ant.* 2.205–217; and to LAB 9.1–10; Tg. Ps. 5; Exod. Rab. 1.13; Seper hazikronot (of Elijah Levita [1468–1549]).

recalls the crossing of the Sea of Reeds; the scene of Jesus's temptation, the entry into the wilderness; and, with the Sermon on the Mount, Matt 5:1, the climbing of Sinai. During the temptation, Jesus fasts for forty days, in parallel with Deut 9:9; he is challenged to command the stones (see Num 20:8); and he is shown the kingdoms (see Deut 34:1; Moses saw only Canaan, however). At the end of his ministry, Jesus gives instructions to his disciples, on the model of Moses in Deut 32 (see v. 48; cf. Matt 10:1-2, 5-6; 11:23). Moses dies outside of the promised land, while Jesus dies in Jerusalem and only returns to Galilee after his resurrection.

All this and more shows Matthew's keen interest in the continuity of the early church with historic Israel. But, as John Meier rightly says, Matthew's church has a broken relationship with the synagogue (Meier refers to Matt 21:33-45 [the vineyard]; 22:1-14 [the wedding feast]; 23:3-36 [invectives, "woe to you"]; 27:25 ["blood on our heads"]).[19] For Matthew, the Jews' rejection of Jesus continues their endemic rejection of the prophets (in addition to the aforementioned texts, see 3:12; 5:20; 8:12). Regarding this latter point, it is important to note that Jewish sectarians claim association with the prophecy of old. This includes contemporary subversive groups of all kinds like the covenanters of Qumran, the sects behind 1 Enoch, the Psalms of Solomon, 4 Ezra, 2 Baruch, and others, and those who followed John the Baptist and Jesus. They are "the righteous," and they oppose "the sinners," "the lawless," and so on. A prophet-interpreter provides the proper understanding of the law of Moses. In 2 Bar. 84, Baruch is Moses redivivus, as Ezra in 4 Ezra 14. In the Jesus birth narratives, the parallels with Moses are omnipresent. Jesus is, here also, Moses redivivus. Roughly half of the fulfillment citations of Matthew are concentrated in this narrative, so we shall meet many of them when we turn to the special section on this topic. Both heroes' births were dramatic. Herod duplicated the pharaoh's attempt at killing the infants (Matt 2:13; Exod 2:15). Joseph and his family return to Israel from Egypt "because it is now safe." Moses also returned to Egypt when assured of his safety (Matt 2:19-21; Exod 4:19-20). Further, both Moses and Jesus are "saviors" of their people.[20] Most important, Jesus is Moses's true interpreter (see in particular the

---

19. The preceding development is indebted to John P. Meier. See his *Companions and Competitors*, vol. 3 of *A Marginal Jew: Rethinking the Historical Jesus*, ABRL (New York: Doubleday, 2001), 32.

20. Jesus is adamant about his role being limited to the "twelve tribes of Israel"!

controversies regarding the respect of the Sabbath and the rules of purity and especially Matt 12 and 15).

*

I have mentioned the sectarian environment of the Jesus movement. The fact is that, while divided and exclusive toward each other, the sects were unanimous in their rejection of contemporary powers—one remembers that Moses also had been considered as a rebel by the Egyptian pharaoh. The leadership then, and now, was corrupt.[21] This brings us to wonder, Who were the people who attended the trial of Jesus before the Sanhedrin and before Pilate? And first, we may wonder about the composition of the Sanhedrin in Jesus's time. We know that, from the time of Queen Salome Alexandra (78–68 BCE), the Sanhedrin was composed of Sadducees (chief priests) and of scribes (that is, Pharisees); see Josephus, *Ant.* 13.408–418 (// *J.W.* 1.110–114; but neither text mentions the Sanhedrin). At any rate, the Pharisees' dominance came to an abrupt halt with the death of the queen. True, *Ant.* 13.17, 288, 296–300, as well as the Talmuds (see m. Sanh.), attribute the leadership at the time to the Pharisees, but this is probably anachronistic. Josephus leads one to think that the chief priests were always the mediating body standing between the Romans and the Jewish populace. They, however, consulted with "the best-known Pharisees" in case of emergency.[22] They must keep order in the temple (Acts 4–6; 23) and in society in general. According to the Mishnah, the composition of the Sanhedrin

---

21. On this, see J. Andrew Overman, *Matthew's Gospel and Formative Judaism* (Minneapolis: Fortress, 1990), ch. 1. The temple personnel's corruption justified the Essene withdrawal into the desert. In a much slower-moving time compared to ours today, some 150 years had elapsed since the high priest Menelaus and the Tobiads had initiated and sustained the religious persecution, generally charged against Antiochus IV (167 BCE). First Maccabees, which reports those events, was written ca. 100 BCE. The circumstances, thus created, left scars (Martin Hengel speaks of "a severe 'collective trauma' ... and this had a decisive influence on the further course of Jewish history," in *Judaism and Hellenism: Studies in their Encounter in Palestine during the Early Hellenistic Period*, trans. John Bowden (Philadelphia: Fortress, 1974), 305. Even down to the Middle Ages, historian Barbara Tuchman writes, "120 years ago was but yesterday insofar as change was expected" (*A Distant Mirror: The Calamitous Fourteenth Century* [New York: Ballantine, 1978], 476).

22. See E. P. Sanders and Margaret Davies, *Studying the Synoptic Gospels* [London: SCM; Philadelphia: Trinity Press International, 1989], 406; see also 441, 444, 315.

was seventy to seventy-two members, but its structure, its powers, and its membership "probably varied with political circumstances.... Diversity and change in Palestinian Jewish life must constantly be kept in mind."[23]

So, if we proceed by elimination (probably partial, I imagine), only Sadducees and some mean-spirited (although "best known" according to Josephus) Pharisees are to be considered as in attendance at Jesus's trial. All the Essenes and the Zealots, the Qumran covenanters and others of the same mind would scorn the authorities involved. The same applies to many contemporary and out-of-favor Pharisees.[24] Thus the crowd dwindles, and when we consider that three-quarters of Israel was already living in the Diaspora, the vociferous mob is hardly representative of "the Jews"! The subsequent persecution of early Christians by *Jewish leaders*—at the exclusion of the Romans—shows that their role in the condemnation of Jesus is authentic.

---

23. Anthony Saldarini, "Sanhedrin," *ADB* 5:979.
24. Let us note that the Pharisees largely disappear from the last chapters of the gospels and play virtually no role in the trial of Jesus (Matt 27:62 and John 18:3 being exceptions).

7
JESUS AND ISRAEL

What has been said of Jesus and the torah applies as well to the relationship of Jesus with his people. The Israel *kata sarka* ("according to the flesh"), of which Paul speaks in his epistles and to which he himself belongs by birth and by choice, incarnates a promise of its own transfiguration "at the end." Historic Israel acknowledges itself to be only the shadow of things to come: the temple, for instance, will be glorified; the land will be Eden restored; Jerusalem will see all its children and all nations coming in to be blessed.

Israel *kata sarka*, therefore, is a reality striving toward its own supereminence, like a chrysalis awaiting its metamorphosis. Here once again Israel, as we saw about the torah, oversteps all limits established by birth. Glorified Israel enfolds all creation, starting with all the nations. Paul concludes: "You are all sons of God.... There is no such thing [any longer] as Jew or Greek, slave or freeman, male or female, for you are all one in Christ Jesus" (Gal 3:26–28). Israel must first regain its promised fullness: the twelve tribes must be regathered, after being dispersed under the Assyrian onslaught and the deportation of the northern tribes, followed by the Babylonian exile of the Judeans. Thus Jesus gathers twelve apostles, who represent the eschatological Israel (see also Ezra 6:17 and, for a comparable reconstitution in Qumran, 1QS 8:1). The advent of the kingdom of God is first and foremost for Israel's restoration to the fullness of its nature—as it was given, according to the rabbis, before the creation of the universe.

In this regard, Jesus's selection of twelve "apostles" (missionaries) is symbolically decisive. Remarkably, the word *mathētēs* ("disciple") does not appear in the LXX, the Apocrypha and Pseudepigrapha, Qumran, and so on. A parallel, however, is found among the rabbis, where disciples of the sages share many a characteristic with Jesus. Shaye Cohen writes, "They would live, eat, sleep, and travel with [the sage].... There was little privacy for either party in this relationship.... In effect, joining a disciple circle was like joining a new family (cf. Mark 3:32–35; 10:29–31)."[1] Jesus's call to discipleship rather resembles Elijah's appointment of Elisha, who must leave behind everything (see 1 Kgs 19:19–21). While a pupil of a rabbi attaches himself to a master by free choice, in the gospel, Jesus always takes the initiative. He addresses a peremptory imperative to a potential follower: Mark 1:16–20; 2:14; 10:17–22; Matt 8:21–22. Another characteristic is Jesus's warning the disciple of "the cost of discipleship" (Mark 8:35 and parr.; Matt 10:38–39; John 12:25; Luke 14:27). The chosen one becomes estranged from his family (see Mark 10:28–30 and parr.; Matt 10:37 // Luke 14:26; John 12:25. Jesus says that he brought "a sword of division"). The demand on the "missionary" parallels Jesus's very experience (Mark 3:20–35). The disciple's commitment is without parallel.[2] Noteworthy is the fact that Jesus selects his disciples from among the 'am ha'arets, not from the sages of the time. This already could only be seen as shocking.

Jesus expected fierce opposition to his doctrine, and this would have an impact on his disciples' welfare. By the way, this context of followers' call is one more warrant as to the authenticity of Jesus's repeated warnings about his tragic destiny. They are not *vaticinia ex eventu* set in Jesus's mouth by the early church. Jesus's frequent confrontations with scribes and Pharisees already belong to his eventual rejection and murder. When, on the cross, he said, "My God, my God, why have you forsaken me?" he meant a divine abandonment not just at that terrible moment but also since the beginning. The Jesus of the gospel is a tragic figure. The statement in Luke 7:31–35 according to which he "ate and drank [and danced]" must be understood as in contrast with John the Baptist's choice of asceticism (v. 33 // Matt 11:19). Jesus's story is the story of a "fall," in the sense of being progressively abandoned by all, including family and friends, and stripped of all protection until he is naked and nailed on a cross.

In summary, Jesus called twelve disciples to be *apostoloi*, which is an ad hoc term for a temporary function of missionaries (see Luke 6:13; Matt 4:18–22 // Mark 1:16–20; Luke 5:1–11). The earliest evidence of this call in the New Testament is 1 Cor 15:5 (a pre-Pauline formula), followed chronologically by Matt 19:28 (twelve thrones set to judge the twelve tribes; note

---

1. Shaye Cohen, *From the Maccabees to the Mishnah*, LEC 7 (Philadelphia: Westminster, 1987), 122.
2. Cf. Alan Culpepper, *The Johannine School*, SBLDS (Missoula, MT: Scholars Press, 1975), 225.

the absence of the figure in Luke; I shall come back to this below in chapter 12, "Jesus Is Betrayed," 211–16, for the important symbolism of the number twelve is emphasized in spite of the elimination of Judas). The names of the disciples are not identical in Matthew, Luke, and Mark (see Matt 10:2-4; Mark 3:16-19; Luke 6:14-16; Acts 1:13). It seems that Jesus spoke of there being twelve disciples, and the church tried to name them. "The 'Twelve' went by that title whether or not there were twelve of them."[3]

In the Synoptics, the Twelve (as a representation of Israel) are an extension of Jesus's person and mission.[4] They are sent to proclaim the approaching kingdom of God, with authority over demons and the ability to heal the sick (see, e.g., Mark 6:7, 12; Matt 10:7). Matthew 7:37-38 emphasizes the point: "The harvest is plentiful, but the laborers are few; therefore ask the Lord of the harvest to send out laborers into the harvest" (also Luke 10:2; cf. Mark 3:13-14).

This notion makes one think of the "remnant" in Scripture (see, e.g., Amos 3:12). In Mic 2:12, the remnant seems to include all Israel, but more specifically the twelve tribes (see also Isa 11:11-12). According to E. P. Sanders, no sect thought of God reducing Israel to the size of their group, but of regathering all Israel "under the covenant rightly understood."[5] He refers to Isa 49:6; 56:8, and others, and in postbiblical literature to 2 Bar. 4:37; 5;5; Sir 36:11; 48.10; 2 Macc 2:18; Pss. Sol. 11:2-7; 17:50; 1QM 2:2-3, 7-8; 3:13-14; 5.1; 11QTemple 18:14-16; 57:5-6; t. Sanh. 3:10. The regathering of the twelve tribes of Israel, promised by the prophets of old, is thus being fulfilled.

Jesus and the Pharisees

The gospels provide neither a definition of the term "Pharisee" nor the origins of Jesus's conflict with some of them. Likewise, the relative absence

---

3. Sanders, *Jesus and Judaism*, 101. Note that the same could be said of the twelve tribes of Israel in Scripture, where the lists vary and often include thirteen names (see Gen 46:8-27; 48:5-49:28; Num 1:1-43; 26:1-50). They are ten in Deut 33:6-29; 2 Sam 19:43; Jud 5:14-18. They are eleven in 1 Kgs 11:31. "There are more than twenty variant lists in the Old Testament.... The tradition of the twelve is maintained in most of the lists (Gen 35:22-26; Deut 27:12-13; 1 Chr 2:1-2; Ezek 48:1ff.)." See C. U. Wolf, "Tribe," *IDB* 4:698-701.

4. See Matt 10:40: "He who accepts you, accepts me, and he who accepts me accepts the one who sent me" (cf. Luke 10:16; Mark 9:37; John 13:20).

5. Sanders, *Jesus and Judaism*, 96.

in the gospel of other parties, like the Essenes and (in part) the Sadducees, reflects the situation after 70 CE. Note that the Johannine term "the Jews" refers mostly to the Pharisees. As noted above, Jesus takes meals with some of them (Luke 7:36; 11:37).[6] At times some Pharisees approve him (Luke 14:1–15; see 13:31); they are absent from the passion narratives,[7] and they respectfully bury his body.

The designation of the religious sects as "parties" comes from Josephus (see 103 n. 110). He saw them as philosophical schools and clearly over-compartmentalized them. Since he mentions Pharisees less than twenty times in his books, he considers them as playing a minor role in society of the time. He does credit the Pharisees, however, for trying to prevent the cessation of sacrifices for Rome in the temple and thus to thwart the revolt that would occasion its destruction by the Romans (see *Ant.* 13 and 18). Josephus is rather favorable to the Essenes, and his information about them became very important with the discovery of the Dead Sea Scrolls and their sectarian attribution.[8] As for the Sadducees, in *Jewish Antiquities*, he asserts that they controlled the high priesthood. This may be correct, especially from the beginnings of the Persian period until the Maccabean revolt. Josephus says that they rejected the Pharisaic tenet of the Oral Torah (*Ant.* 13.297), to which we shall return. But first let us note that, in Acts 23:6–8, Sadducees sit with Pharisees "in the council." We find a similar situation in both Mark and Matthew. Concurring with Josephus's analysis, rabbinic literature displays a sharp opposition between the two "parties," especially as regards the concepts of purity, civil law, and the Sabbath observance.[9]

---

6. As also with marginalized people (see Matt 26:6; Mark 14:3).

7. Unless we interpret Mark 15:1 as meaning that Pharisees came to the Sanhedrin in the morning of the day following the nightly pretrial.

8. Much of what we have learned about the "covenanters" agrees with the information provided by contemporaries like Philo and Josephus. Philo (*Prob.* 75) says that they do not sacrifice animals; Josephus says rather that they "perform their sacrifices among themselves" (*Ant.* 18.18–22). The Essenes put the accent on purity through frequent ablutions with a pure intent (1QS 3:4–9). Their communal meal is essential (1QS 6:3–5; Josephus, *J.W.* 2.128–133) since it has an eschatological dimension (1QSa 2:19–22). Their exclusivity (they even had a different calendar) accommodated their distinct asceticism and dualism.

9. On purity, see m. Yad. 4:6, 7; m. Nid. 4:2; so also in the Tosefta (from ca. 250 CE). On civil law, see m. Yad. 3:7; m. Mak. 1:6. On the Sabbath, see m. 'Erub. 6:1.

Other remarks by Josephus on the Sadducees may be of interest to us in this inquiry. The Jewish historian says of them that they are "more heartless" than the other Jewish parties (*Ant.* 20.199); their interpretation of the torah was literal, and socially they had the "confidence of the wealthy" (cf. *Ant.* 18.17 and ARN [A] 5). Their relationship with the priesthood is a moot question. Clearly, there were also Pharisees among the priests. The downfall of the Sadducees is not necessarily due to the destruction of the temple in 70 CE, but to their involvement in the war against Rome and the destruction of Jerusalem.[10]

To return to the Pharisees, they were a minority (some six thousand in the time of Herod, around the year 30 CE, according to Josephus, *Ant.* 17.2.42), but they enjoyed a real popularity, due to their piety and earnestness as well as to their lay composition. Paula Fredriksen is right to say that it is difficult to imagine them stalking Jesus everywhere and beleaguering him.[11] This conclusion, however, does not necessarily attribute their seeming omnipresence to anachronism. The "Pharisees" in the gospel often stand for a certain attitude. Thus this label indicates an umbrella concept covering a diversity of opinions. As such it allegedly finds a "justification" in the later historical controversy between early Christians and Pharisees. This distinction between earlier and later "Pharisees" is important.

The truth of the matter is that we know little about the first-century CE Pharisees. They are sometimes mentioned in rabbinic literature as *perushim* or *perushin* (meaning "separatists"). But the term is ambiguous, as it designates also other sectarians and even "heretics." On the Pharisees being opposed to the *ṣadduqim*, "Sadducees," see m. Yad. 4:6–8.[12] The Mishnah always sides with the Pharisees, but the number of cases is minimal.

The Pharisaic tenet is that, along with the written torah, there are venerable traditions, unwritten but originating from Moses (what was later called "Oral Torah"). These traditions govern the everyday behavior of the pious and explicate the rules of the torah. Jacob Neusner offers an attractive—but perhaps unsubstantiated—theory that the Pharisees were a

---

10. See Gary P. Porton, "Sadducees," *ABD* 5:892–95; and Anthony J. Saldarini, "Rabbinic Literature," *ABD* 5:602–4

11. See Paula Fredriksen, *From Jesus to Christ: The Origins of the New Testament Images of Jesus* (New Haven: Yale University Press, 1988), 106.

12. The Sadducees were mainly recruited in priestly and aristocratic milieus of Jerusalem. Typically, the only reported clash between Jesus and the Sadducees, in Mark 12:18–27 and parr., occurs in the Jerusalem temple.

group of people who extended the temple's rules of purity and holiness to everyday life. They ate their food in a state of ritual purity (Lev 19:2), "You shall be holy, for I, the Lord your God, am holy." At any rate, it seems clear that they were especially concerned with matters of purity with regard to food and its vessels,[13] contact with corpses and tombs,[14] the cult apparatus in the temple,[15] tithing,[16] the observance of Sabbath and holy days,[17] and marriage and divorce.[18]

The Pharisees were eager to convince the general populace to adopt their set of *halakot* ("rules"). In contrast to the Sadducees and the Qumranites, they were "democratic" in their approach, as was Jesus.[19] This explains in part their mutual opposition, since all three were trying to win the souls of the people. The Pharisees had quite a reputation for their strict interpretation of the torah, as testified by Josephus (see *Ant.* 13.297) and Paul (see Gal 1:13-14; Phil 3:6). A parade example is provided by the parenthetical remark in Mark 7:3, followed by Jesus's denunciation of these Pharisaic rules. Nevertheless, Jesus and the Pharisees stood on the same foundation of "Judaism." Their debates were legal and ethical, not doctrinal.

As I have just noted, both the Pharisees and Jesus were "democratic." This fact, as far as Jesus is concerned, is particularly well attested in texts like Luke 14:15-24, a parable on the invitation to a banquet. Jesus comes with the subversive idea of egalitarian commensality. John Dominic Crossan stresses this point.[20] On the microlevel, he says, the parable speaks of food; on the mesolevel, the common table; and on the macrolevel, society. "To subvert either of the former is a calculated attack on the latter.... Open commensality profoundly negates distinctions and hierarchies

---

13. See, e.g., Mark 7:1-23; Matt 23:25-26; m. 'Or. 2:12.
14. See Matt 23:27-28.
15. See, e.g., Matt 23:16-22; m. Ker. 1:7.
16. See Matt 23:23; m. 'Ed. 1:2.
17. See, e.g., Mark 2:23-28; 3:1-6; Luke 13:10-17; 14:1-6; John 5:1-18; 9:1-34; m. 'Erub. 6:2.
18. See, e.g., Mark 10:1-12 and parr.; m. Yad. 4:8; m. Giṭ. 9:10.
19. Some documents attributed to the Pharisees are conspicuously absent in the library of Qumran, like Psalms of Solomon, 1 Maccabees, Judith, and all of the pro-Hasmonean literature. This is all the more important since the extant scrolls were written by hundreds of different hands.
20. John Dominic Crossan, *The Historical Jesus: The Life of a Mediterranean Jewish Peasant* (San Francisco: HarperSanFrancisco, 1991), 263.

between female and male, poor and rich, Gentile and Jew."[21] Regarding commensality, he adds that it was "a strategy for building or rebuilding peasant community on radically different principles from those of honor and shame, patronage and clientage. It was based on an egalitarian sharing of spiritual and material power at the most grass-roots level."[22]

As the interpretation of the torah became a central issue after 70 CE, Jesus's earlier interpretation is of major interest to the historian in terms of being perhaps prodromic. As Amy-Jill Levine writes, we cannot

> suggest that Jesus simply recapitulates conventional sayings and deeds; to the contrary, had he not said or done some things that proved memorable, distinct or arresting, it is unlikely we would have records of his teachings. Nor, however, could he have been completely anomalous; were he so, he would have made no sense either to those who chose to follow him or those brought into the movement after his crucifixion.[23]

The core of the question was interpreting the torah's aim. What does the torah expect from Israel? Jesus answered: compassion. Love is the heart of the law; everything else is commentary. He quotes Hos 6:6, "For I desire steadfast love and not sacrifice." While the Pharisaic notion of obedience to the law is in part "introverted"—in the sense that it is geared to self-sanctification—compassion transcends all boundaries, since it is by its nature "extroverted" and thus all-encompassing. Anyone and anything can be its object. There is, of course, no way to accuse Pharisaism of ignoring compassion. The love of the neighbor set in parallel with the love of God constitutes the Golden Rule (acknowledged, e.g., by the lawyer in the parable of the Good Samaritan).[24] What Jesus apparently experienced was a gulf between theory and practice among those who are called "Pharisees." Taking this into account helps to realize that Jesus's critique applies to many more people than to "Pharisees"!

---

21. Ibid., 344.

22. Ibid.

23. Amy-Jill Levine, introduction to *The Historical Jesus in Context*, ed. Amy-Jill Levine, John Dominic Crossan, and Dale C. Allison (Princeton: Princeton University Press, 2006), 1.

24. See further Rabbi Aqiba on Lev 19:18 in Gen. Rab. 24.7 ("the greatest principle of the law").

Yet what kind of "Pharisaism" are we to imagine in the first century CE? There was a variety of religious stances under that umbrella.[25] In a less than scholarly argumentation, unfortunately, Harvey Falk produced an intriguing book title and with it a still more intriguing thesis: *Jesus the Pharisee: A New Look at the Jewishness of Jesus*.[26] The author focuses in his thesis on the severe clash in Jesus's day between the so-called house of Shammai and the house of Hillel. Falk is convinced that Jesus was a "Hillelite" in conflict with "Shammaite Pharisees" (deceptively called "the Pharisees" in the gospel). The fact is that, according to talmudic sources, the two "houses" clashed some 316 times in one century—let us note, however, that the late composition of the Talmuds relativizes the accuracy of Falk's conclusion. To his credit, all rabbinic sources insist on Shammai being strict at the extreme (see, e.g., Yoma 77b; Beṣah 16a).

In my opinion, Falk's argument would have been more aptly applied to the conflict between Pharisees and Sadducees. Most relevant for us is that the Sadducees apparently had the upper hand until the destruction of the temple in 70 CE. Their influence in the time of Jesus should not be ignored, although we know little about them prior to the Jewish revolution. Their role in the disastrous revolt of 66–70 against the Romans is reported in Josephus, *J.W.* 2.408–410. They shunned the opposition of the then high priests[27] and chief Pharisees (2.15.2–4 [§§315–324]). Their preponderance at that point is evident. They were virulently opposed to all non-Jews—but, more specifically, to the Romans. The Sadducees supported the leader of the revolt, Eleazar, governor of the temple (2.17.9).

---

25. Note that the case is far from unique. Nascent Christianity as well was multifaceted. Along with a "Hellenized" branch in the early church, we find more Jerusalem-oriented traditions. I concur with Christopher Tuckett's assessment of the source Q: "Certainly Q reflects a strongly conservative Jewish-Christian group within primitive Christianity" ("Q, the Law and Judaism," in *Law and Religion: Essays on the Place of the Law in Israel and Early Christianity*, ed. Barnabas Lindars [Cambridge: James Clarke, 1988], 100).

26. Harvey Falk, *Jesus the Pharisee: A New Look at the Jewishness of Jesus* (Mahwah, NJ: Paulist Press, 1985). The thesis is that Jesus was a Hillelite rabbi concerned with spreading Judaism among the gentiles. Thus he preached the adherence to the Noahide laws. By so doing he minimized the torah in its wholeness, which in fact applies only to Jews. The gentiles would have been crushed under the 613 commandments, so Jesus tried to make out of them the just of the nations.

27. The plural noun "high priests" designates the sacerdotal aristocracy; see Luke 23:13; Josephus, *J.W.* 6.111–117.

Although both Sadducees and Pharisees were members of the Sanhedrin, they were antagonists according to Acts 23:6, especially regarding the Pharisaic doctrine of the resurrection of the dead.[28] Josephus also insists on this divisive issue in *J.W.* 2.8.14 (§163), as does m. Sanh. 10.1. The Pharisaic concern with general resurrection indicates a vivid interest in eschatology. They were expecting the advent of "last days" with reward and punishment after death. Further, Paul shows that they expected the coming of a promised messiah, at which time the cosmic consummation of history would come. Meanwhile, Israel was to obey the law of the Lord in preparation for the great judgment.

Pharisees' opposition to the Sadducees is no fiction. In Acts 23:12, 20, 27; 24:9; 25:7, and other passages, the Sadducees want to kill Paul while the Pharisees want to save him. The high priest Ananias is among the Sadducees (see Acts 23:2; 24:1), who are in collusion with chief priests and elders—not with scribes, however, who were mostly Pharisees. It is a blatant exaggeration when Festus, the Roman procurator, says that the whole Jewish populace is against Paul (25:24), since the issue continued to be the resurrection of the dead. All this recalls the judicial procedure against Jesus, where Caiaphas the high priest and president of the Sanhedrin is also a Sadducee. In Matt 26:3, elders accompany him, but the scribes are absent. In Mark 14:1, however, they participated in the plot to kill Jesus. But we do know from Josephus that Pharisaic opposition helped to curb the Sanhedrin (*Ant.* 18.180).[29]

Let us note that, according to John, most of the Pharisaic activities occurred in and around Jerusalem, since they congregated in the capital. There is little attestation for their presence in Galilee in early first century CE. It may be that Jesus's clashes with them took place in Jerusalem when Jesus went there on pilgrimage. Galilee, as a matter of fact, constituted a separate province from more than one viewpoint. It had only been reintegrated into the Jewish pale, with Jerusalem as capital, under the Hasmoneans. Furthermore, no Roman army was stationed in Galilee during Jesus's time. Herod Antipas (*regnit* 4 BCE to 39 CE) ostensibly presented himself as a pious Jew, in spite of his illegal marriage with Herodias, the wife of his brother Philip (Matt 14:4) and the beheading of John the Baptist (Matt

---

28. The earliest reference to the doctrine of resurrection is in 1 Enoch 22–27 (ca. 164 BCE).

29. Furthermore, when Jesus proclaims the advent of the kingdom, he eliminates as a result the Sanhedrin and the high priesthood!

14:10). Caiaphas was then the high priest in the temple, and Pilate was Roman governor over the whole country from 26 to 36 CE; both played a major role in the death of Jesus.

How does this affect "the Jewishness of Jesus"? We remember that Falk tries to put a Pharisaic label on the teaching of Jesus. He presents examples of Jesus adopting a "Hillelite" stance. Matthew 12:9–14, for instance, shows Jesus healing a man on the Sabbath and being blamed by some for doing so. The latter, Falk says, were Shammaites (but, as I have said, why not rather Sadducees?). Furthermore, in Matt 15:5–9, Jesus protests a *qorban* ("sacred offer") that would impoverish the family of a man with good conscience. Such a criticism is valid only as regards a Shammaite stance on the matter (see b. Naz. 9a, according to a principle in b. Šabb. 127b that was held by the very conservative Rabbi Eliezer [a rabbi of the first century CE who preserved early legal traditions, y. Yebam. 3:3, 4d; for him, intention is not decisive, but action is, m. Ker. 4:3]).

As I mentioned earlier, Pharisees opposed the cessation of sacrifices on behalf of Caesar in the temple. On this score they again found themselves clashing with Sadducees. Below, in the section "Jesus and the Temple" (158–64), I shall expound on Jesus's "cleansing" of the temple by overturning the tables of the moneychangers in the Court of the Gentiles (Matt 21:12–13). To anticipate here this coming development, it is clear that a coalition of lower priests and Zealots, led by some upper-class priests and by the temple governor Eleazar ben Ananias (the high priest), who was headquartered in the temple, stopped offering sacrifices to Caesar (and thus were ultimately responsible for the destruction of the temple by the Romans, says Josephus). Then, Sadducees and Zealots colluded, since both forbade all intercourse with the Gentiles, as we saw above. Both parties loathed the Jews who collaborated with the Romans, such as tax collectors and customs collectors (m. B. Qam. 10:1; B. Qam. 113a; m. Sanh. 3:3; Sanh. 25b). Chances are that such an attitude was not novel on their part, and we can assume that Jesus encountered it during his ministry.

As could be expected, the Sadducees had no qualms about having the moneychangers sit in the Court of the Gentiles. Note that "Caiaphas had moved the vendors previously located on the Mount of Olives into the Court of the Gentiles."[30] Jesus declared, on the basis of Jer 7:11 and Isa

---

30. Amy-Jill Levine, *The Misunderstood Jew: The Church and the Scandal of the Jewish Jesus* (San Francisco: HarperSanFrancisco, 2006), 152–53; cf. Bruce Chilton, "Caiaphas" *ABD* 1:803–6, 805b.

56:7, that the temple should be a house of prayer for all nations, a stance that definitely favors the Pharisees, rather than the Sadducees.

More impressive, I believe, is m. B. Qam. 8:1 followed by b. B. Qam. 83b–84a, on the *lex talionis*. In y. B. Qam. 8:1, 6c, we read, "One who acts inadvertently pays money compensation." In the discussion that ensues, the conclusion is that money compensation applies in all cases. In B. Qam. Gemara 83b–84a, a lengthy discussion shows that nearly all the rabbis agreed about a monetary compensation for injuries to someone else.[31] The only dissident opinion mentioned comes from the same, all-demanding R. Eliezer, who states that the law of Exod 21:24–25 must be followed "literally"! It is within this perspective, I suggest—in spite of being expressed decades after Jesus—that Jesus tells his audience, "You have heard that it was said, 'An eye for an eye and a tooth for a tooth,' but I say to you ..." (Matt 5:38–39). What the people have heard is a strictly conservative voice.

After 70 CE, Beth Hillel prevailed in all decisions (see t. Yebam. 1:13; y. Ber. 1:3, 4b). The talmudic tradition is thus one-sided: *beth-Shammai bimeqom beth-Hillel eynah mishnah* (Ber. 36b; Beṣah 11b; Yebam. 9a). The modern use of its by now Hillelite interpretive texts should be made with caution.

The dispute between Jesus and the Pharisees, as we saw, boils down to the notion of *paradosis* ("tradition"): the one of the former and the other of the "elders."[32] In Matthew and Mark, Jesus says that the *paradosis* in question comes from humans, not from God (Mark 7:1–13; Matt 15:1–9; cf. Luke 11:37–52). Of course, this is not true for the written tradition in the Tanak, especially in the Torah. Against the background of a strict, meticulous observance of the commandments, Jesus's insistence on the unevenness in importance of biblical commandments and prohibitions is all the more intriguing.

This issue is highlighted in Matt 22:34–40, in the discussion on the "greatest commandment" (22:36). To recall, Jesus states that the core of the torah is love, and he combines Deut 6:5 and Lev 19:18, which merge the love of one's neighbor with the love of God. The former is the condition for

---

31. So, e.g., R. Dosthai b. Judah, R. Simon b. Yohai, the school of R. Ishmael, the school of R. Abbaye (273–335) and R. Hiyya (1065–1136).

32. See Josephus, *J. W.* 1.110; 2.162; *Life* 191; *Ant.* 17.41. See also Acts 26:5 ("strictest party"); 22:3.

the latter.³³ The Pharisees do not react to this in the Matthean text, but, in the Markan text, "one of the scribes" approves Jesus's summary and adds, "this is much more important than all whole burnt offerings and sacrifices" (12:33). We thus can assume that at least one type of Pharisee generally agreed with Jesus's insight. I would add that, although J. Andrew Overman's sociological analysis of the Matthean community is admirable, he might have overlooked the fact that the Pharisees were at that time involved in a *formative* Judaism. Thus the possibility exists that the Matthean interpretation of the law was not entirely a defensive argument but also an attempt to bring the "opponents" to accept Jesus's understanding and thus to influence the formation of what would eventually become "rabbinic" Judaism. Who knows whether texts such as m. 'Abot 3:10, m. Yoma 8:9, and Gen. Rab. 93.1,³⁴ which parallel Matt 5:41–48, have not been influenced accordingly. As Overman states, Jesus did not break the law; he broke with Pharisees over the interpretation of the law.³⁵

Moreover, Jesus's discussion of the torah's meaning is, at least to a certain extent, Pharisaic. Both he and they acknowledge the full authority of the torah. They only differ on its interpretation.³⁶ Consider Mark 2:21–22, which speaks of new cloth on an old cloak and new wine in old wineskins. This saying comes after Jesus has rejected the "Pharisees'" criticism that his disciples are not fasting (2:18–20; Gos. Thom. 104). Jesus says that the disciples do not fast while "they have the bridegroom with them." They will fast when "the bridegroom is taken away from them" (Mark 2:19–20). Ritual cannot supersede the dictates of actual circumstances. Rituals, like the Sabbath, are made for humans. Their virtue is flexibility. When Jesus celebrates his last Passover, for example, the gospel turns the festival into

---

33. See 1 John 4:20–21; Matt 7:12; 19:19; 24:12; 25:34–40. For Matt 23:28, one may be scrupulous in keeping the law and still be *anomos*: cf. 7:17; 12:33; 21:43.

34. Amy-Jill Levine and Marc Zvi Brettler, eds., *The Jewish Annotated New Testament* (Oxford: Oxford University Press, 2011), ad loc., provides these texts.

35. See J. Andrew Overman, *Matthew's Gospel and Formative Judaism* (Minneapolis: Fortress, 1990), 81. Cf. Jacob Neusner: "The Christian and rabbinic tradents around the destruction of Jerusalem exhibit much the same literary and formal tendencies" (*The Pharisees: Rabbinic Perspectives* [New York: Ktav, 1973], 186).

36. See Mark 10:2–9; Matt 5:39; Mark 2:26; and esp. Mark 7:14–15 (on purity and impurity). For Luke, the Pharisees are entitled to exegete the law; see Luke 7:36; 11:37; 13:31–33; 14:1; 17:20. See Christopher M. Tuckett, "Q (Gospel Source)," *ABD* 5:570. See also, in particular, Matt 22:23–32, where Jesus refutes the arguments of the Sadducees and assumes a Pharisaic position.

Yom Kippur![37] This is not a rejection of the Passover per se but a call to realize that there is a time for laughter and a time for tears. Jesus consistently affirms the supersession of life over ritual. The latter must always submit to existential imperatives. So, "if you remember that your brother or sister has something against you, leave your gift there before the altar and go; first be reconciled to your brother or sister, and then come and offer your gift" (Matt 5:23-24). Life always comes with "new cloth" or "new wine." The old cloak and the old wineskin are not *ne varietur*. At the extreme, Jesus says that "something greater than the temple is here" (Matt 12:6), "something greater than Solomon/Jonah is here" (Matt 12:41-42; Luke 11:31-32), and this "something" prophets and kings wanted to see (Matt 13:16-17; Luke 10:23-24). Whether or not this saying is authentic, its radicalism, which verges on blasphemy, cannot be lightly dismissed.

Another source of dispute is the accusation by some that Jesus thrived in the company of "sinners" (Mark 2:17 and parr.), a motif that is probably historical. Jesus uses the term "the poor"—although tax collectors were certainly not poor!—that is, the powerless (Matt 11:5 // Luke 7:22; 4:18 [also Isa 61:1-2]; 6:20 [were the disciples really wretched and famished? Here, the word "poor" is metaphorical]). As to "sinners," the term is highly derogatory. The Hebrew equivalent is *resha'im*, that is, the "wicked," and the term in the gospel depends on the interpretation one gives to it. *Resha'im*, normally, are heinous, unrepentant sinners. Behind this accusatory slur is the image of Jesus as "a glutton and a wine-bibber" (Matt 11:19; cf. Luke 7:34). But Jesus claims that his mission is precisely to "the lost" and "the sinners"—so he ironically adopted the terms used by his foes.

Sanders forcefully rejects the current confusion among New Testament scholars between "sinners" and *'amei ha'arets*, which is conducive to a grave misreading of the Jewish traditional literature. The rabbis of old called "wicked" the oppressors, not the oppressed. True, one can find in the literature here and there an expressed hostility between the learned and the unlearned (see, e.g., Pesaḥ. 49b). The *'amei ha'arets* are contrasted with the *haverim* (something like a right wing of the Pharisees) and the *hakamim* ("the learned ones"). But Sanders rightly contends that the unlearned are not thought of as "wicked." They are common people, who must be distinguished from "sinners."

---

37. See ch. 13 below, "The Trial of Jesus and His Passion," 217-38.

At this point, James Dunn is especially helpful.[38] He points out that any sect did and does call "outsiders" *hamartōloi* ("sinners"). This term is sometimes used as synonym for gentiles (Ps 9:17; Tob 13:8 [6]; Jub. 23:23–24; Pss. Sol. 1:1; 2:1–2; Luke 6:33 = Matt 5:47; Mark 14:41 and parr.; Gal 2:15). It designates those who are, from the standpoint of the sectarians, lawless. So, in Jubilees [ca. 100 BCE], those who observe a "wrong" calendar are considered nonobservant sinners (6:32–35; 23:16, 26; in 1 Enoch 89:73, all offerings in the temple were impure).[39] In 1 Enoch 82:4–7; CD 1:13–21; 1QS 2:4–5, for example, the Pharisees are the "sinners." In the Psalms of Solomon, the "sinners" are the Sadducees: they defile the temple, are hypocrites, and are impure (e.g., 4:1–8; 8:12); they have no part in Israel's inheritance. In the Testament of Moses (contemporary with Jesus's day), the sectarians say, "Do not touch me, lest you pollute me!" (7:3, 9–10).[40]

In spite of Josephus's declarations about the Pharisees' influence among the people before 70 CE,[41] it must be said, with Sanders again, that the Pharisees in Jesus's time had no power to effectively exclude any other group from the pale. Arguably, they never thought of denying salvation to those who did not belong to their party. But, if the "Pharisees" of the gospel were not able to exclude, they were able to despise. Of course, this

---

38. See James D. G. Dunn, *Jesus, Paul, and the Law: Studies in Mark and Galatians* (Louisville: Westminster John Knox, 1990), 61–88.

39. Further, as John J. Collins writes, "The notion of a priestly messiah [in Jubilees and Qumran literature] implies some dissatisfaction with the current High Priest and the operation of the temple cult" (*The Scepter and the Star: The Messiahs of the Dead Sea Scrolls and Other Ancient Literature* [New York: Doubleday, 1995], 95). See also 4QFlor, which arguably designates the Qumran community as an intermediary temple straddling that of Solomon, made desolate by foreigners, and the now eschatological "sanctuary of the Lord" (with reference to Exod 15:17). In 11QTemple 29:9, the temple described is "for an interim period" before the eschaton.

40. In his monumental three-volume *The Rabbinic Traditions about the Pharisees before 70* (Leiden: Brill, 1971), Jacob Neusner shows that 67 percent of the halakah deals with dietary laws, including purity for meals, which select who is in and who is out. According to Josephus, Pharisaic behavior is characterized as *akribeia* ("scrupulousness"). Paul also speaks of their *zēlos* ("zeal") and thus of their sense of superiority (esp. in Acts 22:3; Rom 2:17–20, 23; Gal 1:14; Phil 3:5–6 [texts provided by Dunn, *Jesus, Paul*, 73]).

41. Josephus, *Ant.* 18.12–15 (esp. 15) and 13.288. On the Pharisees' doctrines, *J.W.* 2.162.

does not reflect a flawed religion called "Judaism." Hypocrites and narrow-minded bigots are ever present among the religious and the nonreligious.

This point, however, should not be exaggerated.[42] During his ministry, Jesus actually confronted bigots from various religious sects, including, of course, Sadducees and Pharisees. (After his death, Christians would no doubt produce their own bigots.) This is not what brought him to the cross, but rather his commerce, shall we say, with "dubious characters,"[43] added to the unease many felt about him. But uneasiness is not necessarily hatred and bloodthirstiness. Other ingredients were needed to make of Jesus the threat that his opponents saw in him. I attempt to spell out the crucial ingredient in chapter 15, "The Great Cry of Jesus on the Cross," below (147–61). This, I contend, is more credible in its determination than other suggestions.[44]

The centrality of Jesus as God's kingdom on earth is the crucial point. He thus "forces" an option that supersedes the fifth commandment (Matt 8:21–22 // Luke 9:59–60: the man who would first bury his father before following Jesus). His presence as "bridegroom" also supersedes the law on fasting (see Lev 16:29, and then Mark 2:19 and parr.). In John 15:3, Jesus says, "Already you are pure through the word that I have spoken to you." The same is suggested in Jesus's declaration to one of those who

---

42. It is an exaggeration, e.g., to state, "We cannot find, in the question of ritual purity, the source of a conflict with Jewish leaders" (Sanders, *Jesus and Judaism*, 210). If it is not the source, then it is arguably a source, as Luke 11:37–41 and Matt 23:25–26 attest.

43. I was about to write "outcasts," but the term is too often misunderstood. Tax collectors, e.g., cast themselves out as "[people] who violate the welfare of the community," as Levine and Brettler say in *The Jewish Annotated New Testament*, 503. They appear with "sinners" in the gospel (Luke 18:10). As regards the gentiles, Jewish elders recommend a centurion to the care of Jesus (Luke 7:1–10)!

44. An example is the emphasis on the word order "forgiveness–repentance" rather than "repentance–forgiveness" (as is usual in biblical and Jewish tradition in general). Another example is Sanders's theory that Jesus did not require repentance at all (*Jesus and Judaism*, 206; see my remarks in ch. 5, "Jesus and Torah" above [71–130]). The nugget of truth in this statement is that the touchstone for salvation was now heeding Jesus, whether formally repenting or not. Note the parallel with Paul concluding that gentile sinners (Gal 2:15) did not need to become proselytes through circumcision, but their acceptance of Jesus would suffice. Yet their conversion required them to become blameless and keep the whole law—or is it the Noahide rules? (e.g., 1 Thess 3:13; 5:23)—and this sheds some doubt on Sanders's exoneration of repentance and restitution (see his *Jesus and Judaism*, 283).

was crucified with him, "Today, you will be with me in paradise" (Luke 23:43), that is, without any other merit than to have recognized Jesus as the central Jew.

Jesus's opposition to Pharisees turns amazingly harsh in Matt 23. Indiscriminately, all Jewish teachers are declared murderers (vv. 29–39), hypocrites (vv. 13–15, 23, 25, 27, 29), blind guides and fools (vv. 16, 24), as well as corrupt and lawless (v. 28).[45] Such rhetoric is not unique. Jesus, as prophet, follows in the line of Amos and Hosea. Furthermore, his outburst of invectives betrays the "dangerous" attraction to the "scribes and Pharisees" of the early Christians. This attraction, by the way, continued through at least the fourth century CE. The number of patristic *Adversus Judaeos* writings testifies to this continuation. These caricatures, notwithstanding, become perilously anti-Semitic and even lethal. As far as Matthew is concerned, however, they amount to a kind of Oedipal rebellion against a parent group. Besides, Matt 23 starts by acknowledging that the scribes and Pharisees are "sitting upon the seat of Moses!" This sounds like legitimating their leadership (vv. 2–3), but the praise is only for what they say, not what they do. While scribes and Pharisees bind heavy burdens on others (v. 4), they are content to receive honors at parties (v. 6). All the same, the kinship between the doctrines of Jesus and the Pharisees deserves emphasis. As David Flusser writes, "Jesus was sufficiently Pharisaic in general outlook to consider the Pharisees as true heirs and successors of Moses.... [Jesus's] moral beliefs are similar to the Pharisaic school of Hillel which stresses the love of God and neighbor."[46]

Andrew Simmonds has brilliantly discussed Jesus's use of this literary device against his adversaries in his essay "'Woe to You ... Hypocrites!' Rereading Mt 23:13–36."[47] Jesus is, he says, censuring by means of pretended praise. Each "woe" starts with a positive statement, immediately followed by a negative one. The whole series follows four controversies: Matt 21:23–27 (Jesus answers a question with another question); 22:15–

---

45. See in the same vein, Jer 9:1–8; T. Levi 10:3; 14:4–6; 16:2–4; Liv. Pro. 3:15; 15:6; 16:3; 2 Bar. 25–30; 4 Ezra 7:22–24. The hypocrites are associated with the killers of prophets. I add y. Ber. 9:5, 14c, which lists five negative types of Pharisees and only two types of positive ones.

46. David Flusser, "Jesus," *Encyclopedia Judaica*, ed. Cecil Roth, 16 vols. (Jerusalem: Keter, 1972), 10:13.

47. Andrew Simmonds, "'Woe to You ... Hypocrites!' Rereading Mt 23:13–36," *BSac* 166 (July–Sept 2009): 336–49.

22 (Jesus evades the question and has a coin give the answer); 22:23–33 (Jesus rebukes the Sadducees on the issue of resurrection); 22:34–40 (Jesus challenges Pharisees on the greatest commandment). The principle is to demonstrate that the opponents condemn themselves through their own speech and action. For instance, they "absurdly admitted that they are the descendents of those who killed the prophets … [but] they require *their own* new prophets to kill and persecute, both to satisfy their own perversity and to carry on their family tradition."[48]

The number of occurrences in the gospel of the issue of Sabbath shows that the break between Jesus and the Pharisees is particularly evident regarding the interpretation of this commandment. Jesus's "violation" of the Sabbath is frequently criticized by the Pharisees. The issue for them is the contextual absence of urgency. Jesus's healings on the Sabbath could have waited a few hours, they thought, until the Sabbath was over. Jesus disagrees because the kingdom of God is already present and, therefore, the constraints of the Sabbath are transcended. But there are precedents in the Scriptures. When King David, for instance, was hungry, his kingship allowed him to transgress the priestly prerogatives of eating the showbread—even in a shrine dedicated to YHWH—Jesus may thus claim that his own kingship eclipses David's. The episode at Nob becomes a prophetic projection of things to come, which are now present in the person of Jesus. To wait for the Sabbath to be over would deny the whole kerygma of Jesus's preaching and consciousness. Jesus, in his person, is the kingdom that he announces. He proclaims that the Sabbath has been given to humans, not they to the Sabbath. An echo of this is found in Yoma 85b and Mek. 9.1 (on Exod 31:13). Note that we learn also from the talmudic Yoma 35b that the rabbis Shemaya and Abtalion—the former, at any rate, of heathen descent in the first century BCE—transgressed the Sabbath for the sake of Rabbi Hillel (also of the first century BCE), who would become their pupil and successor (ca. 30 BCE). Pointedly, Naz. 23b states, "The transgression [of a precept] for serving God is more important than to fulfill it without the same intent."

It bears notice for our purpose that the Talmud also severely criticizes sham Pharisees for their vanity and hypocrisy, their mistaken ordering of priorities, their casuistry, their "good conscience," their lack of firmness in

---

48. Ibid., 345.

the faith, and their ostentation.[49] The fact is that both parties, Pharisees and early Christians, were too close for comfort. They were too similar to allow them to enjoy a peaceful coexistence.[50]

Jesus and the Temple

As E. P. Sanders writes, "The principal function of any temple is to serve as a place for sacrifice, and ... sacrifices *require* the supply of suitable animals."[51] Notwithstanding, we can find harsh criticisms of the Jerusalem temple personnel in different places. Malachi 3 comes to mind (the Levites were impure, etc.; see vv. 3, 7–10). Psalms of Solomon extends this criticism to the priesthood (8:9–19).[52] It is also true in 1QpHab 12:8–9 and CD 5:6–8. But such charges are absent from the gospels, with the exception of Mark 11:17 (reckoned as a later addition). Jesus's attacks on the system are *symbolic*. We must realize that, in the so-called temple cleansing scene, Jesus overturns only a few tables: it is clearly to make a point, which is a prophecy of destruction (with an eventual restoration).[53] The cleansing of the temple and the cursing of the fig tree (Mark 11:12–21) must be read together. As such, they spell an eschatological judgment on the temple. The "fig tree" is metaphorical (see Mark 13:2, 28–29): it symbolizes the temple and ensures that Jesus was not calling for a religious reform and purification but was actualizing a prophetic judgment. As Jesus threatens the destruction of the shrine, so the temple authorities want to destroy

---

49. See also Soṭah 22b; Ber. 24b.
50. See Overman, *Matthew's Gospel and Formative Judaism*, 148. Christians continued to pray among Jews; see Matt 10:17; 23:24. But the Matthean community felt that they were losing ground (ibid., 155).
51. Sanders, *Jesus and Judaism*, 63.
52. See Pss. Sol. 1:8 (the psalmist's children, secretly, "defiled the temple of the Lord with defilement"); 2:3 (cf. vv. 1–13), "The sons of Jerusalem defiled the sanctuary of the Lord." They are accused of hypocrisy (4:6, 8, 19–20). In 8:13 it says, "There was no sin greater even than those of the nations that they did not commit." In fact, the defilement has been inaugurated by the "nations" in Jerusalem. Some Jews, thus increasing the devastation, immediately imitated them. No doubt, the author is alluding to "collaborators" with the Romans. So the purification must be on two fronts. Pss. Sol. 17.32 expresses hope in the restoration of "their king who will be the Lord Messiah."
53. See Mark 13:1–2 superseded by Matt 26:60–61; 27:40 // Mark 15:29; Acts 6:14 (Stephen's); John 2:18–22 ("the temple of his body").

Jesus (Mark 11:18 // John 2:14–20 [here, without the motif of the fig tree]). The prophetic act of Jesus calls for the end of an unjust system in preparation for the kingdom of God.[54] The lucrative commerce in the Court of the Gentiles distracts people from realizing that the temple is a place of prayer. It has become a marketplace where business matters more than worship. The beneficiaries are the priestly aristocrats, and the exploited are, once again, the peasants.

Sanders also asks: did Jesus predict or did he threaten the destruction of the shrine? "Both point towards the destruction of the present order and the appearance of the new."[55] Chances are that the prediction was construed as a threat. For Jesus, *God*, who would send a new temple from heaven, would destroy the temple. That Jesus as such did not reject the temple's legitimacy is shown by the fact that Jesus daily taught—and the early church worshiped—in the Jerusalem temple (e.g., Luke 19:47; John 18:20; Acts 2:46; 3:1; 21:26).[56]

But the words and actions of Jesus in this respect were offensive to many. They "resented his personal self-assertion."[57] I would insist on the word "personal" because the priests' attitude shows that their hostility is ad hominem rather than ad causam. They look for a motive to kill Jesus, but they do not find any (Mark 14:55; Matt 26:59; Luke 22:66–71). They must have recourse to a direct interrogation: Are you or are you not? The same occurred with Pilate (cf. Matt 27:11 [which Paul interpreted positively in 1 Tim 6:13]). To say the least, Jesus's responses are ambiguous. He says, "It is you who say that [not I]," and this puzzles the questioners. It certainly

---

54. So Crossan, Horsley, Wright, others.

55. Sanders, *Jesus and Judaism*, 73.

56. This shows that, at least in the beginning of the church's existence, Christianity was not a sect, for a sect would demand a strict adhesion to the group, separation from all others, strict discipline, and threats (and practice) of exclusion. All these elements are present at Qumran but not in the early church. See Eyal Regev, "Were the Early Christians Sectarians?" *JBL* 130 (2011): 781–92. He writes, "[M]any early Christians regarded themselves as an integral part of the larger Jewish society and did not attempt to create a distinct *social system*" (792, emphasis original). This statement should be tempered, however, as regards the Matthean community; see Matt 23. As to the paradoxical attachment of the early Christians to the temple after their Master's threat of its destruction, the analogy is that the expectation of the end of the world does not prevent anyone from living in the present world with a sense of awe before it.

57. Sanders, *Jesus and Judaism*, 76.

means something like, "Anything I would say one way or the other will not change your mind. It is already set in advance."

Let me add a few reflections on "prediction" versus "threat." Among the different versions of the temple "cleansing" in the gospel, the *lectio difficilior* is the one with a threat of destruction, rather than just a prediction of it (Mark 14:58). The Synoptists show their embarrassment and try to water down the impact of the saying: when Jesus predicts the temple's destruction, he acts as a prophet.[58] John 2:19 has Jesus saying, "Destroy this temple, and in three days I will raise it up." The threat, however, is more than oracular; it is sovereign, and Jesus's role here is apocalyptic. He fills the part, not simply as a prophet, but as the Son of Man–judge of Dan 7.[59]

If the case is such, the stance adopted by Jesus almost demands what we shall see below was his decisive assertion of his sovereignty before the high priest (*egō eimi*; see ch. 13, "The Trial of Jesus and His Passion," 217–38). The trial of Jesus, seen from an all-important point of view, is a clash of powers with religious and political potentates.

Put in the aforementioned context of ritual and life, the declaration that there is more than the temple is consistent with Jesus's general doctrine. What is "more" is not just the person of Jesus, but also the human being in general, the "son of man," whoever he or she may be. The "Son of Man" and the "son of man" are more than the temple. Like the Sabbath, the temple has been made for her, not her for the temple.

As we saw above, Jesus's prophecy about the destruction of the temple is not per se a condemnation of the cult in the temple, but it announces the end of an era that was centered on the Jerusalem temple. As long as the temple is erect, Jesus and his disciples visit it regularly to pray, to teach, to heal, and presumably also to offer sacrifices. We cannot speak of the temple as a "domination system." If it had been, Jesus no doubt would have avoided visiting it and, more generally speaking, the populace would not have put themselves at grave risk in opposing Roman moves of desecration (see Josephus, *J.W.* 2.184–198; *Ant.* 18.318–339).[60]

---

58. Threats against the temple are found in the prophets; see Mic 3:9–12; Jer 26:1–6. For Jesus as a prophet or as the prophet, see below in ch. 16, "Jesus and the Resurrection," 263–72.

59. In Sib. Or. 5.425, the builder of the new temple is "a blessed man from heaven."

60. On this, see Levine, *The Misunderstood Jew*, 153–57.

7. JESUS AND ISRAEL

Yet, while the temple is holy, its personnel are not necessarily beyond reproach, especially the well-to-do among them. There is a real consistency in Jesus's mistrust of the upper classes.[61] For one thing, we can imagine a certain unevenness of honesty and earnestness in a bureaucracy that employed, directly or indirectly, some twenty thousand people! The moneychangers are not generally considered as moral exemplars. They sell unblemished doves for sacrifices, but the poor and the gentiles cannot afford them. The temple was not just the religious shrine we imagine, but also a marketplace, the treasury and the national bank—in short, a sort of Vatican City before the fact. By "cleansing" the temple precincts, Jesus confronted religious heads and denounced their corruption. He was "destroying the temple" (at least in their eyes). I am indeed inclined to agree with scholars like E. P. Sanders[62] and Paula Fredriksen[63] that, rather than a "cleansing" act, Jesus's overturning of the tables of the moneychangers symbolized the destruction of the temple. As Fredriksen writes,

> In sum: Jesus' gesture (overturning tables in the Temple court) near the archetypal holiday of national liberation (Passover) in the context of his mission ('The Kingdom of God is at hand!') would have been readily understood *by any watching Jew* as a statement that the Temple was about to be destroyed (by God, not human armies, and certainly not literally or personally by Jesus himself), and accordingly that the present order was about to cede to the Kingdom of God.[64]

From this perspective, we can better understand the recurring motif of the accusation by a couple of "witnesses" that Jesus threatened to destroy the temple.[65]

Jesus's attitude toward temple personnel could easily be extended in the popular mind to the temple itself. In a text unique to Matthew, collectors of taxes ask him whether he pays the temple tax at all! The response of Jesus is somewhat backhanded (Matt 17:24–27). He claims that, being himself the Son (of God), he should not have to pay the *didrachmon*

---

61. Without, however, principally excluding the rich. Some people around Jesus are in that category: e.g., Jairus, the anointing woman, Zacchaeus, Joseph of Arimathea.
62. Sanders, *Jesus and Judaism*, 62–63.
63. Fredriksen, *From Jesus to Christ*, 112–13.
64. Ibid., 113.
65. Of course, the text of the gospel is based on Zech 14:21: the temple is reformed, and this coincides with the end of an era—or is it with the end of history?

(17:26, "the sons are free," thus including the disciples as well; cf. Matt 6:9–5; 13:38–43). For the sake of peace (so as not "to scandalize them," 17:27) he pays the tax.

Although Jesus kept his distance from the political front, his attitude and fate are tinged with ambiguity. Not only is he crucified as a *lestēs* ("rebel"), but, being an apocalyptic preacher, he cannot remove the political dimension of the apocalypse qua critique of the present order. Yet Jesus is pacifistic.[66] "My kingdom is not of this world," stresses that point. In contradistinction to a warrior messiah, "son of David," one also expected a spiritual messiah (see Isa 11 and Zech 12), humble, lowly, and saintly (see m. Šabb. 6:4; Psalms of Solomon; 4 Ezra).

This is how the gospel presents Jesus after 70 CE. A number of scholars (especially S. G. F. Brandon) have suggested that such an idyllic image by the evangelists was due to the fear of confusion of Christianity with Jewish revolutionaries of 66–70. But, they continue, as far as the alleged scene of the trial before the Roman governor is concerned, it could not, as expected, assuage Pilate's suspicion regarding the implied consequences for Roman occupation of having such a person around. For, being apolitical according to the invoked criteria, Jesus's "kingdom of God" is, on another level, a political-religious metaphor,[67] and thus a challenge to all kingdoms. Perceptively, Marcus Borg recalls the petition in the Lord's Prayer for bread and remittance of debts (Matt 6:11–12), that is, "the two central survival issues in peasant life" constantly jeopardized by the "king's" abusive taxation. God's granting bread and freedom from debts is the good news for the poor (see also, among the Beatitudes, Matt 6:20–23), but it is "bad news for the wealthy and powerful." The poor are "hungry for righteousness," that is, for justice, as it prevails in the kingdom of God.[68] So Jesus is con-

---

66. See Fredriksen, *From Jesus to Christ*, 125. By "pacifism" I mean that Jesus was anxious not to be confused with self-proclaimed messianic leaders of military rebellion against the Roman occupiers, like Theudas (Josephus, *Ant.* 20.97), or the so-called Egyptian (Josephus, *J.W.* 2.261–262; cf. Acts 21:38), or again Judas the Galilean (Acts 5:36–37 [with a chronological confusion]), John of Gishala (Josephus, *J.W.*, e.g., 2.556–646), Simon bar Gioras (Josephus, *J.W.*, e.g., 2.517–522), Eleazar commander of the Sicarii (Josephus, *J.W.* 7.252–274), etc.

67. So, Marcus Borg, *Jesus: Uncovering the Life, Teachings, and Relevance of a Religious Revolutionary* (San Francisco: HarperSanFrancisco, 2006), 187. He refers to Sib. Or. 2.

68. See Borg, *Jesus*, 188, 190, 252. After Herod's death, there was a widespread revolt against the high taxes—among other complaints (Josephus, *J.W.* 2.55–65; *Ant.*

demned as a *lestēs* and crucified between two other "brigands" (in modern parlance, "terrorists") under the *titulus* "King of the Jews." Furthermore, say the same critics, there was a Simon "the Zealot" among Jesus's disciples (Luke 6:15; Acts 1:13).

Brandon's argument falters, however, when we remember Matt 5:44 on the love of the enemy, and the presence among the disciples of the former tax collector, Levi, as a counterbalance to Simon.

Along with Jewish aristocrats, Jesus also dragged the Roman authorities into the abyss of irrelevance, for they were like hand and glove regarding policy and economics. The worldly successes of both aristocrats and authorities induced them to regard themselves as in no need of "the physician," even as righteous in their own eyes (Matt 9:12–13) but certainly not as "lost" (Luke 19:10). Accordingly, Jesus says that the kingdom of God is for the poor (Luke 6:20; Matt 5:3), for wealth poses great spiritual danger (Luke 12:15–21; 18:23–27; cf. 14:33).

Incidentally, when Jesus says, according to John 18:36, "my kingdom is not of this world [*ek tou kosmou toutou*]," we must understand that the kingdom of God does not fulfill the criteria of this world. The statement has the same sense as in Qidd. 2b, for example, where it is said that the marriage is *qiddushim*, that is, the husband subtracts his wife from this world to dedicate her to the sanctuary.[69] The kingdom forecast by Jesus involves the renewal of heaven and earth in the eschaton. Of this, several texts serve as background. Sanders cites Isa 49:5–6; 56:1–8; 60:3–7, 10–14; 66:18–24; Mic 4; see esp. Tob 14:5; 1 Enoch 90:98–99; 91:13; Jub. 1:15–17; T. Benj. 9:2; 11QTemple 29:8–10; Sib. Or. 5:414–433.[70]

Another fact must be taken into consideration: Jesus alone was arrested and eventually crucified. His disciples, although very much fearing for their safety (remember Peter's triple denial of belonging to Jesus's group), were not persecuted; they could remain untroubled in Jerusalem. I suggest that the authorities considered Jesus's pacifism. It may even explain

---

17.269–285). After that the Romans collected tribute directly. Eventually, Florus coerced tribute from the temple treasury and thus caused the war (*J.W.* 2.293–296). Economic aspects of the revolt included poverty and overtaxation. The Sicarii burned houses of the rich and the public archives, "to cause a rising of the poor against the rich, sure of impunity" (*J.W.* 2.425–429). The revolt, therefore, was also class warfare of peasants against estate holders and other aristocrats.

69. See Claude Gruber-Magitot, *Jésus et les Pharisiens* (Paris: Laffont, 1964), 411.
70. Sanders, *Jesus and Judaism*, 79.

why the enthusiastic crowd accompanying Jesus's entry in Jerusalem was not immediately dispersed or crushed by the Romans. Jesus as leader was not issuing a call to arms. *On the contrary.* After all, the hailing crowd brandishes palms and willow branches (*lulavim*, palms and *ethrog*, lemon, willow, myrtle, were waved while reciting Ps 118:25, "save us!"), not swords and spears, sickles and hammers. To a certain extent, this could have been reassuring to the Romans. Then the role played by the temple personnel in delivering Jesus to the Roman authorities as a seditious figure becomes more understandable. Their hostility to Jesus had to be explained. Hence, the gospel elaborated the whole scene of Jesus before the Sanhedrin and before Pilate. We must note the comparative scarcity of references to the Sanhedrin in the gospel texts. It is present only once in Luke (22:66) and Matthew (26:59), and twice in Mark (14:55 and 15:1). Luke does not mention the Sanhedrin's verdict against Jesus. In John, the Sanhedrin is absent.

Though the trial is fraught with inconsistencies, at least its scenario suggests some of the motives invoked by both religious and political authorities for eliminating a troublemaker. Furthermore, any inconsistencies might be somewhat mitigated if the proceedings were merely fact-finding and not a formal trial. The latter occurred before Pilate.

Formative Christianity and Formative Judaism

While formative Judaism tended more and more toward an ahistorical and an atemporal stasis, especially in the Mishnah, the Christian missionaries insisted on the historical and prophetic traditions of Scripture, in addition to historical-biographical testimony about the Nazarene. This conflict between the two traditions is in part responsible for the respective emphases of each, one on the escape from history,[71] the other on the continuity of the unique thrust from beginning to end of the *Heilsgeschichte* since Abraham and even Adam. Rabbis saw themselves compelled to affirm an Israelite identity transcending time. So, for instance, after the messianic fever of the first and second centuries CE, the Mishnah comes (around 200 CE) with a harsh judgment on that wild explosion.[72]

---

71. See Yosef H. Yerushalmi, *Zakhor: Jewish History and Jewish Memory* (New York: Schocken, 1989 [1982]). See also Martin Hengel, *Judaism and Hellenism: Studies in their Encounter in Palestine during the Early Hellenistic Period* (Philadelphia: Fortress, 1974), e.g., 150, 175.

72. See Neusner, *Messiah*, 226. Regarding the messianic expectations, there had

7. JESUS AND ISRAEL

So, even before we turn to details of Jesus's "biography" in the gospel, we note the decisive role of the story of Jesus as told. Such a story may be a literary patchwork in the present form of the gospels—hence our difficulty in retrieving the historical Jesus—but it is beyond doubt what constitutes the foundation of the Christian movement. We must reconcile this with the relative disinterest of the Nazarene himself in his people's past history! The fact is that he believed that a new era had commenced, whose history was all-important, in relative contrast to what preceded it. Further, Jesus is influenced by the historic promotion of the individual over the collective, as we have seen. The weakness of the Israelite nation within the Roman Empire also plays a nonnegligible role.

As to the Nazarene's life, Paul, formerly a strict Pharisee, may be less interested than others in the New Testament about the "details" of Jesus's "biography," but his whole doctrine is an elaboration on the decisive meaning of Jesus's death and resurrection.

True, the term "biography," as we saw above, must be qualified in view of the biased narrative of the gospel. The latter, for instance, frequently refers to texts of Scriptures in an ex post facto way: "Jesus did/said this or that as it is written in Scriptures." True, formative Judaism also refers constantly to Scriptures, but it does so to predict things in advance—for instance the coming occurrence of political events.[73] It can also "explain" why some things happened—such as the destruction of the temple. This puts the onus on Israel's sins, and thus, as Neusner judiciously remarks, it emphasizes that Israel controls its own destiny. Strikingly, Jesus weeps over Jerusalem about to be destroyed as a consequence of rejecting him.[74] There is some circularity here, which Christianity shifts to teleology and inscribes within the trajectory of history. The so-called fulfillment citations are apologetic and an efficient defense against formative Judaism.

---

been a widespread belief during the Maccabean period that one was living in the messianic times. This would be followed by even more remarkable events at the "end." For the mentality prevailing after the Maccabean era, see the Psalms of Solomon, and for after 70 CE, see 2 Baruch, 4 Ezra, and Sib. Or. 5.

73. See Qidd.. 72a; Yoma 10a; 'Abod. Zar. 2a–b (Neusner, *Messiah*, 202–5).

74. See Luke 19:41–44; cf. 13:34. Note also Matthew; from Matt 2 onward, "Jerusalem" is aligned with Jesus's opponents. Chances are that the Sadducees' controversy with the Pharisees over the Oral Law reflects the priestly claim of authority to interpret the torah. This tended to pit "Jerusalem" against the *chora* (countryside) (Josephus, *Ant.* 13.293–296; 18.180).

The *process* by which the fulfillment is ongoing, with Christians embodying Christ (a continuity much stressed by Paul), is remarkable.

Excursus: John's Use of the Term "the Jews"

Everyone agrees that the word "Jew" etymologically designates the inhabitants of Judea in the region of Jerusalem. It is, therefore, a possible sense of the term in the Gospel of John. In this excursus, I shall not go beyond a quick survey of this possibility, since this does not directly contribute to the purpose of this book.

Clearly, John situates Jesus in Galilee[75] and insists, as also the other gospel writers do, on the fact that Jesus was a Galilean. Judea is another "country," of which inhabitants are seen as arrogant burgers "with an attitude."[76] They tend to be hostile toward Jesus (see John 8:48, 52; 9:18) and, more generally, toward Galileans (cf. Mark 14:70; John 18:17). In other words, we are witnessing the perennial and universal rivalry between "provincials" and "metropolitans." Within this perspective, Pilate's massacre of Galilean pilgrims reported in Luke 13:1 did not make lots of waves! It is not even mentioned in secular history, except for Josephus's allusion to something similar in *Ant.* 18.60–87.

At times, John identifies "Judeans" and "Pharisees" (see, e.g., 9:13–17). Now, the Pharisees were city dwellers and concentrated in Judea, especially, of course, in Jerusalem, where Jesus clashes with some of them and also where his opponents plot to kill him. In this respect, John 7:1 is illuminating: "Jesus went about in Galilee. He did not wish to go about in Judea because the Judeans were looking for an opportunity to kill him." He stays as much as he can in Galilee, and his brothers—moved by less than a candid motive—tell him that he should leave the Galilean periphery and face the potential publicity in metropolitan Judea, "Leave here and go to Judea." To which Jesus responds, "My time has not come yet" (7:2–3).

---

75. See John 1:43, 47 (Jesus, an Israelite without duplicity: an implied criticism of the Judeans?); 4:3 (Jesus leaves Judea and returns to Galilee); same situation in, e.g., 4:43–47; 7:52. See John 7:41–42: Jesus should have been born in Bethlehem, and this is to be set in the context of the sociological rivalry between Judea and Galilee. The Judeans ("Jews" in John's current translations) would never accept a Galilee-born messiah.

76. Hellenistic influence was mainly evident in Jerusalem. Among chief priests and rich lay aristocrats, it contributed to a feeling of superiority toward "provincials."

When, however, he goes up the Jerusalem, it is "in secret," for the Judeans are looking for him. Among the latter, some nevertheless believe in him (7:31; 8:31), so that John avoids, at this point, the term *Ioudaioi* and uses the periphrasis "some inhabitants of Jerusalem" (7:25). The festivals are celebrated in Jerusalem, and therefore John calls them "of the Judeans" because of their traditional location in the temple. This explains why Jesus risks his life by going up to Jerusalem (e.g., 2:13, 23; 5:1–2, 18; 6:4; 11:55).

It is true that some Johannine texts with *Ioudaioi* are more ambiguous. So, in 4:22, Jesus speaks with a Samaritan woman and tells her, "Salvation comes from the *Ioudaioi*" (to be translated here "from the Jews," but Jesus is thinking of the temple in Jerusalem, hence the use of the term here). The basic text is Isa 2:3, which speaks of Zion/Jerusalem; it helps to explain why the term appears in John 4:22. Furthermore, in John 6:41, 52, 59, we find *Ioudaioi* in Capernaum! There is, of course, no impossibility of Judeans living in Galilee and vice versa. Besides, the situation is not clear-cut; Jesus has friends in Judea (11:1, 18; 12:1) as well as many foes (11:54).

The latter chapters of the Gospel of John take us to Jerusalem, whither Jesus eventually goes while knowing that this decisive move will be fatal ("the hour has come," 12:23; 13:1). After the dramatic trial and crucifixion of Jesus, John completes his gospel, by *inclusio*, in Galilee, where Jesus appears to his disciples (21:1).

In conclusion, I choose to translate most instances of *Ioudaioi* in the Johannine texts by "Judeans" (from the perspective of the Galilean that John was like his Master). In general, scholars detect behind the texts with *Ioudaioi* a historical rivalry between the Johannine church and the Jewish synagogue that John retroverted to the time of the historical Jesus. This scholarly reconstruction is not impossible; I suggest, however, another reading that spares us from a speculation that is not buttressed by anything we know historically.

8
Jesus Taught in Parables

What is a parable? It is a short story characterized by verisimilitude and conveying a lesson, usually moral. A parable is, in Hebrew terms, a haggadic or midrashic *mashal*. The whole of Jewish tradition is bidimensional; it is built into the halakah (legal dispositions) and the haggadah (paradigmatic stories illustrating the meaning, impact, and relevance of a biblical theme or text). Historically, it must be said that preference has been given by Jewish readers to the halakic side of the tradition because of its obvious bearing on ways of life according to the divine order. Great revivalist movements in Judaism, however, were typically based on a rediscovery of the variegated message imbedded in the haggadah. Suffice it to think of the thirteenth-century kabbalah, of the sixteenth-century Lurianic reform in Safed, of the sixteenth-century magisterial work of the Maharal of Prague, as well as of the magnificent Hasidic movement of the eighteenth century. Now, preceding them all, Jesus's teaching in parables is to be considered as inserted, like the subsequent Jewish reforms, within a line of tradition called haggadic or midrashic.

The midrash builds on a biblical text or theme by narratively expanding its message or by highlighting for the audience one or more aspect deemed particularly relevant in the Singer of Tales' eyes. As far as Jesus's kerygma is concerned, his main point throughout is that the kingdom of God has come, with a decisive impact on the world and human life. The "notion" of the kingdom is readily concretized within the existential.

Jesus, in the view of the gospel, taught only in parables (see Matt 13:3, 13; Mark 4:34 [that is, a haggadic teaching]).[1] Matthew 13:34 is basic: "Jesus

---

1. There are between thirty and forty parables and more than one hundred aphorisms, to mention only these categories of Jesus's teaching. Marcus Borg calls attention to the fact that these were repeated from place to place "many times and then expanded upon" (*Jesus: Uncovering the Life, Teachings, and Relevance of a Religious Revolution-*

told the crowds all these things in parables; without a parable he told them nothing"; then follows a quotation of Ps 78:2 in the LXX text, where the Greek term is *parabolē* rendering the Hebrew *mashal* (in the second part of the verse, *hiddoth* means riddles). It claims that the parable reveals secrets hidden from the foundation of the world. In the LXX, the word *parabolē* renders the Hebrew *mashal* ("proverb, byword" [Deut 28:37], "allegory" [Ezek 24:3], "simile" [Ps 49:13], and "fable" [Ezek 17:2]). But a pure parable like the one the prophet Nathan told to David in 2 Sam 12:1–6 is not called *mashal*! Thus *mashal* needs interpretation. The first thing that we learn, therefore, is that the matter only makes sense against a Judaic backdrop. Jaroslav Pelikan speaks of the parable as situated "between rabbinic tradition and prophetic innovation."[2] In the teaching of Jesus, the parable sets comparisons between the kingdom (kingship) of God and the human humdrum of daily life.

In general, two realities are set in parallel so as to be mutually explained by means of their resemblance (cf. the rabbinic rule of *gezera shawah*). The parable is a didactic illustration of a truth (cf. 2 Sam 12:1–4; 14:4–7; 1 Kgs 20:39–40). "What is truth?" asks Pilate (John 18:38). Marcus Borg astutely stresses the point that Jesus's parables teach his hearers to understand things *differently*. He refers to Job 42:5; John 9:25; and Acts 9:18.[3]

Rabbinic parables were committed to writing some two centuries after Jesus, but they reflect much older traditions (one estimate suggests that there are some two thousand rabbinic parables), and they closely resemble Jesus's parables in format.[4] Typically, they start with the words, "To what is this case comparable? To someone who ..." Often they make only one

---

ary [San Francisco: HarperSanFrancisco, 2006], 157). See Luke 18:9–14; 14:11. Add to Jesus's aphorisms, the healings, exorcisms, direct dialogues, and a reaction to events of all kinds, the conclusion is that it takes a protracted time to accomplish all this.

2. Jaroslav Pelikan, *Jesus through the Centuries: His Place in the History of Culture* (New Haven: Yale University Press, 1985), 15.

3. Borg, *Jesus*, 133.

4. Gary G. Porton, "The Parables in the Hebrew Bible and in Rabbinic Literature," in *The Historical Jesus in Context*, ed. Amy-Jill Levine, Dale C. Allison Jr., and John Dominic Crossan (Princeton: Princeton University Press, 2006), 206–21, refers to the following in the Hebrew Bible: Judg 9:7–15; 2 Sam 12:1–14; 14:1–20; 1 Kgs 20:35–43; Isa 5:1–7 (some critics add Ezek 17:3–10; 19:2–9, 10–14; 23:3–5; Judg 14:14; Isa 1:5–6; Hos 2:2–15). Among the rabbinic parables, Porton cites m. Sukkah 2:9; Sipra Qedoshim 11:14; Mek. 2.3, 2.4, 2.5; Sipre Num. 84; Gen. Rab. 8.27; 86.2; Šabb. 153a; Ber. 31b; B. Qam. 79b; Qoh. Rab. 3.11; y. Ber. 2.8, 5c; Deut. Rab. 2.24; ARN (A) 24.

clear point. They are distinct from allegory, but a tendency toward allegory is already perceptible (Mark 4:15; 12:5; Matt 13:36–42; 21:34–36; 22:6–7; 25:21, 23, 30; Luke 14:22–23; 19:12–15, 27), at least in the stereotyping of key characters. The king, the master, the father always represent God; the servants and the flock, his people; the court of justice and the harvest, his judgment; the banquet and the wedding feast, the messianic times.

In the Synoptics some thirty *different* parables—whether or not they are called by that name in the texts[5]—later added developments of selected traits, but these remain rather modest. They reflect the new situation prevailing in the Christian church of the evangelists' time. See, for instance, a number of clues as to the break with Judaism and to the mission to the gentiles (Matt 21:43; 22:7, 10, 14; Luke 14:22–23). In addition, messianic themes are present in the rendition of Israel as a vineyard (John 15:1–8) and of Jesus as the good shepherd who gives up his own life (15:12–13). This latter motif is dramatically highlighted as Jesus's message became more and more of an irritation to the religious establishment of the time (cf. Matt 11:16–19; 22:1–10; Mark 12:1–9). Jesus is without illusion as to his mission's failure but at the same time is fully convinced of its eschatological triumph. He says that the latter comes like a thief in the night (Matt 24:43–44) or like a delayed bridegroom (25:1–13), but the wedding joy is actually coming (22:1–13).

At this point we may ask, why did Jesus speak in parables? First, it was certainly not in contempt of the halakah, as the Sermon on the Mountain demonstrates. But the fact is that the parable is nondogmatic and nonsystematic. It leaves open a large margin of interpretation. In other words—the point is important—there exists no monolithic truth; truth is variegated and multilayered.[6] Evidently, the kingdom of God cannot be reduced to a formula. No definition could embrace the infinite diversity of its reality, as diverse indeed as life itself.[7]

---

5. Mark 4 presents a collection of parables.

6. In the words of Abraham J. Heschel, "One truth comes to expression in many ways of understanding" ("No Religion Is an Island," *USQR* 21 [1966]: 127). A. N. Wilson (*Jesus: A Life* [New York: Fawcett Columbine, 1992], 250), writes, "Something which Western minds have found it almost impossible to come to terms is the unsystematic nature of Jesus' thought." Wilson also says (249), "Once the idea of Jesus had been given to the Gentiles, they adopted him as a saviour, in whose human biography they took small or no interest."

7. From another angle, N. T. Wright says that the relative lack of definition of the kingdom of God in the NT is due to the general knowledge of the concept among the

This is the beauty of the parable. The only way to speak of the kingdom is to say, "It is like...." Only terms of comparison will suggest what the kingdom actually is. It can be seen as a grain of mustard, as the seed sowed by a sower, or as the yeast in dough, that is, as something that begins very small but that has a startling outcome. It can be a lost and retrieved coin or a royal banquet. One of the most telling suggests a comparison with a high-priced pearl (see Matt 13:44–46; in the Gos. Thom. 109). In order to acquire it, the potential buyer is willing to sell all his possessions. Nothing in life can be more important or more precious. Once he has spotted the "treasure in heaven," all becomes secondary, even trivial in his eyes. "All the rest is commentary," said the rabbis. The kingdom is the key to a full human existence.

Jesus uses different similes so that they can correct each other's trajectory. As a "pearl," the kingdom could be misunderstood as an object, an item for a collector. But the kingdom escapes the misinterpretation; it is also a plant or a tree that grows (Mark 4:31); it is unpredictable like a royal invitation to a banquet (Matt 22:2); it is like yeast in the dough (Luke 21:7). The common denominator of all the kingdom similes is that it is life-changing. Strikingly, what Jesus says of the kingdom is parallel to what the rabbis say of the Shekinah, the divine presence.[8]

The parables are notoriously obscure to those who are "outside." Harold Bloom calls them "enigmatics" and their author Jesus "poet of the riddle."[9] Mark 4:10–12 in Jesus's mouth quotes Isa 6:9–10, "Keep listening but do not comprehend, keep looking but do not understand ... so that they may not look with their eyes and listen with their ears, and comprehend with their minds, and turn and be healed."[10] Both the prophet of the eighth

---

Jewish people of the time. It was "part of a story" (*Jesus and the Victory of God* [Minneapolis: Fortress, 1996], 227). Wright also mentions "Jesus in his new way of being Israel" (229).

8. When the kingdom of God is mistaken as a possession (something like, "our conception is the only truth there is, all other interpretations are heresy") it may be useful to turn to John Steinbeck's short story "The Pearl." It is a sort of prolongation of the parable of Jesus. The possession of the pearl—or of the truth—becomes a murderous curse (cf. Mark 12:1–11, the murderous vinedressers). There is only one way of salvation: the throwing away of the best that has become the worst. It is, to be sure, a terrible loss, but at least it is an honest one. That is why the "dechristianization" that is so severe in the West is not irreparably negative.

9. Harold Bloom, *Jesus and Yahweh: The Names Divine* (New York: Riverhead, 2005), 10 and 19.

10. This saying of Jesus inadvertently opened the door to a gnostic interpreta-

century BCE and the prophet of the first century CE use riddles to sift the wheat from the weeds (cf. Matt 13:25–30; Gos. Thom. 57), *a procedure that recalls the priests sorting out the pure from the impure.* Here again, the ethical has eclipsed the ritual. The crux of the matter is not external purity but the ability to cope with the new situation as proclaimed by Isaiah and now inaugurated by the Nazarene. True, neither Isaiah nor Jesus is referring to an intellectual capacity.[11] The distinction between those who hear and those who do not hear is grounded on a *will* to hear or to be deaf, and it is well known that no one is deafer than one who is unwilling to hear.

The point is that the utter simplicity of a parable can be deceptive. It is so for those "outside" who get a taste of the truth but miss the profundity of the kerygma.[12] As a result, what is intrinsically revelatory becomes a veil hiding the mystery, and the parable, which should open the eyes, the ears, and the heart, eventuates in blinding, deafening, and hardening the heart.[13] The case is comparable to someone who becomes immune to the *pharmakon* through its misuse. Then the *pharmakon*'s poisonous capacity prevails.

Mark 1:22 tells us that Jesus "taught them as one having authority, and not as the scribes." This is paradoxical, since scribes and official teachers taught what to do and not to do, while Jesus's parables are not directly halakic but haggadic. They call for an interactive dialogue. The narratival has displaced the imperatival. The former is clearly more respectful of the audience, which, considering its low social status, is not accustomed to being "consulted" or asked, "What do you think?" Jesus's teaching has a

---

tion. So the Gospel of Thomas begins by stating, "These are the hidden sayings that the living Jesus uttered.... Whoever finds the meaning of these sayings will not taste death" (saying 1; cf. John 8:52). Note, with John P. Meier, Thomas's "rejection of salvation history, of a privileged place in that history for Israel, of the significance of OT prophecies, etc." (*The Roots of the Problem and the Person*, vol. 1 of *A Marginal Jew: Rethinking the Historical Jesus*, ABRL [New York: Doubleday, 1991], 134).

11. "The difference between what is and what is not" in the words of Philo, *On the Life of Moses*, quoted by Bloom, *Jesus and Yahweh*, 74, is of the same essence. It has little to do with a sharp or a dull intelligence.

12. What Joseph Klausner calls "an esoteric significance" (*Jesus of Nazareth: His Life, Times, and Teaching* [New York: Macmillan, 1925; repr., New York: Bloch, 1997], 265).

13. A sure sign of the legal experts' hardened hearts is that they never marvel at the healings they witness. They are not amazed; they show no eagerness to see someone crippled being whole again.

certain flavor of popular wisdom,[14] but it unexpectedly subverts conventional wisdom; it is as if it were a "counter wisdom."[15] It is not often that we find in the book of Proverbs or Qoheleth a call to compassion similar to Jesus's parable of the prodigal son, where compassion is the primary quality of God and also the primary quality of the human response to God (Luke 6:36; cf. Matt 5:48).[16] This theme is also central in parables like the good Samaritan (Luke 10), the indebted servant (Matt 18:23–34), and the sheep and goats (Matt 25). The lesson does not seem to be hard to understand, but Jesus's friends are obdurate, and they would like their Master to adopt another way, other than by riddles, of speaking.

Mark's subtlety is once more evident. He is careful to depict the disciples that were close to Jesus as being puzzled by their Master's teaching. They did not understand, or at least they were not sure they understood. Thus, even those who *want* to hear do not end up constituting an elitist caste ("I believe; help my unbelief!" Mark 9:24). They join the "cloud of witnesses" that struggle with their unbelief while realizing that no other way is open to them. In the words of Peter, "Lord, to whom [else] should we go?" (John 6:68; cf. Gos. Thom. 38).

The parables in the gospel are not limited to storytelling. Jesus's relationship with his followers resembles performed parables and psychodramas. One of the most moving such scenes involves the prostitute anointing Jesus's feet in Luke 7. "Her sins, which are many, are forgiven, for she loved much" (7:47). Another is the dialogue of Jesus with the adulterous woman, whom bystanders plan to stone to death (John 8:3–11). Jesus is writing in the sand, seemingly unconcerned, seemingly absent-minded, until he addresses the self-appointed judges and executioners: "Let anyone among you who is without sin be the first to throw a stone at her" (John 8:7), "and Jesus was left alone with the woman standing before him. Jesus straightened up and said to her, 'Woman, where are they? Has no one condemned

---

14. Cf., e.g., Matt 5:13 and parr.; 6:22 and parr.; 15:14 and parr.

15. So Borg, *Jesus*, 167. Luke 6:20–26; 12:15, 16–21, 33–34; Mark 10:17–31 contrast with conventional wisdom as in Prov 10:4; 13:21; 15:6; 19:15; 22:4, all of them equating wealth with blessing!

16. Incidentally, let us note here that Schalom Ben-Chorin interprets the parable on the prodigal son on the model of Ber. 34b, "In the place where those returning stand, even the completely righteous cannot stand" (*Brother Jesus: The Nazarene through Jewish Eyes*, trans. Jared S. Klein and Max Reinhart [Athens: University of Georgia Press, 2001], 78–79).

you?' She said, 'No one, sir.' And Jesus said, 'neither do I condemn you. Go your way, and from now on do not sin again'" (8:9–11).

The midrashic ambiance introduced by Jesus's teaching permeates even the history-like narratives of the gospel. The evangelists have a distinct tendency to "parabolize" the events they report. The constant declaration that biblical texts and themes have been fulfilled by those events is a case in point. As it has accurately been said, the narratives are *ad probandum*,[17] not *ad narrandum*.[18] The scene at Gethsemane in Luke 22

---

17. See John 20:31. In *The Quest of the Historical Jesus: A Critical Study of the Progress from Reimarus to Wrede* (2nd ed., trans. W. Montgomery [London: Black, 1911], 349), Albert Schweitzer wrote (in reaction to a negative critique of the less than elegant style of the gospels), "The chaotic confusion of the narratives ought to have suggested the thought that the events had been thrown into this confusion by the volcanic force of an incalculable personality, not by some kind of carelessness or freak of the tradition."

18. The phrase comes from Quintilianus (ca. 35–90 CE). See, e.g., John 19:35; 20:31. But this is the "99 percent" of the gospel's nonhistoricity! Regarding the evangelists' "inventiveness" in reporting Jesus's words, it has been, I believe, vastly exaggerated. See, approvingly, Wilson, *Jesus: A Life*, 135. David Flusser, *Judaism and the Origins of Christianity* (Jerusalem: Magnes, 1988), 233, writes, "One thing is clear: in the Synoptic tradition Christological motifs, though existing to some extent, are not developed." In her turn, Amy-Jill Levine writes that such historical claims "presume that the 'original' audience or the 'original intent' determines the meaning" (*The Misunderstood Jew: The Church and the Scandal of the Jewish Jesus* [San Francisco: HarperSanFrancisco, 2006], 115). See also G. B. Caird, *Jesus and the Jewish Nation* (London: Athlone, 1965). In this respect, the presence in the gospel of "embarrassing" statements such as disparaging remarks about gentiles, or explicit predictions of the imminent end of the world, should be strongly emphasized. They certainly come to the credit of the evangelists and illustrate their "professionalism" as "biographers." True, in parallel, e.g., with the midrashic in the Synoptics, John makes Jesus's doings into "signs"; in John 19:28, at the foot of the cross, Ps 22:15, "I thirst" is "midrashized." In both cases of the Synoptics and of John, this does not amount simply to putting words in Jesus's mouth. Another example in John's Gospel is his concluding simile of Jesus as the ultimate fisherman. The nets bring ashore 153 fish (John 21:11)—the very number of members of John's church at the time? It is how John interprets an event that indeed reflects a trivial but actual occurrence. The midrashic tendency in the gospel induced Rudolf Bultmann and his followers to conclude that the gospel is all mythology! Bultmann actually said, "The community created such scenes in the spirit of Jesus" (*The History of the Synoptic Tradition*, trans. John Marsh [Oxford: Blackwell, 1968], 54), while Martin Hengel called attention to the fact that we know as little to the development of the tradition in early Christianity between 30 and 70 CE as we know of Jesus. Too often, critics "dissolve well-attested tradition in the Synoptic Gospels in

and the birth narratives in Matthew and Luke are prime examples, as we shall see below.[19]

Let us recall at this point that this book is about "the historical Jesus"; hence what is important in the sources we examine is what Jesus actually said and did. Nevertheless, this, which seems like a truism, is somewhat deceptive, for the genuine sayings of Jesus never existed independently of being interpreted. What Jesus said and did was witnessed by his followers, and he solicited their response ("repent," etc.). Hence, his message was always "performed," always dialogical. Therefore, what the evangelists tell us in terms of encountering Jesus is important. There is no Jesus in history in isolation from his interpreters. The historical Jesus is the Jesus interpreted, the Jesus seen by Peter, by the Twelve, by the female followers, then by Matthew, Mark, Luke, and John (and sometimes by an extracanonical gospel like Thomas's).[20] Even a saying like "Let the dead bury their dead" is not neutral or aphoristic. It was remembered because it was puzzling, as were a number of parables, and the disciples interrogated Jesus as to their meaning.[21] The quest for the *ipsissima verba* is sometimes a distrac-

---

the anonymous 'community tradition'" (*The Charismatic Leader and His Followers*, trans. James Greg [Edinburgh: T&T Clark, 1981], 85). Let me add that, in many cases where the gospel's statements cannot be confidently ascribed to historical Jesus, a true portrait of his thinking about himself may be detected. As an example, whether or not Jesus thought of himself as the Messiah or the Son of God, it is how his disciples saw him, and the point is all-important.

19. So, e.g., Herod's order to massacre infants less than two years of age is not historical. It is modeled on the Pharaoh's orders in Exodus 1. But the myth fits what we know of Herod's insensibility and cruelty.

20. Timothy Polk writes, "It matters not whether the compositions are the product of the historical Jeremiah [alt. Jesus] himself or later redactors. In my opinion, it violates the integrity of the text, *qua* poetry, to replace the given literary context with the conjectured historical occasion of the writing process and to construe the text as referring to authorial circumstances rather than to the subject as it is literarily defined" (*The Prophetic Persona: Jeremiah and the Language of the Self* [Sheffield: JSOT Press, 1984], 165; on the next page, Polk rejects the equation of "authentic" with *ipsissima verba*). As Northrop Frye says, "A work of art ... is contemporary with its own time and ... is contemporary with ours" (*Anatomy of Criticism: Four Essays* [Princeton: Princeton University Press, 1957], 51).

21. John Dominic Crossan writes, Jesus "was a very problematic and controversial phenomenon, not only to his enemies but even to his friends" (*The Historical Jesus: The Life of a Mediterranean Jewish Peasant* [San Francisco: HarperSanFrancisco, 1991], 311).

tion that isolates Jesus from his people (that is, his interpreters), making him a philosopher uttering abstract truths. The distinction between what is reported in the gospel and what Jesus "actually said" is legitimate, but is of severely limited use. A radical view could arguably claim that we never have the *ipsissima verba* of the Nazarene. The same is true of the pharisaic/rabbinic traditions. Jacob Neusner, speaking of the reported sayings of Rabbi Aqiba, states that we must assume that he actually did say so (by suspension of disbelief, as Samuel Taylor Coleridge would say). "Otherwise, we should have continually to say, 'The circle of 'Aqiba attributed to 'Aqiba the following.'"[22]

Since the present book depends on *sociohistorical exegesis*, it is by way of gathering a constellation of motifs that we may apprehend the sociological reality of Jesus's time and, hence, something of his mentality and of his symbolic world. Gerd Theissen in particular insists on the practicality of Jesus's sayings in the Christian communities, starting with the tradents themselves.[23] Incidentally, Theissen notes that, while people of power generally write history, the gospels, to the contrary, come from the lower layer of society.[24]

In fact, the midrashic composition of narratives spelled big trouble when the Christian church betrayed more and more of its Jewish roots. For the "Greeks" disliked the imprecision implied in "a large margin of interpretation" characteristic of the parable/haggadah. What they wanted were hard facts with a margin of interpretation that was as narrow as possible. The fathers of the church rushed to "solidify" the narrated events into the *historisch* category. The haggadic shifted into the literal; the paradigmatic into the idiosyncratic; the kerygmatic into the biographical. There occurred a metamorphosis from "office" to "nature." Yes, Jesus was born from a virgin mother; yes, he was literally the Son of God; yes, he actually walked on the waters of the lake; yes, he resurrected Lazarus; and so on. The result of such a "cult of the personality" was to mythologize Jesus, henceforth uprooting him from his Jewish basis and meaning.[25] The process, it is true, is already incipient in the gospels.

---

22. Jacob Neusner, *The Pharisees: Rabbinic Perspectives* (New York: Ktav, 1973), 148.
23. See Gerd Theissen, *Studien zur Soziologie des Urchristentums*, WUNT 19 (Tübingen: Mohr Siebeck, 1989), 79–105.
24. Ibid.
25. The "fireworks"—in the second century onward—of fantasies and follies in the apocryphal "gospels" shows an amazingly early corruption of the life and teaching

When the emperor Claudius passed an edict in 49–50 that only the pagans who converted to Judaism could stay in Rome at the exclusion of the native Jews (see Acts 18:2), his edict sanctioned the divorce between Christians and Jews. Eventually, the fact had a backlash effect on the Christians, as they became a sect and an association, which no longer being Jewish became unlawful in the Rome of Nero.

The Work of Luke

According to scholarly consensus, the Gospel of Luke, along with a second volume called the Acts of the Apostles, was written around 90 CE. The author of the so-called Luke Gospel is in fact anonymous, but all elements point to a non-Jewish composer, most probably the physician Luke, a convert and friend of Paul.[26] His *euangelion* seems to have been written in Antioch. Its audience is composed of non-Jews (at least in majority), but Luke is eager to mention Jewish traditions, both biblical and nonbiblical. It may be in response to Marcion and his disparaging opinion of the "Old Testament." It is therefore probable that Luke used a Jewish-Christian pre-Lukan document.[27] This is particularly obvious in the canticles of Luke 1. Proper to Luke are important passages like the parable of the good Samaritan (Luke 10), and of the prodigal son (Luke 15), as well as accounts of Jesus's resurrection and ascension. During his ministry, Luke says, Jesus showed a keen interest in the disenfranchised, tax collectors, sinners, gentiles, women, children,[28] the sick, and the disabled. Luke presents a Jesus who embraces universalism (see 7:1–11).[29]

---

of Jesus. Suffice it here to mention the Protevangelium of James with its fancy "Infancy Gospel." As soon as the Jewish "magisterium" was ignored, everything became possible, even the grotesque. Even the Gospel of Peter, so celebrated by John Dominic Crossan (see *The Cross That Spoke* [San Francisco: HarperSanFrancisco, 1988]) is a pastiche of traditions drawn from the canonical gospels.

26. See Col 4:14; cf. 2 Tim 4:11; Phlm 24.

27. So, in part, Raymond Brown, *The Birth of the Messiah: A Commentary on the Infancy Narratives in Matthew and Luke* (Garden City, NY: Doubleday, 1977).

28. Jesus blesses the children (Mark 10:13–16 // Matt 19:13–15 // Luke 18:15–17). The kingdom of God is for them, that is, for those who are humble enough to be counted among them (Matt 18:1–4). The children in the gospel are the pendant of the poor; see Luke 6:20; Matt 5:3; Jas 2:5; Gos. Thom. 54.

29. Cf. 1QM, in which there shall be justice and peace for the poor and oppressed.

8. JESUS TAUGHT IN PARABLES

Not surprisingly, Luke is Paulinian.[30] Early on, he indicates his expectation of the conversion of gentiles to Christianity. Thus Simeon praises the infant Jesus in the temple by saying that he is to be "in the presence of all peoples, a light for revelation to the gentiles and for glory to your people Israel" (2:31–32; cf. Isa 49:6; 46:13). Also Luke 3:6 (in John the Baptist's message) quotes Isa 40:3–5, "all flesh shall see the salvation of God."[31] Further, in his gospel, Luke is eager to mention pious non-Jews: the Roman centurion, builder of a synagogue (7:5; cf. Mark 8:5–13); the Ethiopian eunuch (Acts 8:27–29); and Cornelius (Acts 10:1–4).

Luke contrasts prophetic Judaism with those hardened Jewish crowds that are always ready to murder God's prophets. These include Moses—and, hence, the torah—with the prophets (e.g., 1:55, 73; 16:9–31; Acts 3:12; 26:22). In Luke, Jesus entertains good relations with both the Pharisees and the general populace. The veritable foes are scribes, priests, and Sadducees who, moreover, act through ignorance (Acts 2:17; 13:27). This, however, is not true of the Diaspora Jews; their persecution of the church is the fact of people who "act from malice and jealousy against [Luke's] church,"[32] and their synagogues are places of violence. As for some Pharisees, they are caricatured as being blind, corrupt, hypocritical, and violent. But it happens that even such a negative attitude can be deemed as providential: it prompted the apostles to spread the gospel among the gentiles (hence, the book of Acts).

Within the Lukan conception of the mission to the gentiles, the evangelist is "de-eschatologizing the kerygma" by "divest[ing] the terms *kingdom* and *Son of Man* almost entirely of apocalyptic significance."[33]

After the death and resurrection of their Master, the apostles were "continually" in the temple (Luke 24:53). This, for Luke, constitutes the link between Scripture and Christ. Jesus was circumcised (2:21); his mother went to the rites of purification forty days after the child delivery (2:22,

---

T. Dan 5:7–13 (with signs of Christian reworking). In t. Demai 3:4, the tax collectors cannot be members of the *havurah* (Pharisaic community).

30. This is not surprising after the tremendous work of Paul's mission among the gentiles. Recall that Paul sent collections to Jerusalem as a tribute from the gentiles to Israel.

31. On the present development, see Paula Fredriksen, *From Jesus to Christ: The Origins of the New Testament Images of Jesus* (New Haven: Yale University Press, 1988), 191ff.

32. Ibid., 194.

33. Ibid., 196.

cf. Lev 12); Jesus was "presented" in the shrine, an allusion to the *pidion ha-ben*, the ransom for a son (2:22; see Exod 13:2, 12, 15; Num 18:15–16: Neh 10:35–36). In short, Jesus's parents fulfilled "everything required by the law of the Lord" (2:39; see also 2:41–51, on the Passover in the temple). In Luke 2:42, Jesus at twelve years old—that is, even before his religious maturity at thirteen, according to m. 'Abot 5:25—recalls the legends of heroes with great wisdom, especially Moses.[34] True, the temple must be transcended (7:49–50; cf. Isa 66:1–2), but Jesus calls it "my Father's house" (2:49, which, incidentally constitutes Jesus's first rebuke of his parents).[35] Again in the temple, the prophetess Anna (2:36) recalls other female prophets of Scripture: Miriam (Exod 15:20), Deborah (Judg 4:4), Huldah (2 Kgs 22:14), Isaiah's wife (Isa 8:3), and Noadiah (Neh 6:14).

John the Baptist marks the transition from the ancient to the new Judaism for Jesus, who is, from the beginning, "son of the Most High" (*'el 'elyon*, 1:32). He is "son of God" (1:35), by *adoption*; Adam, for example, was already a "son of God" (see 3:38; cf. 2 Sam 7:14; Ps 2:7; 4QFlor 3:10–13).

Finally, as Fredriksen writes, Luke emphasizes the role of the Spirit. The Spirit safeguards the apostolic succession from the beginning (see, e.g., Acts 3:38; 9:17).

Raymond Brown says, "Neither [Matthew nor Luke] knew the other's work."[36] It seems to me inconceivable, however, that both independently created, ex nihilo, a virginal birth story or haggadah. A "popular tradition" must have existed, as is evident in apocryphal gospels. As we know, most of these popular myths about Jesus's childhood, replete with petty prodigies such as reviving dead birds or the boy that Jesus had killed, were felicitously rejected in the canonical gospels. I would say that stories on Jesus's birth are an exception to the general sobriety of the gospel stories. It is true that the Matthean and the Lukan versions display great literary qualities that single them out. They also provide a cento of Scripture texts

---

34. See Josephus, *Ant.* 2.230; Philo, *Mos.* 1.21; or, about Cyrus, Herodotus, *Hist.* 1.114–115; about Alexander the Great, Plutarch, *Life of Alexander* 5. In Luke 2:52, "Jesus increased in wisdom." This parallels Moses, once again; see Josephus, *Ant.* 2.231; and Philo, *Mos.* 1.19.

35. This is not to be confused with what Erik Erikson termed "negative [deviant] identity" (cf. *Identity: Youth and Crisis* [New York: Norton, 1968]). It is rather an echo of the competition between the spiritual and the natural.

36. Brown, *Birth*, 497.

and thereby build a wonderful bridge between the "old" and the "new." Furthermore, they pay homage to the extraordinary character of the one who, in the evangelists' opinion, is the Messiah of Israel. They also include an ex post facto encomium to Mary, who belatedly joined the ranks of the early Christians (Acts 1:14, a kind of "by the way" mention of "Mary the mother of Jesus and his brothers"). She is not an exemplar of a "virginal" conception, but of humble surrendering to God's will. In the early church, it was imperative to show a "continuity of the Christian movement with Israel," and "Mary will embody that continuity," says Brown.[37] Indeed, Mary's procrastination and resistance during her son's life builds a portrait of the Jewish temporary "blindness," which will end, as it did indeed symbolically, when she joined the church.[38]

Much more needs to be said about the Gospel of Luke, especially as regards his narrative on the birth of Jesus, where his literary genius is in full play, as we shall see. Luke also uses a mosaic of scriptural themes that he builds into the passion narrative. His composition is thus bifocal: Scriptures are prophecies of Jesus. Luke draws from Genesis, Judges, 1 Samuel, Daniel, Isaiah, and other books. This is one of his main two sources (for the discrete E presentation). The other comprises the events of the ending episodes in Jesus's life. They are now artistically applied to the time of the birth and infancy, in the image of the birth and infancy of the Christian church, while at the same time prophetically announcing the end, both of Jesus's life and of history.

All the puzzle pieces—deliberately and coherently specified in the infancy narrative—are meant to be reassembled into another coherent narrative of the last stage of Jesus's life. In fact, this latter is the original and natural seedbed for the former. It is only for the sake of chronology that the pieces are made to fit for the beginning as well as for the end. The infancy narrative thus becomes a pesher (or haggadah) of the passion. Each of these parts of Luke's composition mirrors the other. It is a tour de force to have made the birth narrative a midrash both of Scripture *and* of

---

37. Ibid., 499.

38. If indeed there had been an annunciation from heaven or from an angel as described in Luke 1:26–38, Mary's stubbornness before her son's prophetic proclamations (Mark 6:4) becomes incomprehensible. The transition between the embarrassed mother of Jesus seen as a mad man (see also Mark 3:20–21, 31–35), and the believing Mary at the end, is facilitated in Luke by Mary's inner wavering about "all these events" (Luke 2:19, 51; cf. Jacob on his son Joseph's dream in Gen 37:11).

the end. The Scriptures are seen as pointing to Jesus as the Messiah,[39] and the ultimate events in Jesus's life as giving form in retrospect to his whole existence, including his birth and even his conception in utero. The intervention of the Holy Spirit in the conception of Jesus is a clear reminiscence of the birth of the universe by the *ruah 'elohim* that *merahephet 'al penei hamayim* (Gen 1:2). Jesus's birth is a new creation, that is, the advent of the world to come.[40]

---

39. See Luke 2:25: "waiting for the consolation of Israel" in relation to Luke 23:51: "waiting for the kingdom of God"; cf. 2:30: "waiting for the redemption of Jerusalem [alternatively, "Israel"]."

40. Brown, *Birth*, writes about the Gospel of Luke that the "Old Testament type" figures of Zechariah and Elizabeth, Simeon and Anna, as well as Mary's hymn of the remnant (1:54) "form a chorus to hail the new era" (242).

9
The Birth Narratives

Were I writing my book in the nineteenth century, I could have come with a typically explicit title such as "The Retrospectively Set Birth Stories in the Beginning of Jesus's Ministry by Matthew and Luke." As I said earlier, the gospels are written from the perspective of the death and resurrection of their main character, so that the end is the beginning and the beginning is the end. In other words, for the evangelists, Jesus's death was no ordinary death, and so his birth was no ordinary birth.[1]

With Matthew and Luke's birth narratives, however, we enter the literary genre of legend or, more precisely as we shall see, the midrashic genre. Both Matthew and Luke consciously start and end their gospels with myth (see Matt 28:2–10; Luke 24:6–12). The final words of Matthew's Gospel, "I am with you always," echo the beginning narrative on Jesus's birth, where he is called "Emmanuel" (1:23). In fact, the miraculous conception of Jesus in Matthew and Luke serves the purpose of stressing God's prior creative act, that is, the divine initiative.[2]

Earlier I referred to the birth narrative as a midrash. The style in Luke 1–2, however, is different from that we find in the body of his gospel (where the midrash is far from absent). If we follow Paul Winter in an

---

1. Daniel Boyarin says, "The rabbis considered the birth one enormous signifying system, any part of which could be taken as commenting on or supplementing any other part.... The new stories, which build closely on the biblical narratives but expand and modify them as well, were considered the equals of the biblical narratives themselves" (*The Jewish Gospels: The Story of the Jewish Christ* [New York: New Press, 2012], 76).

2. See Charles H. Talbert, "Miraculous Conceptions and Births in Mediterranean Antiquity," in *The Historical Jesus in Context*, ed. Amy-Jill Levine, John Dominic Crossan, and Dale C. Allison (Princeton: Princeton University Press, 2006), 79–86.

article he published in 1954,[3] these two chapters of the gospel are from a different author. He argues that someone very aware of the Jewish social, religious, folkloric, traditions and customs, as well as of the local topography, wrote them. He cites eight texts to prove his thesis, including Luke 2:8 (shepherds in the countryside of Bethlehem keeping watch over their flocks by night). These texts show that this particular author was familiar with Palestinian topography, a familiarity absent from the rest of Luke's Gospel. The author needed to place Jesus's birth in Bethlehem on the basis of Mic 4:9-10 ("from the city … in the open country"). He understands Micah correctly as referring to the king who will save the small remnant of Israel. It is Mic 4:10 ("the open country"), for instance, that dictated the motif that there was no room in the inn for Mary about to give birth to Jesus. Noteworthy is John 7:41-42 reporting a messianic tradition with Bethlehem as its center.

The late Professor Otto Betz suggested to me another, complementary approach. Luke's narrative may be a midrash on 2 Sam 7 (the eternal covenant with the house of David), in which case Mary plays the role of David. In 2 Sam 7:12 (LXX), God says to David that his successor will come *ek tēs koilias sou* (from your belly/uterus [*sic*]), and in Luke 1:42 Elizabeth greets the one who is coming *ek tēs koilias sou*. Further, the angel's apparitions fill the role of the prophet Nathan.

This brings us to mention the presence of "miraculous births" in the Hebrew Bible and elsewhere. Texts like Gen 4:1 (Eve); 16:2 (Hagar); 17:16 (Sarah); 18:14 (Sarah); 21:1-6 (Sarah; LXX: *kai kyrios epeskepsato ten Saran*); 25:21 (Rebecca); 29:31-33 (Leah); 30:2, 6, 8, 17-18, 20, 22-24 (Rachel and Leah);[4] and 1 Sam 1:5, 11, 19 (Hannah), may be cited. We shall return to this biblical theme, particularly well emphasized by Philo in *De cherubim* 48-49 and *De posteritate Caini* 78. At any rate, this motif proved fertile ground for further haggadah. Note that the midrash is everywhere present in the birth narrative of Matthew as well: see Matt 2:1-12, based on Num 24:17; Matt 2:13-15, on Hos 11:1 (note the typical transposition); 2:16-18, on Jer 31:15; 2:23, on Nazareth, building a pun with Nazarene

---

3. Paul Winter, "The Cultural Background to the Narrative in Luke 1 and 2," *JQR* 45 (1954): 159-67, 230-42.

4. On Gen 30, see my "Une descendance manipulée et ambiguë (Genèse 29,31–30,24)," in *Jacob*, ed. Jean-Daniel Macchi and Thomas Römer, Commentaire à plusieurs voix / Ein mehrstimmiger Kommentar zu / A Plural Commentary of / Gen. 25–36, Mélanges offerts à Albert de Pury (Geneva: Labor et Fides, 2001), 109-27.

(see below). The gospel may also draw a parallel with the haggadic tradition that the Hebrews in Egypt voluntarily abstained from sexual relations so as not to provide Pharaoh with infant victims: Exod. Rab. 1.22 and 10.7 (on 1:15 and 2:25); Yoma 74b; Sop. 11b; cf. B. Bat. 60b. This particular midrash bears notice for our purpose: "Mary" recalls the name and the person of Miriam, who in the midrash is credited for the birth of the savior Moses. In Luke 2:51 ("Mary kept those things in her heart") falls in parallel with Miriam's behavior ("to see what would happened to [Moses or her prophecy]").[5] Mary is visited by an angel (Luke 1:26–38; Miriam has the vision of a man clad in linen, the angel Gabriel). Joseph is said to be *dikaios* ("a just man"), like Amram, who is credited with being one of the "Seven Just" who brought back the Shekinah on earth.[6] Mary and Joseph remain chaste until Jesus's birth (Matt 1:18, 25), a theme that recalls the Israelites' decision to refrain from sexual relations (see above). To bring about the birth of Moses, Amram and Yokebed remarry! (Note that King David is a descendant of Miriam [1 Chr 2:18].) Exodus Rabbah 15.1 says that Moses is Israel to whom Yokebed gave birth. Along this line, note that in the midrash on Jeremiah's birth, his mother is Zion (see beginning of the midrash). In the Zohar, the messiah's mother is the Shekinah, also identified with the community of Israel.[7] (Incidentally, the Zohar adds that the sages will at first not believe the messiah, but when he resurrects Nehemiah son of Shealtiel,[8] they believe him.)

I mention alongside these a legend about very old parents giving birth to Isaac.[9] God orders the angel to shape Isaac's embryo exactly on the model of Abraham. But there are people who are suspicious of Abraham's paternity and say, "Look at this old couple! They picked up a foundling on the highway, and they pretend he is their son!" According to Philo—for whom, by the way, a woman after menopause reverts to virginity if she had no children (cf. Gen 18:11 cited in *Post.* 134)—Isaac is "son of God" ("The Lord begot Isaac"). See also *Leg.* 3.218–219; cf. *Cher.* 45 regarding Sarah.

---

5. So, e.g., in the Mekilta; cf. Exod. Rab. 1:22; Num. Rab. 13.20; Meg. 14a.
6. See, e.g., Tanh. B ad Numbers, p. 16; Num. Rab. 13.2; Pesiq. Rab. 5.
7. Sefer Zerubbabel, in Beth ha-Midrash 2:54–57; Zohar, Ra'aya Mehemma, 3:67b–68a; see Raphael Patai, *Messiah Texts* (New York: Avon, 1979), 125–30.
8. Perhaps, Rabbi Nehemiah (between 135–170 CE), student of Rabbi Aqiba. According to Sanh. 86a, he stands behind all anonymous statements of the Tosefta.
9. See Louis Ginzberg, "The Birth of Isaac," in *Legends of the Bible: A Shorter Version* (Philadelphia: Jewish Publication Society, 1992), 121.

This type of story is also found in other cultures. Pythagoras was "conceived by Apollo," Iamblicus says, and his virtues made "it reasonable to call him the son of a god" and to speak of his "divine nature."[10] It is not that Apollo had sex with Pythagoras's mother, but Pythagoras goes through a transfiguration.[11] Only a divine witness can understand—in contradistinction to disciples, who misunderstand—according to "the principle of like knowing like."[12] See also the legend of Bacchus's divine birth, which gave him divine healing power. And, if we feel that we are going overboard in "fishing" for non-Jewish parallels, see early third-century Origen, *Against Celsus* 1.37: "It is not absurd to employ Greek stories to talk with Greeks, to show we Christians are not the only people who use a miraculous story like this one [about Jesus's conception]. For some (Greeks) think it proper ... to relate even of recent events that Plato was the son of Amphictione, while Ariston was prevented from having sexual intercourse with his wife until she gave birth to the one sired by Apollo."

Is there in the gospel a clue that some saw Jesus's birth as that of an illegitimate child? It is clear, according to Matt 1:19, that Joseph could have taken Mary to justice for adultery, but he does not want to bring the whole matter to a public display (*deigmatisay*). The question is tied with the gospel episodes around Jesus's mother Mary (see below). At any rate, there is in Jewish tradition very little speculation about the mother of the future messiah.[13] She remains mainly anonymous. But in a talmudic story she is called Hephzibah and is the wife of the prophet Nathan. Her son Menahem (Comforter) is, however, the son of another man by the name of 'Amiel, son of David!

Clearly, the midrash cannot be compared with pagan myths. While the latter take the reader to the beginning of time, the midrash takes place within the experiential time. There are a protagonist and one or more

---

10. Iamblicus, *Vita Pythagorica* 10, p. 8.20–30.

11. Iamblicus, *Vita Pythagorica* 7, p. 7.22–24.

12. See Jonathan Z. Smith, "Good News Is No News: Aretalogy and Gospel," in *Map Is Not Territory: Studies in the History of Religions* (Chicago: University of Chicago Press, 1993), 34, 35. Smith adds that, in both the Greco-Roman *Vitae* and the Christian gospels, there is "discrepancy between [the readers'] understanding and the protagonist's self-understanding" (37).

13. In Pesiq. Rab Kah. supp. 6's "stunning hymn" to the [coming] messiah (Jacob Neusner, *Messiah in Context: Israel's History and Destiny in Formative Judaism*, The Foundations of Judaism: Method, Theology, Doctrine 2 [Philadelphia: Fortress, 1984], 157), we find, "Blessed is the womb whence he came!"

antagonists in midrashim. In the gospel, the antagonism is the unexpectedness and irrationality of the event announced. It is also the potential scandal of Mary's pregnancy.[14] Eventually, the antagonism is personified in Herod.

Note that Jesus is mentioned in the Tosefta (fifth century); see t. Hullin 2:22, where we find the famous hoax of "Jesus, son of Pantera," and in 2:24, "Jesus ben Pantiri [sic]." In the view of Joseph Klausner,[15] the expression *huios tēs parthenou* may have been changed by mockery into "ben Panthera."

On Mary, Mother of the Nazarene

Evidently the birth narratives in Matthew and Luke are based on the LXX version of Isa 7:14: "Behold a virgin shall conceive in the womb and shall bring forth a son, and you shall call his name Emmanuel." About the term "virgin" (*parthenos*) in the LXX, we shall note that it renders no less than three Hebrew words: *bethulah*, *na'arah*, and *'almah*. It designates a virgin, but also a girl still unable to conceive although married because she is not yet pubescent.[16] In m. Nid. 1:4, the question is raised, "Who is the virgin? Any girl who never in her life saw a drop of [menstrual] blood, even though she is married." In t. Nid. 1:6, "Who is a virgin? Any girl who never in her life, and even if she is married and had children, I call a virgin, until she will see the first drop [of menstrual blood]. It comes out that they did not refer [in the Mishnah] to virgin in respect to the tokens of virginity but a virgin in respect to menstrual blood" (cf. y. Nid. 1:3, 49a; b. Nid. 8b).[17] In the second century CE, Trypho already responded to Justin that *'almah* means

---

14. Matthew mentions "scandal" apropos Mary's pregnancy. This seems to associate her with the four questionable female characters of Jesus's genealogy (1:3–6). The Prot. Jas. 17 seems to be aware of the possibility of Jesus's illegitimate birth ("I am ashamed of her," says Joseph).

15. Joseph Klausner, *Jesus of Nazareth: His Life, Times, and Teaching* (New York: Macmillan, 1925; repr., New York: Bloch, 1997), 24. Morton Smith rejected this hypothesis in *Jesus the Magician* (New York: Gollancz, 1978), 47.

16. Cf. y. Nid. 1:3, 49a. Geza Vermes reads Luke 1:34 ("How can it be, for I know no man?") as meaning that she is "a minor, awaiting the right biological moment to change to the status of wife" (*Jesus the Jew: A Historian's Reading of the Gospels* [New York: Macmillan, 1973], 221).

17. See Jacob Neusner, *Are There Really Tannaitic Parallels to the Gospels*, USFSHJ (Atlanta: Scholars Press, 1993), 97.

young woman and that "the whole Isaianic prophecy [there] refers to King Hezekiah."[18] In later Greek versions of Isa 7, *'almah* is rendered by *neanis*.

Trypho was right as regards *'almah*. The term designates a female human being *before* her first child. So the first conclusion to draw from the Hebrew text is that Emmanuel is a firstborn child.[19] *'Almah* is not necessarily a virgin, as made evident in Prov 30:19–20.[20] Furthermore, the LXX commonly uses the term *parthenos* as a simile for Israel as a collectivity. Her identification is beyond the scope of this study. It remains, however, that in Luke 1:48 Mary is "[God's] servant," and so is Israel in 1:54 (cf. Isa 44:1; Ps 136:22; 1 Chr 16:13). Note again the association of Mary with Israel in Luke 1:66 ("the hand of the Lord" like in Exod 9:3; 16:3; Josh 4:24; 22:31; Isa 41:20; 66:14). In Luke 2:7, Jesus is a "firstborn son" (*prōtotokos*), like Israel in Exod 4:22. This point is clearly expressed in John 3:1–21, that is, the dialogue of Jesus with Nicodemus. He exhorts Nicodemus to be born again, from above (*anōthen*), that is, to be begotten by the heavenly Father, like the Son of Man himself (3:31).

This point sheds light on the reason why Matthew and Luke chose to weave a midrash around Isa 7:14. Both wanted to make the point that Jesus's sonship of God was ab initio. Jesus was Son of God even before his birth. So his developing messianic consciousness is like the growth of a plant whose seed was preexistent.

Anthropologically speaking, the Mediterranean system of honor and shame involves the "almost mythological importance of virginity" of marriageable females.[21] Hence the quasi-mythological, supreme status of Mary as virgin-mother, that is, maternity without loss of virginity. Therefore, Mary rises above competition with other females.

It warrants mention, however, that nearly all the gospel references to Jesus's relationship with his family are conflictual, especially with his mother. Some of his kin even declared him mad, at least at the beginning of his ministry (see Luke 8:20; John 7:5 [cf. 10:20]). But in contrast to Mark's

---

18. Note that the term *bethulah* appears in Isa 23:4, 12; 37:22; 47:1; 62:5; so the LXX in Isa 7 deliberately chose *parthenos* for *'almah*.

19. In the Vulgate of Matt 1:25, we find the words, "filium suum [Joseph's] primogenitum" (influence of Luke 2:7, see below).

20. See also Gen 34:3 LXX: Dinah is said to be a *parthenos* just after she had intercourse!

21. John Dominic Crossan, *The Historical Jesus: The Life of a Mediterranean Jewish Peasant* (San Francisco: HarperSanFrancisco, 1991), 14.

negative judgment on Jesus's family (Mark 3:21–32), Matthew's birth narrative describes Jesus's parents as the first witnesses of Jesus's divine sonship (1:20–25; 2:10; Matt drops Mark 3:21, Jesus as "out of his mind"!). After Mark 3:31–35, no family contact with Jesus is any longer reported. Furthermore, some of Jesus's declarations regarding his family are striking in their total originality. In Luke 8:20, for instance, he says, "My mother and my brothers are those who hear the word of God and do it."[22] Luke 14:26 (softened in Matt 10:37) speaks of "hating father and mother, wife and children, brothers and sisters, yes, and even life itself, [otherwise one] cannot be my disciple."[23] As José Pagola reminds us, "Outside the family an individual was unprotected, unsafe. One's true identity came from the family."[24] Jesus never addresses his mother other than as "woman" (John 2:4; 19:26)!

It is remarkable how Jesus's mission continuously sparked conflict, both in Galilee (Mark 2; 3; 7: scribes and Pharisees) and in Jerusalem (chief priests, elders, and scribes). Jesus speaks of himself as a prophet rejected in his own land and house (Matt 13:5; John 4:44; cf. Matt 21:10; Luke 24:19).

The early Jerusalem church (the Ebionites) under the leadership of Jesus's brother, James, did not believe that Jesus had been born of a virgin, nor in the divinity of Christ, but saw him rather as a prophet. David Flusser comments, "It could be supposed that such early Christian groups [the Ebionites and the Nazarenes] ... saw salvation mainly in the future."[25]

The Genealogies of Jesus (Matthew and Luke)

In the Matt 1 genealogy of Jesus, we find that four names have been omitted after David-Solomon. Further, in 1:8, Joram did not father Uzziah, who was his great-grandfather. As to Josiah, he was not the father but rather the grandfather of Jechoniah. In Luke 3:36 introduces Cainan, a name that is not extent in the MT, but is present in the LXX. We shall also note the lapse in Luke 1:31–33: Jesus is said to have David as his father,

---

22. This declaration must be central in all reflection on a theory of marriage, for instance.

23. See Matt 10:34–35; 23:9; 25:40; Mark 1:19–20; 3:32–35; Luke 9:61–62; 12:51–53.

24. José A. Pagola, *Jesus: An Historical Approximation*, trans. Margaret Wilde (Miami: Convivium, 2009), 58. See Mark 3:34–35; Matt 23:9.

25. They were declared heretics by Irenaeus in the second century.

which presupposes that he is the son of Joseph of the lineage of David (see Luke 3:23 and Matt 1). On Jesus's Davidic descent, see, a contrario, John 7:40–42 and Mark 12:35–37, contrasting with Mark 10:47 and 11:9–10. Remarkably, the genealogy of Jesus cites, among non-Jews like Abraham, Tamar, Rahab, and Ruth, questionable characters—female and male—like Bathsheba. Joseph—here the father of Jesus—is mentioned among kings, descendents of David, so as to make fourteen generations from the exile to Christ.

Was Jesus born in Bethlehem? Not so in John 7:41–43. Bethlehem is absent in Mark. For Matthew, the birth in Bethlehem would fulfill the prophecies (see Mic 5:1), as does the flight to Egypt (see Hos 11:1) and the move to Nazareth ("he'll be called the Nazarene" in Matt 2:22–23, a "quote" of a nonexistent text!).

By the way, the term *Nazōraios* in Matt 2:23; 26:7—eight times in Luke-Acts and three times in John—is not without ambiguity. Four times in Mark and two times in Luke, we find *Nazarēnos* (Mark 14:67 // Matt 26:71). The basic meaning may be "from Nazareth." But, on the model of *pharisaios* or *saddoukaios*, the term may designate Jesus's belonging to a sect of that name, as it appears in Acts 24:5, where the Christians are called *Nazōraioi*. It seems safe to conclude that "from Nazareth" suggests a messianic pun on the term *nazir* in the Hebrew Bible (that is, one being vowed to divine service: Num 6:1–21; cf. Luke 1:15 on John the Baptist). In the LXX, *nazir* is translated *Nazir/Nazeiraios* (cf. Mark 1:24; Luke 4:34; John 6:69).[26] To be added to the dossier is Mark 1:24, where Jesus is called *ho hagios tou theou*, the very terms used by the LXX to translate *nazir elohim* (in the case of Samson, cf. Judg 13:7; 16:17). Along the same line, the *qedishey 'elohim* of Dan 7:18, 22, 25, 27 is translated in Theodotion by *hagioi (tou) theou*. So, when Jesus is called *ho hagios tou theou* in Mark 1:24, there is an allusion to the *nazir* of the Hebrew Bible—a man totally dedicated to the service of God—and to Isa 11:1, where the Hebrew root *nṣr* means "to keep, to watch" (hence, in a fifteenth-century Dutch MS now in Cambridge, Joseph is said to keep "[Mary] to protect her." This text agrees with the Protevangelium of James).[27]

---

26. On all of this, see Raymond Brown, *The Birth of the Messiah: A Commentary on the Infancy Narratives in Matthew and Luke* (Garden City NY: Doubleday, 1977), 212.

27. Cited by Matthew Black, *An Aramaic Approach to the Gospels and Acts*, 3rd ed. (1946; repr., Peabody, MA: Hendrickson, 1998), 224–25.

9. THE BIRTH NARRATIVES

In conclusion, the midrashic nature of the birth narratives in both Matthew and Luke is beyond controversy. These stories were never intended to be read literally, as indeed they were later by non-Jewish "Greek" Christians, anxious to transpose their former culture, with gods mingling with human females, into their newfound but all-too-Jewish traditions. The result has proved disastrous for Christendom, thus favoring a literal, superficial reading of texts that actually are allusive and metaphorical.[28] As we saw earlier, a basic hermeneutic rule is made explicit in Mek. 6.8 on Exod 20:12 (God descended on Mount Sinai [and left the heavens empty]!). We then said that the literalist is called a *shomea'*, that is, one who sticks to the literal meaning of the text. The latter he explicates with additional "conclusions" that are unwarranted and belong only to the narrow, literal interpretation. To this the rabbinic authority reacts by saying, *'amartha*, "you must [rather] say." It is echoed by Jesus's "but I say unto you."

---

28. John P. Meier (*Law and Love*, vol. 4 of *A Marginal Jew: Rethinking the Historical Jesus*, ABRL [New Haven: Yale University Press, 2009], 652) speaks of "the partial transformation of a Galilean rabbi into a Gentile guru."

10
Jesus's Baptism

In the view of New Testament scholars, the baptism of Jesus by John is most probably historical, if only for the simple reason that it is inconceivable that the early Christian church would have invented such an embarrassing story about Jesus going through a "sacrament" of repentance for the remission of sins. Although the Fourth Gospel all but ignores the episode, the three Synoptics more or less reluctantly report it. It is even presented as an important event, marked by a theophany declaring Jesus the Son of God. Historically, we may imagine that Jesus at that point was seized by an intimate illumination, decisive enough to stir the conviction that he had to engage in a preaching ministry.

At any rate, Jesus's decision to be baptized by John shows clearly that Jesus's self-consciousness started, so to speak, at point zero. When he comes to John, he is unassuming about his own vocation, and his attitude betrays a deep piety (he is then about thirty years old) with a clear inclination toward the subversive religiosity represented by John the Baptist. John's baptism, as Josephus says (*Ant.* 18.116–118), was "for the purification of the body; supposing still that the soul was thoroughly purified beforehand by righteousness" (117). Josephus adds that Herod was so afraid that John's influence on the people would stir rebellion that he puts him to death in Machera (118; cf. Mark 6:17–29).

The Gospel of Mark (10:38–39) provides an interesting interpretation of Jesus's baptism, clearly alluding to Jesus's passion. He was baptized in the "waters" of death.

As I have said, Jesus's baptism is the springboard into stage two of his self-consciousness. It is the door that opens on his teaching mission, after an illumination that the gospel translates as an epiphany (Mark 1:9–11 and parr.).[1] Strikingly, the inner transformation in a human is such that it induces a taut temptation to power, which by the way would negate the meaning of recent "baptism of repentance for the forgiveness of sins"! The devil in the desert uses the revealing formula, "If you are the Son of God ..." (Matt 4:3, 6 and parr.).[2] In short, things may go one way or the other as far as Jesus's options are concerned. The ending of the scene of temptation ominously declares that the devil departed "until an opportune time" (Luke 4:13). During his trial, at the other end of the trajectory, Jesus reminds Pilate that he could order legions of angels to intervene in his favor (Matt 26:53, "[God] will at once send me more than twelve legions of angels").

From start to finish, being the Son of God implies Jesus's existential choice of weakness and death. It is from this perspective that we are to read his repeated announcements to that effect. (Mark has Jesus anticipating his fatal destiny in Jerusalem three times: 8:31; 9:31; and 10:33–34; see, e.g., Matt 16:21–23 and parr.; 17:12, 22–23; 20:18–19 and parr.; Luke 24:6–7.) Whether these statements are seen as historically authentic is not decisive. The point is that Jesus clearly knew that a certain way of life is not conducive to triumph and public recognition. Individual innocence makes everyone else ill at ease, embarrassed, and sometimes cruel. There is no innocence without an implicit or explicit resistance to group pressure.[3]

Inevitably, the group takes its revenge and selects the just as its scapegoat. "This is the one who comes through water and blood" (John 5:6), the baptism of Jesus was already an immersion in blood (see for the image Rom 6:3). This is why Jesus's baptism was an absolute necessity. It was a spiritual ritual, like a rite of passage.

Hence, I don't believe that the question of Jesus's sinfulness or non-sinfulness, or again, perhaps in a less vexing way, whether Jesus had the (wrong) feeling of being himself sinful, is a true problem. Rather, the baptism certainly emphasized the all-important unity of Jesus with his people. Jesus was convinced, as much as John, that Israel was sinful and needed to

---

1. In Luke 3:22, the celestial voice says, "In whom I am well pleased." The Codex D of the Western text says, "On this day I begot you."

2. The scene of Jesus in the desert is modeled on Moses and Elijah. Jesus dwells there forty days like Moses spent forty years in the wilderness, and Elijah forty days in the desert of Horeb.

3. See the striking text of John 7:7 ("I testify against the world that its works are evil").

truly repent in preparation for the coming of the kingdom of God.[4] Both John and he were also conscious of belonging to that sinful people. Focusing our attention exclusively on Jesus is a mistake.

In other words, the theologoumenon according to which Jesus was sinless means very little here. Jesus is a Jew among his people. Excluding himself from the group of repentant Israelites would entail an enormous consequence: the non-Jewishness of the Nazarene.

If so, the criterion of embarrassment that the exegetes conjure up must be reassessed. What is embarrassing is not the questioning of a dogmatic statement, but the issue of Jesus's total Jewishness. It was a necessity that the central Jew be baptized with all those who were repentant, lest he belong to another people. We stumble again on the continual gospel problem of the Jewish roots of Christianity. An embarrassing issue indeed![5]

Right after his baptism, Jesus spent forty days in the wilderness, where "the angels waited on him"—thus duplicating the episode of Elijah in 1 Kgs 19:5–8. There is an Elijah-like aura around the baptism by John and the temptation of Jesus that follows. Later on, at the time of Peter's confession, we once more learn that some people believe that Jesus is Elijah redivivus. This motif's recurrence implies a persistent wavering of opinion between Jesus considered as Messiah or as precursor of the Messiah. Decisively, Peter tips the scale toward Jesus's messiahship: "You are the Messiah" (Mark 8:27–29; see also 6:15).

Incidentally, Jesus's question to the disciples as to who people think he is was neither innocent nor "academic." Jesus's quest betrays his anxiety and his uncertainty about his own identity. At times, the disciples are the sounding board for Jesus's troubled heart.[6] From this perspective, Peter's confession that, indeed, he is the Anointed One is a decisive event. Jesus is revealed to himself (even though he must correct the confession's trajectory). This is when he decides to travel to Jerusalem, where he will risk his all.

---

4. Furthermore, Jesus's repentance would not be more "outlandish" than God's repentance (see Gen 6:6; Exod 32:12, 14; Deut 32:36; plus several times among the Prophets and the Psalms).

5. Understandably, John's Gospel has purposely omitted Jesus's baptism by John, if only because of its mild polemics against the diehard disciples of John the Baptist.

6. Many times they serve as a foil to Jesus's call to lose one's life for the sake of the reign of God. They display a self-centeredness and an avidity of power characterized as "thinking the things of men."

Meanwhile, the notion of the Son of God, common to narratives of both baptism and temptation, emphasizes their consistency (Mark 1:11; Luke 4:3). As Marcus Borg writes, "The personification of evil as Satan does reflect the fact that evil is 'bigger' than any of us."[7] Jesus rebukes Satan and his threefold attempt to subdue him. He successively quotes Deut 8:3; 6:16; and 6:13. The whole scene thus becomes a meditation on the Deuteronomic text. Whether or not Jesus lived that experience in the desert is less important than the typological use of Scriptures to characterize Jesus's venture. The Qumranic pesharim come to mind. While the rabbinic commentary on the Torah draws halakic wisdom from the texts, both Qumran and Jesus read the texts as referring to themselves, since they contain their own eschatological fulfillment.

These biblical quotes must be seen as *preceding*—but not just chronologically—the literary elaboration of the birth narratives, which were composed to fit the requirements of the Hebrew texts. The new story weaves in the contributions of Isaiah, Jeremiah, Numbers, and others.

The rabbinic reading is not thereby invalidated, but it must be deemed incomplete, since it perpetuates the status quo. Hence Jesus emphasizes his "I" ("I say unto you") that no rabbi would find appropriate in his eagerness to appeal to the tradition.[8] Per contra, Jesus speaks from within his consciousness when the tradition has already reached its teleological goal.[9] Then he speaks with an amazing authority that demonstrates his self-consciousness.

---

7. Marcus J. Borg, *Jesus: Uncovering the Life, Teachings, and Relevance of a Religious Revolutionary* (San Francisco: HarperSanFrancisco, 2006), 123.

8. See, e.g., 'Abot 1 and ARN (A) 1.

9. See Matt 5–6, "It was said ... but I say" (six times in the Sermon on the Mount); Matt 11:2–6, 9–15.

11
JESUS'S SELF-CONSCIOUSNESS

At the risk of being anachronistic, I shall begin by evoking Hayim Vital (sixteenth–seventeenth centuries). This eminent disciple of Rabbi Luria said that the messiah will grow in righteousness and that finally "he will recognize himself as such. His messiahship had not been known [to him] before, but now it will be revealed [to him]. Others, however, will not recognize him." Vital takes Moses as an example, who ascended to heaven for forty days and was "unknown" by others, so the messiah "will be raised to heaven." Then he will reveal himself fully, and all Israel will recognize him.[1]

"All Israel." In contrast to an individual-centered psychological analysis of Jesus, it must be affirmed that his self-consciousness is inseparable from the realization that Israel collectively faces the ever-present potentiality of actualizing the kingship of God on earth. If there is anything like a "messianic consciousness" in Jesus, it is not confined to his personal accomplishment—although the latter belongs crucially to the prodromes of collective messianism.[2] Jesus's insistence on the apostolic role before

---

1. See Gershom Scholem, *Sabbatai Sevi: The Mystical Messiah*, trans. R. J. Zwi Werblowsky (Princeton: Princeton University Press, 1973), 53. Note, however, that Vital sees the servant of the Lord as a figure of Moses, not as the messiah, as his teacher Moses Alsheikh did. On the parallel drawn between Jesus and Moses, see Samson H. Levey, *The Messiah: An Aramaic Interpretation*, HUCM 2 (Cincinnati: Hebrew Union College Press, 1974), 13.

2. Jacob Neusner writes, "The figure of the Messiah bears within itself the shared view of a society that bonds family to family, village to village, and the whole into 'Israel'" (*Messiah in Context: Israel's History and Destiny in Formative Judaism*, The Foundations of Judaism: Method, Theology, Doctrine 2 [Philadelphia: Fortress, 1984], xiii). The collective dimension of messianism fuses with the notion of history. As regards Jesus, Mark 3:21, 31–35; and 6:1–6 show clearly that his communion with his community amounts to interdependence.

and after his death points in the same direction. The disciples will experience the same fate as their Master. Mark especially emphasizes this: Mark 13:9-11 (disciples) corresponds to 9:31 (Jesus); and 13:9 to 8:31, also 10:33-34 and 13:13 to 9:12 (Jesus). The Son of Man will die (8:31; 9:31; 10:34), and the disciples must take up their crosses (8:34).[3] The notion of "corporate personality" comes to mind. Although we should use this expression carefully (especially avoiding confusion with some kind of primitive mentality), the intrinsic relation of individual and group helps to illuminate some Hebrew texts. I refer, for example, to Gen 19 (Sodom); Josh 7 (Achan); 2 Sam 24 (collective punishment for David's census); and Ezek 28:2, 12 (the king represents all his people). To avoid inherent confusion in the formula, N. T. Wright uses rather the term "incorporative."[4] He writes, "The Messiah, the anointed one of Israel, represents his people and sums them up in himself, so that what is true of himself is true of them."[5]

First Peter 1:4 is an amazing text that speaks of human participation in the divine nature.[6] It clearly is a becoming, a process moving toward its fulfillment. Jesus, along the same lines, speaks of the Son of Man in the third person singular.[7] It is a mission that Jesus may or may not fulfill. It puzzled the disciples then as it does us today (John 12:34). When this teleological point is reached, however, then the "son of man" Jesus becomes

---

3. See Lloyd Gaston, *No Stone on Another: Studies in the Significance of the Fall of Jerusalem in the Synoptic Gospels* (Leiden: Brill, 1973), 370-409.

4. N. T. Wright, *The Climax of the Covenant: Christ and the Law in the Pauline Theology* (Edinburgh: T&T Clark, 1991); and Wright, *Paul: in Fresh Perspective* (Minneapolis: Fortress, 2005). In this respect, the use of the Greek preposition *en* + person name or pronoun in LXX and in Paul is important (e.g., *en Christō, en Dauid, en soi, en tō basilei*).

5. N. T. Wright, "The Messiah and the People of God: A Study in Pauline Theology with Particular Reference to the Argument of the Epistle to the Romans" (PhD diss., Oxford University, 1980), 4. Crossan also stresses the point: "The Kingdom [is] not ... an individual dream but ... a corporate plan. My wager is that *magic and meal* or *miracle and table* constitutes such a conjunction and that it is the heart of Jesus's program" (*The Historical Jesus: The Life of a Mediterranean Jewish Peasant* [San Francisco: HarperSanFrancisco, 1991], 304).

6. One may interpret Gen 28:12 as meaning that the angels (on Jacob's ladder) connect the earthly man with his celestial nature, like Christ's *doxa* with his *phanerosis* on earth in John 2:11 (so Hugo Odeberg, *The Fourth Gospel: Interpreted in Its Relation to Contemporaneous Religious Currents in Palestine and the Hellenistic-Oriental World* [Chicago: Argonaut, 1929], 36).

7. So, in 1 Enoch 71:17, Enoch himself becomes the Son of Man.

the Messiah. Mark 14:61–62 is crucial (cf. Matt 26:64; Luke 22:69): as long as the glorious Son of Man tarries, the Messiah has not come. *So, strictly speaking, as far as Jesus is concerned, the Messiah has not come yet!* The church's proclamation of Jesus as the Messiah is anticipative. He is already the Messiah now because of "the firm assurance" of his coming in glory. The glorious Messiah will not be other than the one who, here and now, is identified with the poor, the hungry, the thirsty, and the captive (Matt 25:31–46). The present and immediate meeting with the Messiah occurs in the restoration of the kingdom of God through love of God and love of the neighbor.

Such is Jesus's reinterpretation of messiahship. From the notional we pass to the dynamic. Messiahship is the name of the in-between "magnetic" field of I and Thou. Messianic love is unlimited; it eventuates with the cross—the gate to glory. Initially a "son of man," Jesus has become the "Son of Man." Jesus's consciousness is his call to become fully human, as every human must. No messianic consciousness of his would single him out. What happens to him must necessarily happen to all those who are the Son of Man with him. The Messiah is *continuus* and *inclusus* (see Mark 10:45; Luke 22:14–30; Gal 2:20).

In summary, Jesus's reinterpretation of messiahship is underpinned by the conviction that no glory is possible short of being anticipated by suffering and death (see Mark 8:31–33). As such, his message is clearly apocalyptic.[8]

Paul certainly shows his keen understanding when he dares to declare, "In my flesh I am completing what is lacking in Christ's afflictions for the sake of his body, that is, the church" (Col 1:24; cf. Rev 5:9–10; in Luke 22:28, Jesus tells his disciples, "You are those who have continued with me in my trials"). Translated in nonmessianic language—say, in the Hasidic masters' idiom—he is completing "Adam's initial stature [*qomah*]." It is certainly from the same perspective that Jesus proceeds to "repair the breaches" [*tiqun*] in the good creation of God (see ch. 4 above, "Jesus as Healer," 53–70). This mending must be complete *before* his messiahship can be recognized. Before the cross, *Jesus's messiahship is in the process of becoming.*[9] Let's again defy chronology and cite Rabbi Moshe Hayim

---

8. On the book of Daniel and its typology destruction/restoration, see my *Daniel in His Time* (Columbia: University of South Carolina Press, 1988), ch. 6.

9. His baptism attests to this much. John's baptism is "of repentance for the forgiveness of sins,"; cf. Mark 1:4–11; Matthew shows his embarrassment by adding an

Luzzato (eighteenth century), who said that to the human being, God "gave all the things of this world to his[or her] use, because by this [use] they also are repaired and the power of holiness drawn by him[or her] is spreading also over them."[10]

Rather than otherworldly, the kingdom announced by Jesus entails a here-and-now redemption, hence his pressing exhortations for the ethical. "Today" is a recurrent theme. The "spreading all over" of messiahship overshadows individual self-consciousness. The Synoptics record a constant wavering between proclamation and restraint, including Jesus commanding his disciples *not* to proclaim to others that he is the Messiah.[11]

The Gospel of Mark

Mark is an "interpreter of Peter,"[12] and this will be of particular importance when we turn to the trial of Jesus. Several New Testament schol-

---

initial protest by John (3:13–17); Luke does not tell who baptized Jesus (3:19–22); and John ignores the baptism altogether (see 1:29–34). In the second century CE, Justin Martyr has the Jew Trypho say, "Even though the Messiah has been born and is living somewhere, yet he is still unknown. Indeed, he does not even know himself, nor has he any power until Elijah comes, appoints him, and reveals him to all" (*Dialogue with Trypho* 8; cited by Geza Vermes, *Jesus the Jew: A Historian's Reading of the Gospels* [New York: Macmillan, 1973], 138). See Vital's comment above.

10. See Isaiah Tishby, *Studies in Kabbalah and Its Branches* (Jerusalem: Magnes, 1992), 3:985 (Heb.), quoted by Moshe Idel, *Messianic Mystics* (New Haven: Yale University Press, 1998), 208.

11. This is especially true in Mark's Gospel (see 3:12; 8:30); by contrast, the appellation "Son of Man" appears thirteen times here; in Matthew, see 16:20: "Then he sternly ordered the disciples not to tell anyone that he was the Messiah" // Luke 9:21. See Frank Kermode, *The Genesis of Secrecy: On the Interpretation of Narrative* (Cambridge: Harvard University Press, 1979). The collective dimension of messiahship is "spreading all over" all Israel's generations; it is an ongoing messiahship—Le messie n'en finit pas de venir! Cf. Rudolf Bultmann: The kingdom is always future and always determines the present; see *Jesus and the Word* (New York: Scribner's Sons, 1958), 51–52; more to the point, although coming from a novelist who is not a theologian or a biblicist, Michael Chabon writes, "A Messiah who actually arrives is no good to anybody. A hope fulfilled is already half a disappointment" (*The Yiddish Policemen's Union* [New York: HarperPerennial, 2012], 349).

12. So according to Eusebius (early fourth century) quoting Papias (second century), who quotes "the presbyter" (= the presbyter John?), see Eusebius, *Church History* 3.39.15.

ars consider Mark as a collector of tradition.[13] More than this, however, he is a storyteller addressing a large audience. For Erich Auerbach, Mark has a peculiar view of reality; that is, he goes beyond the surface events (in contrast to Homer, Petronius, or Tacitus) to their sensory effect. What interests him is the sensory result of Jesus's life. Peter's reactions provide an example. In fact, everyone must take sides one way or the other.[14]

Peter may have written a gospel before 70 CE, that is, when the temple was still standing. On that (shaky) basis, George D. Kilpatrick advances the idea that Jesus's prevision of the destruction of the temple appeared to his contemporaries as false.[15] But the situation is complicated by the fact that Mark's version of the saying entails also the reconstruction "in three days ... not made with hands" (13:2; 14:58). I shall deal with this issue in more depth in chapter 13, "The Trial of Jesus and His Passion" (217–38).

First, as I have said earlier, the call for secrecy is especially well attested in Mark (see 1:44; 2:1–10; 5:35–43; 7:31–37; 9:2). This Markan insistence on secrecy is generally explained as a later reaction of the early church to the lack of recognition of Jesus and of Christianity. Paula Fredriksen sees in this motif a hidden anti-Semitism; the Markan Jesus did not want the Jews to know about his true identity (she invokes Mark 4:10–12).[16] But even if this were right, for the argument to be valid there must be some congruence with the traditional reports of Jesus's teaching. It is only by way of interpretation of the Nazarene kerygma that Mark can make of the command of secrecy such a central motif. This means that we must dig deeper and ask what actually stands behind the motif. There is an unmistakable parallel with the secrecy in which God himself stands: see Matt 6:6 on the basis of 1 Kgs 8:12 (God dwells in darkness); Isa 45:15 (God's hiddenness); the issueless holy of holies with God's throne; and so on. Furthermore, obviously, Jesus loathes publicity. His messiahship will affirm itself by other means, that is, through his life, his teaching, and his fate, not

---

13. See, e.g., Vincent Taylor, *The Gospel According to Saint Mark*, 2nd ed. (New York: Palgrave Macmillan, 1982), 53.

14. See Erich Auerbach, *Mimesis: The Representation of Reality in Western Literature*, trans. Willard Trask (Princeton: Princeton University Press, 1953), 47–48.

15. George D. Kilpatrick, *The Trial of Jesus* (Oxford: Clarendon, 1952), 10. In reality, Mark was most probably written shortly after 70 CE.

16. Paula Fredriksen, *From Jesus to Christ: The Origins of the New Testament Images of Jesus* (New Haven: Yale University Press, 1988), 49.

by a more-or-less efficient public proclamation. Characteristically, demons loudly and clearly herald his identity; they must be silenced.

Second, if we allow that Jesus's messianic consciousness grew in time until becoming a certainty in Jerusalem at his last Passover celebration, any untimely public proclamation of his messianism becomes a manipulation, a forcing of the issue. In view of what was to happen in Jerusalem, especially when confronting the high priest, one can understand the reluctance of Jesus to precipitate his own murder "before the time has come." The ambiguity of his self-reference as the son of man (Son of Man) and his use of riddles suggest that Jesus was biding his time. To an extent, this reticence blunts Jesus's self-proclamations.[17]

Third, Donald Juel is certainly right to say that Mark's concern with secrecy is a device to create a bilevel understanding of the gospel. The secret is at surface level addressed to the characters of the story; the deeper level, the one of the readers, however, is not affected. The reader knows what the characters don't. There is thus a deep irony in the limited understanding of Jesus's protagonists—even his disciples—on the one hand and the informed penetration of the "secret" on the part of the reader[18]—see the ambiguity of the royal robe of Jesus at the praetorium,[19] of his crown of thorns, and of his being hailed with the title "king of the Jews" (Mark 15:2, 9, 12, 26). The mockery (including at the foot of the cross, 15:29) is "simply another testimony to the truth."[20] Mikhail Bakhtin's notion of the "unfinalized" (until the end) comes to mind. While the story unfolds, Jesus remains for all unfinalized.[21] True, according to Mark, Jesus knew about his messiahship, but he was wary of popular misinterpretations regarding

---

17. See David Rhoads, Donald Michie, and Joanna Dewey, *Mark as Story: An Introduction to the Narrative of a Gospel* (Philadelphia: Fortress, 1982), 84–85.

18. Donald Juel, *Messiah and Temple: The Trial of Jesus in the Gospel of Mark* (Missoula, MT: Scholars Press, 1977), 47.

19. Helmer Ringgren (*The Messiah in the Old Testament*, SBT 18 [London: SCM, 1961], 13) says, "It is probable that the garment of the High Priest, as described in Exodus 28, is a post-exilic copy of the royal robe." James Frazer discovered that in the remote past, tribes used to kill their king as he showed weakness or aging (see *The Golden Bough: A Study of Magic and Religion*, abridged ed. [London: Macmillan, 1922], 348–73).

20. Juel, *Messiah and Temple*, 48. See also Matt 27:11, 29, 37, 42.

21. Mikhail Bakhtin: often in his works. I refer to Gary Saul Morson and Caryl Emerson, *Mikhail Bakhtin: Creation of a Prosaics* (Stanford: Stanford University Press, 1990), 36ff.

the messiah. Unavoidably, Jesus appears as a mysterious figure, shrouded in mystery, until the secret is lifted at the cross (14:61–62; 15:39).

There is something of the Menippean satire in the mockeries. As a matter of fact, the satirist multiplies the oxymorons, characteristic of the genre. So the religious and civil authorities act as conspirators; the real king is derided as a sham ruler, recognized only thanks to his purple tunic; the Son of Man is accused of blasphemy, while the accusers are the real blasphemers; and so on. From this perspective, the multiple times Jesus's clothes are changed during his kangaroo trial is remarkable. His original clothes are changed on the order of Herod into a white tunic (Luke 23:11). Then Pilate's soldiers, in derision, put a purple robe on him (Mark 15:17). Finally, Jesus puts back on himself his original clothes before the crucifixion. This changing of garments, says Schalom Ben-Chorin, alludes to the high priest's procedure at Yom Kippur; see m. Yoma 7:3–4.[22] There is here a striking combination of the priestly, the kingly, and the martyrial.

Fourth, the notion may go back to the preexistence of the Son of Man according, for instance, to 1 Enoch 62:7, "From the beginning, the Son of Man was hidden." In Pesiq. Rab Kah. 49b, we find expressed a comparable thought, "R. Berakia [ca. 340] said in the name of R. Levi [ca. 340]: As it was with the first liberator (Moses) so also will it be with the last one (the messiah). As the first liberator revealed himself to Israel and then hid himself from them, so also the last liberator will reveal himself and then hide himself."

And fifth, what people around Jesus understood by "messiah" does not correspond with his understanding. Before well-meaning but unwise enthusiasts spread the wrong message, an unambiguous order must be given to stop, in ovo, what could become a hoax.[23] As a counterproof,

---

22. Schalom Ben-Chorin, *Brother Jesus: The Nazarene through Jewish Eyes*, trans. Jared S. Klein and Max Reinhart (Athens: University of Georgia Press, 2001), 166–67.

23. See Vermes, *Jesus the Jew*, 149: "There is every reason to wonder if [Jesus] really thought of himself as [the Messiah]." Later, of course, there was no hesitation in the early church to identify Jesus as the Messiah: see Acts 2:36, which added the notion of suffering (2:19–31; 3:17–18). In John also, "Yet, the fourth gospel still stops short of asserting that Jesus declared in public that he was 'Christ'" (See John 4:25; 17:3). Vermes concludes, "The positive and constant testimony of the earliest tradition considered against its natural background of first-century Galilean religion, leads [to] Jesus the just man, the *zaddik*, Jesus the helper and healer, Jesus the teacher and leader, venerated by his intimates and less committed admirers alike as prophet, lord and son of man" (ibid., 225).

after curing a *gentile* in the country of the Gerasenes, Jesus tells him to spread the news to his friends (Mark 5:19). In other words, the instruction of silence could have been, at least in part, motivated by a false Jewish interpretation of messiahship at the time. As to the rationale behind the miracle, it is, we see once again, the restoration of the normal conditions in the created world. If it does not constitute "proof" of messiahship; it at least shows the power of God at work.

All this, to be sure, does not detract from a pro domo Markan argument in which some traces of anti-Jewishness can be detected. The onus, of course, is on Mark, not on Jesus. The alleged "difficulty" of the parables (Mark 4:10–12) is no anti-Semitic device. Surprisingly, Fredriksen fails to mention the Isaianic pronouncement that Mark closely parallels (see Isa 6:9–10). Scripture dictates to the evangelists themes that they "midrashize" in their gospels.

There is an evident paradox in simultaneously calling for keeping secret some events and sayings, while sending disciples to proclaim the gospel to all Israel (see Mark 4:22; Matt 13:33 and parr.; 13:44 and parr.; Mark 6:7; Luke 10:1; 22:35). As N. T. Wright says, "[Yahweh's plan was] not through the Herodian dynasty, not through the Pharisaic movement, not through high-priestly activity in the Temple, nor yet in the plotting of holy revolutionaries, but in Jesus's own proclamation and activity."[24] Incidentally, let us note that "secrecy" in a way continues beyond Jesus's death and resurrection, for in his transformed "body," the risen Jesus is not directly recognizable (see Luke 24). His body is now "spiritual" (see John 20:14–15; also John 21, which is an appendix by another writer).

Further, secrecy as regards messiahship is also well attested in other Jewish documents, both preceding and following the time of the gospel, for example 4 Ezra 7:28 and 1 Enoch 62:7; and in the Talmud Pesaḥ. 54b and Sanh. 97a. In the words of Moshe Idel, "The masses had to learn that the real nature of the Messiah is not the manifest but the hidden dimension."[25] In contrast to an elitist orientation of a sophisticated messianism, Jesus's itinerancy attempts to reach the masses. Idel, on the basis of Jesus's spiritual experience interwoven with the historical experience of the people—especially by an overwhelming appeal to the Scriptures—says that the combination creates symbols, such as internalized and

---

24. N. T. Wright, *Jesus and the Victory of God* (Minneapolis: Fortress, 1996), 238.
25. Idel, *Messianic Mystics*, 259.

eschatologized circumcision, purity, death, torah, and, for that matter, "Israel" (Matt 3:9, "God is able from these stones to raise up children to Abraham!"). This set the teaching of Jesus in disharmony with that of the rabbis. This is all the more so since the accent set on the personal responsibility before God—often contrasted with other emphases among Pharisees and Essenes—implied deemphasizing notions like the land of Israel and the temple. Not that these ideas became meaningless, but they needed no philosophical or ritual consecration. To a certain extent, these ideas obscured the veritable and existential *mitsvoth* to be fulfilled now that the kingdom has come near. The present events transcend the temple and its rituals. The "descent" of the kingdom of God (or of the Shekinah) brings with it a sense of urgency. True, the torah is not obsolete ("Do not think that I have come to abolish the Law or the Prophets; I have come not to abolish but to fulfill" [Matt 5:17]), but, at the same time, nothing is the same as it was before ("It was because you were so hardhearted that Moses allowed you to divorce your wives, but from the beginning it was not so" [Matt 9:8]; above all, see the impressive series of "You have heard that it was said ... but I say to you" in the Sermon on the Mount [Matt 5–6]). The time for preparing the way of the Lord is over; the rules now are those of the divine household. Jesus's appeal to "(from) the beginning" is revealing. If Moses indeed made allowance for the weakness of the recipients of his torah, it is evident that the law must at some time reach its absolute status.[26] Something now "precedes" (in importance) the Mosaic torah, as it also does David and even Abraham ("Before Abraham was, I am," John 8:58). The same principle is true regarding the present state of the universe, which the kingdom of God eternally precedes. It belongs to the essence of the created reality. Its unveiling reveals the soul of the matter, of all matter.

To return more specifically to the issue of individual versus collective redemption, the essence of the *tselem* ("image of God") is unveiled. With the advent of the kingdom, the *hashlemah* ("completion") of the *tselem* becomes possible (for the first time? Or once again?).[27] The whole doctrine of the Maharal of Prague is based on that hoped for fulfillment (*themimah*) of the vocation-promise of the human soul. If Jesus had stressed

---

26. A large part of the messiah's function, as expected, is the revelation and fulfillment of the absolute torah.

27. The *tselem* is restored in its fullness to Moses descending from Mount Sinai (Exod 34:29–35), but it was "a fading splendor" in the view of Paul (2 Cor 13:12–13).

his Davidic ancestry—a kind of "by-the-way" affirmation of the gospel—the atemporality of his messiahship would have been annulled. The mystical was played against the political. It appears that for Jesus the Roman Empire was an evanescent shadow, like all the powers that be. It was a minor, even fleeting problem.

When Paul speaks of the "body of Christ," he means something much more spiritual than just social cohesion. The "saints" continue "in their flesh" what "is missing" in the individual messiahship of Jesus of Nazareth. Discipleship means that each Christian becomes a "limb" of the body, that is, a part of the Messiah.[28] In other words, Christ activates a collective messiahship that includes, mirabile dictu, the non-Jews as Paul insists. In actuality, as any such a "spread over" sanctity is at best sporadically successful, Paul puts his trust "in Christ" (*en christō*), that is, in the only one able to replace the transience of death with the permanence of life. The secret lies in the hypostatic unceasing activity of the Messiah.

The movement of the pendulum between individual *themimah* and collective *hashlemah* is not without parallels in Jewish literature. The mystic tradition in Judaism insists, alternatively, on collective and individual redemption.[29] Although the later Christian tradition has too often disregarded the collective dimension of messiahship (the notion of the church as the gathering of "born again" individuals comes to mind), that is what needs to be rediscovered. Let us take here as a counterexample Jesus's irritation about the witnesses around him. In a nutshell, the irritant is focusing on the external ritual to the neglect of ethical commitment—like the circumcision of the flesh substituting for the circumcision of the heart, or the washing of the hands substituting for inner purity. The Nazarene is incensed because the *messianic people* corrupts its vocation with

---

28. Cf. E. P. Sanders, *Jesus and Judaism* (Philadelphia: Fortress, 1985), 117: "The teaching attributed to Jesus is markedly individualistic." As Gerd Theissen stresses, the relationship with Jesus belongs to the category of "personal-charismatic," i.e., spontaneous and, initially, without any other foundation than the personal conviction of its truth. This is called "faith." It transcends all social and natural limits; see Gal 3:18. See Gerd Theissen, "Vers une théorie de l'histoire sociale du christianisme primitif," *ETR* 63 (1988): 119–225, reprint with corrections in *Histoire sociale du christianisme primitif: Jésus, Paul, Jean* (Geneva: Labor et Fides, 1996), 267.

29. For the NT, "because individual instances of salvation occur, the presence of the end can be proclaimed here and now" (Gerd Theissen, *The Miracle Stories of the Early Christian Tradition*. Translated by F. McDonagh [Edinburgh: T&T Clark, 1983], 280).

good conscience. It so happens that a non-Jew's faith may become a model for the Israelites as in Matt 8:10, "Truly I tell you in no one in Israel have I found such faith. I tell you, many will come from east and west and will eat with Abraham and Isaac and Jacob in the kingdom of heaven"! This discovery goes beyond pronouncing an encomium for the Roman centurion. It is the statement of a scandalous twist in the divine covenant. Against the backdrop of the denounced failure of the messianic community—a failure perpetuated in the eyes of the early church by the relative scarcity of Jewish converts to Christianity—Jesus proclaims the precedence of individually oriented hope of redemption.[30] John the Baptist had come to the same conclusion and baptized individual Jews in order to reconstitute an authentic "Israel" with repentant men and women, thus setting a favorable terrain for the messianic advent. Such a conception was not exempt from danger though, since it questioned the unconditionality of Israel's election. That is why the Baptist's tradition is somewhat besmirched in the gospel. Mark 11:18 (and parr.) draws a contrast between the personalities of John and Jesus. Although both address "this generation," they do so in different ways. John the Baptist preached an ascetic call to repentance, but Jesus comes as "jolly."[31] His broadmindedness goes to extremes as described by Jesus's opponents—verse 19 even speaks of Jesus being a "glutton and drunkard"! At any rate, this unexpected portrait of Jesus makes the pericope seem authentic.

The issue of the individual versus the collective dimension of redemption is, in my opinion, one of the criteria of authenticity or historicity of the gospel traditions. John P. Meier offers, helpfully and carefully, other criteria. I already mentioned above the touchstone of "embarrassment" or "contradiction" when dealing with Jesus's baptism. The early church was certainly uneasy with this. Another case is provided by Jesus's saying that he himself does not know when the end-time will be coming (Mark 13:32; see Matt 24:36; the theme is absent in Luke and negated in John [see, e.g., 5:6; 6:6; 8:14]). Also embarrassing, prima facie, is Jesus's cry on the cross quoting Ps 22:1 (see Mark 15:34; Matt 27:46). Luke replaces it with Jesus commending his spirit to the Father; and John replaces it with "It

---

30. The Hasidic spiritualistic interpretation of redemption also comes in the eighteenth century on the heels of the Sabbatean disaster. Once more, popular messianism had come to an impasse.

31. The contrast between the eighteenth-century-CE Hasidim and Mitnagdim comes to mind.

is accomplished!" (19:30). Meier thinks that, in itself, the "cry of dereliction" may not have been embarrassing to its hearers, but mishearing and/or misunderstanding that Jesus was calling for Elijah seems to invalidate Meier's argument on this point.

A further criterion, of "dissimilarity" or "discontinuity" (from Judaic and early Christian traditions), applies to logia that can be surprising, or somewhat unrealistic, such as the prohibition of all oaths (Matt 5:34, 37), of voluntary fasting (Mark 2:18–22 and parr.), of divorce (Mark 10:2–12), and the command to turn the other cheek when being slapped in the face and to run another mile when someone "forces you to go one mile" (Matt 5:41).[32]

"Multiple attestation" or "cross section" refers to a theme that is recurrent in several sources, like the "kingdom of God/heaven" (Mark, Q, M, L, John; cf. echoes in Paul). Similar examples can be found in other situations, in Jesus's words at the Last Supper (Mark 14:22–25; 1 Cor 11:23–26; cf. John 6:51–58); in the prohibition of divorce (Mark 10:11–12; Luke 16:18; 1 Cor 7:10–11); in Jesus's oracles against the temple (e.g., Mark 13:2; 14:58; John 2:14–22); and so on.

The criterion of "coherence" or consistency includes, for instance, the sayings about the coming of the kingdom and the disputes over legal observance, which we find in all the New Testament testimonies.[33] Using this particular criterion, I have at times chosen the extant text over its

---

32. An important caveat is sounded by Daniel J. Harrington in his presidential address to the Catholic Biblical Association in 1986: "The Jewishness of Jesus: Facing Some Problems," *CBQ* 49 (1987): 1–13, here 10: "The problem with this criterion is that it makes Jesus dissimilar to or discontinuous with Judaism (and the early church). It wrenches Jesus out of his Jewish context and turns him into a kind of creative genius or eccentric ... transcending his culture." Crossan, after Theissen, sounds the same warning and touts instead the criterion of plausible historical context, that "requires only a demonstration of positive connections between the Jesus tradition and the Jewish context, i.e., between Jesus and the land, the groups, the traditions and the mentalities of the Judaism of that time" (Theissen, cited by Crossan, *The Historical Jesus*, 12–13). Hans Conzelmann agrees with Perrin (*Jesus*, trans. J. Raymond Lord, ed. John Reumann [Philadelphia: Fortress, 1973], 16 [= "Jesus Christus," *RGG*, 3rd ed., vol. 3, cols. 619–53]), but on the next page (17) he states, "Jesus moves almost exclusively within the framework of Palestinian Judaism"!

33. William Freedman adds the self-explanatory criteria of "frequency and avoidability [sic]." See Freedman, "The Literary Motif: A Definition and Evaluation," *Novel* 4 (1971): 123–31.

modern criticism. True, we cannot substitute the history of tradition for the history of the Nazarene, but the division between the two is not always clear. What would be an acute issue of distinction of sources as far as rabbinic traditions are concerned is considerably less so as regards evangelistic elaborations. In the former case, the historian is dealing with a protracted time of composition, involving a large number of masters/sages/rabbis. In the latter case, the period under consideration is reduced and is much more manageable as the master/sage/rabbi is unique. We have to deal with the issue case by case. As Cardinal John Henry Newman wrote, "Literature expresses, not objective truth, as it is called, but subjective; not things, but thoughts."[34]

The litmus test for "rejection and execution," that is, which of the historical deeds and words of Jesus explain his eventual trial and condemnation, constitutes the final criterion. (There may be other so-called criteria, helpful in conjunction with the above-mentioned ones but secondary in and of themselves.)

---

34. John Henry Newman, "Literature" (1858), in *The Idea of a University* (Notre Dame: University of Notre Dame Press, 1982), 273.

12

JESUS IS BETRAYED

The fate of both Jesus and the temple is—at least in the eyes of some early Christians—clearly consolidated into one large-scale event. John 2:21 says that, when Jesus spoke of the coming destruction of the temple, he was speaking of his own body. Witnesses at his trial accused him of forecasting the end of the temple—which in fact occurred some forty years later. It seems reasonable to conclude that both the cross and the temple ruins after 70 CE were seen as a dual inauguration of a new and final chapter in Israel's history. True, the accusation at the trial is brought about by *false* witnesses, say the texts. What is "false" is not the substance but its alleged implication, namely, that Jesus hailed the end of biblical Judaism. What is false is the conclusion that Jesus was a cryptic Zealot or even an anarchist. His antiestablishment stance was turned against him.[1] Paradoxically, the gate was thus opened for gentile anti-Judaism in the Master's alleged image. Jesus loses with foes and friends alike.[2] In fact, witnesses for both the prosecution and the defense are false witnesses! The whole trial became a great betrayal. The people who knew Jesus well after years of discipleship could have put things straight, but they were conspicuously absent! Jesus's failure was total. All conspired to kill the central Jew.[3]

---

1. Speaking of the "eschatological priest," 4Q541 frag. 9 reads, "They will speak many words against him and they will invent many [lies] and fictions against him."

2. As gentiles achieved a critical mass within the church, the interpretation became skewed. As Amy-Jill Levine says, "Comments spoken to Jews became perceived, by the Church as well as the Synagogue, as comments spoken against Jews" (*The Misunderstood Jew: The Church and the Scandal of the Jewish Jesus* [San Francisco: HarperSanFrancisco, 2006], 111).

3. True, Jesus died at the hands of the Romans, but the gospel makes it clear that the conspiracy was not bounded by race. The circle around the center has vanished; the central Jew became the isolated Jew.

In reality, Jesus was apolitical.[4] His female entourage was another unmistakable sign that he "was not planning to found a paramilitary movement to overthrow the Romans."[5] Jesus had been misunderstood every step of the way, and if some of his friends used the term "messiah," the confusion became total. When he preached the advent of the kingdom of God, for instance, to a crowd of five thousand that he had fed with a few loaves and fish—as Israel of old was fed by the manna in the desert—the crowd was ready to use force to make him their king (John 6:15) and to take the lead in an uprising against the Romans. Jesus flees and goes in hiding.

Then comes Judas. A sinister figure in the gospel, Judas is nevertheless a scapegoat who assumes the role of universal betrayer of the Master. Conveniently, the collective guilt of Jesus's disciples was borne by one "bad" individual, whose name, no less conveniently, means "the Jew"! The whole affair looks suspicious. Judas may be a pure fiction, but at any rate he was not the sole betrayer,[6] and, moreover, one of Jesus's brothers was also called Judas (see Mark and Matthew).

Scholars are divided on the authenticity of the Judas episode. Phillip Vielhauer, for instance, agrees that the betrayal by a disciple was invented on the basis of Ps 41:10 (in Hebrew; LXX 40:10), which speaks of betrayal by a table companion. Mark 14:18 alludes to this psalm.[7] But Matthew and Luke do not seem to be interested in this connection (see Matt 26:20–25

---

4. In this, Jesus behaved like the Pharisees, who were little involved in politics—although consistently opposed to in the opposition to, and irritated by, the Sadducees "flirting" with Rome. The Pharisees saw government (even foreign) as the keeper of civil order, without which social chaos would occur (cf. Paul in Rom 13). We should remember that, more than once, uprisings against Rome had come from Galilee. The so-called Judas the Galilean in 6 CE incited the people not to pay tribute to Caesar (contrast Mark 12:17).

5. A. N. Wilson, *Jesus: A Life* (New York: Fawcett Columbine, 1992), 152.

6. Joel Carmichael also believes that Judas is in fact "the Jew par excellence" (*The Death of Jesus* [New York: Pelican, 1966], 26). "Iscariot" may mean "the one who delivers" (root *skr*, see Isa 19:4 echoed in Matt 26:15).

7. Phillip Vielhauer, "Gottesreich und Menschensohn in der Verkündigung Jesu," in *Festschrift für Günther Dehn zum 75. Geburtstag am 18. April 1957 dargebracht von der Evangelisch-Theologischen Fakultät der Rheinischen Friedrich Wilhelms-Universität zu Bonn*, ed. Wilson Schneemelcher (Neukirchen: Kreis Moers, 1957), 62–64. We may also remember that Judas's namesake in the Scriptures is Joseph's brother, the one who advised selling him as a slave.

and Luke 22:21–23). E. P. Sanders suggests that the betrayal by Judas is authentic since it created a serious embarrassment for the church because it involves one of Jesus's intimates and also because of its impact on the symbolic number of "twelve" apostles. (Note that Luke omits the number twelve in 22:30.) Thus it was indeed predicted by Jesus, and it was indeed the fulfillment of Scripture.

To the extent that we may trust the historicity of the Judas theme, it seems right to reconstruct it as follows. Publicly, Jesus was a more or less obscure preacher in Galilee, exhorting his audience to repent and to extend mutual love. There is, at any rate, no need for violence. However, Jesus grew increasingly convinced that he himself was the "Son of Man" whose advent he himself proclaimed. This resulted in a progressive shift toward referring to himself in speeches in third person rather than first person.

With the coming of the Passover festival, Jesus left Galilee, his home space and the area of his private teaching, and exposed himself and his disciples to the thousands of pilgrims in Jerusalem.[8] This created a certain popular restlessness, especially when he proceeded to "cleanse" the temple precincts. He thereby set the ax to the very root of the religious institution—which was itself gravely compromised with the Roman regime (for the sake at least of peace and order). The very importance of the temple makes, of course, of the symbolic act of the Nazarene a programmatic as well as formidable impact. From "marginal," Jesus became—to his own peril and that of his followers—a central character. Whether Jesus himself felt overwhelmed in the process is a moot question. The fevered pitch in any case spiraled higher and higher.[9]

Bart Ehrman is certainly right in thinking that Judas faced a dilemma.[10] More active and determined than most, Judas tried to temper his Master's

---

8. There may have been some thousands of pilgrims in Jerusalem for any given festival, but especially for Passover (cf. m. Hag. 1:1). This explains why Pilate as governor came to Jerusalem with troops and resided in the Antonia Tower, ready to intervene in case of civil disorder. Josephus (*J.W.* 6.222–223) eloquently says, "The temple was the fortress dominating the city, and the Antonia tower dominated the temple." Jesus's humble entry into Jerusalem is a satire of the triumphal Roman procession into the Antonia.

9. Gershom Scholem speaks of the "dazzling but highly dangerous amalgamation of mysticism and the apocalyptic mood" (*Major Trends in Jewish Mysticism*, rev. ed. [New York: Schocken, 1946], 329–30).

10. Bart D. Ehrman, *The Lost Gospel of Judas Iscariot: A New Look at Betrayer and Betrayed* (Oxford: Oxford University Press, 2006).

ardors by having him taken into protective custody until after Passover. He led the authorities to Jesus's retreat and kissed him, not necessarily as a fake sign of affection, but perhaps to ask forgiveness in advance. At this point, continues Ehrman, Jesus and the remaining eleven seem stunned by the turn of events. In fact, the situation suddenly got out of hand for all concerned, including Judas, when he learned that the Master had been delivered to a court of justice, which proceeded to condemn him. This development was totally unexpected. It was the Jewish high clergy that betrayed, not Judas. The eleven dispersed, and Judas was devastated to the point, perhaps, of committing suicide.[11] He had become a scapegoat in the hands of temple leaders.

Retrospectively, early Christians expressed certain uneasiness with what looked like the collusion of Jesus with those who betrayed him, as well as with those who came to arrest him. The gospel describes Jesus as knowing in advance that Judas is about to deliver him to the authorities. It also reports that Jesus invited his disciples to purchase swords—but only two for the whole group (Luke 22:36–38). This is a ridiculously small number of weapons for purposes of self-defense, but enough to raise the suspicion that Jesus is a *lestēs*! Besides, a disciple uses his sword against the servant of the high priest (Mark 14:47–48; Luke 22:49–52; Matt 26:51–52, 55). In each of these contexts, Jesus blamed the mob that came with sticks and swords to seize him as if he were a brigand or rebel.[12]

In fact, it was a certainty that the challenge of cleansing the temple precincts would not remain unanswered. Was this a search for martyrdom? Rather, Jesus staked everything on the outcome that God had in store for him—perhaps with the idea of forcing that outcome in a nonviolent way. With only two swords, the effort seems to be little more than that of "paper tiger."

---

11. As Mikhail Bakhtin says (in *Author and Hero in Aesthetic Activity in Art and Answerability: Early Philosophical Essays*, ed. Michael Holquist and Vadim Liapunov, trans. Vadim Liapunov, supplement trans. Kenneth Bostrom [Austin: University of Texas Press, 1990]), the hero "stops coinciding with himself." His passions move him to folly.

12. Jesus's question about the swords in the disciples' "arsenal" resembles his inquiry in other contexts, like about the five loaves of bread and the two fish for the four thousand people (Mark 8:1–9; or over five thousand of them, Matt 14:13–21 // Luke 9:10–17). In all these occasions Jesus's question evokes a ridiculous circumstance. It is the same, I contend, with the "two swords."

Is that also what Judas thought he was doing (to the extent that the episode is historical)? At this point, Jesus becomes conscious of being a *skandalon* (Luke 12:49–53; Matt 10:34–37). But we must realize that, as far as Jesus's message was concerned, it could have been prolonged till his natural death, and Jesus would have been a preacher and a reformer, or at most a prophet. The only way to fulfill his destiny was to force the issue, and that is what was accomplished.[13]

With time, Judas became the villain par excellence. His kissing Jesus was seen as the apex of duplicity. Judas is the antichrist. Since his name is foreboding, he provided a golden opportunity for early Christians to reframe the whole trial of the Galilean as a Jewish conspiracy. As a proof, the Synoptic Gospels assert that the crowd had a choice between Jesus the Nazarene and Jesus bar-Abbas, that is, "the son of the father"! John 18:40 says that bar-Abbas was a bandit.[14] The popular choice goes in favor of another kind of "Son of the Father"—but he is a hoodlum, a murderer (Mark 15:7). The non-Jew centurion at the foot of the cross (Mark 15:39) presents a stark contrast. No surprise then that "those intent on antisemitic propaganda have depicted [Judas] as the prototypical Jew."[15]

Let us again stress that the details of Judas's treachery appear to be literary constructs. We are dealing with a midrash based on Zech 11. His designation by Jesus at the meal table, his collusion with the religious and political authorities (while probably being a Zealot himself), his being paid thirty pieces of money, his kissing Jesus as a signal for the religious police, his throwing the money at the feet of the chief priests and his hanging himself—a sad parody of his Master's impending fate—all of these follow the model of Zech 11. No other chapter in Jesus's story—with the exception of the birth narratives—is more fraught with the legendary.

Judas's actions and their result were preceded by an exuberant popular demonstration of adulation. The mob's mood had reached a feverish high pitch. The religious and political provocation of cleansing the temple precincts was prolonged in the streets of Jerusalem, where the crowd brandished palms and willow branches while shouting "Hosanna," as in the

---

13. On Jesus and/or Judas forcing the issue, see the rabbis about Eleazar ben Dinai, who wanted "to bring on the coming of the end by force" (Cant. Rab. 2.9.3).

14. The two men crucified with Jesus are also "bandits" (Matt 27:39–44).

15. Ehrman, *Judas*, 180.

liturgy of Sukkoth![16] This cry is surprising since, in the present context, it sounds like a triumphant praise, something like "Hallelujah." In fact, "hosanna" means "please, save!" It is a play on words with the very name of Jesus, *yehoshu'a—hoshia'na*. It is then followed here by the preposition "to," a clear translation of the Hebrew *le-* before the addressees "son of David" and the "Highest."

Such a preposition is difficult to justify, but Marvin Pope has demonstrated that it amounts to a vocative, not "to the son of David," but "O son of David," not "to the highest," but "O, the Highest" (God). In other words, the cry "save us!" is addressed to Jesus riding on a donkey and thus seen as king, Messiah, and Son of David (on the basis of Zech 9).[17] The cry is also directed to God, "the Highest." This "was politically and religiously provocative, to both Jews and the Roman rulers, especially at the paschal season celebrating the great rescue of the past and the hope of present liberation from Roman rule."[18]

During the last days of the Nazarene, we find ourselves, as usual, in full ambiguity (see Matt 21:8 // Mark 11:8–9 // Luke 19:38). Is Jesus really proclaiming his kingship? Why is there a gap of several days between this triumphal (and provocative) entry into Jerusalem, and the arrest of Jesus? After the gospel report, Jesus's every move has become highly symbolic: riding on an ass, making declaration(s) about the temple, the actual "cleansing" of it, the last meal as a sign of the final banquet, and so on. We shall have to plunge into this thicket of questions.

---

16. Matt 21:15 ("in the temple"); Mark 11:9 // John 12:13; see Ps 118:25–27; m. Sukkah 4:3–6.

17. There are two texts in the MT where *hoshia'* is addressed to the king: 2 Sam 14:4 and Ps 20:10. Note that the name "Jesus" (*yeshu'a*) is built on the same root (see, e.g., Ezra 2:6, 36, 40; 8:33).

18. Marvin H. Pope, "Hosanna," *ABD* 3:290–91.

13
The Trial of Jesus and His Passion

According to Marcus Borg, Jesus's entry into Jerusalem was a counter-demonstration, as Pilate's troops were also entering the city from the opposite direction to reinforce the garrison on the Temple Mount during Passover. Jesus's entry, modeled on Zech 9:9–10, symbolized the peaceful kingdom of God. Peaceful, yes, but with active resistance through public criticism and symbolic acts. For, to our surprise, Jesus has recourse to violence in the temple! His pacifism must thus be qualified: it is "bifocal." Toward the Roman occupation, its aspect is of nonresistance, but toward the temple personnel and the perversion of their mission, it is active resistance.[1] Asked whether to pay tax to the Romans, Jesus traps the Herodians: they carry a graven image of the emperor as "son of god" (Luke 20:22; see 23:2). To render unto God what is God's means everything (Ps 24:1), but what, then, does belong to the emperor? Nothing.

As to the accusation that Jesus was in collusion with the Zealots, the scene of the temple cleansing supports this suspicion of political subversion—despite his protest. There can be no doubt that some considered him to be a crypto-Zealot, just waiting for the right time to unveil his activism. "Palm Sunday" seemed to confirm such expectations, although it turned to nothing, in large part because of Judas. Hence the popular frustration and the total reversal of its attitude: "Crucify, crucify!" As a matter of fact, the crowd in question is not necessarily different from the one that acclaimed Jesus on Palm Sunday. The paradox is even starker when we remember that Jesus led the protest against the dominating system that was oppressing the people (see Col 2:5). The crowd then turns against its liberator and compromises itself with the oppressors! Ironically enough, such reversals

---

1. See "a den of robbers," Mark 11:17; see Isa 56:7; Jer 7:5–7, 11, about the oppressive system hidden within the temple as a "safe house."

are historically redundant. Time and again, people vote in favor of those who victimize them. "They do not know what they are doing."

"It is expedient," says the high priest Caiaphas, "that one dies for the people" (John 11:48–50), and thus Jesus's torturers make him the savior of his race.² The ambiguity is such that Jesus finds himself "between a rock and a hard place." The crowd wants him to die because he is not a Zealot,³ and the Romans want him to die because he is! No escape is possible. The trial is a trap. The indirectness of Jesus's responses to the high priest and the Roman governor ("I am [and you will see the Son of Man] …" or, "You say so!") added to the awkwardness of the whole scene. A different outcome risked resolving the ambiguity and reducing the passion to a commedia dell'arte. But perhaps it was a comedy anyway, a dark one, in which everyone concerned is a dramatis (comoediae?) persona. Jesus knew that whatever he said would not make any difference; *les jeux sont faits*!

It is thus understandable—whether the New Testament reports are authentic or not—that at his trial Jesus was "tossed" from one leader to another, from Charybdis to Scylla, so to speak. The lesson is clear. It is also clear why Jesus chose to remain silent at times and ignored the prosecutors' accusations, and even at times to throw back at them their own statements: "You are the one to say so"; or "indeed, I am [what you just said]." This confusion of the elements of the trial intensifies its ambiguity even more.⁴ Who condemns Jesus? On what counts? Why were these Jews so obstinate in their intention to kill, and why was there so much reluctance on the part of the Romans?⁵ The texts focus on Jesus's silence or, alternately, on his provocative responses—both subject to different interpretations—to the high priest and to Pilate. Shall we follow Joel Carmichael

---

2. See A. N. Wilson, *Jesus: A Life* (New York: Fawcett Columbine, 1992), 219.

3. See Nils A. Dahl, *Das Volk Gottes: eine Untersuchung zum Kirchenbewustsein des Urchristentums*, new ed. (Darmstadt: Wissenschaftliche Buchgesellschaft, 1963), 161: It may well be that the crowd around Jesus was composed of "messianic Zealots" who "did not understand … Jesus' intention."

4. Confusion and inconsistencies prevailed, as noted below. In contrast to Mark's narrative, there could not be a trial on the day of Passover, nor a nighttime summoning of the Sanhedrin. No sentence was allowed the same day as the instruction. Also noncredible is the intervention of Herod the Tetrarch (as in Luke and Gospel of Peter); Pilate would never defer authority to him. Incidentally, Luke 13:1 notes Pilate's natural cruelty.

5. Acts 2:23 puts this succinctly, "This man … you crucified and killed by the hand of those outside the law."

and imagine that, originally, the texts charged the Romans but were later doctored into anti-Jewish polemics?

There are even inconsistencies in the gospels' calendars regarding the pretrial and the trial of Jesus. The conflict, however, is possibly solved if Jesus followed the Qumranic solar calendar, that is, celebrating Passover one day earlier than the Sadducees and Pharisees. It would also shed light on the fact that the Seder meal was celebrated, à la Qumran, in the absence of women.

Jesus faced two charges: he allegedly threatened to destroy the temple of Jerusalem and he claimed for himself an exalted status. The latter, I contend, is based on his statement *egō eimi*, which identifies him with the divine.[6] This is, in the eyes of the high priest, the ultimate blasphemy. Our task now is to determine how the two charges relate.

Rudolf Bultmann, from a form-critical point of view, thinks that Mark 14:61 (the question of the high priest) hangs without logic after 14:59 (the witnesses cannot mutually agree).[7] But the fact is that Mark 14:59 concludes that an impasse had been reached. The testimonies of the "witnesses" were inconsistent, so the high priest shifts strategy and comes with another issue, *without obliterating the former one*. There is thus no reason for assuming with Bultmann that verses 57–59 are "secondary." Nor are there any grounds for sundering the two charges.[8] John Donahue has shown that repetition of the falseness of testimony is thoroughly Markan; he calls the pattern "insertion technique."[9] T. A. Burkill's explanation of why the testimonies are "false" is well put: "[Mark wants to portray the trial as illegal inside and out,] hence he reports that the witnesses testify falsely and that their evidence proves incoherent (14:59), not because their

---

6. Cf. John 19:7. Even the episode of Jesus walking on water, for that matter, is in conformity with God marching on the sea in Job 9:8 (cf. Hab 3:15; see Matt 14:22–34 // Mark 6:45–53 // John 6:16–21). Nature is restored in its function as the servant of the humans. For Johann F. Schreiber, the divine sonship is the real issue at the trial. See "Die Christologie des Markusevangeliums," *ETK* 58 (1961): 154–83. See also here below.

7. Rudolf Bultmann, *The History of the Synoptic Tradition*, trans. John Marsh (Oxford: Blackwell, 1968), 270–71.

8. We find the same opinion in Eta Linnemann, *Studien zur Passionsgeschichte* (Göttingen: Vandenhoeck & Ruprecht, 1970), 109–10.

9. John Donahue, *Are You the Christ? The Trial Narrative in the Gospel of Mark*, SBLDS 10 (Missoula, MT: Scholars Press, 1973), 77–84. On false witnesses, see Ps 27:12; 35:11, but there is here no verbal similarity with Mark.

allegation is a misrepresentation of what they actually heard, but because they are opposed to the prisoner and are unable to grasp the mysterious import of his words."[10] Burkill calls Mark 15:38 to witness on the tearing of the temple veil (to which we shall return below). He writes, "And now in supernatural fashion, the temple itself sets the scoffers at naught by bearing witness to the doom to which it is condemned."[11]

The problem, as a matter of fact, is that the witnesses are called *pseudomartyroi* in spite of Mark 13:2. But witnesses can be, at the same time, both false and prophetic. Their failure to reach a consensus is highly significant. It betrays the hasty manipulation by the chief priests in a precipitously arranged trial. It also casts suspicion on the legitimacy of the legal procedure itself, as we have seen. It is in this case spurious and amounts at least to a miscarriage of justice but perhaps even to a conspiracy.

A closer look at the testimony itself is needed. Donald Juel has called attention to Mark's carefully chosen words when speaking of the temple.[12] When referring to the whole temple complex, Mark uses the term *hieron* (see Mark 11:1–14:49). When the central holy of holies is intended, he uses *naos* (see 14:58; 15:29, 38). The witnesses against Jesus confuse these terms. In 13:2, Jesus spoke of the *hieron*; the witnesses, of the *naos* (14:58, cf. 15:29). Eventually, it is the veil of the *naos* that is torn.

Jesus spoke of the destruction of the *hieron*, and an aura of mystery surrounds this prediction. First, notice that any declaration to the effect that the temple will be destroyed remains an empty threat as long as there is no relation between the speaker, Jesus, and the content of his speech, the temple. The prediction must be taken seriously only when Jesus claims ownership by adding that he will build a new temple "not made with hands" (Mark 13:2; 14:58). John astutely states that Jesus was speaking of his own body (2:21). This, however, complicates the matter. For this announcement does not come from a fanatic as the "false" witnesses intimate (Mark 14:56–59), but from someone who claims ownership. How could Jesus "own" the temple? By being the Son of God, that is, the heir

---

10. T. A. Burkill, "The Trial of Jesus," *VC* 12 (1958): 8 (see also *Mysterious Revelation* [Ithaca, NY: Cornell University Press, 1963]; and Burkill, "St. Mark's Philosophy of the Passion," *NovT* 2 [1957]: 245–71).

11. Burkill, "St. Mark's Philosophy of the Passion," 267 (cited by Donald Juel, *Messiah and Temple: The Trial of Jesus in the Gospel of Mark* [Missoula, MT: Scholars Press, 1977], 37).

12. Juel, *Messiah and Temple*, 127ff.

of the true proprietor. Thus the temple's status is radically changed. It is no longer an object, a building representing power, which a revolutionary would hope to destroy along with its symbolism. It is, so to speak, an extension of Jesus's person, and thus John's identification of the temple as Christ's body is correct.

Jesus's prediction about the temple refers to the indissolubility of the bond between the Herodian building *and* his body. It is on this model that Paul can speak of the human body in general as the temple of the Spirit (see 1 Cor 6:19). Jesus, in other words, envisages the transcendence of the shrine that has so far only adumbrated its own transfiguration.[13] And according to Christian tradition, echoed by John, he also speaks of his own resurrection. In both cases—the building and the body—what was "made with hands" (that is, by natural means, cf. Acts 7:48) reaches out to its fulfilled and definitive form.

It is within this context that we should approach the mocking of Jesus as prophet after the sentence was passed. Jesus made a double "prophecy." He forecast the destruction of the *hieron* and he prophesied the imminent glorification of the Son of Man. As we acceded to the eschatological telos with the theme of a temple "not made with hands," so the announcement of the Son of Man's glory takes us to the same end-time. Jesus's saying is based on Dan 7:13–14, which advises, "All peoples, nations, and languages should serve him. His dominion is an everlasting dominion that shall not pass away, and his *kingship* is one that shall never be destroyed" (emphasis added; we are still in a royal environment). Aside from Daniel, Jeremiah is also in the background. When Jesus is baptized, we saw that a *bath qol* proclaimed him Son of God. Such a divine pronouncement amounts to a prophetic vocation, as we find illustrated in the Hebrew Scriptures. Combining this with Matthew and Luke's birth narratives, the calling of Jeremiah comes to mind (see Jer 1). John the Baptist also had been called to a prophetic mission, and Luke 3:1 clearly depends upon Jer 1 (LXX).

Jesus's opponents mocked him as a prophet at his trial and at the foot of the cross. In the words of Joachim Jeremias, "Jesus was in the eyes of his opponents a false prophet."[14] In the best of cases, even Jesus's friends summarize well their disappointment: "We had hoped that he was the one to redeem Israel" (Luke 24:21). Now, Jewish tradition has kept alive the

---

13. Recall Jer 7:4: "Here is the temple, the temple, the temple!"
14. Joachim Jeremias, *The Eucharistic Words of Jesus*, trans. Norman Perrin (London: SCM, 1964), 79.

potentially accurate motive of the accusation of Jesus. He was "deceiver, sorcerer, seducer of the people" (see Ber. Sanh. 43a); in Matt 27:63, he is allegedly an "impostor" (NRSV), a *planos* (see also John 7:12).

Notwithstanding this, it may well be that the inconsistencies in the gospel narratives reflect unexpected *historical* inconsistencies. Against the legal arguments that make the New Testament reports on the trial of Jesus suspect, actual circumstances to the contrary should be contemplated. A glaring example is the Jewish persecution of the early church, to which Paul testifies as an early participant (Gal 1:13, 23; 1 Cor 15:9; Phil 3:6). From a legal point of view, it does not make sense—but it happened! (Acts 4:1–23; 5:17–42). On that score, Stephen's trial (Acts 6:8–14) and his death by stoning (7:54–60) retrospectively shed doubt on a radical modern critique of the evangelical account of Jesus's trial. The religious-political passions at the time had reached a fever pitch. It is not unthinkable that passions overwhelmed legal constraints such as a nighttime session of the Sanhedrin. This implies the absence of the populace since it was Jesus's fame that prompted the authorities to act at night in the first place. Implied also is the fact that, by secretly doing their dirty business, and thus breaking several rules, they show their utter hypocrisy in accusing Jesus of being a lawbreaker. At the apex of the trial, Jesus is accused of blasphemy, but when he is crucified, the gospel returns the indictment to Jesus's judges: they are those who commit blasphemy (Mark 15:29–32; Matt 27:39–44, 49; Luke 23:34–38).

Further, Paul himself was subsequently arrested in the temple, and the mob pressured the Sanhedrin to kill him, thus forcing the Romans to put him in protective custody (Acts 23:12–24; 9:19–30; 26:10–12). This latter event certainly passes muster if the Stephen incident may be deemed a copy of Jesus's sentence. And if we needed a further example, Josephus (in *Ant.* 20.9.1) tells us that the high priest Ananus arrested James, the brother of Jesus, and others, dragged them to the Sanhedrin, and executed them.[15] On this basis, Hans Lietzmann claims that the Sanhedrin had the authority to execute capital offenders—for blasphemy it would be by stoning (and, indeed, John 11:8 lets us know that Jesus was almost stoned to death in Judea). He concludes that Mark's scene of Jesus's trial is not historical.[16] Such a radical judgment is uncalled for. The Roman policy regarding

---

15. Pharisees (!) protested the illegality of the action. Ananus was deposed. The illegality of Pilate's crime, of course, could not be protested!

16. Hans Lietzmann, *Der Prozess Jesu*, SPAW (Berlin: de Gruyter, 1931), 313–22.

capital punishment may have varied. John 18:31 records that "we [Jews] are not permitted to put anyone to death," reflecting the Roman policy of execution during the time of Jesus.[17] In Stephen's days, a relaxation of this rule allowed his stoning. M. Sanh. 7:2, 23c reports the burning alive for adultery of a priest's daughter. Furthermore, the circumstances of Jesus's trial were extraordinary. Whether we deem them "irregularities" or "inconsistencies," or give allowance for temple personnel's precipitous arrangements in order to eliminate a troublesome but popular charismatic, deference to the Romans makes good sense if the Jewish authorities want to "pass the buck" and maintain a good image vis-à-vis the populace. Note that, in that case, the Christian grudge toward "the Jews"—that is, the Jewish hierarchy—is less "anti-Semitic" than it appears.[18]

Excursus: Does the Mishnaic Tradition Shed Light on Jesus's Trial Irregularities?

If we take for granted the rabbinic tradition on jurisprudence, Jesus's trial as reported by the gospel is full of irregularities. This tradition, however, was written down some two hundred years after the Nazarene's trial. There is thus no guarantee that its stipulations were already applied in the first half of the first century CE. Furthermore, even if we could antedate the strict rabbinic restraints regarding the courts of judgment (see below), we cannot exclude the possibility that the Sanhedrin, in the case of Jesus, did not apply them. We know that the Jewish authorities wanted to avoid any popular disturbance, so they proceeded, by stealth, to arrest Jesus. Nighttime sessions of the Sanhedrin and a death sentence on the eve of a festival (Passover) are not necessarily impossible.

1. m. Sanh. 4:1: Trials must be held during daytime; so must the verdict. They cannot be held on the eve of a Sabbath or a festival. A conviction can be reached only on the second day of the debate.

---

17. According to y. Sanh. 7:2, 23c, the Jews lost the right to judge capital cases "forty years before the temple was destroyed." Ta'an. 6 tells us that, in 66 CE, such authority was restored.

18. See John 19:11, "The one who handed me over to you [Pilate] is guilty of a greater sin."

2. m. Sanh 7:5: There is blasphemy only when the full Name (Tetragrammaton) is pronounced.
3. m. Sanh 11:2: The designated place for trials is the "Chamber of Hewn Stone."
4. m. Sanh 4:5: The witnesses must be carefully vetted.

All this is impressive, but we must remember that the Mishnah was composed at the end of the second century for the use of Pharisaic Judaism. Further, this may be an idealization (but for the substantiation of two witnesses, which has a scriptural warrant). Jesus appeared in a Sadducee court, and chances are that the applied procedures were different. One thing, however, should have been true for Sadducees as well as Pharisees: the prohibition of holding court on the eve of a festival.[19] Further, the unanimous condemnation of Jesus would already invalidate the death sentence according to the Sanhedrin text. Was the remanding of Jesus to the Roman authorities a way to dodge the illegality of their own procedures, a sort of "hand-washing?"[20] If so, whether or not the Jews at the time were habilitated to perform the death penalty is the wrong question (cf. John 19:6). As to the pretrial occurring at night, again in spite of the (Pharisaic) rabbinic protocol, it is to be noted that Sadducees organized the procedure. They did not summon the Pharisees until the morning of the following day, if we may infer that much from Mark 15:1. Schalom Ben-Chorin is right in pointing out, "In the tractate Sanhedrin, we have an example of ideal trial procedure, though it was by no means always followed."[21]

Jesus before the High Priest and the Governor Pilate (Matt 26:62–66)

In general, Jesus remained silent before his Jewish accusers (see 26:63). Only through deference to the high priest, who solemnly demanded a response, Jesus answered, *su eipas*, which is an evasion: "[That's what] you

---

19. On all of this, see Eduard Lohse, "συνέδριον," *TDNT* 7:867–68. See also the strong caveat of Martin Hengel, *The Charismatic Leader and His Followers*, trans. James Greg (Edinburgh: T&T Clark, 1981).

20. See Ps 26:6; Matt 27:24.

21. Schalom Ben-Chorin, *Brother Jesus: The Nazarene through Jewish Eyes*, trans. Jared S. Klein and Max Reinhart (Athens: University of Georgia Press, 2001), 162.

say." Jesus's silence recalls that of the servant of the Lord in Isa 53:7 (cf. Acts 8:32–33).

We have stepped into the domain of language. Jesus's interlocutors bring a semantic understanding that they want to impose on him. So the high priest says something like, "In summary, what you have said amounts to a proclamation that you are 'the Messiah, the son of God.'" But these words are intended as a trap. He is determined to find Jesus guilty and thus liable to the death sentence. His words are loaded with implications. Pilate, later, tries another formula: "In summary, Jesus, all you are about is to be the 'king of the Jews.'" From Pilate's mouth, this is a lapidary legal sentence to a politically motivated death (see Mark 15:26). Some one hundred years before, the Hasmonean priests had carried this title during the Maccabean rebellion (143–63 BCE), as did Herod the Great (37–4 BCE). Accusing Jesus of making this claim portended danger. But since there are some sparks of theological truth in those simplistic definitions of Jesus's identity, the Nazarene's reply is neither yes nor no: "[Those are] your words! [Not mine. It is your conclusion drawn from your particular standpoint, which I cannot endorse as such]" (Mark 15:2–5 // Matt 27:11 // Luke 23:3).

In another text—close to the scene of the trial—we find Jesus answering Judas (Matt 26:25) with the same words, *su eipas*, to be here understood as, "You just said it!" This is addressed to someone who, unwittingly, just expressed his temptation to betray his Master. Judas's exclamation, "God forbid that it be I!" sets him at the center. Psychologically, the matter would have been different, had he said, "God forbid that it be any of us!" But, as it now stands, Judas's oath corresponds to the secret wish of everyone present: "Surely, not I" (Matt 26:22). Hence, in spite of Jesus's words, his co-disciples do not question Judas.

Here and there, as I said, we are treading the ground of language. To his opponents' semantics (those of the high priest, the priests, Pilate and Judas), Jesus responds, either with a disapproving silence, or with a corrective statement about the triumphant Danielic Son of Man (Matt 26:64). In the context of Judas's betrayal—a mini-trial of Jesus in its own way—Jesus claims that, on his request, God would "at once send [him] more than twelve legions of angels—but how then would the Scriptures be fulfilled?" (see Matt 26:53; cf. John 18:36). More than ever, these discrete semantic understandings are contiguous, but they never fuse. While Judas, the priests, the high priest, and Pilate remain within their own logic—amazingly uniform, even as regards Pilate—Jesus demands the "destruction" of such logic (as of the temple precincts, earlier on). He says to the high priest (in Matt 26:63), *su eipas plēn* ("your words, but"). *Plēn* means, "except that."[22] Since Jesus cannot say an unqualified no to being the Messiah or the Son of God, he adds an interpretive explication. So *plēn* does not mean "on the contrary." Here again, Jesus acknowledges some traces of truth in his interrogators' formulas. Yet the question posed to Jesus needs clarification. In Luke, Jesus does it by raising a question of his own. It is meant to help form the right question, "You should rather ask...." In Mark, this eventuates with Jesus's use of the scandalous *egō eimi* on the model of Exod 3:14.

Since Jesus spoke Aramaic, we must ask what Semitic substratum lies behind the Greek *egō eimi*. There is no literal Hebrew or Aramaic equivalent. The Peshitta text of Mark 15:62 has the impossible *'ana 'ana*, which, however, presents the advantage of stressing the first person singular of the speaker, leaving no doubt about the Exodal origin of the declaration. Jesus may have answered with the apparently neutral *'ani hu'* (*'ana he'*), which, as we shall see, cannot be neutral. This explains why the high priest theatrically tears his vestments and declares Jesus a blasphemer.

Can Jesus both refuse and accept the same thing? Let us turn to another text, Mark 8:27–33, where Peter confesses, *su ei ho christos* ("you are the Messiah"). This is a case in point: Jesus seems to accept the title *christos*, but then he forbids publicizing it (v. 30). Then, as usual, he shifts focus to the Son of Man and his coming sufferings, a shift that casts a dark shadow over Peter's proclamation (v. 31). Hence, Peter's reaction and rebuke of Jesus (v. 32), followed by Jesus's rebuke of Peter, whom he calls Satan (v. 33). All this occurs in rapid succession, leaving the reader with the uncomfortable feeling that Jesus has both accepted and refused the title "Messiah." This same ambiguity is present in the parallel synoptic pericopes. Matthew 16:16 has Peter use the formula, "Messiah, the son of the living God," which will become famous in the high priest's questioning at the trial (Matt 26:63). Luke 9:18–22 drops the words "son of the living God" and instead uses "the Messiah of God." Each gospel gives prominence to the coming sufferings of the Son of God, a flagrant contradiction to the messiahship proclaimed by Peter![23]

---

22. Cf. Matt 11:22, 24; Luke 10:14 (plus a half dozen times in Luke). Matt 26:39: "Yet not what I want but what you want."

23. But this messiahship was acknowledged—and much emphasized—by the early church after the resurrection. The background of the messianic sufferings is psalmic (see Pss 22; 31; 69).

13. THE TRIAL OF JESUS AND HIS PASSION

Dialectically, the gospel shows Jesus accepting and refusing the same thing at the same time! Mark takes advantage of this ambiguity and stresses the "secret messiahship" of Jesus. Thus two opposites clash within the concept of messiah. Logically, the themes of the suffering servant and of the glorious messiah were mutually exclusive. These themes have never been associated in the Hebrew and the Jewish traditions. Peter is a faithful reflection of such traditions.

This, by the way, explains why Isa 53 is quoted only twice in the gospel: Matt 8:17 and Luke 22:37—where we note the absence of the Son of Man notion. But references and allusions to the Isaianic text are significant; see Acts 8:32–33; Rom 10:16; 15:21; Heb 9:28; 1 Pet 2:22–25; Mark 9:12 (with the Son of Man). In Matt 17:12–13, John the Baptist's martyrdom becomes that of the (collective) Son of Man.

The only solution for the dilemma of the combining the suffering servant and the glorious messiah is found in life experience. As concepts, messiah and suffering Son of Man cannot be combined. Life, however, transcends conceptualization. So biblical and later traditions do not see an insoluble contradiction in God's judgment *and* love; immanence *and* transcendence; divine predestination *and* human freedom; God relenting *but* not recanting (1 Sam 15:11, 29); and so on. What is impossible to conceive intellectually is realized in Israel's history. The key to the evangelists' demonstrations is that every thread of Israel's expectation in Scripture found its fulfillment in Jesus's life.

Messiahship, at times, constituted *the* temptation of Jesus. This is especially conspicuous in the narrative, mentioned above, on "the temptations in the desert" (Mark 1:12–13 // Matt 4:1–11 // Luke 4:1–13). At that time also, Jesus used the phrase "Be gone Satan" (Matt 4:10). Hence, the faith of the early church in the messiahship of Jesus cannot be traced back to him. It is, instead, a later conclusion that she drew from the "finalized" life-death-resurrection of the Nazarene.

This will take us again to the infamous scene of Jesus's trial, with the pointed questions of the religious and civil authorities as to the true identity of Jesus. As we have seen—and as recognized by the consensus of critics, old and new—the whole scene is skewed and full of inconsistencies.[24]

---

24. Eduard Lohse had found twenty-seven violations of the later Jewish code of law governing the Sanhedrin procedures (*The New Testament Environment*, trans. John Steely [Nashville: Abingdon, 1976]). Sanh. 43a is a rather fanciful text about "Yeshua" and his crucifixion, but it unabashedly says that this happened "on the eve of Passover."

Many suggestions of "solution" have been proposed by scholars, mainly along the line of an evangelistic invention without much of a basis. The whole affair, they are saying, boils down to a miscarriage of Roman justice with the complicity of the Jewish Sanhedrin that led to the horrible Roman torture of the crucifixion. The common ground for this scholarly conclusion is the gospel writers' alleged ignorance of the fundamentals of the Jewish and Roman juridical systems.

Recall, for instance, the striking scene of Pilate washing his hands in Matt 27:24, so as to reject—hypocritically?—all guilt. Scholars stress that this is a Jewish symbolic act, not a Roman one. Furthermore, Pilate alludes to a scriptural text, 2 Sam 3:28–29 (David rejecting all guilt in the death of Abner)! On this basis, many scholars dismiss the Matthean text as inauthentic. The Matthean text, it is true, looks suspect. We should rather speak here of a midrashic composition on 2 Sam 3, with allusions to Deut 21:6 and Ps 26:6 (as we shall further see). Then we realize that this is a Jewish way of telling a story. There is no way to conclude, *on this basis*, whether the theme is historical or fictionalized. Pilate is often presented as a prophet *malgré lui*—remember *ecce homo* and his *titulus* on the cross designating Jesus "King of the Jews."[25] (For Luke, of course, Jesus is the son of David and thus king of Israel.)[26] It is not beyond credibility that a Roman governor of Judea would adopt a customary Jewish ritual to "please" his Jewish allies—that is, the "quislings" among the Jews. Nevertheless, the whole scene, logically speaking, is highly tendentious. No historian would understand it literally. It serves as a gap-filler but does not succeed in hiding a terrible void of accuracy—although we do know that Pilate accepted bribes (see Philo, *Legatio ad Gaium* 302).

This would also be my own conclusion. But recently, Andrew Simmonds has, in my opinion, renewed the historian's scrutiny of the trial of Jesus in the gospel.[27] He sees Pilate washing his hands, on the model of Deut 21:8, as a parody—and the whole scene of the trial as scathingly satirical. In Deuteronomy, the washing of hands is meant to absolve *Israel* (of all guilt in the murder by an unknown murderer); Pilate twists it into his own absolution in Matthew (and thus unwittingly he alludes to murder in the person of Jesus). He also distorts the elders' oath, "our eyes have not

---

25. See John 19:5 and Matt 27:37 and parr.
26. Luke 1:32–34, 54–55, 68–79.
27. Andrew Simmonds, "Mark's and Matthew's Sub Rosa Message in the Scene of Pilate and the Crowd," *JBL* 131 (2012): 733–54.

seen," into "see by yourselves," and although "innocent" in Deut 21 refers to the murder victim, Pilate applies the term to himself in Matt 27.

In fact, Simmonds invites the reader to see in the trial a bitter parody of the Roman system of justice and of gladiatorial games. So Pilate asking the crowd in Mark 15:12 what he should do with Jesus of Nazareth or with Jesus Barabbas is quite similar to Caesar asking the mob what to do with the losing gladiator in the arena. It is also a Roman custom for Caesar to give "warrior" names to gladiators. Pilate/Caesar "gives Jesus' gladiatorial nickname as 'King of the Jews.'"[28]

Jesus Barabbas's release conjures up, for Simmonds, the Roman crowd granting freedom to a gladiator.[29] Only the roles are ironically reversed: the Jews act like Romans, and Pilate, washing his hands, acts like a Jew! This explains why the sub rosa story of the trial demonstrates the total illegality of the proceedings and, especially, the acquiescence of the judge to the wishes of the mob. Further contributing to this literary genre, Jesus is later treated as a carnival king.

We saw that the sole grounds for deferring the execution of Jesus to the Roman governor, Pilate, is found in John 18:31. The Romans, at the time, may have been the only ones with the authority to execute people, so Pilate has the last say in the matter. We can imagine that the Romans insisted on the exclusive right to pronounce the death penalty (*ius gladii*) for fear that Jews would show leniency—and perhaps worse—regarding rebels like Barabbas. Mark's irony is unmistakable in this case, with "the Romans" hesitant and "the Jews" adamantly demanding the killing of Jesus. This reduces all the events at the praetorium and beyond to absurdity.

Mark 14:66 interrupts the scene of the trial with a cameo of Peter in the courtyard. Juel thinks that this highlights the contrast between Jesus's "good confession" and Peter's denial of his Master. Although this reading is perfectly admissible, I would suggest that Mark also intended to tell us that there was a "spying" witness to the Sanhedrin's process.[30] Too often, schol-

---

28. Ibid., 753. On Barabbas in the gospel, see Mark 15:6–15; Matt 27:26; Luke 23:18–25; John 18:39–19:16.

29. Simmonds, "On Mark's and Matthew's," 734. On this, see also Adela Yarbro Collins, *Mark: A Commentary*, Hermeneia (Minneapolis: Fortress, 2007), 720.

30. *Pace* John Dominic Crossan, *The Historical Jesus: The Life of a Mediterranean Jewish Peasant* (San Francisco: HarperSanFrancisco, 1991), 375. See John 18:15–16: Peter *and* another disciple, who, by the way, "was known to the high priest [and] went with Jesus into the courtyard of the high priest," is the one who "brought Peter in."

ars' skepticism leads them to conclude that there was no one to report the deliberations in the Sanhedrin and so the whole story in the gospels is an ex post facto, fanciful reconstruction of what must have been said, without historical backup. I think that this negative judgment is wrong. It must be recalled that Mark was Peter's disciple. The latter is arguably Mark's source of information. Peter's denial is conceivably autoconfessional. Further, the denial may thus have been the only way for him to stay in the courtyard and thus hear the debates within.[31]

The miscarriage of justice and the rejection of value should never be the products of a Jewish court of justice. But this emptiness triumphs through the later emptiness of the tomb. History rebounds. The circle reforms. The veil of ambiguity is lifted. Preaching Jesus as Christ and his kingdom as heavenly no longer entails vulnerability to the accusation of Zealotism. The apostles, James, and Paul—but Paul above all—now have a clear vision of Jesus's historic centrality. Jesus's insistence on his impending suffering and death was part of his self-consciousness (Mark 8:31; 9:31; 10:33 and parr.).[32] We find a warrant for it in Luke 12:50: "I have a baptism with which to be baptized, and what stress I am under until it is completed!" The poignancy of this text is compounded by the ambiguity of the motif, like the one of "being taken away" in Mark 2:20. Is it to be understood like the taking away of Enoch and Elijah, who were lifted to heaven without knowing death?[33] Or is it an allusion to the servant of the Lord "taken" and "cut off," while later being granted length of days after his entombment according to Isa 53:9–10? Mark 14:62 lifts all ambiguity, and all uncertainty ends. The veil of concealment is torn apart by the words "I am he," but this involves a removal from the living (even though, by faith, followed by a coming from above as the glorious "Son of Man"). Thus the New Testament interprets what might otherwise be seen as a total failure, as rather a sacrifice voluntarily offered (Heb 9:14, 28). In this sense, suffering is a messianic experience so intense that it becomes lethal. The cross becomes *ekstasis*.

Note that the early church's insistence on Jesus's death as being more important than his life may also be a way to besmirch his Jewishness. Jesus's life becomes transient, a long preparation for the cross. Death becomes an

---

31. Cf. Matt 26:3, 69–75.

32. In light of 1 Kgs 2:37, Jesus's crossing the brook Kidron in John 18:1 belongs to the same motif.

33. In this sense, see Acts 1:2, 11, 22; Mark 16:19; Luke 24:51; 1 Tim 3:16.

obsession.³⁴ No doubt the church's emphasis is solidly anchored. The cross throws a beam of light on everything that preceded. Too often, however, the light is turned onto itself as if reflected in a mirror. Death is the great equalizer. One does not need to be a Jew to be tortured and killed. In that sense, Jesus's body joins all the corpses since the beginning of the world. It is anonymous, since all have indeed abandoned him.³⁵ His proclaimed resurrection—after the alleged transforming rite of passage of the cross—maybe as a reborn "citizen of the world," who has transcended his Jewish "first" birth!

In that respect, Pilate may have been particularly astute with his inscription "King of the Jews"—an indication, by the way, that the Roman governor saw in Jesus's "sedition" a collective movement, not just an individual's subversion. To be sure, Pilate's intention was derisive—a gladiatorial nickname as we saw—but, in conformity with other utterances and events during the trial of Jesus, the placard turned out to be prophetic.³⁶ Another saying put in Pilate's mouth is similarly much more meaningful than intended, *ecce homo*,³⁷ since, unknown to the governor, it strongly emphasizes an important aspect of the title "Son of Man." The mob's exclamation is on the same level of unconscious prophecy. It is reported in what became the most historically devastating verse of the gospel, namely, Matt 27:25 ("His blood be on us and on our children"). It has provided a trumped up excuse for the protracted murderous persecution of the Jews.

There is no parallel to this text elsewhere. It is allegedly uttered by *pas ho laos*, or *kol Israel* ("all of Israel"), with an unusual inclusiveness embracing all the generations ("and on our children"!). Matthew shifts from the term *ochlos* ("crowd") to *laos* ("nation"), thus making the popular oath all-inclusive. This may be an echo of Amos 9:8 ("The eyes of the Lord God are upon the sinful kingdom, and I will destroy it from the face of the earth"). Kurt Schubert says that the Matthean text needs a gloss, such as we find

---

34. "He was talking of his death" / "of his body" / "that he had to die." Marcus Borg rightly protests, "To think of Jesus's passion as simply what happened on Good Friday is to separate his death from the passion that animated his life" (*Jesus: Uncovering the Life, Teachings, and Relevance of a Religious Revolutionary* [San Francisco: HarperSanFrancisco, 2006], 274).

35. See Matt 26:56; Mark 14:50 ("All of them deserted him and fled").

36. Prophetic intimations, of course, fill the gospels. See, e.g., Mark 5:11; 8:31; 9:9 + 14:14, 21; 10:33–34; Luke 22:48.

37. "Then came Jesus forth, wearing the crown of thorns and the purple robe, and Pilate said unto them, 'Behold, the man!'" (John 19:5).

in Acts 3:17 ("I know that you acted in ignorance") and, especially, Rom 11:1 ("Has God rejected his people? By no means!"). A more direct "gloss" would be Acts 5:28 and Luke 23:34 ("Father, forgive them; for they do not know what they are doing").

Without minimizing the importance of the Matthean text, it must be remembered that three-quarters of the Jewish population of the time were already living abroad. Of the one-quarter that remained, it is inconceivable that all were present at Jesus's trial.[38] So the question is, why did the gospel perpetuate this unconsidered and reckless vilification? Judiciously, J. Andrew Overman[39] refers to Matt 23:34–39, "I send you prophets, sages, and scribes, some of whom you will kill and crucify.... Jerusalem, Jerusalem, the city that kills the prophets and stones those who are sent to it.... See your house is left to you, desolate" (NRSV). Within the context of murderous Jerusalem, Jesus joins the many messengers, prophets, and sages who were martyred in their own land. Moreover, further following the lead of Overman, we turn to the Hebrew Bible texts of 1 Sam 26:9: "Who can raise his hand against the Lord's anointed and be guiltless?" and 2 Sam 1:16, "David said to [the murderer of Saul], 'Your blood be on your head; for your own mouth has testified against you, saying, I have killed the Lord's anointed.'" Thus the crucifixion of Jesus is "the killing of the Lord's anointed [Messiah]." It cannot but bring guilt on the perpetrators, and the city that condoned the crime will "be left desolate."

All this makes a lot of sense. Yet we must examine afresh the text of Matt 27:25. There is in this text an indisputable note of polemic reflecting the schism between local synagogues and local churches after the destruction of the temple by the Romans. In fact, however, the saying underlines once more the inseparability of Jesus and his people. Jesus's blood is also their blood (cf. Luke 2:34, "the fall and rising of many in Israel"; Gal 2:19–20, "I have been crucified with Christ"). Not knowing what they are doing (Luke 22:34) by rejecting the accused from their midst, they make him the very image of their own bloodletting. "His blood be on us and on our children," means that his blood is theirs. Jesus, G. B. Caird says, "was confident

---

38. The modern estimation of the demography of Palestine of the time counts some 500,000 people. Josephus offers the number of 6,000 Pharisees, 4,000 Essenes, while the Sadducees were "not numerous"! The rest of the populace constituted the ʿamei haʾarets ("peasantry").

39. J. Andrew Overman, *Matthew's Gospel and Formative Judaism* (Minneapolis: Fortress, 1990), 115; see also 114.

that in him the whole Jewish nation was being nailed to the cross, only to come to life again in a better resurrection, and that the Day of the Son of Man which would see the end of the old Israel would see also the vindication of the new."[40] Who will henceforth be able to distinguish between Jesus the crucified and the crucified Jews? The Roman officer's spear stabs both an individual and a collective heart. Possessed by a vicious demon, anti-Semites go unrelentingly after the body of the "king of the Jews," who is already dead and beyond death, where they cannot reach him. They are only capable of adding one more barb to the Auschwitz's wire fences.

The preceding paragraph was written when I discovered that Andrew Simmonds concurred by saying that the Jewish crowd uttering Matt 27:25 was "betraying their subconscious affinity with Jesus.... The crowd asserts that the proximity of the blood kinship between Jesus and themselves gives them the right to have Jesus put to death."[41] Simmonds compares this psychologically uncomfortable knowledge of oneself with that of other well-known characters, such as Oedipus and many others who choose to be deaf to the "message" of their souls but, like a Freudian slip, at some point betray it. So Oedipus may ignore for a time all the signs that Jocasta is his mother, and Jocasta may ignore the injuries to Oedipus's feet, but not forever.[42]

But let us return to Jesus's judgment. In a dramatic reversal of mood, the Jewish populace assembled at the court seems to be unanimous in their demand for a capital punishment of the accused. True, such an opportunistic popular turpitude is rather frequent in history, but the phenomenon in the gospel may be more indebted to an imitative reminiscence of Dan 6 (Old Greek text), "If you do not hand over Daniel, we will kill you and your whole household!" (v. 29). Such is the alleged pressure on Pilate. This, by the way, does not conflict with what we saw earlier about the gospel's parody of the Roman mob attending a gladiatorial game, for there are several levels of understanding to this. Let us say, however, that it contributes to casting doubt on the historicity of the gospel scene. That the drawing of a parallel between these two documents of the Old and the New Testament is warranted is confirmed by the gospel mention of the sealing of Jesus's grave stone (Matt 27:66) on the model of Dan 6:18.[43]

---

40. G. B. Caird, *Jesus and the Jewish Nation* (London: Athlone, 1965), 22.
41. Simmonds, "Mark's and Matthew's," 754.
42. Ibid., 753. See p. 234 below for another such statement by Simmonds.
43. Something that Lawrence Wills deemed a practical impossibility! (*The Jew in*

On the deeper meaning of the popular oath in Matt 27:25 ("His blood be on us and on our children!"), both Amy-Jill Levine and Andrew Simmonds offer significant help. In her *The Social and Ethical Dimension of Matthean Salvation History*,[44] Levine connects the saying in Matt 27:25 with Jesus's discourse on the institution of the Eucharist (Matt 26:28): "This is my blood of the covenant." So, "The crowd has, in very ironic circumstances, bestowed a blessing upon itself and its offspring" (269). Simmonds agrees with this in "Uses of Blood: Rereading Matt. 27:25": the crowd is, as it were, divinely inspired and thus corroborates Jesus's pronouncement at the Last Supper as far as they are concerned. In fact, there is a clash between Pilate and the crowd on the matter of "blood." Pilate is eager to be absolved of the "blood of this just man" through the parody of hand-washing.[45] The people respond with their understanding of the covenantal blood "thrown on" the participants in the temple sacrifice (see Exod 24:8, "Behold the blood of the covenant" [see also Zech 9:11; Matt 26:28; 1 Cor 11:25; Heb 9:19–22]). They even challenge Pilate by demanding the liberation of the murderer Barabbas and the condemnation of the just Nazarene, thus insisting on a blatant miscarriage of justice. The Jewish chief priests, scribes, and elders proclaiming, "He is Israel's king" (Matt 27:42) adds to the ambiguity of the popular attitude toward Jesus! In other words, there is here, on the part of the *laos*, an unwitting acknowledgment of facts, of which there are many examples in the Scripture.[46] In parallel with the ancient Near Eastern conceptions of treaties, the contract indeed is unilateral and unconditional: "The intent of the promisor is irrelevant and only the precise words count," says Simmonds.[47] This figure of speech is called *peripeteia*, reversal of intention. Externally, the story of Jesus's trial seems to depict the Romans as more beneficent and the Jewish crowd as more sinister, while the reverse is true to the Jewish audience.

---

the Court of the Foreign King [Minneapolis: Fortress, 1990], 136). In addition to the Danielic text mentioned, see also Ps 89:51; and Pss 22; 31; 69, all read messianically by early Christians.

44. Amy-Jill Levine, *The Social and Ethical Dimension of Matthean Salvation History* (Lewiston, NY: Mellen, 1988).

45. See the discussion of Pilate's hand-washing above (228).

46. Isaac's blessing of Jacob instead of Esau (Gen 27:13, Rebekah: "Upon me be thy curse, my son: only obey my voice"); Jacob's marriage with Lea instead of Rachel; the treaty with the Gibeonites mistaken as non-Canaanites; and so on.

47. J. Andrew Simmonds, "Uses of Blood: Rereading Matthew 27:25," *Law Critique* 19 (2008): 184.

When Pilate asks Jesus, "Are you the King of the Jews?" Jesus answers *su eipas* ("you say so"), an ambiguous formula that "suggests triply that, indeed, Jesus is the King of the Jews, that Pilate recognizes it, and most tellingly that Pilate's recognition of the fact helps make it so."[48]

At this point, the trial has degenerated into ordeal. We remember the scriptural prescription for a woman suspected of infidelity through ordeal in Num 5:12–31. The suspected adulteress is made to drink a potion prepared by the priest on a parchment. Among the imprecatory words of Num 5 is the ineffable Name of God, erased in the beverage, so that the woman, as it were, drank God with either positive or negative consequences (cf. 1 Cor 11:27–34 on the Eucharist). The woman keeps silent, like Jesus at his trial-ordeal, as she does not attempt to avoid her fate. "As in an ordeal, in the Agony in the Garden, Jesus drinks the bitter cup and puts his fate in the hands of God, 'thy will, not mine' (Matt. 26:39)."[49] The crowd around "seeks a sign" (Matt 12:38) from the test: Is Jesus the Messiah? "It is the crowd's subconscious awareness of the simple truth that they should free Jesus and condemn Barabbas that, along with Pilate's stimulus by using the words 'blood' and 'Christ', produces the crowd's choice of means to mock Pilate in their oath. They choose the oath that reflects their quintessentially strong bond with Jesus called Messiah."[50]

*

Jesus, Harold Bloom says, "wisely decided not to become the king of the Jews, but ironically may have suffered as such by Roman hands."[51] However, Jesus's entry into Jerusalem on Palm Sunday (Matt 21:1–11 // Mark 11:1–10 // Luke 19:29–38 // John 12:12–16) suggests a comparison with royal procession. Matthew and John quote Zech 9:9 in relation to this event, which is remarkable, since this text from Zechariah is not used messianically in either Qumran texts or in the Pseudepigrapha. It is used so in Sanh. 98a for the first time outside the New Testament. Furthermore, let us note that the Zechariah text includes the words, "[Jerusalem's king] shall command peace to the nations" (9:10; cf. Mark 11:17, quoting another Hebrew text: Isa 56:7).

---

48. Ibid., 182.
49. Ibid., 189.
50. Ibid., 190.
51. Harold Bloom, *Jesus and Yahweh: The Names Divine* (New York: Riverhead, 2005), 19, speaks of "a fatal destiny."

Royalty is the central theme in the last chapter of Jesus's life. It is as "king" that Jesus is arrested, tried, convicted, mocked, and put to death. "King of the Jews" appears six times. This is a Roman title,[52] but it is found only twice in Josephus's works and never in association with messiahship. The corresponding Jewish term would be "king of Israel," which actually appears in John 1:49 and 12:13.

We must turn to the strange figure of "ben Yoseph," also called Messiah ben Ephraim, to find any correspondence, in the main Jewish traditions, to the messianic understanding of the suffering servant in the Second Isaiah's songs. He is a warrior anointed, descendent of Rachel (Gen 30:24), and he dies by the hands of Gog and Magog (Ezek 38–39). The Messiah ben David raises him. The model text is Dan 9:24-26 (v. 26 reads, "After the sixty-two weeks, an Anointed one will be cut off." The same character becomes the dying messiah in 4 Ezra 7:27-30. There were also speculations about Moses, model of the messiah, dying by the hands of his own people. See, for example, y. Suk. 5:1, 55b and 5:1, 52a.[53] At any rate, suffering associated with the messianic event is common to both Judaism and Christianity (see Pesaḥ. 118a).

Who are the people shouting at the trial? The answer is somewhat muddled by the discrepancies in reports. For Mark and Matthew, the interrogation occurs at night. Luke's setting is in the morning of the following day. The high priest raises two questions and, in parallel, Pilate raises two questions. We find two statements about false testimonies against Jesus. The accusation that Jesus predicted the temple's destruction is repeated at the foot of the cross (Mark 15:29 // Matt 27:39-40). It pops up again at the Stephen's trial (Acts 6:13-14). For John, Jesus was actually speaking of "the temple of his body" (2:19-21). This alleged will of

---

52. In Matt 2:2, the foreign "wise men" ask Herod about the "king of the Jews." The context demands it. On mockery of a person as a royal figure, see Philo, *In Flaccum* 36–40: a certain insane man called Karabas.

53. See Raphael Patai, *The Messiah Texts* (New York: Avon, 1979), 167. Later the messiah was split in two. True, there are only few texts in the old Jewish tradition that elaborate on the suffering messiah, and there are no texts on a suffering Son of Man. See Zech 12:10; 4Q540-541; T. Benj. 3:8. The figure of the "Messiah ben Yoseph" may derive from early Christianity, according to Lazarus Goldschmidt, *Der Babylonische Talmud* (Berlin: Harz, 1897), 399. The oracles of Zechariah play an important role here (esp. chs. 11–13). Schalom Ben-Chorin may be right that "from Jesus' entry into Jerusalem to the Last Supper to the crucifixion, the source is a Midrash to the book of Zechariah" (*Brother Jesus*, 128).

13. THE TRIAL OF JESUS AND HIS PASSION

Jesus to destroy the temple is one of the main accusations leading to his crucifixion. Here again, the midrashic is far from absent. The model text is Jer 26:5–24 (LXX: 33:5–24),[54] in which nearly all the elements—regarding the prediction of the temple's destruction, the arrest of Jeremiah and the "unanimous" ("all the people") demand for his death, the shared guilt in shedding an innocent blood, and so on—are all present in the trial of Jesus. At his trial, the testimony of the witnesses may be fraudulent, but, on another level—which was probably misunderstood by the "witnesses"—Jesus's cleansing of the temple on the Day of Palms was, for all practical purposes, a symbolic destruction. Jesus stopped temple operations, at least for a while. It is clear that this cleansing triggered the arrest of Jesus and his precipitously arranged trial. The witnesses to Jesus's intent to destroy the temple perjured themselves, but the issue of the temple appears again here. Earlier, Jesus actually called the temple a den of thieves (Mark 11:17).[55]

The inner complexity of the scene is further stressed when the high priest questions Jesus as to his real identity, thus begging the question: is there a correspondence between messianism and the demise of the temple? "Are you the Christ, the son of the Blessed One?" First, we should discard any idea of an antitemple piety similar to that in Qumran. This is out of the question, if only in view of the infancy narratives, especially in Luke (see also Luke 21:38). In Matt 17:24–27, Jesus pays the half-shekel tax to the temple, in order "not to offend," although he should be exempt from it because he is Son of God. There is no contempt here and no offense. Then what?

In "Jesus and Torah" (ch. 5, 71–130) and "Jesus and Israel" (ch. 7, 141–68) above, I insist on the intrinsic dynamism of both the torah and Israel. Neither has reached its ultimate identity, and both strive toward fulfillment. A transcendent torah and a transcendent Israel are on the horizon, as is a transcendent temple. The Qumran covenanters in the time of Jesus were not the only ones to contemplate the coming destruction of the Herodian temple and its replacement by a celestial temple, descending to earth from heaven. The torah, Israel, and the temple are eschatological realities and, as such, are preexistent. Their end is within the image of

---

54. See also Mic 3:12; 1 Enoch 40:28.

55. Jesus was not the only one to criticize aspects of the commercial arrangements in the temple. Peṣaḥ. 57a denounces high-priestly rapacity. See also Josephus, *Ant.* 20.204–214 (on the high priest Ananias).

their origin. Suffice it, here, to refer to second-century texts like 1 Enoch 90:28–29 and Jub. 1:27.[56]

We do not need to theorize about any association between Jesus and the Zealots.[57] The high priest and company found it easiest to understand Jesus's words as referring to a violent uprising against the authorities. It is in this sense that the witnesses at the trial are false witnesses. Their testimony is false because Jesus was actually speaking of the coming of the celestial temple at the end of time.

Before turning to the dialogue of Jesus with the high priest in the Sanhedrin, let us note that one of the main stumbling blocks for New Testament scholarship is determining the actual grounds on which Jesus was condemned and killed. On the basis of his teaching—including his parables—it is, indeed, difficult to fathom how anyone could accuse him of blasphemy. So most critics would agree with Martin Hengel that a *misunderstanding* led to the crucifixion, while Jesus's intent was *innocuous*.[58] I beg to differ.

At one level, innocuousness may suggest a lack of depth. In that case, Jesus was tragically killed on the mistaken assumption that he meant one thing, while in fact he meant another! Sanders raises another set of objections,[59] but in general he follows Hengel here. I believe that the theories of these two eminent New Testament scholars show one thing: the consensus reading leads to an impasse. True, Hengel comes closer to the truth when he says that Jesus stood in God's stead. This was a "unique, underivable claim to authority, grounded in God himself.... He [Jesus] is incommensurable."[60] I shall now suggest another track altogether.

---

56. See David Flusser, "The Temple Not Made with Hands in the Qumran Doctrine," *IEJ* 9 (1959): 99–104; Kurt Schubert, *Jesus im Lichte der Religionsgeschichte des Judentums* (Vienna: Herold, 1973) (see section "Jesus Appears before the Sanhedrin").

57. As S. G. F. Brandon did in *Jesus and the Zealots* (New York: Scribner's Sons, 1967); and *The Trial of Jesus of Nazareth* (London: Batsford, 1968). On Jesus's rejection of Zealotism, see Mark 7:15 // Matt 15:17 (on purity).

58. See Hengel, *Charismatic Leader*, 59. Blasphemy is, nevertheless, a crucial notion in the Gospel of Mark, where it serves as an *inclusio* of the whole book; see 2:7 and 14:64.

59. Sanders (*Jesus and Judaism*, 229) dismisses the idea of a general misunderstanding on the part of the disciples. Jesus spoke clearly of the kingdom in a new age (in 1 Thess 4, "in the air"), that is, an eschatological one. Its utopist character explains, in particular, why Jesus's followers were not rounded up and killed.

60. Ibid., 68–69.

14

EGŌ EIMI IN THE MOUTH OF JESUS

Jesus answers the high priest's question about his true identity with the words *egō eimi* (Mark 14:61–62), which is a troubling echo of Exod 3:14 ("*egō eimi* has sent me to you").¹ The high priest and his company chose to understand that Jesus pronounced the forbidden name of God—which, according to 1QS in Qumran, to Josephus,² and to m. Sanh. 7:5 constitutes blasphemy.³ The high priest himself, we note, avoids pronouncing the name. He uses a periphrasis, "the Blessed One," in Hebrew *hameborak* (see m. Ber. 7:3: Ber, 50a, where it functions as a participle; only in 1 Enoch 77:1 is it used as a divine title, as in the Markan text). This unusual title attracts keen attention to itself, which makes sense in a context where the name is at issue. The scholarly opinion that this paraphrase was a pseudo-Jewish expression is baseless. Such an opinion is symptomatic of the prevailing tendency among modern scholars to look at ancient authors of both Hebrew and Greek Scriptures as "principally collectors, vehicles of tradition, editors."⁴ The expression "the son of the Blessed One" stands clearly for "Son of God," a messianic title in 4QFlor 3:10–13 (on 2 Sam 7).

---

1. Ephraim of Sedylkov, the grandson of the Baal Shem Tov (eighteenth century), wrote about Gen 28:16, "The word 'anokhi ('I') which ... comprises the totality of the Torah, stands for the ineffable name of God who is revealed through the revelation of the light of the Torah" (quoted by Gershom Scholem, *The Messianic Idea in Judaism, and Other Essays on Jewish Spirituality* [New York: Schocken, 1971], 201).

2. On Jesus in the works of Josephus, see *Ant.* 20.200. More disputed is the text in 18.63–64 (= Testimonium Flavianum). For Josephus, Jesus was a *sophos anēr* due to his miracles and effective teaching. According to the Testimonium, Jesus had a large following before his trial. That would relativize John P. Meier's skepticism as to who was present at Jesus's trial and could report what had occurred there.

3. See also m. Sanh. 90a: he who utters the four-letter name shall not inherit the world to come (R. Abba Shaul).

4. See Martin Dibelius, *From Tradition to Gospel* (New York: Scribner's, 1935), 3.

Jesus answers with the stunning words *egō eimi*, which carry tremendous weight.[5] But the text is fraught with difficulty. First, a variant of Mark 14:62 has *su eipas hoti egō eimi*, which sets Mark in parallel with Matt 26:64 and with Luke 22:70 (*hymeis legete ...*): "you say that [so] I am." For some critics, the addition of "Son of Man" in 14:62 is a qualification for messiahship in terms of an eschatological office.[6] If we accept this version of Jesus's response, the irony is unmistakable. But most commentators believe that the "lean" version in *egō eimi* is the original. Mark's sense of irony further highlights the contrast between the high priest's accusation of blasphemy and Jesus's warning in Mark 3:29 that rejecting him is blasphemy against the Holy Spirit.

Franz Delitzsch translates Mark 14:62 in a bona fide Hebrew *'ani hu'* with the expected meaning of "yes." But *egō eimi* is followed by a verb in the future tense, "you will see." Hence, a possible Hebrew correspondent is not *'ani hu'* but *'ehyeh hu'*. Jesus's subsequent use of the periphrasis "the power" (Delitzsch: *hageburah*) is in deference to the high priest's reluctance. Mark's text thus falls in parallel with Matthew and Luke's version of the dialogue. David Catchpole's opinion about Luke is worth mentioning at this point: "Luke 22:67–70 belongs to circles where divine Sonship is a repugnant concept sealing the doom of the claimant."[7] Note that Luke does not mention blasphemy at all. This, I think, is significant. Mark apparently went "too far" in the eyes of his contemporaries. He himself seems to have backed down when using the term "the power." At the same time, the notion conveyed by *egō eimi* reappears in yet another form, namely, the image of the Son of Man being enthroned in heaven with God himself.[8]

The notion of blasphemy appears especially in Mark 2:7; 3:18; 15:29. In 2:7, Jesus's blasphemy is attached to his forgiving sins (a prerogative of God alone). Here, *egō eimi* is absent, but *epi tēs gēs* ("on the earth") refers to the heavenly setting of the Son of Man. Hence, this incident initiates a plot against Jesus (3:6), and indeed, in 3:28–29 the matter discussed is

---

5. Ethelbert Stauffer, *Jesus and His Story*, trans. Richard Wilson and Clara Wilson (London: SCM, 1960), thinks that it is a self-application of the ineffable name.

6. See Ferdinand Hahn, *The Titles of Jesus in Christology*, trans. Harold Knight and George Ogg (New York: World, 1969), 285; and John Donahue, *Are You the Christ? The Trial Narrative in the Gospel of Mark*, SBLDS 10 (Missoula, MT: Scholars Press, 1973), 548.

7. David R. Catchpole, *The Trial of Jesus*, StPB 18 (Leiden: Brill, 1971), 200.

8. So Rabbi Jose in Sanh. 38b.

blasphemy (see 15:29).⁹ As we saw, Luke 23:35 typically avoids the term "blasphemy," substituting the Greek verbs of LXX Ps 21:7–8 (comp. the vocabularies), while Mark exposes his neck again by reiterating the verb "to blaspheme."¹⁰ The same occurs in Acts 7:55–58, where Stephen is stoned to death, but Luke again avoids the term "blasphemy." As a result, it becomes hard to see why Stephen's statement as it stands about the Son of Man of Dan 7:13 would result in his stoning.

The problem with *egō eimi* is clear when the expression stands without a predicate, as it does time and again in the gospel (especially in John). In this case, Augustine had already tied the formula to Exod 3:14 (*ego sum qui sum* in Latin).¹¹ Besides, Exod 3:14 is not the sole text to refer to in this connection. Deuteronomy 32:39 reads, "I, even I, am he; there is no god beside me."¹² And Isa 43:10 and 48:12 have the text *'ani hu'* ("I am he"), while Isa 45:18 has *'ani yhwh*, the three texts being translated *egō eimi* in the LXX. True, the LXX shied away from the absolute form and tended to add a predicate like *kyrios* ("lord"). *Egō kyrios* appears 171 times and *egō eimi kyrios* 63 times. In view of this situation, Eduard Schweizer, for example, comes to the negative conclusion, "For the LXX translator, *ego eimi* was no formula reserved for the sacred (hymnic, for instance) use."¹³ We must rather follow Heinrich Zimmermann and distinguish the absolute use of *egō eimi*, in which one recognizes the formula of divine revelation (*Offenbarungsformel*). In the background is *'ani yhwh*.¹⁴

In the New Testament, as we already know, John in particular insists on the formula. John 6:20: "I am, do not be afraid." John 8:28: "You will realize that I am." John 8:58: "Before Abraham was [*genesthai*], I am [*egō*

---

9. In fact, the accusation of blasphemy is leveled against Jesus by an "establishment" afraid that the Nazarene represented or could be seen as a messianic activist. It thus applies to a religious label to cover what was perceived as a political threat to its authority.

10. Hence, Donald Juel is right again (*Messiah and Temple: The Trial of Jesus in the Gospel of Mark* [Missoula MT: Scholars Press, 1977], 103): those who mock Jesus on the cross are the real blasphemers.

11. Augustine, *Johannis Evangelium, Tractatus* 38.8 (PL 35:1678–79).

12. The Tg. Ps.-Jon. on Deut 32:39 has, *'ana hu' dehawi* ("I am he who is").

13. Eduard Schweizer, *EGO EIMI… Die Religionsgeschichtliche Herkunft und Theologische Bedeutung der Johanneischen Bildreden, zugleich ein Beitrag zur Quellenfrage des vierten Evangeliums* (Göttingen: Vandenhoeck & Ruprecht, 1939), 24.

14. Heinrich Zimmermann, "Das absolute Ego eimi als die neutestamentliche Offenbarungsformel," *BZ* 4 (1960): 69.

eimi]." John 13:19: "that you may believe that I am." John 18:6: "When Jesus said to them 'I am,' they stepped back and fell to the ground." And so on. God has given his name to Jesus (17:11-12), so that God and Jesus are one (10:30, 38). But this is blasphemy for "the Jews," so they want to stone Jesus (10:33). Besides, from the start, John has stated that Jesus is *ho christos, ho huios tou theou*, thus stressing the kingly and preexistent character of his messiahship (see the Prologue to John). This, of course, amounts to Hellenistic Jewish speculation. Jesus is a god or the emanation of God (cf. Phil 2; 1 Cor 8:6).[15]

The Gospel of John is not alone in making the point. We turn, for instance, to Mark 13:6, where Jesus warns his disciples against false messiahs. These imposters will imitate Jesus and say, *egō eimi*.[16] Matthew 24:5 softens the formula by adding the words, "the Messiah" ("I am the Messiah"), but Luke 21:8 keeps the expression intact. Mark 14:62 brings us to the crucial scene of Jesus's dialogue with the high priest. The latter asks, "Are you the Messiah, the Son of the Blessed One?" Jesus answers, *egō eimi*.[17] Right away, the high priest accuses Jesus of blasphemy. Note the Lukan softening, "You say that I am" (22:70; the word "blasphemy" does not appear again).

In conclusion, it seems incontrovertible that, at the end of his ministry, and perhaps occasionally before, Jesus claimed to be the incarnation, or the presence (*shekinah*), of God's being. Or if we take seriously the imperfect tense of *'ehyeh* and *yhwh* in the supreme revelation to Moses in Exod 3:14 ("I shall be/become"),[18] Jesus claimed to be, in his person, what indeed God had historically become.[19] Jesus's self-proclamation is the blasphemy that justified his murder in the eyes of Jewish authorities. In fact, the claim was so unexpected that the Synoptists themselves felt

---

15. See Adela Yarbro Collins and John J. Collins, *King and Messiah as Son of God: Divine, Human, and Angelic Figures in Biblical and Related Literature* (Grand Rapids: Eerdmans, 2008), 181.

16. In wisdom literature, the I-saying of wisdom in Prov 8 is imitated by folly in Prov 9:4-5, 16.

17. It is conceivable that Jesus at this point shifted from Aramaic to Hebrew *'ani hu'*.

18. In 1967, I wrote a book with the title *Le Devenir de Dieu* (Paris: Les Editions Universitaires).

19. "The last" in Isa 41:4; 48:12. Ethelbert Stauffer ("ἐγώ," *TWNT* 2:350-52) writes, "Jesus is the acting Subject of the history of God ([John 8] v. 58).... [He is] God's definitive representative in the absolute ego eimi—the purest and fullest expression of his incomparable significance." (B, 6).

uneasy with it (or anticipated a negative reaction from their audience) and tended to dull its sharpness. This is particularly evident in their report of the "loud cry" of Jesus on the cross, as we shall see below.

Furthermore, I have earlier suggested that a back-and-forth movement occurred between early Christianity and the evolving Judaism of the time, resulting in the latter distancing itself from Christianity and vice versa.[20] Hence, the Mishnah strongly emphasizes that there is blasphemy only when the unutterable name is spelled out. This, I believe, could be seen as a direct confrontation of a Christian tradition according to which Jesus did just that at his trial and on the cross.[21] For the Jewish sages, Jesus's claim would amount to making himself equal to God (*meshaveh 'atsmo le'elohim*). An echo of this is clearly sounded in John 5:18 (in the mouth of opponents): "He is making himself equal to God [*isōn heauton poiōn tō theō*]." Jesus replies in 5:19 by evoking his compliance with God's will.

This point is particularly important regarding the use of the expression "Son of God" in so-called pre-Christian Judaism. However, the targumic avoidance of this title in 2 Sam 7 and in 1 Chr 17:13, for instance, should not be seen as "pre-Christian"! The Jewish messianic use of the title is clearly displayed in 4QFlor. Besides, it seems evident that the expression in the gospel (esp. in Mark 14:62) is employed—in full force and without restriction—in its literal meaning. Of note is its belonging with other Father/Son imagery (see 13:32; Matt 11:27 // Luke 10:22).

In this respect, the Qumranic literature is helpful. The Hodayot, for example, evoke the constant fellowship of the community with angels (see 1QH 3:21–22; 11:10–12, a realized eschatology; cf. 11:5–9). The covenanters shared a concept of a messianic figure that is heavenly. For 1QS ("treatise of

---

20. The mutual influence is also alluded to by Joseph Klausner in *The Messianic Idea in Israel, from Its Beginning to the Completion of the Mishnah*, trans. W. E. Stinespring (London: Allen & Unwin, 1956), 442. About the pangs of the messiah, he notes that the times of the persecutions that precede the advent of the messiah (under Hadrian) stirred similar expressions in the mouths of both talmudic sages and Christian fathers. Possibly, they borrowed from each other. Similarly, the later belief that the torah would be restored under a new form may be due to a Christian influence; see Pesiq. Rab. 15; Cant. Rab. 2.13; Yal. Isa. 26 (Klausner, *Messianic Idea in Israel*, 442–46).

21. David Daube writes about a Jewish midrash on "I the Lord" in Exodus: "'What flesh and blood cannot possibly say.' This is manifestly directed against Christianity" (*The New Testament and Rabbinic Judaism* [London: Athlone, 1956; repr., Peabody, MA: Hendrickson, 1990], 327).

the two spirits"); 1QM 13; 17:7; and 11QMelch, it seems that Michael and Melchizedek and also the Prince of Light are the same figure; to which we can add "the messenger" in the Testament of Moses.[22] In 4Q491, there is a character that is reckoned among the *'elim* ("gods").

In all of these examples, it is important to realize that the "divinity" of some earthly figures is *a matter of status, not of nature*.[23] So, the king in Israel could be called *'elohim* (Ps 2:2). At any rate, as Raymond Brown writes about *egō eimi*, "this usage goes far beyond ordinary parlance."[24] Mark 14:62 or Luke 22:70 "provokes the charge of blasphemy—a charge that would be more understandable if Jesus were claiming a divine name rather than simply affirming messiahship."[25]

A similar judgment applies to the Markan term *ho christos* in the absolute (8:29; 12:25; 14:61; 15:32) in contrast to pre-Christian literature. In fact, three texts in Mark pair Son of Man and Christ: 8:29-31; 13:21-27; 14:61-62.[26] Mark uses the term "Christ" for the first time in 8:29, as a qualification of Peter's confession; it is accompanied by a prediction of suffering, while Jesus's coming vindication is addressed in 13:21-27 and 14:61-62. (His resurrection or parousia is prophesied; hence the taunting of Jesus as prophet in 14:65.) Psalm 110:1 and Dan 7:13 again provide the background for 14:62.

Against this background, the high priest's tearing off his vestments and crying blasphemy is more than a theatrical gesture.[27] Wherein lies the

---

22. See John J. Collins, *The Star and the Scepter*, 176.

23. In spite of Rudolf Bultmann, "The Divinity of Christ, His Divine Nature," in *Theology of the New Testament* (New York: Scribner's Sons, 1951), 1:128-29. De facto, Jesus is the incarnation of the Word of God (John's Prologue), and of his judgment (John 5:22; 8:16; 9:39).

24. Raymond E. Brown, *The Gospel According to John 1-12*, AB 29 (Garden City NY: Doubleday, 1966), 533. Although, in the Synoptics, "the evangelist seems to play on both a banal and a deeper use of ego eimi" (ibid., 538).

25. Ibid. Note that divine appellations were applied to kings in Israel. We find terms like *'elohim, 'adon, ben 'elohim*; see Ps 45. We must think in terms of adoption by God and of the names as paying respect to the king's vocation. He represents his people's election. Fundamentally, it is Israel that is *ben 'elohim*. A parallel may be drawn with Prov 8:22-36, which in a mythopoeic language speaks of Wisdom as begotten, not made. Thus she is both divine and human.

26. The following paragraph owes much to Juel, *Messiah and Temple*, 115-16.

27. As seen above, the Pharisees saw three grounds only for applying the death penalty: blasphemy by uttering the unutterable name (see Sanh. 6:5), invitation to

blasphemy in Jesus's words? It does not consist in Jesus speaking of resurrection to a Sadducee high priest (Mark 14:61-62), in which case all the Pharisees and the Essenes would have been liable to death for irreverence.[28] In John 8:57-58, Jesus declares, "Before Abraham came into being, *egō eimi*," and the crowd is immediately ready to stone him (for blasphemy). I shall return to the stark ambiguity of this formula in Jesus's mouth, below in chapter 15, "The Great Cry of Jesus on the Cross" (247-62).

These are confusing elements, but one thing seems clear: Until this point Jesus's foes were disorganized, while now, with his arrest, his enemies have united. They are identified as members of the temple personnel, that is, essentially the Sanhedrin. They are called high priests, elders, and scribes and represent the Jewish political and religious supreme rulers.[29] Jesus had provoked their ire, at least indirectly, by "cleansing" the temple (Mark 11:15, with the reaction of the authorities in 11:18 // Matt 21:12, reaction in 21:15 // Luke 19:45, reaction in 19:47-48 // John 2:13-22, reaction in 2:18-20). The parallels with Amos (3:13-15; 7:10-17) and Jeremiah (7:1-15) are striking. The cleansing fulfills Zech 14:21 (on the "Kenaanim," "Canaanite merchants," according to the Buber-Rosenzweig translation). The final provocation came with the declaration in *egō eimi*.

Then came Pilate. As Kurt Schubert says, the religious language used at the Sanhedrin had to be translated into a political language for the Roman governor: "king of the Jews." The civil trial is clearly biased. Pilate allegedly tried to save the accused, for he could not find guilt in him. This version is a Christian charge against "the Jews," which holds that they are the truly disloyal people. Pilate would have preferred to crucify Barabbas.[30]

---

idolatry, and premeditated murder. The tearing of the robe as a sign of being scandalized by an outrageous saying is illustrated in Sanh. 7:5 (blasphemy).

28. Was the high priest in personal competition with the messianic claim of Jesus? A document like Sipra (to Leviticus)—among all the writings of formative Judaism, such as the Mishnah, the Tosefta, the Jerusalem Talmud—catalogs some one hundred references to the "Messiah," every one of which refers to the high priest! David Flusser says that there is an "inevitable tension between charismatic miracles ... and institutional Judaism," because of the former's nonconformism. Charismatics posed a threat, by their unrestrained authority, to the upholders of the established religious order (*Jesus* [New York: Herder & Herder, 1969], 56).

29. The Romans, who chose whomever they pleased, appointed the high priests. From 6 to 66 CE, they elected eighteen high priests in succession!

30. See David Flusser "Sepher Hadash 'al Mishpat Yeshu," *Tarbiz* 31 (1961): 107-117 (Heb., a position close to Paul Winter's in *On the Trial of Jesus* (Berlin: de Gruyter,

For Matthew, "all the people" took responsibility (27:25). The tendentiousness of the account is still stronger in the Gospel of Peter, where the tetrarch Herod is the one who imposes the capital punishment.

1961). We must remember that the Jewish festivals were the ideal times and places for the Sicarii to commit their political murders. They did that, according to Josephus, even in the temple (*Ant.* 20.163–166). Josephus, and no doubt many others, saw this as a desecration of the shrine. It is thus improbable that the Romans would release an insurrectionist on a Passover holiday, when there was a great crowd of Jewish pilgrims from all over the Mediterranean basin. The episode makes of Jesus a scapegoat. Barabbas shares the name Jesus with the Nazarene; strikingly, so does Jesus ben Ananias, who, according to Josephus (*J. W.* 6.300–310) was also arrested, refused to answer any questions (cf. Isa 53:7), was released as a maniac, and was eventually murdered. Of note is the fact that he also was arrested by Jewish leaders and handed over to the Romans for judgment.

15
THE GREAT CRY OF JESUS ON THE CROSS[1]

Jesus is reported to have uttered several cries while being crucified. One of them is especially memorable. Jesus quotes in Aramaic—the vernacular language of the Jews of Palestine at that time—Ps 22:1, "My God, my God, why have you forsaken me?" (*eloi, eloi, lemah savakthani*; in Hebrew, *eli, eli, lamah 'azavthani*).[2] These moving words are fraught with their own set of problems, starting with the hard-to-believe note that the crowd thought Jesus was calling the prophet Elijah.[3]

But I want to deal now with the second exclamation of the Crucified that, although it was "a great cry" (*phōnē megalē*), is left unspecified in the gospel. This great cry comes with the momentous last breath of the martyred Jesus and is, within this very context, most intriguing. Be that

---

1. A more elaborate study of the "great cry of Jesus in Matthew 27:50" is in my essay with this title in *Putting Body and Soul Together: Essays in Honor of Robin Scroggs*, ed. Virginia Wiles, Alexandra Brown, and Graydon F. Snyder (Valley Forge, PA: Trinity Press International, 1977), 138–64.

2. See Matt 27:45; Mark 15:34. For Luke 23:46, he rather said, "I commend my spirit." Matthew and Mark report two cries, the second one without words (Mark 15:37; see Matt 27:50, which adds the word *palin* (again), "Jesus cried again with a loud voice [*phōnē megalē*] and let go his spirit").

3. The only possibility in this regard is to refer to an abbreviation of the name Elijah into Eli as Jewish inscriptions in Rome show. A theory developed successively by Harald Sählin, Thorleif Boman, and Xavier Léon-Dufour, has Jesus in fact saying in Hebrew *eli 'athah* ("You are my God," like in Pss 22:11; 63:2; 118:24; 140:7) understood as in Aramaic by the crowd as *eliya tha* ("Elijah, come!"). See Thorleif Boman, "Das letzte Wort Jesu," *ST* 17 (1963): 103–19; Xavier Léon-Dufour, "Le dernier cri de Jésus," *Etudes* 348 (1978): 666–82. At any rate, the mention of the name Elijah as the first of the sayings on the cross sets the whole context under the shadow of the temple, at least of the cultic (see the Passover expectation of Elijah's visitation bringing closure to the recurrence of the festival).

as it may, "[It] is the most historically certain memory in the tradition," José Pagola writes.[4] He refers to all the Synoptics, the Gospel of Peter, and Heb 5:7.

Since the gospel writers leave the cry without specification, commentators tend to bypass it, as if the Synoptists meant by it an outcry from pain. While this may be possible,[5] it sounds rather redundant after the *eloi, eloi* invocation. Something much more breathtaking (pun intended) may be hidden here, and I'd like to explore the possibility of lifting the veil. My thesis is that Jesus on the cross uttered the unutterable name of God or, at least, some words considered as equivalent to the Tetragrammaton.[6] If so, the "great cry" could be envisaged as parallel to the equally ambiguous saying of Jesus to the high priest, which the latter immediately declared as blasphemous and deserving death. We must, therefore, go back to the scene of the trial and focus on the accusation of blasphemy.

Until his entry into Jerusalem on "Palm Sunday," the remonstrance of the scribes to Jesus is rather minor—namely, not waiting until the end of the Sabbath before healing the sick, eating ears of grain on a Sabbath, not ritually washing hands before a meal (Mark 7:1 and parr.), and not fasting with the Pharisees (Mark 2:18 and parr.). With his summons before the Sanhedrin, however, everything is reaching a climax. On this, Mark 14 is illuminating. At first the Sanhedrin is "looking for testimony against Jesus to put him to death, but they found none" (14:55). All is changed with the high priest's question as to his true identity, to which Jesus answers with highly loaded words; at that very point, the audience considers Jesus's declarations as blasphemous. Jesus, we read, had responded by saying, "I

---

4. José A. Pagola, *Jesus: An Historical Approximation*, trans. Margaret Wilde (Miami: Convivium, 2009), 382.

5. This is especially true as regards the partially non-Jewish audience of Matthew; to the Jewish section, however, the "double entendre" was all that mattered: the tearing of the temple curtain opening the gates to the new messianic era, heralded by Elijah; the resurrection of the dead; the reversal of all powers; the integration of all nations into the elect people; and so on. Matthew's narrative is conceived so that noninitiates could understand it, while at the same time alluding, for the sake of the Jewish Christians of his audience, to exegetical and midrashic traditions.

6. Hans Conzelmann writes, "Jesus does not know the Jewish fear of pronouncing God's name" (*Jesus*, trans. J. Raymond Lord, ed. John Reumann [Philadelphia: Fortress, 1973], 56 [= "Jesus Christus," *RGG*, 3rd ed., vol. 3, cols. 619–53]). I believe that he does but dares going beyond his fears.

am" (*egō eimi*).⁷ This, we saw, is the crux of the matter. True, it is possible to understand the words as simply affirming his messiahship (see 14:54), but *this would not normally constitute grounds for blasphemy*, and certainly would not make one subject to capital punishment.⁸

It is another matter if *ego eimi* ("I am") is a shorthand formula for "I am Who I am," or in the Hebrew third person, "YHWH" (see Exod 4:14). Similarly, in John 8:58–59, Jesus states: "Before Abraham was, I am," and in John 10:30, "I and the Father are one." Immediately following these words, his adversaries prepared to stone him for blasphemy! Other examples include Matt 14:27 (*ego eimi*), to which Peter remarkably exclaims, "Lord!"⁹ Strikingly, a text like John 13:13 comments: "You call [*phoneite*] me teacher and Lord [*ho kyrios*]—and you are right, for I am [*eimi*]" (see also John 4:26; 8:24, 28; 12:36; 13:19; 18:5, 8). In John 18:6, hearing the uttered words *egō eimi*, the detachment of soldiers "stepped back and fell to the ground."¹⁰

If we take these statements by Jesus seriously, the high priest's accusation of blasphemy makes sense, since we find in m. Sanh. 7:5, "No one is guilty of blasphemy but if he fully and distinctly spells out the Name of God." Whether Jesus indeed spelled out the name "fully and distinctly" is debatable, but Jesus aggravated his case considerably by applying the divine claim to himself. Or did he? The ambiguity is at its apex. What is clear is that Jesus affirms his messiahship by associating himself with the

---

7. Already through the healing of the paralyzed man, "scribes and Pharisees" reckon Jesus's "remission of sins" as blasphemy (Matt 9:2; Mark 2:3; Luke 5:20).

8. Unless we understand that the title "messiah" is synonymous with rebel, since all the guerrilla leaders of the time were proclaiming themselves messianic. But then, their pretension cannot be called "blasphemy," for the self-proclamation as messiah is not considered as such.

9. In Matt 24:5, false messiahs will come "in my name" and claim *ego eimi*! Note the purposeful ambiguity of the word "Lord" in Luke (see 1:15, 76; 3:1–2; esp. 20:41–44; Acts 2:25–36, a text that shows that Jesus's messianism is a church construction). Incidentally, see Josephus's stunning attribution of messiahship to Vespasian (*J.W.* 6.312–313).

10. After bypassing several texts in *ego eimi*, *The Jewish Annotated New Testament* (ed. Amy-Jill Levine and Marc Zvi Brettler [Oxford: Oxford University Press, 2011]) finally singles out John 8:28 and says, "A divine claim, alluding to the theophany of Exod 3:14" (175). At Matt 14:27, the note laconically says, "Exodus 3:14." By contrast, the NBS in French is much firmer (and more useful) about these texts as alluding to Exod 3:14 (see, e.g., 1406).

divine being. This decisively substantiates his claim. As a result, the high priest "tore his clothes" (Mark 14:63).

As I insisted above, Jesus's appearance before the tribunal was marked by a number of irregularities. The high priest's reaction reveals to all present a foregone conclusion. Now, the talmudic treatise of Sanhedrin (4:2) prescribes that the lower judges speak first and then vote, so as not to be manipulated by higher authorities in the tribunal. In addition, Sanh. 17a casts a grave doubt on a unanimous condemnation, not only as an unlikely occurrence but also as a questionable verdict. Rab Kahana (third century CE) says that, in such a case, the condemned one must be set free. Rabbi Aqiba (second century CE), according to Mak. 1:10, said that one death penalty in seven years comes from a "bloody" court of justice. At any rate, he rejected the death penalty altogether.

Can we trust that the *egō eimi* declarations reported in the gospels are historical? As far as I know, no ancient Jewish tradition mentions anyone who dared to pronounce the unutterable name *apart from the high priest on Yom Kippur in the most sacred place of the temple*.[11] The existence of this taboo—which explains the reluctance of the gospels to spell out the great cry on the cross; what was Jesus's prerogative did not extent to his "biographers"—attributes to the testimonies of the gospels a measure of authenticity. True, it has been argued that Mark 14:55–64 cannot be historical because of the christological elements it contains. But without these words precisely, the Sanhedrin's outrage lacks a motive.

Thus Jesus's response to the high priest is consistent with the whole context of the gospel. "You will see the Son of Man seated at the right hand of the Mighty One and coming on the clouds of heaven" (Mark 14:62; cf. Ps 110:1; Dan 7:13). Jesus signals that the End has come; everything has changed, and the old formulas are obsolete. His is the discourse of a visionary. Jesus's messianic consciousness during his career may be debated, but not his consciousness of the End and his decisive contribution to it. One element is particularly important, namely, the distinction to be made between the Master's private and public discourse. When the boundary between the two realms risks being blurred, Jesus forbids those who would put it at risk to persist on that tack.[12] To the crowds, he speaks

---

11. Sabbatai Zwi, however, in the seventeenth century, uttered the name in his claim of being the messiah: a remarkable occurrence.

12. See Matt 10:27, "What I say to you in the dark, tell in the light, and what you hear whispered, proclaim from the housetops."

of the Son of Man in the third person (see, e.g., Mark 2:10, 28; 8:38; 10:46). Privately, to the Twelve, Jesus speaks as an apocalyptist, and prophetically announces the coming of the kingdom of God. It is only toward the end that, for him, the moment has come. He then shifts to the first person, thus emphasizing his growing conviction that he is the expected Son of Man, who is also the Son of God in a special way.

The text of Mark 8:38 (// Luke 12:8-9) bears notice for our purpose. There are three personae: "me," "the Son of Man," and "the angels of God." The identification of Jesus with all three is clear. The emphasis is on *en emoi* and *me*, and on the contrast between *anthrōpoi* and *angeloi*, as well as between the *huios tou anthrōpou* and the *anthrōpoi*. The Son of Man belongs to the angels of God (as in Dan 7). At the center of the picture is the "I" of Jesus. In the following verse (Luke 12:10), a fourth persona is introduced: *to hagion pneuma*, in whom we again recognize Jesus. On this, Mark 3:28 is crystal clear: "Everything will be forgiven to the sons of man ... but to those who blaspheme against the Holy Spirit, it will never be forgiven ... for they said, 'he has an impure spirit.'" No logion could be more limpid regarding the celestial claim of Jesus. Robert Frost writes (in a poem called *Kitty Hawk*):

> God's own descent
> Into flesh was meant
> As a demonstration
> That the supreme merit
> Lay in risking spirit
> In substantiation.[13]

As another example, I shall follow Bruce Chilton's focus on Luke 4:16-30, a text already mentioned above (with a note of scholarly skepticism as to its "authenticity"). It is about Jesus's sermon in Nazareth's synagogue on Isa 61:1-2. The alleged "inauthenticity" of the passage must be reassessed when it is realized that, with the backing of the Syriac gospels, Jesus manipulates the personal pronouns of the Hebrew model text. Now, the ones who are commissioned by the Spirit of the Lord are "you," but you failed, and now "I," or "me," am the one who will free the broken with release and so on. The "me" is now assuming the charge that the people,

---

13. Robert Frost, *Speaking on Campus: Excerpts from His Talks 1949-1962*, ed. Edward Connery Lathem (New York: Norton, 2009), 93.

here called "you," refused. The "I" is the anointed one, while the "you" are anointed as messiahs. The emphasis on both the first person singular and the second person plural is striking.[14]

Are there other texts conveying Jesus's daring self-proclamation in *egō eimi*? Although these words are obscured in the gospel on the grounds that they are extremely offensive in the eyes of all Jews (and not just those of the high priest), Jesus's claim was so central that it could not be bypassed. It was the veritable cause of the Jewish authorities' demand for the death penalty for a blasphemer. Thus Jesus's proclamation had to be handled gingerly in documents that were addressed as much to Jewish Christians as to gentile Christians. Further, the discreet veil cast over the formula emphasizes the shrouding ambiguity surrounding the last days of the Nazarene.

More in-depth: if indeed Jesus associated himself intimately with his "Father" by using his name, *while being conscious that he was about to die*, the blasphemy becomes a scandal of heretofore unheard proportion. On the cross, he is taunted by some witnesses, "He saved others; he cannot save himself" (Matt 27:42 // Mark 15:30 // Luke 23:35). This may or may not allude to his self-claimed divine relationship, but then a text like Phil 2:9–11 is incontrovertible: "God … gave him the name that is above every name, so that at the name of Jesus every knee should bend, in heaven and on earth and under the earth, and every tongue should confess that Jesus Christ is *Lord*, to the glory of God *the Father*."[15]

In 1 Enoch 48:2–3, we find this great text about the Son of Man: "And in that hour, that son of man was named in the presence of the Lord of Spirits; and his name before the Head of Days. Even before the sun and the constellations were created, before the stars of heaven were made, his name was named before the Lord of Spirits." And in verse 7, "For in his name they are saved, and he is the vindicator of their lives."[16]

The invocation of Jesus's name is well attested in the gospels, as well as in Acts and in Paul's letters.[17] See Rom 10:13, where Joel's invocation

---

14. Bruce Chilton, "Targum, Jesus, and the Gospels," in *The Historical Jesus in Context*, ed. Amy-Jill Levine, John Dominic Crossan, and Dale C. Allison Jr. (Princeton: Princeton University Press, 2006), 238–55.

15. NRSV (emphasis added). Note that the kingdom is indifferently Jesus's kingdom, God's kingdom, or the Son of Man's kingdom (cf., e.g., Matt 19:28 with Luke 22:28–30).

16. First or second century CE, possibly composed by a Jewish Christian.

17. See, e.g., Matt 18:20; 19:29; Mark 9:38; 13:6; John 12:28; 14:13; Acts 2:21; 3:16;

of God's name (Joel 3:5) has become, for Paul, the invocation of Jesus's name (see also 1 Cor 1:2; 2 Tim 2:22; see especially the amazing 1 Cor 8:6; Titus 2:13). This survey, I believe, is conclusive. Whether the theology of Jesus's name in the early church originated from Jesus's actual saying—in particular his answer to the high priest's question—or, on the contrary, influenced the gospel narrative of Jesus's trial is a moot question; it must remain unanswered.[18] But this does not detract from the fact that we can identify the Sanhedrin's accusation of blasphemy (that is, the pronouncing of the unutterable divine name) as the grounds for Jesus's condemnation.[19]

As we know, the high priest's query was not the first time the question of Jesus's real identity was raised. Matthew 16 in particular describes the memorable scene of Jesus interrogating his disciples on that issue. The puzzlement of even the closest of his acquaintances—including the one of whom it was said, "the one that Jesus loved" (John 13:23; 19:26; 20:2; 21:7, 20)—is astounding. They express various opinions, although, to be sure, they had had plenty of time to reflect on the question. We could have even thought that there was nothing more urgent for them to do. When directly asked, however, they start giving voice to an anonymous crowd behind which they hide themselves: "Some say ... and others say ..." (Matt 16:14). "'And you?' Jesus said to them." The disciples remain voiceless. Only Peter proclaims (Matt 16:16): "You are the Messiah, the Son of the Living God"—almost by default, as if to say (in the words of John 6:68), "Lord, to whom [else] can we go?" Besides, after being highly praised for

---

4:7, 12. But in Mark 10:17 and parr., Jesus refuses to be called "good" as only God is good, he says.

18. Mark gives an account of the divine sonship at the time of baptism, but the possibility remains that this is an ex post facto conclusion of the early church. Along the same line, the disciple Thomas vents his suspicion about "seeing" the Lord resurrected until "seeing" the physical marks of his martyrdom. At that point, he cries, "My Lord and my God"—using a formula intended for the Caesars (the emperor Augustus was called, "god, son of god, savior, and father")—for only a god can rise from the dead (John 20:25, 28; the rest of the text is a play on the verb "to see"). The closest ancient textual witness I can think of is in the book of Daniel, when "King Nebuchadnezzar fell on his face, worshiped Daniel, and commanded that a grain offering and incense be offered to him" (2:46; Daniel does not protest).

19. A. E. Harvey, however, considers Jesus's response to the high priest as "manifestly unhistorical" (*Jesus and the Constraints of History* [Philadelphia: Westminster, 1982], 32, 136, 170, also cited by E. P. Sanders, *Jesus and Judaism* [Philadelphia: Fortress, 1985], 299).

his insight, Peter is rather harshly rebuked (Matt 16:23). The rebuke is extended to all the disciples in Mark 8:30 and Luke 9:21, since the order not to speak of him as the Messiah is followed by a description of a fate that the apostles do not want to know about. John adds the dramatic note, "Because of this, many of his disciples turned back and no longer went about with him" (6:66).

Mark 11:28; Matt 21:23; and Luke 20:2 show Jesus confronted by chief priests, scribes, and elders. What is remarkable in these texts is Jesus's ambiguous response to the question, "By what authority are you doing these things? Who gave you authority to do them?" The reader is expecting a direct answer, but instead Jesus questions the high clergy about the authority of John the Baptist.

Note that this scene takes place inside the temple, that is, on the turf of Jesus's foes. Depending on what he says about the source of his authority, Jesus will either be dismissed as a quack or accused of intolerable arrogance. Since the high clergy never reached consensus regarding John the Baptist's magisterium, what good would it do for Jesus to provide an answer as to his own authority, an answer they will certainly reject? The high clergy are not looking for the truth but for an excuse to arrest him. His unwillingness to answer says clearly that his authority comes from heaven, without saying it expressis verbis.[20]

Now, facing the high priest, Jesus's discourse becomes direct and "private," as if the priest were one of his disciples. Jesus is no longer an obscure Galilean preacher, for the time has come for all to prepare for the advent of the kingdom.[21] No circumlocution is permitted. Jesus is seized not only by a sense of an ending, but also by a sense of urgency. Note that he is not necessarily certain of dying at this point, but he is convinced that a final event—like the Son of Man riding on the clouds—is imminent. The future tense he uses is not necessarily a remote future, but perhaps a close one. Apocalypse now!

---

20. I have already mentioned the text of Matt 9:6 and Mark 2:10 about the paralytic man whose sins are forgiven by the authority of Jesus. See also Matt 28:18 (all authority in heaven and on earth); Mark 1:22: "He taught them as one having authority, and not as the scribes"; Luke 4:36 (Jesus has authority over the unclean spirits).

21. Before, in the words of John, his "hour is not yet come" (2:4; 7:16, 30; 8:20), not to be confused with fatalism. The final *kairos* is of his own choosing or, at least, acceptance (see, e.g., Matt 26:2, 12).

15. THE GREAT CRY OF JESUS ON THE CROSS

*

It's time now to return once more to the great cry on the cross. To recall, it appears in Matt 27:50 with parallels in Mark 15:34–37; Luke 23:45–46; and Gos. Pet. 5:19 and is each time reported as shouted with "a loud voice." This expression, *phonē megalē*, is well attested in the Septuagint (LXX), as we shall see. This matter is important since Matthew, as is well known, is more "Jewish" in his account of the passion than the other evangelists. It is furthermore notable that, as the outcome of the great cry, Matthew introduces apocalyptic phenomena (see also John 5:28; 11:43).

Phonē megalē in the LXX and the New Testament is found in cultic and apocalyptic contexts.[22] The great cry in Matthew and Mark occurs at the very time of the afternoon prayer in the temple ("at the ninth hour"; see Ps 30:6; cf. Jdt 9:1). *Phonē* in Matthew has been used prior for the prophetic voice of John the Baptist and the following voice of God (3:3, 17; 17:5; it is the *bath qol* of rabbinic literature). But Matthew reserves the whole expression *phonē megalē* for the passion narrative. Matthew 24:31 says that, at the End, angels will be sent with a trumpet sound and "a great cry."[23] In short, the Hebrew backdrop of the cry is less *tsaʿaqah* ("a shriek") than *teruʿah* ("a shout, a battle cry"), the sacred and cultic war cry accompanied by the sounding of the shofar.[24] This fits the ethos of Matt 24:31, which describes the ultimate battle that will be waged by the Son of Man, with the help of his angels. Further, the accompanying apocalyptic manifestations echo those that follow God's shouts, by which he reveals himself in Amos 1:2; Jer 25:30; Ps 45:7; and Joel 4:16.

To be sure, the great cry of Matt 27:50 is not uttered in a pure context of war, but it is still in the context of the cult (see v. 46) and hence still within the ethos of the *teruʿah*. Remarkably, *phonē megalē* in Matthew, as in the LXX, like the *teruʿah* in the MT, always introduces a major revelation. It breaks the walls of ignorance and incomprehension, so that at the foot of the cross, the Roman centurion (a representative of the *goyim*)

---

22. In Dan 5:7 Old Greek, the king *ephonēse phonē megalē kalesai* ("with a great uttered cry, summoned") the "enchanters, magicians, Chaldeans, and the soothsayers."
23. See Isa 18:3 LXX (same vocabulary). See the striking texts of 1 Thess 4:16; 1 Cor 15:52.
24. See Amos 2:2; Zech 1:16 ("a day of the *shofar* and the *teruʿah* against the fenced cities").

responds with a confession of his own.[25] With regard to this all-important saying from the mouth of the Roman officer, Matt 24:30–31 is illuminating: "Then the sign of the Son of Man will appear in heaven, and then all the tribes of the earth will mourn, and they will see 'the Son of Man come on the clouds of heaven' with power and great glory. And he will send out his angels with a loud trumpet call" (a habitual accompaniment of the great cry). As Otto Betz wrote, "It is probable that Mark regarded as an epiphany the loud cry with which Jesus died on the cross."[26] This is indeed an epiphany that marks the end of darkness (Mark 15:37; see below). As Matt 27 makes clear, the centripetal temple becomes centrifugal and extends itself to the ends of the earth. The apocalyptic events around the cross spell out the demise of the exclusionary temple and, with it, a whole era. The "desolating abomination," spoken of by Dan 9:27, sits in the temple (Matt 24:15) and must be eradicated. "No matter what Jesus thought, said, or did about the temple, he was its functional opponent, alternative, and substitute," John Dominic Crossan says.[27]

I have mentioned in a preceding footnote the striking text of 1 Thess 4:16, which describes the coming down of "the Lord," "with a cry of command, with the archangel's call [*en phonē archangelou*], and with the [sound of the] trumpet of God [*en salpingi theou*]." The cry calls for the dead to rise. The clouds, once more, serve as a vehicle "in the air." The parallel with Matt 24:30–31 is evident.

Along the same line, the texts stress the presence of earthquakes (in Matthew, two pairs of them, 21:10 echoed in 28:4 and 27:51 echoed in 28:2), as the old world sinks into darkness with the sound of a shriek, and a new world is born at the sound of a *teruʿah*—the same cry with two faces, like Janus. In Matt 27:52, the rocks are split. We remember that, for

---

25. See the *inclusio* it builds with Matt 4:16 (on the basis of Isa 9:1–2). A further *inclusio* exists with Matt 27:42–43 regarding the chief priests' "wish" to see Jesus come down from his cross as king and Son of God so that they may believe. The response to the question of the high priest whether Jesus is "the Messiah, the Son of God" (Matt 26:63) is given by a Roman officer! At this point, four things simultaneously happen: the great shout, the darkening of the skies, the rending of the temple curtain, and the confession of the centurion. Four powers are overcome: the temple establishment, nature, death, and Rome (i.e., the religious, the cosmic, the ontological, and the political).

26. Otto Betz, "φωνή," *TDNT* 9:293.

27. John Dominic Crossan, *The Historical Jesus: The Life of a Mediterranean Jewish Peasant* (San Francisco: HarperSanFrancisco, 1991), 355.

15. THE GREAT CRY OF JESUS ON THE CROSS

Zechariah (14:4), the splitting in two of the Mount of Olives is a prelude to the resurrection of the dead.[28] This theme is reinforced with the mention of darkness at noontime.[29] The darkness is that of Gen 1:2–4: it is the chaos that precedes creation, which is "light," that is, revelation and self-disclosure of the Creator. When Jesus is about to die, the cosmos reverts to chaos. Darkness lingers for three hours (Matt 27:45), as many hours as the number of days that Jesus will stay in the grave.[30] After that, there is a new creation, ushered in by a new earthquake (28:2). In other words, Jesus pulled the whole world into his tomb with him, where it would have stayed forever, were it not for the fact that, as death was unable to hold Jesus in its sway (Acts 2:24), the just come back to life (Matt 27:52–53) as forerunners of those who will share in the new world.[31]

The double entendre of the motif of darkness depends on the tearing of the curtain that covered the *debir* (holy of holies). Dialectically, once it is rent, the darkness of the sacred place (see 1 Kgs 8:12; Ps 18:12)[32] invades the world. In concomitance with this, God leaves the temple at the moment of Jesus's death, just as he deserted the First Temple, which, in consequence, was destroyed by Nebuchadnezzar.[33] Thus the other face of the event is revealed: at the moment of the contact with the sacred, the earth quakes, it loses its grip on the dead, and they enter Jerusalem, as did the revived dry bones in Ezekiel's vision of chapter 37 (v. 13). The holy of holies is extended to the whole earth. This is inaugurated by the *teru'ah* that the true high priest shouts on the Day of the universal Atonement. Let us here make reference to T. Levi 18:10–11, in the view of which the last

---

28. See, e.g., Pesiq. Rab. 31; Tg. Cant. 8:5 (the resurrection will happen when the Mount of Olives is cleft); Josephus, *Ant.* 9.222–227; 20.167–172.

29. See Amos 5:18–20; 8:9; Isa 13:9–16 (on God's judgment); Jer 4:5–6, "Blow the trumpet [*shofar*] through the land; shout aloud," and so on.

30. The darkness for three hours alludes to the apocalyptic: the sun and the moon will become dark and so on; see Amos 8:9; Jer 15:9. Darkness or blindness plays a major role in Jesus's polemics. The leaders of the time are blind guiding blind (Luke 6:39; Matt 15:14; darkness: Matt 6:22–23; Luke 11:34), while, in John, Jesus is "the light of the world" (9:5; see 1:9).

31. Pesiq. Rab. 40.5 reads, "On the Day of Atonement I will hold you guiltless, regarding you as a newly made creature" (William G. Braude, trans., *Psikta Rabbati* [New Haven: Yale University Press, 1968], 2:711).

32. In the LXX, see Exod 26:31–33; 30:6; 35:12; 39:34; 40:21; Num 4:5.

33. See Tacitus, *The Histories* 5.13; Josephus, *J.W.* 6.299; 2 Bar. 8:1–2.

high priest "will open the gates of paradise ... and will give to the holy ones to eat from the Tree of Life."[34]

So far I have concentrated on the atmosphere of the Day of Atonement surrounding Jesus's passion. Now it is true that Matthew, instead, sets his narrative ostensibly within the framework of Passover. This transformation of the festival into Yom Kippur is only compositional![35] Matthew does not hesitate before such metamorphoses. In Matt 21:15, the reported popular cries of hosanna in the streets are usually shouted in the temple at Sukkoth, while this scene happens on the eve of Passover.[36]

We find confirmation of the Yom Kippur setting for the passion in the Epistle to the Hebrews. Hebrews 5:7 tells us that Jesus cried *meta krauges ischuras* ("with a loud *teruʻah*") his "prayers and petitions." This direct reference to the liturgy of Yom Kippur, "entirely devoted to prayers and petitions ... and humble entreaty in which one seeks earnestly to propitiate God," as says Philo,[37] explains why Yom Kippur is called "the day of the *teruʻah*" in Num 29:1. This is the day when the high priest annually shouts the Tetragrammaton in the *debir*. On that day, Jews practice self-oblation,[38] the very theme of Heb 5 and 10 as regards Jesus, seen both as high priest and as sacrificial victim.[39] So, while the appointed high priest and his cohorts in the Sanhedrin show their total incompetence and corruption—the words "high priest" are used no less than fourteen times in Matt 26–27—they are being replaced by the true high priest, who offers no other sacrifice but himself and who will shout the sacred name in a most unexpected and paradoxical "holy of holies," namely, the cross of Golgotha. At this very moment, he expires; it is the apocalyptic moment par excellence, when shout and silence, darkness and light, the same and the other, life and death, meet.

---

34. Rev 11:19 and 15:5 speak of the opening of the heavenly temple. See also Heb 10:19–20; and especially Mark 1:10.

35. Matthew's transposition of a festival for another is present in 21:9, where the people acclaim Jesus with Sukkoth's *hallel* and waive bundles of boughs.

36. Cf. m. Sukkah 3:9 on the singing of the *hallel* of Ps 118.

37. Philo, *The Special Laws* 2 (Colson, LCL).

38. *Weʻinnithem ʻeth naphshoteychem* ("you shall torment your souls"), at Yom Kippur, Lev 23:26, 16:29; Num 29:7.

39. Barn. 7 compares Jesus's passion with the scapegoat of Yom Kippur; in fact, says the text, there were two scapegoats, one sacrificed on the altar, the other cursed and sent into the desert. (This may shed light on the strange popular choice made between Jesus bar-Abbas and Jesus king of the Jews).

Matthew accommodates his double audience with double entendres. He does not spell out the great cry so that it is open to double interpretation. The crucifixion of the Nazarene is the same horrible torture it is for all who are executed in his manner. But the great cry evokes another perspective: it is the ultimate *teru'ah*, replacing the one the high priest shouted three times on the Day of Atonement. Then the whole universe enters into convulsions.[40] Just as Rabbi Aqiba, who died at the hands of the Romans in the second century CE, prolonged, in his last breath, the last word of the "Shema," *ehad* ("one"), so Jesus died before him with the sacred name on his lips.

"Jesus gave a loud cry and breathed his last, and the curtain of the temple was torn in two, from top to bottom" (Mark 15:37–38). The curtain (*katapetasma*) surely designates the inner veil of the holy of holies (see Heb 6:19; 9:3; cf. 10:20). This fits nicely with my theory about the bearing of *egō eimi*: access to God's presence is secured by Jesus's death. True, there is a Jewish tradition of the tearing of the outer veil signaling the impending doom of the temple.[41] But the Josephus text, as well as y. Yoma 6:3, 43c = m. 6:3 (*dalthoth ha-heykhal*), and Yoma 39b have "gates" not "veil." In contrast to Donald Juel's judgment here, it is preferable to see Mark 15:38 referring to the inner curtain and to see Hebrews as correct in its interpretation.

The truth of the matter is that the veil of the temple has a double-faced meaning. The Hebrews interpretation is one side of the notion. This takes us to a much more positive meaning of the removal of the curtain than just an omen on the temple's destruction. The stress is on the access "behind the veil" to the holy of holies, where Jesus has become the high priest, that is, the one who alone is entitled to penetrate the *naos* at Yom Kippur. The correspondence with the *egō eimi* as *'ehyeh* is unmistakable. Hebrews 10:20 confirms this reading.

The other face of the veil is backed up by the customary use of "tearing" in 2 Kgs 2:12 and Matt 26:64–65; Mark 14:62–63. In 2 Kgs 2, Elisha rends his clothes when Elijah goes to heaven. On that model, the rabbis

---

40. The martyrdom of St. Stephen in Acts 7:59–60 is depicted on the very model of Jesus's passion. Even the great cry is shouted here again.

41. See Josephus, *J.W.* 6.290–296; Yoma 39b; y. Yoma 43c; Tacitus, *The Histories* 5.13. Note, however, that it is a question of the "doors of the shrine," not of its veil or curtain. That we must distinguish between "veil" and "gate" in this respect is clear from m. Zebaḥ. 9:14: "Most holy things were eaten within the [temple] veils, lesser holy things and second tithe within the wall."

prescribed the renting of one's clothes on the occasion of the death of a parent, or of one's teacher, of the patriarch (*nasi*), of the father of the court (*'ab beth din*), of blasphemy (see m. Sanh. 7:5), of a scroll burning, of the destruction of the temple, or of Jerusalem (Mo'ed Qat. 25b–26a). I have emphasized the importance of the high priest rending his vestments during the trial (Matt 26; Mark 14). In conclusion, the temple veil torn from top to bottom signals a deep sorrow. In the New Testament, the mourning is for Jesus's death or, according to *Clem. Recogn.* 1.41, for instance, for the temple's end.[42]

We should not rush to interpret the "temple not made with hands" as designating the Christian community (*pace* Juel et al.). At the "original" level, the temple is not the church but Jesus himself (Heb 10:20), and the veil is Jesus's flesh (so also John 2:21); besides, the mention of the "three days" before the reconstruction makes it crystal clear (e.g., Mark 14:58). On this particular point I agree with Eta Linnemann.[43] "Not made with hands" (*acheiropoiētos*) refers to a temple of a different order—like the torah written on hearts, for instance (Jer 31:33). Midrash Tehillim on Ps 90 contrasts the temple built by hands of mortals with the temple that God will build and that cannot be destroyed. Similarly, Mek. 3.10 (on Exod 15) says that, while God used only one hand to create heavens and earth (see Isa 48:3), he will use both hands to build the ultimate temple that cannot be destroyed (Exod 15:17),[44] when "the Lord will reign for ever and ever" (15:18).

The nuance is important. In (Pharisaic) rabbinic tradition, the builder of the definitive temple is God, not the messiah. The same is true of the Qumran text 4QFlor 3:2–3: "The house wh[…] is the end of days … which Thy hands have established." For the Qumranic document, the central biblical text is Exod 15:17, not 2 Sam 7:13 (where David is the builder). This one contrasts with the standing one, which was "laid waste," for it was "a temple of man" (*miqdash 'adam*) and was destroyed "because of our sins" (lines 3–4). Per contra, of great import is the Targum on Isa 53:5 which

---

42. See David Daube, *The New Testament and Rabbinic Judaism* (London: Athlone, 1956; repr., Peabody MA: Hendrickson, 1990), 23–26.

43. See Eta Linnemann, *Studien zur Passionsgeschichte* (Göttingen: Vandenhoeck & Ruprecht, 1970), 124.

44. See Judah Goldin, *The Song at the Sea, Being a Commentary on a Commentary in Two Parts* (New Haven: Yale University Press, 1971), 237–39.

states that the messiah is expected to be the builder.[45] In Mark, the builder is Jesus (as King-Messiah). In view of the Markan shift from God to the Messiah, Jesus claims a status that cannot but enrage his opponents.

In a second move, however, Paul and followers apply the expression "not made with hands" to the Christian community (e.g., 1 Cor 3:14; 2 Cor 6:16; Eph 2:20-22 // 1QS 8:8-10; 9:3-6; 5:5-7; CD 3:18-4:10; 1QpHab 12:3, in which texts the Qumran community is the living temple of God). The correspondence between Qumran's and Jesus's claim spells out similarity, but with a different object. It is only through Jesus as Christ that what is identified as his becomes applied to the church, his "body," a Pauline conception. The church thus becomes the living temple. Even Christian individuals are temples for the Spirit, hence their sanctity. Bypassing this Pauline interpretation risks ignoring the communal dimension of Jesus's messiahship. It is by being bound to Israel, like a graft to a tree trunk, that the church becomes the ultimate temple not made with hands, according to Paul (see Rom 9–11). There can be no shortcut.

---

45. The verb *halal* in Isa 53:5 is read with the meaning "be profaned," not "be wounded." The corruption, eventually the destruction, of the temple is the feat of gentiles. So the messiah is not the destroyer, it is already in ruins (after 70 CE, as a reinterpretation by the Targum). By contrast, Mark for one denounces the actual temple personnel as bringing about the destruction of the shrine in their rejection of the veritable "owner" of the temple, the Son of God.

16
Jesus and the Resurrection

A number of texts in the Scriptures present death as irremediable (see Pss 49:20; 88:9; Job 7:9–10; 14:7–22), but for Dan 12 and the "intertestamental" literature, faith in resurrection is a certainty (see 1 Enoch 51:1; 92:3–5; 2 Macc 7; 14:46; Wis. Sol. 2–4; 4 Ezra 7:32). In Jesus's time, most Jews believed in the resurrection of the dead. Mark 12:18–27 (// Luke 20:27–38) reports Jesus's rebuke of the Sadducees about this issue.[1] The entire New Testament presupposes Jesus's resurrection. The gospel shows the disciples unanimously believing that Jesus, their Master, is alive and well after Easter. After cowardly fleeing to Galilee, they come back to Jerusalem—a dangerous place for them, but also the place where Jesus had been entombed—to proclaim Jesus's resurrection. The Synoptic texts use two terms: "awakening" (*egeirein*) and "raising" (*anistanai*) as metaphors. In early Christian liturgical hymns, the preferred term is "exalting" (*hyperypsoun* in Phil 2:9; cf. 1 Tim 3:16).

While in general winners write history, the early church was far from a position of power when it proclaimed Jesus's resurrection. It brought concomitantly the testimony that the event occurred to the embarrassment and faithlessness of an obtuse community of former disciples, ill prepared for it. Furthermore, early Christians died rather than renege on their faith in Jesus's resurrection: Would anyone die for what they know to be a fabrication?

"Christ is risen!" anticipates the eschatological universal resurrection and therefore is itself an eschatological event. On this score, once again, Jesus's resurrection harbors a collective component, just as his death was

---

1. Jesus uses the surprising argument that Exod 3:6 speaks of the resurrection. No Jewish tradition, before or after Jesus, ever used that text as an ad hoc argument (see Sanh. 90b–92).

"for all" (1 Tim 2:6) or "for a multitude" (Mark 14:24).[2] On the basis of Isa 53:11, Paul concludes that Christ "was raised for our justification" and "so that he might be Lord of both the dead and the living" (Rom 4:25; 14:9). The resurrection is the seal authenticating the early witnesses' testimony (Matt 28:16-20; Acts 10:42).

Yet the church, to its own benefit, arrogated exclusively to itself the collective character of Jesus's messiahship. The church alone became the body of Christ. The setting in life of such a move is the supersessionist complex of non-Jewish Christianity. However, when we retrieve—even in part—the original intent of the Nazarene and his insistence on his mission on behalf of the lost sheep of Israel,[3] the *unio mystica* of Jesus with the Jewish people appears in its full light.[4]

In other words, the crucifixion of the Nazarene is also the crucifixion of the Jews, as I said above, and Jesus's resurrection is also the resurrection of Israel. It is this communion with the people as a whole that rendered it impossible for death to hold him (Acts 2:24).

There is no other individual resurrection in Judaism:[5] that of Jesus is unique. At the very least, we may speak of an audacious interpretation on the part of the early disciples after the death of their Master for, as Kurt Schubert remarks, Jesus's apparitions could have been otherwise understood than eschatologically.[6] We may add that, had the grave not

---

2. Gershom Scholem (*The Messianic Idea in Judaism and Other Essays on Jewish Spirituality* [New York: Schocken, 1971], 186) writes, "Messianic redemption ... is an essentially public act, consummated by the body of the nation as a whole." And on 194, he says, "Judaism [in contrast to Christianity] saw one of its glories in the rejection of the Messianic character of a redemption on any other than the public, social, and historical plane." Note that for Scholem, the resurrection of the dead is a total cosmic re-creation.

3. See Matt 10:5-6: "Go nowhere among the Gentiles ... but go rather to the lost sheep of the house of Israel." See also Matt 15:24: "I was sent only to the lost sheep of the house of Israel."

4. In a Pauline vein, Luke, in Acts 13:47 (in reference to Isa 49:6), proclaims that if the Jews had not rejected Christ, it would have been unnecessary to "turn to the Gentiles" (cf. Acts 18:6; 28:26-28). A "converted" Israel would have brought the end of the world with the fulfillment of the messianic mission. Thanks to this nonfulfillment, there is the spreading of the "light to the Gentiles." Paul shares the same vision (see Rom 11:11-12; cf. Matt 24:13).

5. In the cycles of Elijah/Elisha, there are miraculous reanimations (1 Kgs 17:17-24; 2 Kgs 4:32-37; 13:20-21).

6. Kurt Schubert, *Jesus im Lichte der Religionsgeschichte des Judentums* (Vienna: Herold, 1973).

been empty, all claims of Jesus's resurrection would have been scornfully rejected. Thus, if we accept that the tomb was found empty, what conclusion is there to draw? In a text like Mark 8:27–33, a distinction may be made between either a genuine announcement by Jesus of the "failure" of his mission or a sheer reflection of the early church's faith (v. 31, on his impending resurrection; cf. Matt 16:13–20; Luke 9:18–21). In this regard, Acts 2:24 is both psychologically revealing and profoundly moving: "God raised him up, having freed him from death, because it was impossible for him to be held in its power."

At this point, it behooves us to consider Jesus's repeated predictions of his sufferings and death. The gospel tends to present those declarations as the fruit of a special divine revelation. By their nature, they certainly are prophetic. Nevertheless, they need not be understood as ecstatic or as *vaticinia ex eventu*. Indeed, it was sufficient for Jesus to realize that the path he had chosen to tread—antipodal to the triumphant one—inevitably led to a fatal clash with all the powers that be. The accent falls less on the impending future than on the present options open to the Nazarene.

Following Juel's study on the gospel of Mark, we shall consider three texts: Mark 8:31; 9:31; and 10:33.

Against the backdrop of Ps 118:22, Mark 8:31 uses the term "rejection." The term is present as well in the parable of the wicked husbandmen (Mark 12:1–12). In both cases it refers to the religious leadership. There is consistency in the accusation repeated in Mark 10:33 (in more detail) and in 11:18. In 12:13, the same foes send Pharisees and Herodians to trap Jesus. In 14:1, they want to kill him; in 14:10–11, Judas betrays Jesus to them (see 9:31); in 15:10, the chief priests act out of envy; in 15:11, they stir up the crowd to demand the release of Barabbas, a murderer; in 15:31, 55–56, they mock Jesus on the cross.

Jesus's antiestablishment stance is bolstered by three elements in the Gospel of Mark: the "cleansing" of the outer courts of the temple, the cursing of the fig tree, and the parable of the wicked husbandmen (12:1–12).[7] In opposition to the contemporary temple personnel, who are apparently corrupt in the postexilic era, Jesus quotes Isa 56:7 (LXX: *pasin tois ethnesin* ["all the nations"]) and Jer 7:11 (LXX, *spēlaiov lēistōn* ["a den of brigands"]). The latter reference may be deemed inappropriate, but Jeremiah's

---

7. Isa 5:1–7, on Israel as a vineyard, has been read as announcing the temple's destruction (see 5:5) in Tg. Isa., ad loc.

denunciation of the sixth-century-BCE temple ideology is decisive, reducing the shrine to a *spēlaiov lēistōn* doomed to destruction.[8]

Jesus's repeated predictions of his death did not require much imagination on his part—Jeremiah was also almost killed, and may have been slaughtered in Egypt, according to a candid Jewish tradition.[9] Jesus's premonition definitely inscribes his destiny within the course of history, the history of his people: what is to happen between him and the populace is envisaged in a tragic mode. The consequences are dire, not only for the one to be crucified, but also for those "who do not know what they are doing" (Luke 23:34). The killing of the "king of the Jews" creates apocalyptic convulsions (Matt 24:1–31 and parr.; 27:51–54 and parr.). The *havelei hamashiah* ("the travails of the messiah") include the crucifiers, so that the murder becomes also a suicide. "They do not know what they are doing"—to themselves.

This incomprehension is even shared by the disciples. They are unprepared to witness the resurrection of their Master (see esp. John 20:24–29; 21:1–14), in spite of its repeated announcements (see Mark 8:31; 9:10, 31–32). It would, of course, be easy to suggest that such prophecies were later put in Jesus's mouth while in fact expressing the early church's convictions. It may be so, but the possibility exists that these prophecies are authentic. This means that the texts stress the uniqueness of the resurrection as being incompatible with the disciples' logic. They understood that Jesus spoke of a "spiritual," not a physical rising from the dead. On that they were not entirely wrong. The gospel insists on the complete transformation of Jesus after his resurrection, so that he is not easily recognizable by those who knew him best (see, e.g., Matt 28:16–20; Luke 24:17–21).

First Corinthians 15:1–5 represents a central development in Pauline Epistles, where Paul carefully situates the individual resurrection of Christ within the doctrine of a general resurrection. Christ is the first among the many and does not constitute an exception. Paul distances himself from the idea of a "removal" of Jesus to heaven à la Enoch, Elijah, and, in a later tradition, Moses.[10] Paul's conviction (shared by the Pharisees, among others) that there is another world beyond this one is basic (see 1 Cor 7:29–31; Rom 6:4 reads, "Just as Christ was raised from the dead by the

---

8. To recall, in Matt 16:14, some people say that Jesus is Jeremiah redivivus.

9. See Heb 11:36–37; cf. Jer 20:37–38; 2 Chr 36:16; S. 'Olam Rab. 20; Tertullian, *Scorpiace* 8.

10. See Deut 34:5, *'al pi yhwh* ("on the mouth of YHWH").

glory of the Father, so we too might walk in newness of life"). Incidentally, the text of 1 Cor 15 presents several Semitisms in its formulation: in verse 4, *tei hemerai tei tritei*, "the third day." It is the day when, according to tradition, God intervenes in favor of the righteous (see Gen. Rab. 91.7, on Gen 42:17–18; 56.1, on Gen 22:4). Furthermore, the Pauline argument suggests a possible annexation of the tradition behind Tg. Isa. 53:5 ("it was given over because of our sins"), for the Targum speaks here of the temple! To the extent that the temple or Christ incarnates the divine on earth, we may say with Martin Buber, "The prophetic idea of man who suffers for God's sake has here given way to that of God Who suffers for the sake of man."[11] It is also on the third day that Jesus's resurrection occurs (e.g., Matt 6:21; Luke 9:22), which corresponds to Hos 6:2, "After two days he will revive us; on the third day he will raise us up, that we may live before him" (note the collective scope). The revival of Jesus that follows his death is interpreted in the light of Isa 53:3–12. It is an atoning death for the sins of others (1 Cor 15:3; Mark 14:22–25) followed by a resurrection, the firstfruits of the general rising from the dead.

About this last point, Jesus's declaration that his death is "a ransom for many" (Mark 10:45) deserves mention. In the wake of the passion's Passover setting, common to all the gospels, it is appropriate to understand "ransom" as referring to the sacrificial lamb slaughtered at the festival in remembrance of the blood that saved the Israelites in Egypt (Exod 12:1–14). Jesus is the Pascal lamb, the "lamb of God" (John 1:29; 1 Pet 1:19). This lamb saves the people, atones for them, redeems them. In other words, the "ransom" motif is directed toward the "many," the beneficiaries, not toward God as an alleged hostage keeper.

In response to John the Baptist's inquiry, "Are you the one who is to come?" (Matt 11:2–6 // Luke 7:18–23), Jesus's powerful statement on the messianic signs (although the term "messiah" does not appear![12]) includes the clause "dead are raised" (v. 5). So in the gospel's testimony Jesus both gives and receives revitalization. The text finds a close parallel in Qumran, 4Q521 (Messianic Apocalypse; see frag. 2, col. 2; and frag. 5, col. 2): "Heavens and earth will listen to his Messiah … freeing prisoners, giving sight to the blind, straightening out the twisted … he will heal the badly wounded and will make the dead alive, he will proclaim good news to the meek."

---

11. Martin Buber, *Two Types of Faith: A Study of the Interpenetration of Judaism and Christianity*, trans. Norman P. Goldhawk (New York: Harper & Row, 1961), 150.

12. See above, page 117.

In the same fragment, we note, "[He makes] the dead of his people rise." Now, the mention of the messianic raising of the dead is noteworthy, for it is a prophetic attribution, not a royal one. It makes one think of Elijah (see 1 Kgs 17:22–23), not of David.[13] Jesus as prophet is well-attested in the gospel (see, e.g., Mark 6:4, 15; John 9:17; Matt 21:11; Luke 4:24; 7:16; 24:19), but two remarks must be made. First, one function does not negate any others: John Hyrcanus II, for instance, was both prophet and king. Second, as the cited Johannine text intimates, there is an important distinction to be made between Jesus being *a* prophet and *the* prophet. There was at the time a doctrine according to which prophecy stopped after Haggai, Zechariah, and Malachi. *The* prophet would come only at the end of times to inaugurate the newness of the messianic era, on the basis of Deut 18:15–20 (see Acts 3:22; 7:37). The designation of Jesus by some as "the prophet" takes all its significance from this perspective (see Matt 21:11; John 1:21; 6:14; 7:40).[14] Along the same line, 1QS 9:11 says, "until *the* prophet comes, and the messiahs of Aaron and Israel."[15]

Jesus, qua prophet, was aware of the crisis of his time and prophesied the advent of the kingdom of God. He places himself in the wake of the great prophets, performing symbolic acts, such as healings, exorcisms, raising the dead, and so on. Even his vicissitudes continue the prophetic sufferings (Matt 23:37; Acts 3:18). We know that some indeed considered him a prophet (Mark 6:15; 8:27–28; Luke 7:16, 39; 24:19; Matt 21:11, 46). In Luke 24:19, disciples on their walk to Emmaus speak of their Master as a powerful prophet.[16] Yet they add that they had hoped Jesus would "redeem Israel," a proof that they had seen Jesus as the Messiah (Luke 24:21). This scene occurs after Jesus's resurrection. The mention of his prophetic charisma is intentional, since a strong tie binds resurrection and messianism. Rising from the dead had become the supreme messianic miracle for the

---

13. See also m. Soṭah 9 (end); y. Šeqal. 3:3, 47b; "in the time of the Messiah" (y. Ket. 12:3, 35b). Ps 146 is in the background.

14. Possibly this is a polemic against the claim of the Baptist's disciples.

15. In the view of Justin's *Dialogue with Trypho*, people believed that Elijah (John the Baptist is identified with him; even their clothes and foods are similar: cf. Mark 1:6 // 2 Kgs 1:8) would anoint the messiah like Samuel did for Saul and David.

16. One does not mention the episode at Emmaus without evoking the striking formula of John Dominic Crossan: "Emmaus never happened. Emmaus always happens" (*The Historical Jesus: The Life of a Mediterranean Jewish Peasant* [San Francisco: HarperSanFrancisco, 1991], 13).

sages as mentioned in, for example, 2 Macc 6:18–31; 7:14, 23; 2 Bar. 30.1–5; Ta'an. 2a; Ketub. 111ab; Tg. Cant. 8:5; Pirqe R. El. 34.[17]

Characteristically, the narratives about Jesus's resurrection are followed by his appearances to his disciples.[18] In other words, the latter have visions of their Master alive and well. Paul also, in 1 Cor 9:1, exclaims, "I have seen the Lord," which for him is the grounds of his apostleship. Paul, however, does not mention the empty tomb, and it is a moot question whether this is significant beyond a lack of emphasis on his part.[19] What is important is the individual and collective experience of the "living one." Truth must not be confused with factuality or historicity.[20] Jesus's resurrection is a theological postulate: "Theology can postulate no historical facts (Tatsachen) and does not need to do so, since it lives by proclamation."[21]

Excursus: Some Theological Reflections on Jesus's Resurrection

Although some reflections on the sense of Jesus's resurrection may seem out of place in this historical inquiry on the Nazarene, the centrality of the notion in the gospel demands an exceptional, although brief, treatment.

The fact that the biblical doctrine on the resurrection of the dead had to wait until the second century BCE (Dan 12) for its full development coincides with the maturation of human self-consciousness. My point is that the former depends on the latter. During the biblical period (until the Hellenization of the ancient Near East), kings, priests, and prophets were more interested in the collective fate of the people of Israel than in individual destiny. The cultural revolution brought by Alexander the Great to the Orient shifted the focus to the person per se. The individual awareness of belonging to a dual history—of the community and of the self—was sharpened: an intimate conviction of one's value as a human being was developed in parallel with this. Such a conception of the self has endured.

---

17. See Raphael Patai, *The Messiah Texts* (New York: Avon, 1979), 199–202.
18. A better English rendition is "he made himself visible," "he made himself be seen"; that is, he let others perceive his presence.
19. But see 2 Cor 5:16.
20. On this, see Marcus Borg, *Jesus: Uncovering the Life, Teachings, and Relevance of a Religious Revolutionary* (San Francisco: HarperSanFrancisco, 2006), 278–79.
21. Hans Conzelmann, *Jesus*, trans. J. Raymond Lord, ed. John Reumann (Philadelphia: Fortress, 1973), 94 (= "Jesus Christus," *RGG*, 3rd ed., vol. 3, cols. 619–53).

Even with its evident and formidable benefits, however, the old/new discovery multiplied anxieties. In particular, the issue of immortality, easier to a certain extent to conceive when dealing with the collective, resulted in individual dread regarding death.

True, from the beginning of humanity, people have been troubled with the problem of their destiny after death. All religions had to deal with the issue. Burial rituals and theological speculations as to the afterlife blossomed everywhere. Arguably, the most widespread religion in the world, until today, has been ancestor worship. The ancestor's immortality is maintained if only as a guaranty of sorts of the descendents' immortality. In the Jewish-Christian way of thinking, nevertheless, short of indulging in the cult of the forebears, the consciousness of one's uniqueness became acute. As Martin Buber says in his classic *I and Thou*, no two tree leaves have ever been similar since the creation of the world. What is true of the leaves and of the flowers of the field is all the more true of humans because of their consciousness. This individual uniqueness is absolute. It is the ultimate nobility of being human. But is this nobility impregnable? Is it not rather fragile and vulnerable? Is not death the incontrovertible demonstration of the vanity of hope? The whole of the biblical revelation, Hebrew Scriptures and New Testament alike, essentially depends on the principle of life as miraculous. Death is the last enemy to be destroyed (see 1 Cor 15:26).

Death is the enemy. It questions human self-consciousness. No systematic enterprise to sterilize the Jewish-Christian conviction of human uniqueness is comparable to that of the Nazi camps. Death was mobilized to make the point that self-consciousness was a myth. The ultimate aim of the Holocaust went beyond mere genocide. Genocide was still a means to a further goal: the eradication of the concept of absolute human dignity, an alleged Jewish invention.

Proving that human beings are fundamentally no more worthy than pigs or mosquitoes, provided that certain circumstances prevail such as imposed in the camps, was seen as decisively debunking the "Jewish myth." Paradoxically, the dehumanization of the other amounted also to being suicidal, as the torturers-murderers themselves were susceptible to being dehumanized and were indeed dehumanizing themselves in the process of exterminating other human beings.

Daniel 12 was composed during the all-out persecution of the Jews by Antiochus IV in the second century BCE. Circumcision and the celebration of the Sabbath and festivals were forbidden; Torah scrolls were burned, as were synagogues. Many Jews became martyrs for their faith, and their premature demise raised the problem of their unfulfilled existence—again bringing the individual to the fore. Resistance to the despot evidently consisted, then as in the twenty-first century CE, in affirming human dignity against all odds. The Danielic apocalyptist voiced the martyrs' proclamation that debasement and slaughter can never rob their victims of ultimate nobility. Beyond their agony, God would restore their lives!

Is this merely a gratuitous affirmation? Neither the apocalyptist nor anyone else—other than Jesus—ever experienced the content of it, let alone reported the *quid* and the *quomodo* of resurrection. This message grew on an existential foundation, namely, the consciousness of human uniqueness qua human.

It is within this particular context that we must approach the meaning of Easter. In the Nazi camps, the inmates could still claim "Die Gedanken sind frei." They could still pray; they could still gather rudimentary means for the celebration of Passover or the Eucharist. They could still show compassion for fellow sufferers. The cardinal virtues of faith, hope, and love were the indestructible means of affirming human uniqueness. Each individual remained a priceless exception, a special jewel on God's crown.

As regards Jesus, his disciples, both then and ever since, realized that "it was impossible that death could hold him," in the words of Acts 2:24. I believe that we may broaden the scope of this Lukan saying. Death cannot annihilate our uniqueness. For the disciples, "Christ is risen" means that Christ is ever-present with them. The tomb is empty; only the dead bury their dead (Matt 8:22 // Luke 9:60). Beyond lies the great mystery of immortality, a mystery expressed in the no-less-mysterious words of Jesus, "Even though they die, they will live" (John 11:25). Paul adds, "He is the firstfruits of those who have fallen asleep" (1 Cor 15:20).

Conclusion

The text of the gospel contains a canto of citations from the Hebrew Scriptures, and this for good reason, for the gospel writers wanted the Jewish roots of its message to be strong and conclusive.[1] Even an apparently non-Jew like Luke is eager to "prove" the authenticity of the messianic identity of Jesus by frequently citing the Hebrew Bible. In fact, this dependence of the gospel on Jewish traditions goes well beyond these quotations. The Hebrew Scriptures provided a rich hermeneutic treasure trove for the evangelists to build pesharim and haggadoth, illustrating the providential events of the life of Jesus, including his very birth and transfiguration. In other words, *Judaica* set the boundaries and became the touchstone for early Christian testimony; *Judaica* built a *siyag latorah* of sorts (a barrier around the torah), if by *torah* we understand the "renewed Torah" mentioned earlier.[2]

---

1. Daniel Boyarin, *The Jewish Gospels: The Story of the Jewish Christ* (New York: New Press, 2012), 21, says, "There is perhaps one feature that constitutes all as members of the Judeo-Christian family, namely, appealing to the Hebrew Scriptures as revelation."

2. See y. Hag. 2:1, 77d: "The Torah is not going to be restored to its fullness until the son of David comes." In a contrasted response to the Christian belief in Jesus as teaching a "new torah," formative Judaism promoted the rabbi "as Torah incarnate, avatar of hope, and model of the son of David" (Jacob Neusner, *Messiah in Context: Israel's History and Destiny in Formative Judaism*, The Foundations of Judaism: Method, Theology, Doctrine 2 [Philadelphia: Fortress, 1984], 3). Harold Bloom's badly concealed anger at the gospel's "usurpation" of the Hebrew Scriptures is somewhat surprising when we realize how thorough a "rabbinization" of all the Jewish traditions, including and especially the Scriptures, is present in the subsequent Jewish writings, starting with the Mishnah (*Jesus and Yahweh: The Names Divine* (New York: Riverhead, 2005). Suffice it to turn to the "stunning metamorphosis" of Dan 8 in t. Miqw. 7:11! More calmly, Neusner says, "The history of Judaism is the story of successive arrangements and revisions of available symbols" ("Defining Judaism," in *The Blackwell Companion*

Through circumstances beyond control of the early church—particularly the reversal of the ratio between Jewish-Christian and pagan-Christian recruits—there occurred a tragic rivalry with the synagogue. The church grew increasingly independent of its Israelite roots. It became, instead of a Jewish sect, a standalone *religion*. As a result of this momentous schism, the nature of the church was transformed. The non-Jewish elements began to rethink the Christian message in non-Jewish categories that were more indebted to Plato, Aristotle, and Plotinus than to Moses. To a certain extent, that revision was unabashedly anti-Judaic, even anti-Semitic.[3] After the Bar-Kokhba's persecution of Christians and Hadrian's decree against the Jews, the Jerusalem church appointed the gentile Mark as its bishop![4]

Although not the most representative of these unfortunate developments, the Gospel according to John, written around the end of the first century, uses the word "the Jews" (sixty-eight times) in a way that makes us very uncomfortable today.[5] And what came after the Gospel of John is even more appalling. The genuineness of sober testimony by the early disciples of the Nazarene degenerates into caricature. Modern psychology has shown that a choice of identity in sheer opposition to the parental is negative and eventually self-denying.[6] It is defining oneself by what one is not. The adolescent, most commonly, wants to become exactly the opposite of whatever his or her parents wished. It is a deviant identity.[7]

Thus, in the course of the second century, a non-Jewish Christian religion emerged, characterized by a non-Jewish messianic ideology heavily influenced by Greek philosophy. Its central point was the relation of Jesus with the divine. It reached its apex with the Nicene Creed (fourth cen-

---

to *Judaism*, ed. Jacob Neusner and Alan J. Avery-Peck [Oxford: Blackwell, 2000], 14; the Tosefta text is on pp. 72–73).

3. Speaking of the "de-Judaization of Christianity," the historian Jaroslav Pelikan writes, "To the Christian disciples of the first century the conception of Jesus as a rabbi was self-evident, to the Christian disciples of the second century it was embarrassing, to the Christian disciples of the third century and beyond it was obscure" (*Jesus through Centuries: His Place in the History of Culture* [New Haven: Yale University Press, 1985], 17).

4. Eusebius, *Hist. eccles.* 4.6.

5. Bloom speaks of the "unsteady veering between love and hate of 'the Jews' within the Gospels" (*Jesus and Yahweh*, 41).

6. See Erik Erikson, *Identity: Youth and Crisis* (New York: Norton, 1968).

7. The phenomenon is particularly blatant in politics.

tury) and the concept of the Trinity. At the end of the same century, Melito of Sardis accused the Jews of deicide. In the fourth century, Jesus Christ became God himself. This was of course a very serious disassociation from the Jewish way of thinking, which emphasizes the uniqueness and oneness of God, and it contrasted with Jesus's declaration in Mark 10:17-21 ("only God is good!").[8] John 20:8, however, tells us that Thomas exclaimed to the risen Jesus, "My Lord, my God!" without being rebuked, and Rom 9:5 declares Christ to belong to his people Israel and to be "over all, God blessed for ever." Clearly, the two proclamations are to be taken together, "God" that belongs to Israel!

This taut paradox is to be approached from the point of view of the differences among *nature, function*, and *status*. When Dan 7 describes the one like a Son of Man riding on the clouds, while elsewhere in the Bible YHWH is the rider (Deut 33:26; Isa 19:1; Ps 68:5, 34; 18:11), there is obviously no usurpation of divinity on the part of the Son of Man, and in Rev 14:14, the "one like a son of man" sitting on the cloud is an angel, not Christ. In the Parables of Enoch, Enoch is called "Head of Days" (46:1-3) and "is a human being in the likeness of the heavenly Son of Man, and is exalted to share his destiny.... Enoch is the first among the earth-born righteous. He must still be distinguished, however, from his heavenly counterpart."[9] In 1 Enoch 48:5, he is worshiped like a deity, and in 4 Ezra 13, the language about him is theophanic. Some rabbis applied to the name of God ("Three are called by the name of the Holy One, blessed be He: the righteous, the Messiah and Jerusalem" [B. Bat. 75b; Lam. Rab. 1.51 on 1:16: "What is the name of King Messiah? R. Abba bar Kahana said, 'YHWH is his name [on the basis of Jer 23:6].'"

Let me conclude with Martin Buber's words: "God shows a human face."[10] The basis for the glorification of the Messiah is well expressed in Rom 11:36, "For from him and through him are all things. To him be the

---

8. Martin Buber sees this text as authentic because it was said in "spite of the Christology opposed to it" (*Two Types of Faith: A Study of the Interpenetration of Judaism and Christianity*, trans. Norman P. Goldhawk [New York: Harper & Row, 1961], 116). Let us add the following decisive text (from Paul!): "When all things are subjected to him [Christ], then the Son himself will be subjected to the one who put all things in subjection under him, so that God may be all in all" (1 Cor 15:28).

9. John J. Collins, *The Scepter and the Star: The Messiahs of the Dead Sea Scrolls and Other Ancient Literature* (New York: Doubleday, 1995), 181.

10. Buber, *Two Types of Faith*, 127-28.

glory for ever." But the gentile-Christian deification of Christ borders on polytheism. There was no big difference for them between function and nature. Note however that, even within the Jewish tradition, this confusion is not totally absent. So, in the kabbalistic literature—under Neoplatonic influence—we find an identification of the Messiah to come with a *Sefirah*, that is, with divine powers. He is preexistent. Like the prelapsarian Adam, he is *elohuth gamur* that the mystic can encounter only by crossing the limits of humanity and entering the realm of divinity. In the *hekhalot* the messiah's body becomes an angel. The same is true regarding the false messiah Sabbatai Zwi (seventeenth century), who claimed to be absorbed into the divine structure. Nathan of Gaza, his prophet, as we saw above, called him "our lord," or "our lord, our king."

In *Two Types of Faith*, Martin Buber touts the contrast between a "Jewish" messiah "ascending" and a "Christian" messiah "descending."[11] Such a statement has only a relative bearing, however. Christ "ascends to heaven" (Luke 24:51; Acts 1:9–11; Mark 16:19). But the early church considered this up-movement as corresponding with a "descent," a *kenosis* (John 3:13; Phil 2), comparable with the Jewish notion of the ascending and descending Shekinah (God's presence). Buber's reference to Jer 1:5 is in a way self-defeating for his argument. Clearly, the prophet is able to speak of his preexisting vocation only in retrospect. It is also in retrospect that Christ may be said to be preexistent and to be identified with the creative Logos. Then the Danielic vision of chapter 7 on the Son of Man can describe him as coming (down) "with the clouds of heaven" (see also 1 Enoch 48:6).

*

One of the main results of the rupture with the synagogue, as far as the church is concerned, was an ignorance—voluntary or involuntary—of the haggadic, metaphorical, or parabolic nature of some ancient texts, such as the infancy narratives that included a virgin birth of Jesus, the use of titles like "Son of God," or again formulas like "this is my flesh ... this is my blood." This ignorance also led to the creation of non-Jewish categories, such as the alleged "double nature of Christ," his "divinity" as seen as belonging to a "Trinity," as well as the "transubstantiation" of bread and

---

11. See ibid., 111.

17. CONCLUSION

wine, and it extended to a conception of the God of Jesus as somehow different from the severe and vengeful God of the "Old Testament." An early example is afforded in Isa 7:14 (the young woman pregnant) used by Matthew and Luke in their birth narratives and reinterpreted in the light of Greek and Roman stories of heroes with divine fathers. Marcion did triumph.

The inevitable result is a mythologized Jesus with superhuman, divine powers, born from a perpetually asexual mother and a castrated father.[12] Through a misinterpretation of Ps 110:1, the Nazarene was identified with YHWH himself. 'Adoni (in reference to the reigning king in Israel or Judah) was read as if the text had 'adonay (a substitute for YHWH). In Luke 1:43, the same confusion occurs. Elizabeth speaks of her Lord—that is 'adoni—as if it were spelled 'adonay, while in 1:45, which is in the close vicinity of the preceding use, "the Lord" is evidently to be understood as 'adonay, and we are dealing with a pun. The confusion went so far as to consider Mary as "mother of God" (mirabile dictu)!

The moment Christianity cut its moorings with Judaism (decisively in the fourth century but beginning long before that), it lost its "virginity" and began to harbor an incipient pagan mythological ideology.[13] The main victim, I believe, was Jesus, the central Jew. Jesus inaugurated the eschatological era, but the "new" church put a brake on time. It could not face the advent of the 'olam haba' ("the world coming") and "wisely" decided to enter into a compromise with the 'olam hazeh ("this present world") provided that there were still some fragments of the other world as proclaimed by Jesus. The result was that the End was delayed *sine die*.

---

12. At the origin of the clergy's celibacy (fourth century).
13. In the words of Bloom, we continue until this day "to literalize doctrinal metaphors" (*Jesus and Yahweh*, 5).

Bibliography

Abécassis, Eliette. *La Répudiée*. Paris: Albin Michel, 2000.

Abrams, M. H. *The Mirror and the Lamp: Romantic Theory and the Critical Tradition*. Oxford: Oxford University Press, 1953.

Achtemeier, Paul. "The Origin and Function of the Pre-Marcan Miracle Catenae." *JBL* 91, no. 2 (June 1972): 198–221.

Allison, Dale C. *The Intertextual Jesus: Scripture in Question*. Harrisburg PA: Trinity Press International, 2000.

Auerbach, Erich. *Mimesis: The Representation of Reality in Western Literature*. Translated by Willard Trask. Princeton: Princeton University Press, 1953.

Avery-Peck, Allen J. "The Galilean Charismatic and Rabbinic Piety: The Holy Man in the Talmudic Literature." Pages 149–65 in Levine, Allison, and Crossan, *The Historical Jesus in Context*.

Bailey, Kenneth. *Through Peasant Eyes: More Lucan Parables, Their Culture and Style*. Grand Rapids: Eerdmans, 1980.

———. *Biblical Theology of the New Testament*. Translated by D. P. Bailey. Grand Rapids: Eerdmans, forthcoming.

Bakhtin, Mikhail. *Author and Hero in Aesthetic Activity in Art and Answerability: Early Philosophical Essays*. Edited by Michael Holquist and Vadim Liapunov. Translated by Vadim Liapunov. Supplement translated by Kenneth Bostrom. Austin: University of Texas Press, 1990.

Barton, John. "Temporality and Politics in Jewish Apocalyptic Literature." Pages 117–41 in Rowland and Barton, *Apocalyptic in History and Tradition*.

Becker, Ernest. *The Denial Of Death*. New York: Free Press, 1973.

Ben-Chorin, Schalom. *Brother Jesus: The Nazarene through Jewish Eyes*. Translated by Jared S. Klein and Max Reinhart. Athens: University of Georgia Press, 2001.

Betz, Otto. φονή. *TDNT* 9:278–309.

Bickerman, Elias. *Studies in Jewish and Christian History*. Leiden: Brill, 1986.
Black, Matthew. *An Aramaic Approach to the Gospels and Acts*. 3rd ed. Peabody MA: Hendrickson, 1998.
Bloom, Harold. *Jesus and Yahweh: The Names Divine*. New York: Riverhead, 2005.
Boman, Thorleif. "Das letzte Wort Jesu." *ST* 17 (1963): 103–19.
Borg, Marcus J. *Jesus: Uncovering the Life, Teachings, and Relevance of a Religious Revolutionary*. San Francisco: HarperSanFrancisco, 2006.
Bornkamm, Günther. *Jesus of Nazareth*. New York: Harper & Brothers, 1960.
Bourdieu, Pierre. "The Sentiment of Honour in Kabyle Society." Pages 197–215 in Peristiany, *Honour and Shame*.
Boyarin, Daniel. *The Jewish Gospels: The Story of the Jewish Christ*. New York: New Press, 2012.
Brandon, S. G. F. *Jesus and the Zealots*. New York: Scribner's Sons, 1967.
———. *The Trial of Jesus of Nazareth*. London: Batsford, 1968.
Braude, William G., trans. *Psikta Rabbati*. New Haven: Yale University Press, 1968.
Brown, Raymond E. *The Birth of the Messiah: A Commentary on the Infancy Narratives in Matthew and Luke*. Garden City, NY: Doubleday, 1977.
———. *The Gospel according to John 1–12*. AB 29. Garden City, NY: Doubleday, 1966.
Brueggemann, Walter. *A Commentary on Jeremiah: Exile and Homecoming*. Grand Rapids: Eerdmans, 1998.
Bruteau, Beatrice, ed. *Jesus through Jewish Eyes: Rabbis and Scholars Engage an Ancient Brother in a New Conversation*. Maryknoll, NY: Orbis, 2001.
Buber, Martin. *Two Types of Faith: A Study of the Interpenetration of Judaism and Christianity*. Translated by Norman P. Goldhawk. New York: Harper & Row, 1961.
Bultmann, Rudolf. *The History of the Synoptic Tradition*. Translated by John Marsh. Oxford: Blackwell, 1968.
———. *The Presence of Eternity: History and Eschatology*. Edinburgh: Edinburgh University Press, 1975.
———. *Theology of the New Testament*. Translated by K. Grobel. New York: Scribner's Sons, 1951.
Burkill, T. A. *Mysterious Revelation*. Ithaca NY: Cornell University Press, 1963.

———. "St. Mark's Philosophy of the Passion." *NovT* 2 (1957): 245–71.
———. "The Trial of Jesus." *VC* 12 (1958): 1–18.
Buttrick, George A., ed. *The Interpreter's Dictionary of the Bible*. 4 vols. New York: Abingdon, 1962.
Caird, George B. *Jesus and the Jewish Nation*. London: Athlone, 1965.
Cangh, Jean-Marie van. "La multiplication des pains dans l'Evangile de Marc: Essai d'exégèse globale." Pages 309–46 in *L'Evangile selon Marc: Tradition et rédaction*. BETL 34. Edited by M. Sabbe. Gembloux: Duculot, 1974.
Carmichael, Joel. *The Death of Jesus*. New York: Pelican, 1966.
Casey, Maurice P. *From Prophet to Gentile God: The Origins and Development of New Testament Theology*. Louisville: Westminster John Knox Press, 1991.
Catchpole, David R. *The Trial of Jesus*. StPB 18. Leiden: Brill, 1971.
Chabon, Michael. *The Yiddish Policemen's Union*. New York: HarperPerennial, 2012.
Charlesworth, James H. "From Jewish Messianology to Christian Christology: Some Caveats and Perspectives." Pages 225–64 in Neusner, Green, and Frerichs, *Judaisms and Their Messiahs*.
———. *The Historical Jesus: An Essential Guide*. Essential Guides. Nashville: Abingdon, 2008.
———, ed. *Jesus' Jewishness: Exploring the Place of Jesus within Early Judaism*. Shared Ground among Jews and Christians 2. New York: Crossroad, 1996.
Chilton, Bruce. "Regnum Dei Deus Est." *SJT* 31, no. 3 (1978): 261–70.
———. "Targum, Jesus, and the Gospels." Pages 238–55 in Levine, Allison, and Crossan, *The Historical Jesus in Context*.
Chilton, Bruce, and Craig A. Evans. *Jesus in Context: Temple, Purity, and Restoration*. AGJU 39. Leiden: Brill, 1997.
Chilton, Bruce, Craig A. Evans, and Jacob Neusner, eds. *The Missing Jesus: Rabbinic Judaism and the New Testament*. Leiden: Brill, 2002.
Cohen, Shaye. *From the Maccabees to the Mishnah*. LEC 7. Philadelphia: Westminster, 1987.
Collins, Adela Yarbro. "The Messiah as Son of God in the Synoptic Gospels." Pages 21–32 in Zetterholm, *The Messiah in Early Judaism and Christianity*.
———. *Mark: A Commentary*. Hermeneia. Minneapolis: Fortress, 2007.

Collins, Adela Yarbro, and John J. Collins. *King and Messiah as Son of God: Divine, Human, and Angelic Figures in Biblical and Related Literature.* Grand Rapids: Eerdmans, 2008.

Collins, John J. "Messiahs in Context: Method in the Study of Messianism in the Dead Sea Scrolls." Pages 213-30 in Wise, Golb, Collins, and Pardee, *Method of Investigation in the Dead Sea Scrolls and the Khirbet Qumran Site.*

———. *The Scepter and the Star: The Messiahs of the Dead Sea Scrolls and Other Ancient Literature.* New York: Doubleday, 1995.

———. ed. *Semeia* 14: *Apocalypse: The Morphology of a Genre* (1979).

Colpe, Carsten. "υἱός." Pages 1206-24 in *The Theological Dictionary of the New Testament: Abridged in One Volume.* Edited and translated by Geoffrey W. Bromiley. Grand Rapids: Eerdmans, 1985.

———. "ὁ υἱὸς τοῦ ἀνθρώπου." *TDNT* 8:400-477.

Conzelmann, Hans. *Jesus.* Translated by J. Raymond Lord. Edited by John Reumann. Philadelphia: Fortress, 1973 (= "Jesus Christus." *RGG*, 3rd ed. Vol. 3, cols. 619-53).

Cox, Harvey. "Rabbi Yeshua ben Yoseph: Reflections on Jesus' Jewishness and the Interfaith Dialogue." Pages 27-62 in Charlesworth, *Jesus' Jewishness.*

Crespy, Georges. "Sociologie et Théologie des Messianismes." *ETR* 54, no. 2 (1976): 189-210.

Crossan, John Dominic. *The Cross That Spoke.* San Francisco: Harper, 1988.

———. *The Historical Jesus: The Life of a Mediterranean Jewish Peasant.* San Francisco: HarperSanFrancisco, 1991.

———. *In Parables: The Challenge of the Historical Jesus.* New York: Harper & Row, 1973.

Culpepper, Alan. *The Johannine School.* SBLDS. Missoula MT: Scholars Press, 1975.

Dahl, Nils A. *Das Volk Gottes: eine Untersuchung zum Kirchenbewustsein des Urchristentums.* New ed. Darmstadt: Wissenschaftliche Buchgesellschaft, 1963.

Daube, David. *The New Testament and Rabbinic Judaism.* London: Athlone, 1956. Repr., Peabody MA: Hendrickson, 1990.

———. "Three Questions of Form in Matthew V." *JTS* 45 (1944): 21-31.

Delitsch, Franz, trans. *The Hebrew New Testament.* Berlin, Britain and Foreign Bible Society, 1901.

Desroche, Henri. "Contribution à une sociologie de l'attente." In *Dictionnaire des Messianismes et des Millénarismes*. Paris: Mouton, 1969.
Dibelius, Martin. *From Tradition to Gospel*. Translated by B. Woolf. New York: Scribner's Sons, 1935.
Dodd, C. H. *The Parables of the Kingdom*. London: Collins, 1961 (1935).
Donahue, John. *Are You the Christ? The Trial Narrative in the Gospel of Mark*. SBLDS 10. Missoula, MT: Scholars Press, 1973.
Douglas, Mary. *Purity and Danger: An Analysis of Concepts of Pollution and Taboo*. London: Routledge, 1966.
Duhm, Bernhard. *Das Buch Jesaia übersetzt und erklärt*. HKAT. Göttingen: Vandenhoeck & Ruprecht, 1902.
Dunn, James D. G. *Jesus, Paul, and the Law: Studies in Mark and Galatians*. Louisville: Westminster John Knox, 1990.
———. *Jesus Remembered*. Vol. 1 of *Christianity in the Making*. Grand Rapids: Eerdmans, 2003.
Dunn, James D. G., and Scot McKnight, eds. *The Historical Jesus in Recent Research*. Winona Lake, IN: Eisenbrauns, 2005.
Ehrman, Bart D. *The Lost Gospel of Judas Iscariot: A New Look at Betrayer and Betrayed*. Oxford: Oxford University Press, 2006.
Eichholz, Geoffrey. *Jesus Christus und der Nächste*. BibS(N) 9. Neukirchen-Vluyn: Neukirchener Verlag, 1953.
Einstein, Albert. "What Life Means to Einstein: An Interview by George Sylvester Viereck." *Saturday Evening Post*. October 26, 1929, 7 110, 113–14, 117.
Emerson, Caryl, and G. Saul Morson. *Mikhail Bakhtin: Creation of a Prosaics*. Stanford, CA: Stanford University Press, 1990.
Erikson, Erik. *Identity: Youth and Crisis*. New York: Norton, 1968.
Evans, Craig A. "The Misplaced Jesus: Interpreting Jesus in a Judaic Context." Pages 11–39 in Chilton, Evans, and Neusner, *The Missing Jesus*.
Falk, Harvey. *Jesus the Pharisee: A New Look at the Jewishness of Jesus*. Mahwah, NJ: Paulist Press, 1985.
Fischer, John. "Jesus through Jewish Eyes: A Rabbi Examines the Life and Teachings of Jesus." Menorah Ministries. 2004. http://www.menorah-ministries.com/Scriptorium/JesusThruJewishEyes.htm.
Fitzmyer, Joseph A. *The Gospel According to Luke (x–xxv)*. AB 28A. Garden City, NY: Doubleday, 1985.
Fletcher-Louis, Crispin H. T. "Jesus, the Temple and the Dissolution of Heaven and Earth." Pages 117–41 in Rowland and Barton, *Apocalyptic in History and Tradition*.

Flusser, David. *Jesus*. New York: Herder & Herder, 1969.

———. "Jesus." Cols. 10–17 in vol. 10 of *Encyclopedia Judaica*. Edited by Cecil Roth. 16 vols. Jerusalem: Keter, 1972.

———. "Jesus, His Ancestry, and the Commandment of Love." Pages 153–76 in Charlesworth, *Jesus' Jewishness*.

———. *Judaism and the Origins of Christianity*. Jerusalem: Magnes, 1988.

———. "Sepher Hadash 'al Mishpat Yeshu." *Tarbiz* 31 (1961): 107–17 [Heb.].

———. "The Temple Not Made with Hands in the Qumran Doctrine." *IEJ* 9 (1959): 99–104.

Frazer, James. *The Golden Bough: A Study of Magic and Religion*. Abridged ed. London: Macmillan, 1967 (1922).

Fredriksen, Paula. *From Jesus to Christ: The Origins of the New Testament Images of Jesus*. New Haven: Yale University Press, 1988.

Freedman, David Noel. *Anchor Bible Dictionary*. 6 vols. New York: Doubleday, 1992.

Freedman, William. "The Literary Motif: A Definition and Evaluation." *Novel* 4 (1971): 123–31.

Fridrichsen, Anton, et al., eds. *The Root of the Vine: Essays in Biblical Theology*. New York: Philosophical Library, 1953.

Freyne, Sean. *Jesus, A Jewish Galilean: A New Reading of the Jesus-story*. London: T&T Clark, 2004.

Frost, Robert. *Speaking on Campus: Excerpts from His Talks 1949–1962*. Edited by Edward Connery Lathem. New York: Norton, 2009.

Frye, Northrop. *Anatomy of Criticism: Four Essays*. Princeton: Princeton University Press, 1957.

Funk, Robert. *Honest to Jesus*. San Francisco: HarperSanFrancisco, 1997.

———. *Jesus as Precursor*. SemeiaSup 2. Philadelphia: Fortress, 1975.

Funk, Robert, and Roy Hoover, eds. *The Five Gospels: The Search for the Authentic Words of Jesus*. San Francisco: HarperSanFrancisco, 1997.

Gaston, Lloyd. *No Stone on Another: Studies in the Significance of the Fall of Jerusalem in the Synoptic Gospels*. Leiden: Brill, 1973.

———. *Paul and the Torah*. Vancouver: University of British Columbia Press, 1987.

George, Augustin. "Parabole." *DBSup* 6:1149–77.

Gilmore, David D. "Anthropology of the Mediterranean Area." *Annual Reviews of Anthropology* 11 (1982): 175–205.

Ginzberg, Louis. "The Birth of Isaac." In *Legends of the Bible: A Shorter Version*. Philadelphia: Jewish Publication Society, 1992.

Glasson, T. Francis. "Schweitzer's Influence—Blessing or Bane?" *JTS* 2/28 (1977): 289–302.
Goldin, Judah, trans. *The Fathers according to Rabbi Nathan*. New Haven: Yale University Press, 1955.
———. *The Song at the Sea, Being a Commentary on a Commentary in Two Parts*. New Haven: Yale University Press, 1971.
Goldschmidt, Lazarus. *Der Babylonische Talmud*. Berlin: Harz, 1897.
Gollwitzer, Helmut. *Das Gleichnis vom barmherzigen Samariter*. Neukirchen-Vluyn: Neukirchener Verlag, 1967.
Green, William S. "Introduction: Messiah in Judaism: Rethinking the Question." Pages 1–14 in Neusner, Green, and Frerichs, *Judaisms and Their Messiahs*.
Gruber-Magitot, Caude. *Jésus et les Pharisiens*. Paris: Laffont, 1964.
Gunkel, Hermann. *Creation and Chaos in the Primeval Era and the Eschaton*. Translated by K. William Whitney Jr.). Grand Rapids MI: Wm. B. Eerdmans, 2006 (1895).
Hahn, Ferdinand. *The Titles of Jesus in Christology*. Translated by Harold Knight and George Ogg. New York: World, 1969.
Harrington, Daniel. "The Jewishness of Jesus." Pages 123–52 in Charlesworth, *Jesus' Jewishness*.
Harvey, A. E. *Jesus and the Constraints of History*. Philadelphia: Westminster, 1982.
Hengel, Martin. *The Charismatic Leader and His Followers*. Translated by James Greg. Edinburgh: T&T Clark, 1981.
———. *Judaism and Hellenism: Studies in their Encounter in Palestine during the Early Hellenistic Period*. Translated by John Bowden. Philadelphia: Fortress, 1974.
Heschel, Abraham. "No Religion Is an Island." *USQR* 21 (1966): 117–34.
Hirshman, Marc G. "Rabbinic Universalism in the Second and Third Centuries." *HTR* 93 (2000): 101–15.
Hollenbach, David S. *The Common Good and Christian Ethics*. Cambridge: Cambridge University Press, 2002.
Hoover, Roy. Introduction to *The Five Gospels: The Search for the Authentic Words of Jesus*, edited by Robert Funk and Roy Hoover. San Francisco: HarperSanFrancisco, 1997.
Horsley, Richard A. *Jesus and the Spiral of Violence: Popular Jewish Resistance in Roman Palestine*. San Francisco: Harper & Row, 1987.
———. "The Zealots: Their Origin, Relationships and Importance in the Jewish Revolt." *NovT* 27 (1986): 159–92.

Idel, Moshe. *Messianic Mystics*. New Haven: Yale University Press, 1998.
Jeanrond, Werner G., and J. L. Rike, eds. *Radical Pluralism and Truth: David Tracy and the Hermeneutics of Religion*. New York: Crossroad, 1991.
Jemielity, Thomas. *Satire and the Hebrew Prophets*. Literary Currents in Biblical Interpretation. Louisville: Westminster John Knox, 2002.
Juel, Donald. *Messiah and Temple: The Trial of Jesus in the Gospel of Mark*. Missoula MT: Scholars Press, 1977.
Jülicher, Adolf. *Die Gleichnisreden Jesu*. 2nd ed. 2 vols. Tübingen: Mohr Siebeck, 1910 (1888).
Jeremias, Joachim. "Abba as an Address to God." Pages 62–68 in *New Testament Theology: The Proclamation of Jesus*. New York: Scribner's Sons, 1971.
———. *The Eucharistic Words of Jesus*. Translated by Norman Perrin. London: SCM, 1964.
———. *The Parables of Jesus*. Rev. ed. New York: Scribner's Sons, 1982.
Kermode, Frank. *The Genesis of Secrecy: On the Interpretation of Narrative*. Cambridge: Harvard University Press, 1979.
Kilpatrick, George D. *The Trial of Jesus*. Oxford: Clarendon, 1952.
Kittel, Gerhard. *Die Probleme des palästinischen Spätjudentums und das Urchristentum*. Stuttgart: Kohlhammer, 1926.
Kittel, Gerhard, and Gerhard Friedrich, eds. *Theological Dictionary of the New Testament*. Translated by Geoffrey W. Bromiley. 10 vols. Grand Rapids: Eerdmans, 1964–1976.
———, eds. *Theologische Wörterbuch zum Neuen Testament*. Stuttgart, 1932–1979.
Klausner, Joseph. *Jesus of Nazareth: His Life, Times, and Teaching*. New York: Macmillan, 1925. Repr., New York: Bloch, 1997.
———. *The Messianic Idea in Israel, from Its Beginning to the Completion of the Mishnah*. Translated by W. E. Stinespring. London: Allen & Unwin, 1956.
Klawans, Jonathan. "Moral and Ritual Purity." Pages 266–84 in Levine, Allison, and Crossan, *The Historical Jesus in Context*.
Klazen, Thomas. *Jesus and Purity Halakhah: Was Jesus Indifferent to Impurity?* Winona Lake, IN: Eisenbrauns, 2010.
Klostermann, Erich. *Das Lukasevangelium*. 4th ed. Tübingen: Mohr Siebeck, 1975.
Kosmala, Hans. *Essener, Christen: Studien zur Vorgeschichte der frühchristlichen Verkündigung*. Leiden: Brill, 1959.

Kümmel, Werner G. *Promise and Fulfillment: The Eschatological Message of Jesus*. SBT 23. London: SCM, 1957.
LaCocque, André. *The Book of Daniel*. Translated by David Pellauer. London: SPCK; Atlanta: John Knox, 1979.
———. *Daniel in His Time*. Columbia: University of South Carolina Press, 1988.
———. "Une descendance manipulée et ambiguë (Genèse 29,31–30,24)." Pages 109–27 in Macchi and Römer, *Jacob*.
———. *Le Devenir de Dieu*. Paris: Les Editions Universitaires, 1967.
———. "The Great Cry of Jesus in Matthew 27:50." Pages 138–64 in Wiles, Brown, and Snyder, *Putting Body and Soul Together*.
———. "Jesus's Hermeneutics of the Law, Rereading the Parable of the Good Samaritan." Pages 251–76 in *Creation, Life, and Hope: Essays in Honor of Jacques B. Doukhan*. Edited by Jiri Moskala. Berrien Springs MI: Andrews University, 2000.
Leenhardt, Franz. "La Parabole du Samaritain: Schéma d'une exégèse existentialiste." Pages 132–38 in *Aux Sources de la tradition chrétienne. Mélanges offerts à Maurice Goguel*. Neuchatel: Delachaux & Niestle, 1950.
Lenski, Gerhard. *Power and Privilege: A Theory of Social Stratification*. Chapel Hill: University of North Carolina Press, 1984 (1966).
Léon-Dufour, Xavier. "Le dernier cri de Jésus." *Etudes* 348 (1978): 666–82.
Levenson, Jon D. *Creation and the Persistence of Evil: The Jewish Drama of Divine Omnipotence*. San Francisco: Harper & Row, 1988.
Levey, Samson H. *The Messiah: An Aramaic Interpretation*. HUCM 2. Cincinnati: Hebrew Union College Press, 1974.
Levine, Amy-Jill. *The Misunderstood Jew: The Church and the Scandal of the Jewish Jesus*. San Francisco: HarperSanFrancisco, 2006.
———. *The Social and Ethical Dimension of Matthean Salvation History*. Lewiston, NY: Mellen, 1988.
Levine, Amy-Jill, and Marc Zvi Brettler, eds. *The Jewish Annotated New Testament*. Oxford: Oxford University Press, 2011.
Levine, Amy-Jill, Dale C. Allison Jr., and John Dominic Crossan, eds. *The Historical Jesus in Context*. Princeton: Princeton University Press, 2006.
Lietzmann, Hans. *Der Prozess Jesu*. SPAW. Berlin: de Gruyter, 1931.
Lindars, Barnabas, ed. *Law and Religion: Essays on the Place of the Law in Israel and Early Christianity*. Cambridge: Clarke, 1988.

Lindemann, Albert. *Esau's Tears: Modern Anti-Semitism and the Rise of the Jews.* New York: Cambridge University Press, 1997.

Linnemann, Eta. *Studien zur Passionsgeschichte.* Göttingen: Vandenhoeck & Ruprecht, 1970.

Loader, William. *Jesus' Attitude towards the Law: A Study of the Gospels.* Grand Rapids: Eerdmans 2002 (1997).

Lohse, Eduard. *The New Testament Environment.* Translated by John Steely. Nashville: Abingdon, 1976.

Luther, Martin. *On Christian Freedom* (1520). In *First Principles of the Reformation, or The Ninety-Five Theses and the Three Primary Works of Luther Translated into English.* Translated by H. Wace and C. A. Buckheim. 1883. Repr., Digireads.com, 2011.

Luz, Ulrich. *Matthew 1–7.* Translated by J. E. Crouch. Hermeneia. Minneapolis: Fortress, 2007.

Macchi, Jean-Daniel. "Genèse 24–42. La dernière rencontre de Jacob et de Laban." Pages 144–62 in Macchi and Römer, *Jacob*.

Maccoby, Hyam. *Early Rabbinic Writings.* Cambridge: Cambridge University Press, 1988.

Maimonides. *The Guide of the Perplexed.* Vol. 2. Translated by Shlomo Pines. Chicago: University of Chicago Press, 1974.

Manson, T. W. *The Sayings of Jesus.* London: SCM, 1949.

Martinez, Florentino Garcia. *The Dead Sea Scrolls Translated: The Qumran Texts in English.* 2nd ed. Leiden: Brill; Grand Rapids: Eerdmans, 1994.

McArthur, Harvey K. "The Burden of Proof in Historical Jesus Research." *ExpTim* 82 (1970–71): 116–19.

McKnight, Scot, and James D. G. Dunn, eds. *The Historical Jesus in Recent Research.* Winona Lake, IN: Eisenbrauns, 2005.

Meier, John P. *Companions and Competitors.* Vol. 3 of *A Marginal Jew: Rethinking the Historical Jesus.* ABRL. New York: Doubleday, 2001.

———. *Law and Love.* Vol. 4 of *A Marginal Jew: Rethinking the Historical Jesus.* ABRL. New Haven: Yale University Press, 2009.

———. *Mentor, Message, and Miracles.* Vol. 2 of *A Marginal Jew: Rethinking the Historical Jesus.* ABRL. New York: Doubleday, 1994.

———. *The Roots of the Problem and the Person.* Vol. 1 of *A Marginal Jew: Rethinking the Historical Jesus.* ABRL. New York: Doubleday, 1991.

Meyer, Marvin. *The Gospel of Thomas: The Hidden Sayings of Jesus.* San Francisco: HarperSanFrancisco, 1992.

Michaelis, Wilhelm. *Die Gleichnisse Jesu.* 3rd ed. Zurich: Zwingli-Verlag, 1963.

Miles, Jack. Foreword to *The Jewish Gospels*, by Daniel Boyarin. New York: New Press, 2012.
Miscotte, Kornelis. *When the Gods Are Silent*. New York: Harper & Row, 1967.
Moore, George Foot. *Judaism in the First Centuries of the Christian Era*. 3 vols. New York: Schocken, 1971.
Morson, G. Saul, and Caryl Emerson. *Mikhail Bakhtin: Creation of a Prosaics*. Stanford, CA: Stanford University Press, 1990.
Moskala Jiri, ed. *Creation, Life, and Hope: Essays in Honor of Jacques B. Doukhan*. Berrien Springs, MI: Andrews University, 2000.
Neusner, Jacob. *Are There Really Tannaitic Parallels to the Gospels*. USFSHJ. Atlanta: Scholars Press, 1993.
―――. *The Idea of Purity in Ancient Judaism: The Haskell Lectures, 1972–73*. Leiden: Brill, 1973.
―――. *Messiah in Context: Israel's History and Destiny in Formative Judaism*. The Foundations of Judaism: Method, Theology, Doctrine 2. Philadelphia: Fortress, 1984.
―――. "Mishnah and Messiah." Pages 265–302 in Chilton, Evans, and Neusner, *The Missing Jesus*.
―――. *Performing Israel's Faith: Narrative and Law in Rabbinic Theology*. Waco, TX: Baylor University Press, 2005.
―――. *The Pharisees: Rabbinic Perspectives*. New York: Ktav, 1973.
―――. *The Rabbinic Traditions about the Pharisees before 70*. Leiden: Brill, 1971.
Neusner, Jacob, and Alan J. Avery-Peck, eds. *The Blackwell Companion to Judaism*. Oxford: Blackwell, 2000.
Neusner, Jacob, William S. Green, and Ernest Frerichs, eds. *Judaisms and Their Messiahs at the Turn of the Christian Era*. Cambridge: Cambridge University Press, 1987.
Newman, John Henry. "Literature" (1858). In *The Idea of a University*. Notre Dame, IN: University of Notre Dame Press, 1982.
Novenson, Matthew. *Christ among the Messiahs: Christ Language in Paul and Messiah Language in Ancient Judaism*. Oxford: Oxford University Press, 2012.
Odeberg, Hugo. *The Fourth Gospel: Interpreted in Its Relation to Contemporaneous Religious Currents in Palestine and the Hellenistic-Oriental World*. Chicago: Argonaut, 1929.
Ortega y Gasset, José. *The Revolt of the Masses*. New York: Norton, 1957.

Overman, J. Andrew. *Matthew's Gospel and Formative Judaism*. Minneapolis: Fortress, 1990.
Pagola, José A. *Jesus: An Historical Approximation*. Translated by Margaret Wilde. Miami: Convivium, 2009.
Patai, Raphael. *The Messiah Texts*. New York: Avon, 1979.
Pelikan, Jaroslav. *Jesus through the Centuries: His Place in the History of Culture*. New Haven: Yale University Press, 1985.
Peristiany, John G. *Honour and Shame: The Values of Mediterranean Society*. Chicago: Chicago University Press, 1966.
Perrin, Norman. *Jesus and the Language of the Kingdom: Symbol and Metaphor in New Testament Interpretation*. Philadelphia: Fortress, 1976.
———. *The Kingdom of God in the Teaching of Jesus*. Philadelphia: Westminster, 1963.
Philo. Translated by F. H. Colson, Ralph Marcus, and D. H. Whitaker. 12 vols. London: Heinemann; Cambridge: Harvard University Press, 1029–1962.
Pines, Shlomo. "The Parables in the Hebrew Bible and in Rabbinic Literature." Pages 206–21 in Levine, Allison, and Crossan, *The Historical Jesus in Context*.
Regev, Eyan. "Were the Early Christians Sectarians?" *JBL* 130 (2011): 771–93.
Reuman, John. Introduction to H. Conzelmann, *Jesus*. Philadelphia: Fortress, 1973 (= "Jesus Christus." *RGG*, 3rd ed. Vol. 3, cols. 619–53).
Rhoads, David, Donald Michie, and Joanna Dewey. *Mark as Story: An Introduction to the Narrative of a Gospel*. Philadelphia: Fortress, 1982.
Ricoeur, Paul. "Love and Justice." Pages 187–202 in Jeanrond and Rike, *Radical Pluralism and Truth*.
Ringgren, Helmer. *The Messiah in the Old Testament*. SBT 18. London: SCM, 1961.
Römer, Thomas, and Jean-Daniel Macchi, eds. *Jacob. Commentaire à plusieurs voix / Ein mehrstimmiger Kommentar zu / A Plural Commentary of / Gen. 25–36. Mélanges offerts à Albert de Pury*. Geneva: Labor et Fides, 2001.
Rowland, Christopher, and John Barton, eds. *Apocalyptic in History and Tradition*. Sheffield: Sheffield Academic, 2002.
Sabbe, M., ed. *L'Evangile selon Marc: Tradition et rédaction*. BETL 34. Gembloux: Duculot, 1974.

Sählin, Harald. "The New Exodus of Salvation According to St Paul." Pages 81-95 in *The Root of the Vine: Essays in Biblical Theology*. Edited by Anton Fridrichsen et al. New York: Philosophical Library, 1953.
Sanders, E. P. *The Historical Figure of Jesus*. London: Penguin, 1993.
———. *Jesus and Judaism*. Philadelphia: Fortress, 1985.
Sanders, E. P., and Margaret Davies. *Studying the Synoptic Gospels*. London: SCM; Philadelphia: Trinity Press International, 1989.
Schiffman, Lawrence. "The Significance of the Scrolls." *Bible Review* 6, no. 5 (October 1990): 19-27, 52.
Schmid, Joseph. *Das Evangelium nach Lukas*. Regensburg: Pustet, 1955.
Schneemelcher, Wilson, ed. *Festschrift für Günther Dehn zum 75. Geburtstag am 18. April 1957 dargebracht von der Evangelisch-Theologischen Fakultät der Rheinischen Friedrich Wilhelms-Universität zu Bonn*. Neukirchen: Kreis Moers, 1957.
Schneider, Gerhard. *Das Evangelium nach Lukas*. 2 vols. Gütersloh: Mohn, 1977.
Scholem, Gershom. *Major Trends in Jewish Mysticism*. Rev. ed. New York: Schocken, 1946.
———. *The Messianic Idea in Judaism and Other Essays on Jewish Spirituality*. New York: Schocken, 1971.
———. *Sabbatai Sevi: The Mystical Messiah*. Translated by R. J. Zwi Werblowsky. Princeton: Princeton University Press, 1973.
Schreiber, Johann F. "Die Christologie des Markusevangeliums." *ZTK* 58 (1961): 154-83.
Schubert, Kurt. *Jesus im Lichte der Religionsgeschichte des Judentums*. Vienna: Herold, 1973.
Schürer, Emil. *A History of the Jewish People in the Time of Jesus Christ: 175 B.C.-A.D. 135*. Rev. and ed. Geza Vermes, Fergus Millar, and Martin Goodman. 5 vols. Edinburgh: T&T Clark, 1986.
Schweitzer, Albert. *The Quest of the Historical Jesus: A Critical Study of Its Progress from Reimarus to Wrede*. Translated by John Bowden. Minneapolis: Fortress, 2001.
Schweizer, Eduard. *EGO EIMI... Die Religionsgeschichtliche Herkunft und Theologische Bedeutung der Johanneischen Bildreden, zugleich ein Beitrag zur Quellenfrage des vierten Evangeliums*. Göttingen: Vandenhoeck & Ruprecht, 1939.
Scott, Bernard B. *Hear Then the Parable: A Commentary on the Parables of Jesus*. Minneapolis: Fortress, 1989.

Shapiro, Rami M. "Listening to Jesus with an Ear for God." Pages 168–80 in Bruteau, *Jesus through Jewish Eyes*.
Sidney, Philip. *Elizabethan Critical Essays*. Edited by G. G. Smith. Vol. 1. Oxford: Oxford University Press, 1953.
Simmonds, Andrew. "Mark's and Matthew's Sub Rosa Message in the Scene of Pilate and the Crowd." *JBL* 131, no. 4 (2012): 733–54.
———. "Uses of Blood: Rereading Matthew 27:25." *Law Critique* 19 (2008): 165–91.
———. "'Woe to You ... Hypocrites': Rereading Matthew 23:13–36." *BSac* 166 (July–September 2009): 336–49.
Simon, Marcel. *Les sectes juives au temps de Jésus*. Paris: Presses Universitaires de France, 1960.
Smith, Jonathan Z. "Good News Is No News: Aretalogy and Gospel." Pages 190–207 in *Map Is Not Territory: Studies in the History of Religions*. Chicago: University of Chicago Press, 1993.
Smith, Morton. *Jesus the Magician*. New York: Gollancz, 1978.
———. *The Secret Gospel: The Discovery of Interpretation of the Secret Gospel According to Mark*. Middletown, CA: Dawn Horse Press, 1973.
———. *Tannaitic Parallels to the Gospels*. SBLMS 6. Philadelphia: Society of Biblical Literature, 1951.
Stauffer, Ethelbert. *Jesus and His Story*. Translated by Richard Wilson and Clara Wilson. London: SCM, 1960.
Stuhlmacher, Peter. "The Messianic Son of Man: Jesus' Claim to Deity." Pages 325–44 in *The Historical Jesus in Recent Research*. Edited by James D. G. Dunn and Scot McKnight. Winona Lake, IN: Eisenbrauns, 2005.
Taft, Jessie. *Otto Rank*. New York: Julian Press, 1958.
Talbert, Charles H. "Miraculous Conceptions and Births in Mediterranean Antiquity." Pages 79–86 in Levine, Allison, and Crossan, *The Historical Jesus in Context*.
Taylor, Vincent. *The Gospel According to Saint Mark*. 2nd ed. New York: Palgrave Macmillan, 1982.
Theissen, Gerd. *The Miracle Stories of the Early Christian Tradition*. Translated by F. McDonagh. Edinburgh: T&T Clark, 1983.
———. "Le mouvement de Jésus, révolution charismatique des valeurs." *NTS* 35 (1989): 343–60. Reprinted with corrections in *Histoire sociale du christianisme primitif: Jésus, Paul, Jean*. Geneva: Labor et Fides, 1996.

———. *Studien zur Soziologie des Urchristentums.* WUNT 19. Tübingen: Mohr Siebeck, 1989.
———. *Urchristliche Wundergeschichten.* Gütersloh: Gütersloher Verlagshaus, 1974.
Tishby, Isaiah. *Studies in Kabbalah and Its Branches.* 3 vols. Jerusalem: Magnes, 1992 (Heb.).
Tuckett, Christopher. "Q, the Law and Judaism." Pages 90–101 in Lindars, *Law and Religion.*
Vansina, Jan. *Oral Tradition as History.* Madison: University of Wisconsin Press, 1985.
Vermes, Geza. *Jesus the Jew: A Historian's Reading of the Gospels.* New York: Macmillan, 1973.
Vernant, Jean-Pierre. *The Origins of Greek Thought.* Ithaca NY: Cornell University Press, 1982.
Via, Dan O. *The Parables: Their Literary and Existential Dimension.* Philadelphia: Fortress, 1967.
Vielhauer, Phillip. "Gottesreich und Menschensohn in der Verkündigung Jesu." Pages 51–79 in Schneemelcher, *Festschrift für Günther Dehn.*
Vischer, Wilhelm. *Das Christuszeugnis des Alten Testaments.* Munich: Kaiser, 1934.
Wiles, Virginia, Alexandra Brown, and Graydon F. Snyder, eds. *Putting Body and Soul Together: Essays in Honor of Robin Scroggs.* Valley Forge, PA: Trinity Press International, 1977.
Wills, Lawrence. *The Jew in the Court of the Foreign King.* Minneapolis: Fortress, 1990.
Wilson, A. N. *Jesus: A Life.* New York: Fawcett Columbine, 1992.
Winter, Paul. "The Cultural Background to the Narrative in Luke 1 and 2." *JQR* 45, no. 2 (1954): 159–67; 45, no. 3 (1955): 230–42.
———. *On the Trial of Jesus.* Berlin: de Gruyter, 1961.
Wise, Michael O., Norman Golb, John J. Collins, and Dennis Pardee, eds. *Method of Investigation in the Dead Sea Scrolls and the Khirbet Qumran Site: Present Realities and Future Prospects.* Annals of the New York Academy of Sciences 722. New York: New York Academy of Sciences, 1994.
Wright, N. T. *The Climax of the Covenant: Christ and the Law in the Pauline Theology.* Edinburgh: T&T Clark, 1991.
———. *Jesus and the Victory of God.* Minneapolis: Fortress, 1996.
———. *Paul: In Fresh Perspective.* Minneapolis: Fortress, 2005.

———. "The Messiah and the People of God: A Study in Pauline Theology with Particular Reference to the Argument of the Epistle to the Romans." PhD diss., Oxford University, 1980.

Yerushalmi, Yoseph H. *Zakhor: Jewish History and Jewish Memory*. New York: Schocken, 1989 (1982).

Zetterholm, Magnus, ed. *The Messiah in Early Judaism and Christianity*. Minneapolis: Fortress, 2007.

Zimmermann, Heinrich. "Das absolute Ego eimi als die neutestamentliche Offenbarungsformel." *BZ* 4 (1960): 54–69.

Index of Passages

Hebrew Bible

Genesis

1	75, 79, 80, 81, 182
1:2	182
1:2–4	257
1:26–27 (LXX)	32
1:27	75, 79, 80, 95
2	75, 79, 80, 81, 182
2:2–3	65
2:24	75, 79, 95
4:1	34, 184
6:1–4	48
6:6	195
6:24	34
16:2	184
17:16	184
18:11	185
18:14	184
19	198
21:1–6 (LXX)	184
23:3–4	73
25:21	184
27:13	234
28:12	198
28:12–17	13
28:16	239
29:31–33	184
30:2	184
30:6	184
30:8	184
30:17–18	184
30:20	184
30:22–24	184
30:24	236
34:3 (LXX)	188
35:22–26	143
37:11	181
46:8–27	143
48:5–49:28	143
49:10	24, 36

Exodus

1	176
2:15	137
3:1–6	134
3:6	283
3:10	133
3:13	133
3:14	133, 226, 239, 241, 242, 243, 249
3:15	133
4:14	249, 296
4:19–20	137
4:22	34, 188
4:28	133, 133
4:31	116
7:16	133, 143
8:15	67
9:3	188
12:1–14	267
12:15	85
13:2	180
13:12	180
13:15	180
14–15	71
15:2–4	71
15:17	154, 260
15:20	180
16:3	188
16:4	68

Exodus (cont.)		12:3	59
19:2	39	13–14	61, 110
19:3	134	15:19	103
19:6	103	15:25	60, 103
20:2	64	15:27	61
20:5	73	16:19	113
20:5	100	16:29	258
20:10	64, 132	18:1–2	83
20:12	73, 105, 106, 117, 121	18:24–30	104
21:18–19	122	19	63, 95, 119
21:19	122	19:2	146
21: 23–24	77	19:18	95, 119, 123, 127, 132, 147, 151, 151, 155, 161, 183
21:24–25	151		
22:27	123	19:31	104
23:2	132	19:34	119, 123
23:4–5	96	20:1–3	104
24:1–9	134	20:7	103
24:8	51, 234	21:1–3	120, 124, 148
24:13	134	21:17–23	113
24:16	134	21:17–24	7, 110
26:31–33	257	23:26	258
28	202	24:19–20	77
30:6	257	26:14–17	62
32:12	195		
32:14	195	Numbers	
33:19–23	134	1:1–43	143
34:1	3	4:5 (LXX)	257
34:7	64	5:1–4	110
34:14	100	5:12–31	235
34:29–35	205	8:14	110
34:30	134	12.1–16	110
35:12	257	12:7	135
39:34	257	14:37	64
40:21 (LXX)	257	15:37–40	61
		16:19	110
Leviticus		19	104
2:4	85	19:1–22	113
10:10	112, 113, 119	19:11–22	120
11	15 – 104	19:16	124
11:32–47	113	20:8	137
11:44	103	24:17	24, 36, 184
11:44–45	113	26:1–50	143
11:47	112	29:1	258
12	180	29:7	258
12–15	113	31:16	25

INDEX OF PASSAGES

Deuteronomy		Joshua	
5:6	64	4:24	188
5:14	64, 132	7	198
6	119	12:7	135
6:4	127	14:7	135
6:4–5	132	22:31	188
6:5	119, 123, 126, 126, 151		
6:13	196	Judges	181
6:16	196	4:4	180
8:3	196	5:14–18	143
9:9	137	9:7–15	170
9:18	25	13:7	190
10:1	134	14:14	170
10:8	110	16:17	190
14:1	43, 55		
16:3	85	1 Samuel	181
17:1	110	1:5	184
17:9–13	19	1:11	184
18	26	1:19	184
18:15	136	15:11	270
18:15–19	99	15:29	270
18:15–20	268	20:35–38	71
18:18	58, 136	26:9	232
19:21	77		
21	35	2 Samuel	181
21:6	228	1:16	232
21:8	228	3	228
21:23	35	3:28–29	228
24	78, 79, 79, 80, 80, 81	7	184, 239, 243
24:1–4	75, 78, 80, 81	7:12 (LXX)	184
25:17–19	96	7:12–13	36
27:12–13	143	7:13	260
27:26	40	7:14	34, 180
28:37	170	8:14	72
32	137	12:1–4	170
32:8	34	12:1–6	170
32:36	195	12:1–14	170
32:39	241	12:13	64
33:6–29	143	14:1–20	170
33:26	275	14:4	216
34:1	137	19:43	143
34:5	135, 266	22	36
34:6	25	22:10	46
34:11	133	24	198

1 Kings		2 Chronicles	
2:37	230	5:13–14	46
8:10–11	46	7:26–27	58
8:12	201, 257	21:12–15	62
8:35–36	58	29:15–19	113
11:31	143	30:8–20	108
17:8–16	67	36:16	266
17:17–24	68, 264		
17:22–23	268	Ezra	
18	21	2:6	216
18:13	37	2:36	216
18:30–38	21	2:40	216
18:41–45	21	6:17	141
18:42	21	7:6	118
19	130, 134	8:33	216
19:5–8	195		
19:19–21	74, 142	Nehemiah	
20:35–43	170	6:14	180
20:39–40	170	10:35–36	180
22:19–23	48		
		Job	112
2 Kings		1:6	48
1:8	268	2:1	48
2	259	2:7–8	109
2:1	134	7:9–10	263
2:8–10	131	9:8	219
2:12	259	14:7–22	263
2:12–14	131	18:13	109
4:18–37	68	22:8	92
4:32–37	55, 264	38:7	48
4:43–44	67	42:5	170
5:1–14	55		
5:10–14	110	Psalms	
8:12	37	2	30, 45
9:13	30	2:2	34, 244
13:20–21	68, 264	2:7	34, 43, 180
22:14	180	5:7	72
		8:5	63
1 Chronicles		9:17	154
2:1–2	143	18	33, 36
2:18	185	18:11	275
16:13	188	18:12	257
17:13	243	18:21	113
23:13	110	18:25	113
		20:10	216

INDEX OF PASSAGES

21:4	31	76:10	74
21:7–8 (LXX)	241	78:2 (LXX)	170
22	33, 226, 234	79:6	51
22:1	207, 247	80:18	48
22:11	247, 294	82:6	43
22:15	175	88	33
23:1	85	88:9	263
24:1	217	89:7	48
24:3–4	108, 113	89:26–27	34
26:6	224, 228	89:51	234
27:12	219	95:7	33, 90
29:1	34	97:2	46
30:6	255	103	62, 63
31	33, 226, 234	103:3	62
34	275	103:13	43
34:10	85	110:1	38, 43, 244, 250, 277
34:21	8	110:1 (LXX)	38
35:11	219	116	33
36:10	73	118	258
37:9	93	118:22	265
37:11	25, 93	118:24	247, 294
40:10 (LXX)	212	118:25	164
41:4	9	118:25–27	216
41:10 (MT)	212	122:5	46
43:3	134	136:22	188
45	244	139:21–22	96
45:6	31	140:7	247, 294
45:7	255	146	268
49	33	146:7–8	55
49:13	170		
49:20	263	Proverbs	174
50:3	47	6:6–11	63, 74
51	108	8	242
51:4	110	8:22	34
51:9	110	8:22–36	244
51:12	113	8:24–31	34
51:16–17	80	9:4–5	242
56:9	47	9:16	242
63:2	247, 294	10:4	174
68:5	275	10:4–5	74
69	33, 226, 234	10:11	73
69:10 (LXX)	101	13:14	73
72:1–4	72	13:21	174
73:1	113	14:27	73
73:13	113	15:6	174

Proverbs (cont.)	174	35:5–6	55
18:4	73	35:8	109
19:15	174	37:22	188
22:4	174	40:29 (LXX)	25
30:19–20	188	41:4	242
		41:20	188
Qoheleth		42	30
3:11	44	42:1	134
		42:6	24
Isaiah	30, 196	42:7	10
1:5–6	170	43:3–5	31
1:10–17	81	43:10	241
1:10–20	80	43:25	64
1:16	104, 113	44:1	188
1:25	104	44:22	64
2:3	93, 167	45:1	26
4:5	46	45:14	100
5:1–7	170, 265	45:15	201
6:1–2	89	45:18	241
6:5	113	46:13	179
6:5–7	110	47:1	188
6:7	64	48:3	260
6:9–10	66, 83, 172, 204, 208	48:12	241, 242
7	188, 188	49	27
7:14	187, 188, 277	49:2	32
8:3	180	49:5–6	163
9	31, 34	49:6	24, 43, 100, 179, 264
9:1	98	49:10	24
9:1–2	256	49:23	100
11	162	50:4	33
11:1	24, 190	51:16	3
11:1–2	36	53:4–12	27
11:10	36	52:7	68
11:11–12	143	52:13–53:12	112
13:9–16	257	53	25, 25, 33, 33, 78, 227
18:3 (LXX)	255	53:3	109
19:1	275	53:3–12	267
19:4	212	53:5	261
22:22	64	53:7	225, 246
23:4	188	53:9–10	230
23:12	188	53:11	264
29:13	105	53:11–12	31
29:13 (LXX)	105, 105	54:3	100
33:24	15	56:1–8	163
35:3–6	25	56:3–8	104

56:7	151, 217, 235	23:6	275
56:7 (LXX)	265	25:30	255
56:8	143	26:1–6	160
57:15	31	26:1–24	74
58:6	55	26:5–24	237
60:3–7	163	31	72
60:10–14	163	31:9	34
61:1	24, 24, 30, 55, 56, 58, 64, 78	31:15	184
61:1–2	17, 56, 60, 153, 255	31:20	34
61:1–3	25, 56, 65	31:33	260
61:2	10	33:8	104, 115
61:6	103	33:15	24
62:5 (LXX)	188		
63:16–17	72	Lamentations	
64:8	72	4:20	37
66:1–2	77, 180		
66:2	24, 25	Ezekiel	
66:14	188	1:1	30
66:18–24	163	7:24	46
66:21	104	13:9	47
		14:11	109
Jeremiah		17:2	170
1 (LXX)	221	17:3–10	170
1:5	276	17:27–28	85
2:13	73	19:2–9	170
2:23	184	19:10–14	170
4:5–6	257	22:26	110
7	115	23:3–5	170
7:1–15	245	24:3	170
7:4	221	24:15	73
7:5–7	217	27:26	113
7:11	41, 217, 265	28:2	198
7:11 (LXX)	266	28:12	198
7:21–26	136	34:23–24	29
9:1–8	156	36:25–38	15
15:9	257	36:33	104, 113
17:13	73	37:24–25	29
18:18–23	74	38–39	236
20:37–38	266	43:1–9	62
22:13–18	72	44:7	41
22:15–17	72	44:23	110
22:24–30	72	44:25	120
22:30	29	44:27	120
23:5	24	48:1ff.	149
23:5–6	29		

Daniel	181	2:2	255
2:46	253	3:12	143
3:12	46	3:13–15	245
3:14	46	5:18–20	257
3:17	46	5:21–24	104, 132
3:18	46	5:21–25	81
3:25	34	5:21–27	80
3:28	46	7:10–17	245
5:7 (OG)	255	8:9	257
6 (OG)	233	9:8	231
6:17	46	9:11	36
6:21	46		
7	29, 31, 32, 45, 45, 47, 48, 160, 251, 275	Jonah	104, 153
7–12	48	Micah	
7:3–27	47	2:12	143
7:13	27, 31, 34, 36, 46, 48, 241, 244, 250	3:9–12	160
		3:11	19
7:13–14	221	3:12	237
7:18	190	4	163
7:22	48, 190	4:1–4	93
7:25	190	4:9–10	184
7:27	190	5:10–15	100
8	273	6:6–8	81, 132
8:15–16	48	7:6	74
9:9	64		
9:21	48	Nahum	
9:24–26	236	1:3	46
9:27	256		
10:13, 20–21	49	Habakkuk	
12	263, 269, 270	1:13	113
		3:15	219
Hosea			
2:2–15	170	Zephaniah	
6:2	267	3:9	104
6:6	81, 106, 132, 147		
11:1	43, 184, 190	Haggai	
		2:11–13	19
Joel		2:12–19	110, 113
1–2	62		
3:17	100	Hosea	
4:16	255	1:10	34
		11:1	34
Amos			
1:2	255		

INDEX OF PASSAGES

Zechariah	
1:16	255
3:8	24
4:14	25
6:12	24
9	30, 216
9:9	26, 92, 235
9:9–10	217
9:11	234, 279
11	215
12	162
12:10	236
14	104
14:4	30, 257
14:20	118
14:21	161

Malachi	
2:6–7	19
3:7–10	158
3:16	47
3:22–24	99
4:5 [3:24]	27

Deuterocanonical Books

Tobit	17, 82
4:15	96, 129
6:13–15	73
13:8 [6]	154
14:5	163

Wisdom of Solomon	26, 39, 82
14:3	22

Sirach	18, 39
4:10	34
7:8–9	132
18:32–33	74
23:1	22
23:4	22
24:9	34
25:2–3	74
34:18–19	132
36:11	143

40:28–30	74
45:1–5	19
48:10	143

1 Maccabees	99, 138, 146
2:27–28	74
2:39–48	74
4:46	99
14:41	99

2 Maccabees	82
2:18	143
6:18–31	269
7	263
7:14	269
7:23	269
14:46	263

3 Maccabees	82
6:3	22
6:8	22

Ancient Jewish Writers

Josephus, *Antiquities of the Jews*	
2.201–204	54
2.205–217	136
2.230	180
2.233	54
2.331	54
4.326	54, 66
4.329	136, 136
8.354	74
9.222–227	257
11.114–119	120
13.17	138
13.288	138, 154
13.293–296	165
13.296–300	138
13.297	144, 146
13.408–418	138
14.22	21
15.529	79
17.41	151
17.269–285	163

Josephus, Antiquities of the Jews (cont.)	
18.12–15	154
18.17	145
18.18–22	144
18.29–35	120
18.60–87	166
18.63–64	239
18.116–118	193
18.180	149, 165
18.318–339	160
20.97	162
20.118–124	120
20.163–166	246
20.165	123
20.167–172	257
20.186	123
20.199	175
20.200	222, 239
20.204	123
20.204–214	237
20.208–210	123

Josephus, *Jewish War*	
1.110	39
1.110–114	151
2.55–65	138
2.128–133	162
2.162	144
2.184–198	151, 154
2.254–257	160
2.261–262	101
2.293–296	162
2.408–410	163
2.409–421	148
2.418–456	101
2.425–429	101
2.517–522	163
2.556–646	162
4.153	162
4.161	157
6.111–117	101
6.222–223	148
6.283–285	213
6.290–296	102
6.299	259
	307

6.300–310	246
6.312–313	249
7.252–274	162

Josephus, *Life*	
191	151

Philo, *De Abrahamo*	
208	132

Philo, *De cherubim*	
48–49	184

Philo, *De posteritate Caini*	
78	184

Philo, *De praemiis et poenis*	
16.152	39
95	24

Philo, *De vita Mosis*	
1.21	180
2.107–108	132

Philo, *Hypothetica*	
2.63–64	130
7.6	130

Philo, *In Flaccum*	
36–40	236

Philo, *Legatio ad Gaium*	
302	228

Philo, *Legum allegoriae*	
3.218–219	185

Philo, *Quod omnis probus liber sit*	
75	144

Philo, *De specialibus legibus*	
2	258;
2.61–62	39
2.63	132
2.63–64	119

INDEX OF PASSAGES

Philo, *De virtutibus*		48:6	276
51.95	132	48:8–49:3	27
		48:10	27
PSEUDEPIGRAPHA		51:1	263
		52:4	24
Apocalypse of Abraham		56:5–7	46
31	47	61–64	45
		62:7	203, 204
Apocryphon of Ezekiel		62:14	46, 51
frg. 3	22	67:7–9	46
		69:27	46
Assumption of Moses		70:2	50
3:11	25	71:1	24, 50
11:16	54	71:8	47
11:17	25	71:13	47
		71:14	46
2 Baruch	25, 26, 137, 164	71:17	45, 46, 198
4:37	143	77:1	239
5:5	143	82:4–7	154
10:18	64	89:73	154
30:1	26	90:28–29	237
30:1–5	269	90:98–99	163
84	137	91:13	163
		91:15	47
4 Baruch		92:3–5	263
4:4	64	94–104	25
		100:2	74
1 Enoch	137		
1:9	47	3 Enoch	45
5:7	25		
6:62	13	4 Ezra	25, 49, 137, 162, 164
9:35–39	13	3:20–22	72
22–27	149	4:42	88
37–71	13, 24, 27, 34, 45, 46, 49	7:22–24	156
39:5	46	7:27–30	236
40:28	237	7:28–29	26, 204
45–50	45	7:32	263
45:4–5	46	11:42	25
46:1	32	13	26, 45, 275
46:1–3	32, 275	14	137
46:3	55		
48:2–3	252	Jubilees	108, 154
48:3–5	275	1:15–17	163
48:4	24	1:23–28	55, 154
48:5	275	1:24–25	34

Jubilees (cont.)		Testament of Joseph	
1:27	237	18:2	95
6:32–35	154		
23:16	154	Testament of Judah	
26	154	24	24
Liber antiquitatum biblicarum		Testament of Levi	
9.1–10	136	2:5–12	50
		10:3	156
Odes of Solomon	39	14–18	26
		14:4–6	156
Psalms of Solomon	137, 146, 162, 164	16:2–4	156
1:8	158	16:3–5	97
2:13	158	18	25
4:1–8	154	18:10–11	257
4:6	158		
4:8	158	Testament of Moses	154, 244
4:19–20	158	1:14	133
7:3	154	3:12	133
7:9–10	154	10:1	86
8:9–19	158	11	136
8:12	154		
8:13	158	Testament of the Twelve Patriarchs	48
17–19	24		
17:32	158	T. Zebulun	
		6:8	95
Sibylline Oracles	82		
2	162	DEAD SEA SCROLLS	
3.46–48	86		
5	164	1QapGen	17
5.414–433	163		
5.425	160	1QH	
		3:21–22	243
		11:5–9	243
Testament of Benjamin		11:10–12	243
3:3–4	130	18:14–15	25, 25
3:8	236		
9:2	163	1QM	25, 96, 178
		1:1	128
Testament of Dan	178	2:2–3	143
5:3	119, 130, 132	2:7–8	143
5:7–13	179	3:13–14	143
		5:1	143
Testament of Issachar		7:4–5	120
5:2	119, 132	7:4–8	113
7:6	132		

10:9	25	4Q512		108
10:13	25			
13	244	4Q521		25, 55, 267
17:7	244			
		4Q540–541		236
1QpHab	92			
12:3	261	4Q541		25, 211
12:8–9	158			
		4QFlor		154, 239, 243
1QS	42, 239, 244	3:2–3		260
1:9–10	128	3:10–13		180, 239
2:4–5	154			
2:24	128	4QMMT		
3:4–9	144	7:10		18
3:8	103			
3:20–24	62	4QprNab		17, 62, 62
5:5–7	261			
5:13–14	104	4QTest		
5:25	128	16–20		74
6:3–5	144			
8:1	141	4QtgLev		17
8:8–10	261			
9:3–6	261	11QMelch 13		45; 244
9:11	25, 268			
10:26–11:1	25	11QTemple		
		18:14–16		143
1QSa	24	29:8–10		163
1	92	29:9		154
2:5–7	7	50:10–19		103
2:19–22	144	57:5–6		143
1QSb		11QtgJob		17
5:20	24			
		CD		
1Q36		1:13–21		154
9:34–35	72	2:25–3:6		108
		3:18–4:10		261
4Q246	25, 45	4:9–11		108
		5:6–7		
4Q252	24	5:6–8		158
		5:11–12		103
4Q285	24	5:13–14		108
		5:18–19		108
4Q491	244	6:24–26		108
		7:18		24

CD (cont.)		5:3	163, 178
8:16–18	108	5:3–5	25
10:12–13	103	5:3–6	74
10:14–11:18	59	5–6	196, 205
11:16	59	5:7–8	93
11:19–22	103	5:8	113
12:1–2	103	5:9	35
16:14–20	105	5:11	48
		5:12	91
New Testament		5:13	174
		5:17	76, 77, 78, 107, 205
Matthew		5:17–18	23
1	189, 190	5:17–20	79
1–2	26	5:18	76, 78
1:1	31	5:20	21, 137
1:3–6	187	5:21–48	118
1:8	189	5:22	127
1:18	185	5:23–24	132, 153
1:19	186	5:31	79
1:20–25	189	5:31–32	75
1:25	185, 188	5:34	208
2:1–12	184	5:35	25
2:2	236	5:37	208
2:10	189	5:38–39	151
2:13	137	5:38–42	81
2:13–15	184	5:39	152
2:16–18	184	5:41	208
2:19–21	137	5:41–48	152
2:22–23	190	5:43	96
2:23	190	5:43–45	85
3	136	5:44	95
3:3	255	5:44–45	35
3:9	205	5:47	126, 154
3:12	137	5:48	72, 85, 174
3:17	35, 255	6:6	201
4:1–11	227	6:9–5	162
4:3	194	6:9–13	90
4:6	194	6:10	91
4:10	227	6:11–12	162
4:16	256	6:14	86
4:17	63, 111	6:16–18	76
4:18–22	142	6:19–21	7
4:23	53, 117	6:20–23	162
5	118	6:21	267
5:1	137	6:22	174

6:22–23	257	10:31	93
6:24	7	10:34	74
6:25	98	10:34–35	189
6:33	87	10:34–37	215
7:1	86	10:37	74, 142, 189
7:7	87	10:38–39	142
7:12	96, 129, 152	10:40	143
7:15	57	11:2–5	49
7:17	152	11:2–6	25, 58, 196, 267
7:28–29	99	11:4–5	51
7:29	21	11:5	53, 64, 89, 153, 267
7:37–38	143	11:5–6	35, 86
8	74	11:9–15	196
8:1–4	61	11:11	64
8:4	82	11:12–13	91
8:5–13	53, 56, 97	11:13	78, 104
8:8	37	11:13–14	79
8:11–12	51, 84, 89, 97, 98	11:16–19	76, 171
8:12	137	11:19	142, 153
8:17	227	11:21–24	97
8:19–20	31	11:22	226
8:20	45	11:23	137
8:21–22	73, 142, 155	11:24	226
8:22	66, 271	11:27	243
8:25	37	12	138
9:2	62, 115, 249	12:1–8	133
9:5	63	12:5	20
9:5–6	62	12:9–13	56
9:6	254	12:9–14	150
9:8	63, 64, 205	12:10–12	60
9:12–13	163	12:18	25
9:15	76	12:22–23	34
9:18–26	61	12:25–26	49
9:27–31	34	12:26	56
9:35	117	12:28	86
10	136	12:31–32	44
10:1–2	137	12:33	152
10:2–4	143	12:38	235
10:4	100	12:38–39	55
10:5	98	12:39	97
10:5–6	2, 97, 137, 264	12:41–42	97, 153
10:7	50, 91, 143	12:42	48
10:17	117, 158	13	136
10:23	88	13:1–23	66
10:27	250	13:3	169

Matthew (cont.)		16:21–23	194
13:5	189	16:23	254
13:13	169	16:27	46
13:16–17	153	16:27–28	46, 89
13:24–30	84	16:28	84
13:25–30	173	17:1–8	134
13:33	204	17:2	42
13:34	169	17:5	255
13:36–42	171	17:11	27
13:38	97, 99	17:12	194
13:38–43	162	17:12–13	227
13:41	84	17:24–27	161, 237
13:41–43	84	17:26	162
13:44	204	17:27	90, 162
13:44–46	172	18	118, 136
13:47–50	84	18:1–4	117, 178
13:52	118	18:20	252
13:55	17	18:23–34	174
14:13–21	214	18:23–35	82
14:22–34	219	19:3–9	75
14:27	249	19:9	79
14:33	35	19:12	12
15	138	19:13–15	178
15:1–9	151	19:19	152
15:1–20	104	19:28	82, 97, 142, 252
15:5–9	150	19:29	252
15:10–20	77, 112	20:1–16	6, 21
15:11	106	20:18–19	194
15:14	174, 257	20:21	84
15:17	238	20:29–34	34
15:18	114	21:1–11	92, 235
15:19	108	21:8	30, 216
15:21–28	34	21:9	31, 258
15:24	97, 264	21:10	189, 256
15:32–39	67	21:11	30, 268
16	253	21:12	245
16:1–4	55	21:12–13	150
16:9	57	21:15	216, 245, 258
16:13	58	21:23	254
16:13–20	265	21:23–27	116, 156
16:14	12, 99, 253, 266	21:33–45	137
16:16	32, 34, 35, 226, 253	21:34–36	171
16:16–17	118	21:43	152, 171
16:17–19	64	21:46	268
16:20	200	22–23	194

22:1–10	171	25:1–13	84, 171
22:1–13	171	25:21	171
22:1–14	82, 137	25:23	171
22:2	172	25:30	171
22:6–7	171	25:31–46	84, 199
22:7	171	25:34–40	152
22:10	171	25:40	189
22:14	171	26	260
22:15–22	156	26–27	258
22:23–32	152	26:2	254
22:23–33	157	26:3	149, 230
22:34–40	129, 151, 157	26:6	144
22:36	151	26:7	190
23	156, 159	26:12	254
23:2–3	21, 115	26:15	212
23:3–36	137	26:16	109
23:7–12	117	26:20–25	212
23:8–12	117	26:22	225
23:9	189	26:25	225
23:16–22	146	26:28	51, 86, 234
23:23	76, 115, 146	26:39	226, 235
23:24	158	26:51–52	214
23:25–26	107, 108, 146, 155	26:53	194, 225
23:27–28	146	26:55	214
23:27–36	106	26:56	231
23:28	152	26:59	159, 164
23:34–39	232	26:60–61	158
23:37	268	26:62–66	224
24–25	136	26:63	35, 226, 256
24:1–31	266	26:64	45, 199
24:5	242, 249	26:64–65	259
24:11	57	26:69–75	230
24:12	152	26:71	190
24:13	264	27	229, 256
24:14	36	27:11	159, 202, 225
24:15	256	27:24	228
24:24	57	27:25	137, 231, 232, 233, 234, 246
24:29–31	31	27:26	229
24:30	31, 45	27:29	202
24:30–31	89, 256	27:37	202, 228
24:31	255	27:39–40	236
24:34	88, 94	27:39–44	215, 222
24:36	34, 87, 88, 207	27:40	158
24:43–44	171	27:42	202, 234, 252
25	174	27:42–43	35, 256

Matthew (cont.)		1:40–45	55, 61, 113
27:45	247, 257	1:41	55, 61, 62
27:46	207, 255	1:42	62
27:49	222	1:44	62, 201
27:50	247, 255	2	60, 189
27:51	256	2:1–10	201
27:51–54	266	2:1–12	53, 58, 62, 63
27:52	256	2:3	249
27:52–53	257	2:5	115
27:55	12	2:7	238, 240
27:62	139	2:10	251, 254
27:63	222	2:11	59
27:66	233	2:12	63
28:2	256, 257	2:14	142
28:2–10	183	2:15–17	117
28:4	256	2:17	65, 85, 114, 153
28:16–20	264, 266	2:18	248
28:18	254	2:18–20	152
28:19–20	118	2:18–22	208
		2:19	88, 155
Mark		2:19–20	152
1	136	2:20	230
1:4–11	199	2:21	220
1:6	268	2:21–22	152
1:7	15	2:23–28	60, 132, 133, 146
1:9–11	30, 193	2:26	152
1:10	258	2:28	44, 58, 59, 251
1:11	35, 196	3	60, 189
1:12–13	227	3:1–5	56
1:14	13	3:1–6	58, 60, 132, 146
1:14–15	85, 86	3:1–8	39
1:15	50, 86, 94	3:2	94
1:16–20	142	3:4	60
1:19–20	189	3:5	61
1:21–28	56	3:6	240
1:22	21, 173, 254	3:7–12	30
1:23	117	3:11	35
1:23–26	113	3:12	200
1:24	190	3:13–14	143
1:27	21, 97	3:16–19	143
1:34	56	3:18	100, 240
1:39	56, 117	3:19–21	57
1:40	62, 109	3:20–21	181
1:40–42	93	3:20–35	142
1:40–44	113	3:21	189, 197

INDEX OF PASSAGES

3:21–32	189	7	189
3:22	56	7:1	248
3:24–25	49	7:1–13	104, 151
3:28	44, 251	7:1–23	97, 104, 106, 146
3:28–29	240	7:3	146
3:29	240	7:5	105
3:30–31	57	7:9–13	105
3:31–35	181, 189, 197	7:14–15	104, 105, 152
3:32–35	142, 189	7:15	75, 106, 238
4	171	7:16–23	104
4:1–20	66	7:17	105, 107
4:10–12	83, 172, 201, 204	7:18–19	98
4:15	171	7:18–23	105
4:22	204	7:19	105, 106, 112, 114
4:26–29	82	7:20	77
4:26–32	83	7:21–23	106
4:31	172	7:24–30	56, 97
4:34	169	7:27	97
4:35–40	39	7:28	37, 97
5	103	7:31–37	56, 201
5:1–13	110	7:34	17, 62
5:1–20	56	8:1–10	67
5:7	35	8:5–13	179
5:11	231	8:11–13	97
5:15	105	8:15	85
5:19	204	8:22–26	53, 56
5:21–34	113	8:27–28	268
5:21–43	55, 61, 68	8:27–29	195
5:24–34	56, 60	8:27–30	13, 32
5:28	61	8:27–33	226, 265
5:35–43	201	8:28	99
5:41	17, 107	8:29	244
6:1–6	18, 197	8:29–31	244
6:2–3	19	8:30	200
6:3	17	8:31	31, 32, 194, 198, 230, 231, 265, 266
6:4	181, 268		
6:5–6	53	8:31–33	199
6:7	143, 204	8:34	198
6:12	143	8:35	35, 142
6:15	136, 195, 268	8:38	45, 88, 94, 251
6:17–29	193	9:1	88, 89, 91, 94
6:32–44	67	9:2	89, 201
6:45	62	9:2–8	134
6:45–53	219	9:5	18
6:56	61	9:9	231

Mark (cont.)	
9:10	266
9:12	27, 31, 198, 227
9:14–29	56, 66
9:24	174
9:25	66
9:31	31, 194, 198, 230, 265
9:31–32	266
9:37	106, 143
9:38	252
10:1–12	146
10:2–9	152
10:2–12	75, 105, 208
10:3–4	79
10:5	75, 80
10:5–9	79
10:9	81
10:11–12	208
10:13–16	178
10:17	253
10:17–21	275
10:17–22	142
10:17–31	174
10:25	83
10:28–30	142
10:28–34	132
10:29–31	142
10:31	83
10:32	9
10:33	230, 265
10:33–34	31, 194, 198, 231
10:38–39	193
10:45	31, 48, 199, 267
10:46	251
10:46–52	34, 53
10:47	190
11:1–10	92, 235
11:1–14:49	220
11:3	37
11:8–9	216
11:9	216
11:9–10	190
11:12–21	158
11:15	245
11:15–18	115
11:17	41, 158, 217, 235, 237
11:18	159, 207, 245, 265
11:19	207
11:21	18
11:28	254
12:1–9	7, 171
12:1–11	172
12:1–12	115, 265
12:5	171
12:13	265
12:18–27	145, 263
12:25	13, 244
12:28–34	129
12:34	113
12:35–37	13, 34, 38, 190
12:38–40	106, 125
13:1–2	115, 158
13:2	158, 201, 208, 220
13:6	242, 252
13:9–11	198
13:10	36
13:13	198
13:21–27	244
13:24–27	31
13:26	31, 45
13:28	21
13:28–29	87, 158
13:30	88, 89, 94
13:31	62
13:32	34, 87, 88, 89, 207, 243
13:32–33	89
13:33–37	88
14	260
14:1	149
14:3	109, 144
14:3–9	115
14:3–29	8
14:10–11	265
14:14	231
14:16	35
14:18	212
14:21	44, 48, 231
14:22–25	51, 208, 267
14:24	51, 264
14:25	88

14:36	17	15:39	32, 203, 215
14:41	154	15:47	12
14:47–48	214	15:55–56	265
14:50	231	15:62	226
14:53–65	32	16:1–8	12
14:54	249	16:7	12
14:55	159, 164, 248	16:15	36
14:55–64	250	16:19	230, 276
14:56–59	220		
14:57–59	219	Luke	
14:58	62, 75, 115, 160, 201, 208, 220, 260	1	136, 178
		1–2	37, 183
14:59	219	1:15	190, 249
14:61	13, 219, 244	1:23	183
14:61–62	44, 45, 48, 199, 203, 239, 244, 245	1:26–38	185
		1:31–33	189
14:62	45, 46, 230, 240, 243, 244, 250	1:31–35	35
14:62–63	259	1:32	25, 31, 180
14:63	250	1:32–34	228
14:64	238	1:34	187
14:65	244	1:35	180
14:66	229	1:42	184
14:67	190	1:43	277
14:70	166	1:45	277
15:1	144, 164, 224	1:48	188
15:2	32, 202	1:54	182, 188
15:2–5	225	1:54–55	228
15:6–15	229	1:55	179
15:7	215	1:66	188
15:9	202	1:68–79	228
15:10	20, 265	1:73	179
15:11	265	1:76	136, 249
15:12	202, 229	2:7	188
15:17	203	2:8	184
15:26	202, 225	2:11	37
15:29	158, 202, 220, 236, 240, 241	2:19	181
15:29–32	222	2:21	179
15:30	252	2:22	179, 180
15:31	265	2:25	182
15:32	244	2:30	182
15:34	207, 247	2:31–32	179
15:34–37	255	2:34	232
15:37	247, 256	2:36	180
15:37–38	259	2:39	180
15:38	220	2:42	180

Luke (cont.)		6:27	126
2:51	181, 185	6:27–28	95
3	136	6:27–45	63
3:1	221	6:28	85, 96
3:1–2	249	6:31	96
3:6	179	6:32–36	95, 96
3:18	47	6:33	154
3:19–22	200	6:35	35
3:22	35, 194	6:36	85, 174
3:23	18, 190	6:36–38	7
3:36	189	6:37	86
3:38	180	6:39	257
4:1–13	227	7	174
4:3	196	7:1–10	53, 97
4:13	194	7:1–11	178
4:15	117	7:5	179
4:16–21	89	7:9	97
4:16–30	17, 84, 251	7:11–17	68
4:18	153	7:14	107
4:18–21	60	7:16	268
4:24	268	7:18–23	58, 267
4:31–41	84	7:22	10, 89, 109, 153
4:32	21	7:31–35	142
4:34	190	7:34	153
4:36	21, 254	7:36	115, 144, 152
4:41	35	7:36–50	69, 110
5:1–3	128	7:39	268
5:1–11	142	7:47	174
5:12	109	7:49–50	180
5:20	115, 249	8:4–15	66
5:26	63	8:20	188, 189
6:1–5	133	8:24	37
6:4	65	8:28	35
6:5	59	8:40–56	61
6:6	71	8:45–46	128
6:6–10	56	9:2	84
6:13	142	9:8	136
6:14–16	143	9:10–17	214
6:15	100, 163	9:11	84
6:18	56	9:16	62
6:20	84, 153, 163, 178	9:18–21	58, 265
6:20–21	7	9:18–22	226
6:20–26	174	9:19	99
6:22	48	9:20	32
6:23	91	9:21	200

9:22	267	12:15–21	163
9:26	46	12:16–21	7, 174
9:28–36	134	12:22–31	63
9:51–56	98	12:31	87
9:57–58	31	12:33–34	7, 174
9:58	63	12:49	74
9:59–60	73, 155	12:49–53	215
9:60	84, 271	12:50	29, 230
9:60–62	66, 84	12:51	74
9:61–62	189	12:51–53	189
10	21, 108, 119, 174, 178	12:54–56	87
10:1	204	13	66
10:2	143	13:1	166, 218
10:9	49, 50, 84	13:4–5	63, 111
10:11	49	13:10–17	59, 64, 65, 146
10:14	226	13:14	59, 65
10:16	143	13:14–16	60
10:22	243	13:15	21, 132
10:22–24	49	13:18	84
10:23–24	50, 153	13:20	84
10:25	119, 125	13:21	85
10:25–28	129	13:28–29	82, 84, 88, 97, 98
10:25–37	18, 119	13:31	144
10:27	126	13:31–33	152
10:29	119, 129	13:34	165
10:30–37	98	14:1	115, 152
10:31	20	14:1–6	132, 146
10:33	120	14:1–15	144
10:37	120, 129	14:5	21, 132
10:38–42	69	14:11	170
11:2	91	14:15–24	88, 146
11:9	87	14:21	7
11:17–18	49	14:22–23	171
11:20	64, 67, 84, 86	14:26	63, 74, 142, 189
11:31–32	153	14:27	142
11:34	257	14:33	163
11:37	115, 144, 152	15	178
11:37–41	104, 155	16:9–31	179
11:37–52	151	16:13	7
11:39–41	107	16:16	91, 97
11:44	107	16:18	75, 81, 208
12:1	85	16:19–31	7, 85
12:8–9	251	17:11–19	98
12:10	44, 251	17:12–19	109
12:15	174	17:20	87, 152

Luke (cont.)		22:48	48, 231
17:20–21	50	22:49–52	214
17:21	64, 87, 90, 91	22:66	164
17:24	91	22:66–71	159
18:1–8	28	22:67–70	240
18:9–14	170	22:67–72	4
18:15–17	178	22:69	45, 199
18:18	125	22:70	240, 242, 244
18:23–27	163	23:2	217
18:35–43	34	23:3	225
19:10	163	23:11	203
19:11	92	23:13	148
19:12–15	171	23:18–25	229
19:27	171	23:34	232, 266
19:29–38	92, 235	23:34–38	222
19:37	30	23:35	241, 252
19:38	31, 216	23:43	156
19:41–44	165	23:45	97
19:45	245	23:45–46	255
19:47	159	23:46	247
19:47–48	245	23:47	11
20:2	254	23:51	182
20:22	217	24	204
20:27–38	263	24:6–7	194
20:41–44	249	24:6–8	12
21:7	172	24:6–12	183
21:8	242	24:11	11
21:25–28	31	24:12	11
21:27	45	24:17–21	266
21:31–35	91	24:19	189, 268
21:38	237	24:21	221, 268
22:1	85	24:21–23	11
22:14–30	199	24:31	11, 12
22:15–20	88	24:44	18
22:16	88	24:51	230, 276
22:19	52	24:53	179
22:20	51		
22:21–23	213	John	
22:28	199	1–12	68
22:28–30	82, 252	1:9	133
22:30	213	1:12	64
22:34	232	1:14–18	58
22:35	204	1:17	133, 135
22:36–38	214	1:21	268
22:37	227	1:24–42	13

INDEX OF PASSAGES

1:29	112, 267	5:1–2	167
1:29–34	200	5:1–9	53
1:43	166	5:1–18	146
1:45	135	5:6	194, 207
1:47	166	5:9–17	132
1:49	236	5:18	13, 167, 243
1:51	43	5:19	243
2:4	189, 254	5:20	43
2:11	50, 198	5:22	244
2:13	167	5:25	90
2:13–22	245	5:27	13
2:14–20	159	5:28	255
2:14–22	208	5:36	133
2:16	9	5:38	133
2:17	101, 108	5:45	135
2:18–20	245	5:46	135
2:18–22	158	6:1–15	67
2:19	160	6:4	167
2:19–21	236	6:6	207
2:21	211, 260	6:14	58, 136, 268
2:23	167	6:15	212
3:1–21	188	6:16–21	219
3:3	84	6:20	241
3:5	84	6:31–32	133
3:13	13, 276	6:32	131, 133, 135
3:13–14	50	6:35	131, 133
3:13–17	200	6:41	133, 167
3:16	90	6:43	133
3:17	133	6:48	133
3:31	188	6:51–56	133
3:34	133	6:51–58	208
4:3	166	6:52	167
4:4	98	6:59	167
4:7–26	98	6:61	133
4:9	98	6:62	13
4:14	90	6:63–58	51
4:22	167	6:66	254
4:22–24	98	6:68	174, 253
4:24	41	6:69	190
4:25	203	7:2–3	166
4:26	249	7:5	188
4:42	37	7:7	194
4:43–47	166	7:15	17, 19
4:44	189	7:16	254
4:46–54	53, 97	7:20	56

John (cont.)		10:20	188
7:21–23	60	10:30	43, 242, 249
7:22–24	132	10:33	242
7:25	167	10:38	242
7:30	254	11:1	69, 167
7:31	167	11:1–45	55
7:40	268	11:1–46	68
7:40–42	190	11:7	69
7:41	98	11:8	222
7:41–42	166, 184	11:18	69, 167
7:41–43	190	11:21–27	69
7:42	16	11:25	271
7:45–52	98	11:25–26	91
7:52	166	11:27	35, 50
8:3–11	174	11:31	69
8:6	17	11:33–38	69
8:7	174	11:43	255
8:9–11	175	11:45	69
8:14	207	11:47–53	68
8:14–15	26	11:48–50	218
8:16	244	11:54	167
8:20	254	11:55	167
8:24	249	12:1	167
8:28	18, 241, 249	12:1–8	69
8:31	167	12:12–16	92, 235
8:46	112	12:13	31, 216, 236
8:48	123, 166	12:15	31
8:52	166, 173	12:16	12
8:53–58	48	12:23	14, 167
8:57–58	245	12:24–25	14
8:58	205, 241, 242	12:25	142
8:58–59	249	12:27	29
9:1	53	12:28	252
9:1–34	146	12:34	198
9:1–41	63, 111	12:36	249
9:3	112	12:45	43
9:5	257	12:49	133
9:13–17	166	13:1	167
9:14–16	132	13:19	242, 249
9:17	268	13:20	143
9:18	166	13:23	253
9:25	170	14:1–3	14
9:35–39	13	14:6	114
9:39	244	14:9	43
10:10	68	14:13	252

14:20	90	21:11	175
14:26	3	21:20	253
15:1–8	171	21:22	90
15:2	113		
15:3	155	Acts	27, 84, 106, 178, 190, 252
15:12–13	171	1:2	230
15:13	78	1:6	27
15:27	3	1:8	84
17:3	203	1:9–11	276
17:11–12	242	1:11	230
18:3	139	1:13	100, 143, 163
18:5	249	1:14	181
18:6	242, 249	1:22	230
18:8	249	2:17	179
18:15–16	229	2:21	252
18:17	166	2:23	218
18:20	159	2:24	257, 264, 265, 271
18:31	223, 229	2:25–36	249
18:36	84, 163, 225	2:36	37, 203
18:38	170	2:37	125
18:39–19:16	229	2:46	159
18:40	215	3:1	259
19	50	3:12	179
19:5	228, 231	3:13	25
19:6	224	3:15	73
19:7	219	3:16	252
19:11	223	3:17–18	232
19:25	12	3:18	268
19:26	189, 253	3:22	70, 268
19:28	175	3:22–23	58, 136
19:30	208	3:38	180
19:31–42	8	4–6	138
19:35	175	4:1–23	222
19:39–40	8	4:7	253
20:2	253	4:12	253
20:8	275	4:23	138
20:14–15	204	4:27	25
20:24–29	266	4:30	25
20:25	253	5:17–42	222
20:28	37, 38, 253	5:28	232
20:31	35, 175	5:31	37
21	204	5:36–37	162
21:1	167	5:42	68
21:1–14	266	6:8–14	222
21:7	253	6:13–14	158, 236

Acts (cont.)			
7:2–53	135	23:2	149
7:7	75	23:6	40, 149
7:37	58, 268	23:6–8	144
7:48	221	23:12	149
7:54–60	222	23:12–24	222
7:55–58	241	23:20	149
7:56	27, 13	23:27	149
7:59–60	259	24:1	149
8:27–29	179	24:5	190
8:32–33	227	24:9	149
9:2	8, 84	24:11–17	40
9:11	84	24:14	8, 117
9:17	180	24:22	8
9:18	170	25:7	149
9:19–30	222	25:24	149
9:36	12	26:5	40, 151
9:36–43	68	26:10–12	222
10:1–4	179	26:22	179
10:14	77	26:28	117
10:15	113	28:26–28	264
10:36	68	Romans	198
10:37	11	1:1–4	87
10:42	264	1:3	2, 26, 36
11:20	84	1:3–4	26, 31
11:26	117	1:16	98
13:23	37	1:18–32	100
13:27	179	2:17–20	154
13:47	264	2:23	154
15:1	40	3:13	40
15:5	40	3:20	39
16:30	125	3:20–21	39
17:3	37	3:23–24	40
17:24	75	3:27	40
18:2	178	3:28	39
18:6	264	3:31	76
18:18	40	4:25	264
18:25–26	117	5:1	83
21:20–21	101	5:8	42
21:20–30	40	5:9–10	83
21:26	159	6:3	194
21:28	41	6:3–4	131
21:38	162	6:4	266
22:3	40, 101, 134, 187	6:19	109, 113
22:4	8, 117	7	75

7:18–19	75	7:10–16	75
8:3	112	7:17–18	40
8:23	83	7:29–31	266
8:34	26	8:6	242, 253
8:39	42	9:1	269
9–11	23, 261	10:1–2	131
9:5	36, 275	10:1–5	51
10:12	40	10:2	135
10:13	252, 83	11:2	3
10:15	68	11:23–25	116
10:16	227	11:23–26	208
11:1	232	11:25	51, 234
11:11–12	264	11:27–34	235
11:13–16	38	12:13	40, 135
11:36	275	13	115
12:9–21	95	13:7	86
12:14	95	15	267
12:17–20	95	15:1–5	266
13	212	15:3	33, 42, 112, 267
13:8	78	15:3–5	116
13:10	78, 129	15:4	42
14:9	264	15:5	142
14:14–23	109, 112	15:5–8	42
14:20	114	15:9	222
15:3	42	15:20	91, 271
15:8	2, 38	15:26	230
15:16	38	15:27–28	34
15:18	2	15:28	275
15:21	227	15:29	83
15:25	117	15:50	83
16:7	12	15:51	89
		15:52	255
1 Corinthians		15:55	42
1:2	253	16:22	37
1:23	35		
3:14	216	2 Corinthians	
3:16–17	109	1:2	117
4:12	95	3:6	127
4:20	83	3:7–8	136
6:9–10	83	3:11	135
6:12–13	109	3:18	83, 135
6:19	221	4:4	32
7	75	4:16	83
7:10–11	79, 208	5:16	269
7:10–12	99	5:17	83

2 Corinthians (cont.)		2:9–11	252
5:18	42	3:4–11	40
5:21	112	3:5–6	154
6:11	34	3:6	101, 146, 222
6:16	261		
12:9	85	Colossians	
13:12–13	206	1:15	32
		1:24	199
Galatians		2:5	218
1:13	222	2:21–22	105
1:13–14	101, 146	3:11	40
1:14	154	4:14	178
1:23	222		
2:11	109	1 Thessalonians	
2:12	113	3:13	155
2:14	40	3:15	117
2:15	99, 154, 155	4	238
2:16	40	4:5	100
2:19–20	232	4:7	109
2:20	42, 199	4:15	3, 89
3	35	4:16	46, 255, 256
3:10–14	35	5:2	88
3:13	42	5:15	95
3:18	206	5:23	155
3:26	55		
3:26–28	40, 142	2 Thessalonians	
3:26–4:6	35	2:5	3
5:1	96		
5:1–6	40	1 Timothy	
5:11	35	2:6	264
5:14	78, 129	2:6–13	159
5:21	83	3:16	230, 263
6:2	78	6:13	159
6:6	3		
		2 Timothy	
Ephesians		2:22	253
2:17	68	3:8	135
2:19	117	4:11	178
2:20–22	261		
		Titus	
Philippians		1:15	113
2	32, 242, 276	2:13	253
2:5–11	37		
2:6	32	Philemon	
2:9	264	24	178

Hebrews	20, 26, 135	11:19	258
2:5–9	27	14:14	43, 275
3:5	135	15:2–4	135
3:7	90	15:5	258
4:14	112	16:15	88
5	258	20:12	47
5:7	248, 258	22:20	37
6:19	259		
8:5	50	\textsc{Early Christianity}	
9:3	259, 260		
9:14	230	Barnabas	
9:19–22	234	7	258
9:23–25	93		
9:28	227, 230	*Clementis quae feruntur Recognitiones*	
10	258	1.41	260
10:1	50		
10:19–20	258	Didache	
10:20	260	16.6–8	31
11:23	135		
11:36–37	266	Gospel of the Ebionites	
		4	30
James			
2:5	178	Gospel of the Hebrews	
2:8	78	2	30
5:1–6	112		
		Gospel of Mary	
1 Peter		8.11–22	50
1:4	198		
1:19	267	Gospel of Peter	177
2:9	84	5:19	255
2:22–25	227		
3:9	95	Gospel of Thomas	
4:16	117	3	64, 91
		9	66
2 Peter		10	74
3:10	88	14	106, 108
		21	88
Jude		38	174
1:9	135	44	44
		45	117
Revelation		51	91
1:13	43	54	178
3:3	88	57	173
3:5	47	86	31
5:9–10	199	95	115

Gospel of Thomas (cont.)
103	88
104	152
108	64
109	172
113	87, 91

Justin, *Dialogue with Trypho* 8, 187, 199, 268

Protevangelium of James	177
17	187

Tertullian, *Scorpiace*	
8	266

Rabbinic Literature

Abot de-Rabbi Natan A	
1	196
1:1	55
4	64
4:11	42
5	145
16:32	96
24	170
27	98

b. ʿAbodah Zarah	
2a–b	165
10b	68
11a	98
37b	73

b. Baba Batra	
60b	185
75b	275

b. Baba Meṣiʿa	
118a	92

b. Baba Qamma	
5a	80
79b	170
83b–84a	151

110a	132
113a	150

b. Berakot	
24b	158
31b	170
33a	63
34b	21, 23, 56, 174
36b	151
50a	239
53b	108
64a	91

b. Beṣah	
11b	151
16a	148

b. ʿErubin	
13b	65, 113

b. Giṭṭim	
15b	108
90b	79

b. Hagigah	
12a	133
12b	131

b. Ketubbot	
111ab	269

b. Megillah	
7b	68
14a	185

b. Menaḥot	
95b	133

b. Moʿed Qaṭan	
25b–26a	260

b. Nazir	
9a	150
23b	157

b. Nedarim		133b	72
41a	63	151b	71
b. Niddah		153a	170
8b	187	b. Soperim	
31b	98	11b	185
b. Pesaḥim		b. Soṭah	
49b	15, 98	14a	25
54b	204	22b	158
57a	237	45b	121
115ab	108	49b	33
b. Qiddušin		b. Sukkah	
2b	163	26b	108
41	40	27a	108
72a	165	29b	93
		52a	236
b. Sanhedrin			
17a	250	b. Taʿanit	
25b	150	2a	269
26ab	100	6	223
38b	47, 240	21a	121
43a	222, 227	23	22
58b	92	24b–25a	22
86a	185		
90a	239	b. Yebamot	
90b–92	263	9a	151
96b–99a	28, 33	21a	80
97–98	33, 46	90	59
97a	74, 204		
98a	32, 46, 92, 235	b. Yoma	
98b	33	10a	165
108b–109a	121	35b	157
		39b	259
b. Šabbat		53b	21
31a	80, 96, 129	71b	20
31b	110	74b	185
49b	66	77b	148
53	40	85b	157
116b	23		
118b	28	b. Zebaḥim	
127b	150	22b	39
128a	133		
128b	132		

Canticles Rabbah		6	102
2.9.3	215		
2.13	243	m. 'Abodah Zarah	
2.13.4	33	4:9	9
Deuteronomy Rabbah		m. Berakot	
2.24	170	1:5	27
3.17	134	2:2	83
5.3	42	3:1	73, 73, 84
		5:5	22
Exodus Rabbah		5:9	3
1.13	136	7:3	239
1.22	185		
4.18	116	m. Baba Meṣi'a	
10.7	67, 185	1:8	99
15.1	185	3:4–5	99
46	3		
		m. Baba Qamma	
Genesis Rabbah		8:1	151
2.3	133	10:1	132
8.27	170		
24	96	m. 'Eduyyot	
24.7	147	1:2	146
56.1	267	8:4	73
85	136		
86.2	170	m. 'Erubin	
91.7	267	6:1	144
93.1	152	6:2	146
98.9	77		
		m. Giṭṭim	79
Lamentations Rabbah		9:10	79, 146
1.51	275		
		m. Hagigah	
Leviticus Rabbah	77	1:1	213
9.7	77	2:2	9
		2:11	19
m. 'Abot		2:12	110
1	116	2:12–14	113
1:1	55, 80		
2:8	63	m. Keritot	
3:10	152	1:7	146
3:10–11	22	4:3	150
3:14	39		
5:10	33	m. Makkot	
5:25	180, 216	1:6	144

1:10	250	3:9	258
		4:3–6	216
m. Niddah			
1:4	187	m. Taʿanit	
1:6	187	3:8	22, 28
4:2	98, 144		
		m. Yadayim	
m. ʿOrlah		1:1–2:4	108
2:12	146	3:7	144
		4:6–8	145
m. Pesaḥim		4:6	144
3:7	132, 133	4:7	144
		4:8	146
m. Qiddušin			
1:10	25	m. Yebamot	
		16:7	9
m. Sanhedrin			
3:3	150	m. Yoma	
3:10	143	6:3	259
4:1	223	7:3–4	203
4:2	250	8:6	59
4:5	224	8:9	152
6:5	244		
7:2	223	m. Zebaḥim	
7:5	224, 239, 244, 249, 260	9:14	259
10:1	25, 149		
11:2	224	Mekilta de Rabbi Ishmael	185
		1.16	75
m. Šabbat		2.3	71, 170
1:5	59	2.4	170
2:6	110	2.5	170
6:4	162	3.10	260
7:2	132	6.1	39, 131
18:1	132	6.8	117, 191
		9.1	98, 157
m. Šeqalim			
2:5	99	Mekilta de Rabbi Simeon b. Yoḥai	
		on Exod 20:5	73
m. Soṭah			
1:7	86	Midrash Ruth	
9	71, 268	4	125
9:15	22, 27, 33, 91, 99		
		Midrash Tehillim	
m. Sukkah		on Ps 90	260
2:9	170	on Ps 43	134

Numbers Rabbah		Sipra	245
13.2	185	68	132
13.14	46	194 on Lev 19:2, 15	120
13.20	185	Metsoraʿ 5:9	110
		Ahare Mot 13:3	39, 83
Qoheleth Rabbah		Qedoshim 4	119
1.28	131	Qedoshim 11:14	170
3.11	170		
		Sipre Deuteronomy	
Ruth Rabbah		5	133
5.6	33	7:12	38
Pirqe Rabbi Eliezer		Sipre Numbers	
34	269	84	170
		127	124
Pesiqta de Rab Kahana			
4.7	114	t. ʿAbodah Zarah	
21	71	4:9	9
49b	203		
supp. 6	186	t. Baba Qamma	
		9:29–30	95
Pesiqta Rabbati		10:18	132
4	134		
5	185	t. Berakot	
14.14	114	6:3	62
15	243		
31	257	t. ʿEduyyot	
35	3, 33	3:4	103
36–37	33		
40.5	257	t. Hullin	
		2:22	187
Pesiq. Zutra on 8	96		
		t. Miqwaʾot	
Qaddish	91	7:11	273
Seder Eliahu Rabbah	22, 40	t. Niddah	
		1:6	187
Seder Eliahu Zutra	40	4:2	144
Seder ʿOlam Rabbah		t. Sanhedrin	
20	266	3:10	143
		13:2	100
Shmoneh Esreh	91		
		t. Šabbat	
		9	133

17:19	71	Targum Psalms	
		5	136
t. Yebamot		89:27	22
1:13	151		
		Targum Zechariah	
t. Zebaḥim		14:9	82
6:8	95		
		Targum Pseudo-Jonathan	82
Tanḥuma B	185	on Gen 49	27
706	46	on Deut 32:39	241
Tanna de-be Eliahu		Targum Neofiti I	82
48	40		
		Targum Onqelos	82
Targum Canticles			
8:5	257, 269	y. Baba Qamma	
		8:1, 6c	151
Targum Deuteronomy	32, 241	8:2, 6c	122
Targum Exodus		y. Berakot	
15:18	82	1:3, 4b	151
		2:8, 5c	vii, 118, 170
Targum Ezekiel		9:5, 14c	156
7:7	82	5:4–5, 9d	56
Targum Isaiah		y. Hagigah	
5:5	265	2:1, 77d	273
11:8–9	35		
24:23	82	y. Ketubbot	
25:6–8	82	12:3, 35b	268
31:4	82		
40:9	82	y. Niddah	
41:1	35	1:3, 49a	187
42:1	134		
52:7	82	y. Pe'ah	
53:5	260, 267	1:1, 15b	72
Targum Job		y. Sanhedrin	
36:7	82	7:2, 23c	223
Targum Malachi		y. Šeqalim	
2:20	22	3:3, 47b	268
Targum Obadiah		y. Sukkah	
21	82	5:1, 52a	236

y. Sukkah (*cont.*)
    5:1, 55b   236

y. Ta'anit
    1:1, 64a   30
    4:8, 68d   24

y. Yebamot
    3:3, 4d   150

y. Yoma
    6:3, 43c   259

Yalquṭ
    on Isa 26   243
    on Ps 43   134

Zohar   77, 114, 185, 185
    Ra'aya Mehemma, 3:67b–68a   185

Other Ancient Sources

Virgil, *Aeneid*
    1.278–279   88

Index of Subjects

angels   11, 13, 24, 31, 32, 34, 35, 45, 46, 48, 49, 88, 135, 181, 184, 185, 194, 195, 198, 225, 243, 251, 255, 256, 275, 276
animals
  donkey   26, 216
apocalyptic
  cosmic   46, 47, 149, 256, 264
  darkness   92, 96, 99, 128, 201, 256, 257
  light   1, 13, 17, 24, 92, 128, 133, 179, 231, 239, 244, 250, 257, 258, 264
  quake   256, 257
  star   252
authority
  haggadah   40, 169, 173, 177, 180, 181, 184, 185, 273, 276
  midrash   6, 21, 32, 33, 68, 125, 136, 169, 175, 177, 181, 183, 184, 185, 186, 187, 188, 191, 204, 215, 228, 236, 248, 260
  succession   180
  supersession   40, 153, 264
body
  blood   5, 51, 56, 61, 68, 91, 101, 104, 107, 111, 137, 155, 187, 194, 231, 232, 233, 234, 235, 237, 243, 267, 276
  feet   7, 50, 69, 174, 215, 233
  hands   7, 33, 43, 56, 58, 61, 71, 91, 104, 105, 109, 114, 118, 122, 146, 201, 206, 211, 214, 218, 220, 221, 224, 228, 229, 232, 234, 235, 236, 248, 250, 259, 260, 261
clothes   120, 203, 250, 260, 268
  crown   87, 202, 231, 271
  dress   120
  nakedness   8, 142
  robe   202, 202, 203, 231, 245
  tzitzit   56, 61
crowds   12, 17, 30, 58, 64, 65, 67, 93, 105, 106, 128, 131, 139, 164, 170, 179, 212, 215, 217, 218, 229, 231, 233, 234, 235, 245, 246, 247, 250, 253, 265
  poor   7, 9, 10, 25, 33, 64, 74, 84, 85, 88, 89, 102, 112, 120, 122, 124, 147, 153, 161, 162, 163, 168, 178, 199
  populace   58, 121, 138, 146, 149, 160, 179, 222, 223, 232, 233, 266
  rich   7, 83, 85, 120, 147, 161, 163, 166
curse   7, 35, 40, 41, 42, 56, 65, 85, 172, 234, 258
blessing   49, 85, 174, 234
disabilities
  blind   7, 10, 40, 53, 55, 56, 63, 66, 89, 90, 93, 108, 111, 117, 124, 156, 173, 179, 181, 257, 267
  dead   8, 10, 25, 32, 42, 55, 61, 66, 68, 71, 73, 89, 96, 103, 112, 120, 122, 123, 124, 127, 149, 176, 180, 233, 248, 253, 256, 257, 263, 264, 266
  deaf   7, 10, 55, 89, 173, 233
  demon   35, 56, 64, 66, 67, 86, 97, 143, 202, 233
  leper   7, 10, 55, 61, 89, 93, 98, 107, 109, 110, 111, 112, 113, 117
  paralytic   53, 58, 59, 62, 94, 156, 201, 204
early Christianity
  anti-Semitism   156, 201, 204, 223, 233

early Christianity (*cont.*)
  legion   38, 48, 194, 225
  oral tradition   3, 71, 73, 83, 94, 99, 105, 118, 121, 144, 145, 165
  pagan   96, 97, 178, 186, 274, 277
education
  charisma   19, 21, 22, 23, 28, 35, 49, 53, 57, 72, 74, 99, 206, 223, 245
  learn   19, 96, 97, 98, 106, 130, 144, 153, 157, 170, 195, 204, 214
  master   2, 20, 27, 37, 40, 44, 54, 55, 97, 105, 116, 118, 142, 159, 167, 171, 174, 179, 198, 199, 209, 211, 212, 213, 114, 215, 225, 229, 250, 263, 264, 266, 268, 269
  read   3, 4, 5, 8, 9, 17, 18, 19, 26, 33, 42, 45, 46, 50, 55, 64, 69, 89, 94, 97, 107, 108, 119, 125, 128, 132, 136, 139, 151, 158, 167, 169, 175, 177, 186, 187, 191, 194, 196, 202, 211, 226, 229, 233, 236, 238, 241, 248, 254, 257, 259, 261, 265, 266, 277
  school   15, 18, 144, 151, 156
  teacher   3, 6, 19, 20, 21, 23, 26, 37, 59, 116, 118, 119, 132, 134, 173, 203, 249, 260
family
  brother   11, 18, 117, 127, 149, 153, 166, 181, 189, 212, 222
  father   9, 17, 22, 28, 34, 41, 53, 63, 72, 73, 84, 86, 87, 88, 89, 90, 91, 96, 115, 116, 117, 118, 135, 155, 171, 177, 180, 188, 189, 190, 207, 215, 232, 243, 249, 252, 253, 260, 267, 277
  mother   53, 63, 177, 179, 181, 185, 186, 187, 188, 189, 233, 277
  "Woman" (voc.)   175, 189
feasts
  calendar   50, 76, 144, 154, 219
  fast   76, 76, 80, 137, 152, 155, 208, 248
  hour   88, 98, 122, 157, 167, 252, 254, 255, 257

  Kippur   153, 203, 250, 258, 259
  Passover   51, 68, 88, 109, 152, 153, 161, 180, 202, 213, 214, 217, 218, 219, 223, 227, 246, 247, 258, 267, 271
  prayer   17, 22, 24, 27, 28, 41, 58, 59, 77, 81, 90, 91, 111, 122, 125, 151, 159, 162, 255, 258
  Shemoneh Esreh   92
  Succoth   62, 134, 135, 216, 258
food
  bread   68, 97, 103, 135, 157, 162, 214, 276
  drink   68, 76, 88, 101, 235
  fish   67, 68, 175, 186, 212, 214
  food   58, 68, 77, 78, 79, 97, 98, 103, 104, 105, 106, 109, 112, 114, 146, 268
  fruit   83, 88, 91, 265, 267, 271
  kosher   77, 103, 112, 113
  wine   51, 53, 68, 88, 152, 153, 277
functions, religious/social
  Caesar   38, 47, 150, 212, 229, 253
  centurion   32, 37, 53, 56, 97, 155, 179, 207, 215, 255, 256
  governor   32, 48, 148, 150, 162, 218, 224, 228, 229, 231, 245
  high priest   4, 19, 20, 23, 26, 39, 44, 81, 101, 138, 144, 148, 149, 149, 150, 154, 160, 202, 203, 204, 214, 218, 219, 222, 224, 225, 226, 229, 236, 237, 238, 239, 240, 242, 244, 245, 248, 249, 250, 252, 253, 254, 256, 257, 258, 259, 260
gentiles   1, 2, 20, 24, 36, 37, 38, 39, 40, 41, 46, 76, 84, 89, 96, 97, 98, 99, 100, 101, 106, 117, 124, 125, 128, 135, 147, 148, 150, 154, 155, 159, 161, 171, 175, 179, 191, 204, 211, 252, 264, 274, 276
  Syro-Phoenician   37, 97
geography
  Bethany   50, 69
  Bethlehem   16, 166, 184, 190
  chora   7, 165
  Egypt   25, 51, 64, 67, 137, 138, 185, 190, 266, 267

INDEX OF SUBJECTS

Galilee 2, 6, 12, 15, 16, 18, 24, 53, 98, 136, 137, 149, 166, 167, 189, 212, 213, 263
Judah 23, 34, 118, 277
Nazareth 16, 17, 18, 53, 54, 77, 184, 190, 206, 229, 251
Rome 47, 88, 101, 136, 144, 145, 178
Tiberias 98
good/evil
  evil 47, 61, 67, 72, 75, 82, 94, 95, 109, 194, 196
  fulfillment 40, 62, 71, 77, 78, 96, 115, 119, 136, 137, 165, 166, 196, 198, 205, 213, 227, 264
  holy 6, 23, 31, 42, 44, 47, 49, 54, 72, 103, 118, 119, 146, 161, 182, 201, 204, 220, 240, 251, 257, 258, 259, 275
  hypocrisy 107, 157, 158, 222
hermeneutics
  exegesis vii, 6, 82, 91, 109, 177
  fundamentalism 109
  literalism 48, 90, 117, 145, 177, 191, 226, 277
  messianic reading 28, 29, 33, 35, 47, 92, 184, 234, 236
  pesher 24, 181
kingdom of God 9, 10, 13, 15, 19, 25, 29, 31, 38, 47, 49, 50, 51, 64, 71, 72, 74, 79, 80, 81, 82, 83, 84, 85, 86, 87, 88, 89, 90, 91, 92, 94, 95, 97, 98, 99, 113, 115, 123, 129, 141, 143, 149, 155, 157, 158, 159, 161, 162, 163, 169, 170, 171, 172, 178, 179, 195, 197, 198, 199, 200, 205, 207, 208, 212, 230, 238, 251, 252, 254, 258
languages
  Aramaic vii, 4, 16, 17, 31, 37, 38, 43, 72, 83, 100, 226, 242, 247
  Greek vii, 4, 7, 11, 16, 34, 37, 41, 43, 54, 56, 57, 83, 91, 100, 132, 141, 170, 177, 186, 188, 191, 198, 226, 233, 239, 241, 255, 274, 277
  Latin 16, 241
  Syriac 251

maiden
  'almah 187, 188
  child 18, 33, 50, 55, 56, 73, 74, 97, 102, 141, 158, 178, 179, 180, 185, 186, 187, 188, 189, 205, 231, 234
Messiah
  anoint 8, 23, 26, 27, 36, 50, 55, 69, 161, 174, 195, 198, 232, 236, 252, 268
  aura 30, 195, 220
  beatitude 25, 50, 74, 84, 93, 162
  king (title) 13, 23, 24, 26, 27, 33, 34, 35, 37, 45, 46, 48, 54, 57, 71, 92, 93, 163, 171, 190, 202, 203, 212, 216, 217, 225, 228, 229, 231, 233, 234, 235, 236, 244, 245, 246, 248, 261, 266, 275, 276, 277
  servant 25, 25, 26, 27, 29, 32, 33, 40, 97, 109, 117, 135, 171, 174, 188, 197, 214, 219, 225, 227, 230, 236
  shepherd 15, 171, 184
names, proper
  Aaron 20, 67, 136, 268
  Abraham 97, 98, 133, 136, 164, 185, 190, 205, 207, 242, 245, 249
  Adam 26, 47, 48, 54, 93, 133, 164, 180, 199, 276
  Antiochus IV 102, 138, 270
  Aqiba 15, 30, 79, 119, 147, 177, 185, 250, 259
  Balaam 92
  Barabbas 229, 234, 235, 246, 265
  Claudius 178
  Cyrus 26, 180
  Daniel 45, 46, 48, 221, 225, 233, 234, 253, 271, 276
  David 2, 13, 16, 18, 23, 24, 26, 27, 28, 29, 31, 32, 33, 34, 36, 47, 67, 71, 74, 93, 133, 136, 167, 170, 184, 185, 186, 189, 190, 205, 206, 216, 228, 232, 236, 260, 268, 273
  Elijah 3, 21, 57, 58, 67, 68, 74, 99, 131, 134, 135, 136, 142, 194, 195, 200, 208, 230, 247, 248, 260, 264, 266, 268

Elisha 55, 56, 57, 67, 68, 74, 131, 142, 259
Elizabeth 182, 184, 277
Herod 15, 16, 41, 46, 79, 98, 101, 137, 145, 149, 162, 176, 187, 193, 203, 204, 217, 218, 221, 225, 236, 237, 246
Hillel 1, 20, 59, 63, 80, 90, 96, 113, 129, 148, 150, 151, 156, 157
Hanina 21, 22, 28, 56, 63, 116
Hiyya 151
Honi 21, 22, 28
Isaac 97, 98, 185, 207, 234
Jacob 19, 35, 97, 98, 181, 198, 207, 234
James 18, 89, 134, 189, 222, 230
Jeremiah 12, 72, 73, 74, 99, 176, 185, 196, 221, 237, 265, 266
Job 33, 63, 109, 112
Johanan ben Zakkai, R. 18, 23, 42, 102
John the Baptist 3, 11, 12, 15, 19, 23, 26, 30, 49, 64, 74, 78, 79, 87, 91, 92, 97, 116, 136, 137, 142, 149, 179, 180, 190, 193, 195, 207, 221, 227, 254, 255, 267, 268
Joseph 81, 115, 137, 161, 181, 185, 186, 187, 188, 190, 212
Joshua 15, 26, 116, 134
Judith 146
Lazarus 7, 50, 61, 68, 69, 85, 107, 112, 177
Leah 184
Luria 26, 169, 197
Maharal of Prague 80, 169, 205
Mary Magdalena 12
Mary, mother of Jesus 31, 35, 181, 182, 184, 185, 186, 187, 188, 190, 277
Martha 50, 69
Miriam 180, 185
Moses 9, 15, 18, 19, 21, 25, 33, 54, 57, 58, 64, 67, 68, 75, 76, 77, 78, 80, 116, 117, 131, 132, 133, 134, 135, 136, 137, 138, 145, 156, 179, 180, 185, 194, 197, 203, 205, 236, 242, 266, 274
Panthera 187
Paul 2, 3, 5, 8, 13, 14, 23, 27, 35, 36, 37, 38, 39, 40, 42, 55, 75, 76, 79, 83, 85, 95, 97, 99, 100, 101, 105, 106, 109, 115, 116, 129, 135, 141, 146, 149, 154, 155, 159, 165, 166, 178, 179, 198, 199, 205, 206, 208, 212, 221, 222, 230, 252, 253, 261, 264, 266, 267, 269, 271, 275
Peter 13, 32, 58, 64, 68, 89, 90, 95, 134, 135, 163, 174, 176, 178, 195, 198, 200, 201, 218, 226, 227, 229, 229, 230, 244, 249, 253, 254
Rachel 184, 234, 236
Ruth 190
Sabbatai 26, 77, 250, 276
Samuel 268
Shammai 59, 79, 113, 148, 150
Stephen 16, 135, 158, 222, 223, 236, 241, 259
Titus 16, 113
Vespasian 249
professions
  carpenter 17, 17
  laborer 6, 143
  peasant 6, 7, 101, 147, 159, 162, 163, 232
purity
  clean 10, 40, 61, 62, 66, 89, 97, 98, 100, 101, 104, 105, 107, 108, 109, 110, 112, 118, 119, 124, 150, 158, 160, 161, 213, 214, 215, 216, 217, 237, 245, 254, 265
  impurity 57, 60, 61, 75, 80, 85, 93, 94, 96, 97, 102–19, 120, 124, 152, 154, 158, 173
  washing of hands 104, 105, 107, 109, 118, 206, 224, 228, 229, 234, 248
ritual
  circumcision 39, 59, 60, 108, 155, 179, 205, 206, 270
Sanhedrin 13, 22, 32, 115, 121, 138, 144, 149, 164, 218, 222, 223, 224, 227,

INDEX OF SUBJECTS

228, 229, 230, 238, 245, 248, 250, 253, 258
court (of justice) 32, 41, 102, 150, 159, 161, 171, 214, 223, 224, 229, 230, 233, 250, 260, 265
gladiator 229, 231, 233
witness 3, 6, 14, 24, 29, 42, 49, 56, 59, 65, 84, 87, 90, 134, 161, 173, 174, 176, 186, 189, 206, 211, 219, 220, 224, 229, 237, 238, 252, 253, 264, 266

sects
Essene 7, 56, 73, 138, 139, 144, 205, 232, 245
Pharisee *passim*
Qumran 2, 17, 18, 20, 23, 24, 25, 26, 36, 59, 60, 62, 74, 83, 92, 96, 100, 102, 103, 108, 116, 120, 128, 135, 137, 139, 141, 146, 154, 159, 196, 219, 235, 237, 239, 243, 260, 261, 267
Sadducee 19, 20, 57, 98, 100, 103, 115, 138, 139, 144, 145, 146, 148, 149, 150, 151, 154, 155, 157, 165, 179, 212, 219, 224, 232, 245, 263
Samaritan 41, 60, 65, 98, 108, 114, 149, 167, 174, 178
Samaritan, Good 119–30
Sicarius 101, 162, 163, 246
Zealot 100, 100–102

sin
forgive 19, 20, 44, 58, 62, 63, 64, 86, 87, 95, 118, 155, 174, 194, 214, 240, 254

suffering
innocence 27, 93, 97, 126, 194, 195, 229
redemption 64, 122, 182, 200, 205, 206, 207, 264
salvation 28, 47, 83, 98, 131, 153, 154, 155, 157, 172, 179, 189, 206

temple
altar 79, 103, 109, 118, 132, 153, 258
curtain 97, 127, 240, 256, 257, 259

holy of holies 213, 220, 257, 258, 259
naos 220, 259
sacrifice 19, 20, 41, 42, 62, 74, 77, 80, 81, 91, 93, 102, 108, 129, 144, 147, 150, 152, 158, 160, 161, 230, 234, 258
shrine 42, 157, 158, 159, 161, 180, 221, 246, 259, 261, 266
veil 135, 173, 205, 217, 220, 230, 248, 253, 259, 260
tomb 11, 12, 69, 146, 220, 257, 263, 265, 269, 271
burial 270
corpse 8, 103, 107, 113, 120, 124, 127, 146, 231
grave 8, 72, 107, 124, 233, 257, 264
resurrection 9, 11, 13, 30, 32, 36, 37, 49, 54, 61, 69, 91, 113, 131, 137, 149, 157, 160, 165, 178, 179, 183, 204, 221, 226, 227, 231, 232, 244, 245, 248, 257
resurrection, Jesus 263–72

war
destruction 39, 42, 62, 71, 83, 100, 101, 107, 112, 144, 145, 148, 150, 152, 158, 159, 160, 161, 165, 199, 201, 211, 220, 221, 225, 232, 236, 237, 259, 260, 261, 265, 266
lestes 162, 163, 214
massacre 102, 166, 176
peace 35, 90, 93, 158, 163, 178, 213, 217, 235
rebel 91, 101, 138, 156, 162, 193, 214, 225, 229, 249
resistance 181, 194, 217, 271
revolution 34, 41, 80, 101, 113, 115, 148, 162, 204, 221, 269
slaughter 41, 101, 266, 267, 271
spear 164, 233
sword 124, 142, 164, 214

www.ingramcontent.com/pod-product-compliance
Lightning Source LLC
Chambersburg PA
CBHW021818300426
44114CB00009BA/218